BUSINESS FILE PROCESSING!

COBOL, CICS, and SQL

JAMES BRADLEY

Mitchell Publishing, Inc.
Innovators in Computer Education
915 River Street • Santa Cruz, California 95060
(800) 435-2665 • In California (408) 425-3851
"A Random House Company"

Sponsoring Editor: Raleigh S. Wilson
Product Development: Raleigh S. Wilson
Production Management: Burgess and Associates
Interior Design: Linda Robertson
Cover Design: Larry Lazopoulos
Composition: The Laser Edge
Printing and Binding: R. R. Donnelley & Sons Company

Published in the United States by Mitchell Publishing, Inc., a subsidiary of Random House, Inc., New York and simultaneously in Canada by Random House of Canada Limited. Toronto. Distributed by Random House, Inc.

Printed in the United States of America

10 9 8 7 6 5 4 3 2 1

Library of Congress Card Catalog Number: 87-91961
ISBN: 0-394-39217-5

CONTENTS

2 TAPE AND DISK STORAGE MEDIA 29

3 SEQUENTIAL FILE PRINCIPLES AND CREATION 73

4 SEQUENTIAL FILE PROCESSING 111

6 INDEXED-SEQUENTIAL FILE PROCESSING 155

7 SECONDARY KEY ACCESS 200

8 HASH FILES 228

11 COBOL FILE PROCESSING WITH CICS 332

12 FILE PROCESSING WITH SQL 355

13 FILE PROCESSING WITH SQL EMBEDDED IN COBOL 380

APPENDIX 1: IBM DISK DATA 395

PREFACE

Simply stated—this book was written to fill a need for a text devoted to teaching business data processing students the principles of file processing, using sufficient COBOL program excerpts to illustrate these principles in practice. By emphasizing file processing principles, students are freed from unnecessary COBOL coding detail that may obscure programming issues and prevent them from writing efficient, maintainable programs.

BUSINESS FILE PROCESSING! COBOL, CICS and SQL can be used in courses on file processing offered in business programs, and even in some courses in computer science departments. In some cases, an advanced COBOL book will have been used in previous years. I believe that in many of these courses, instructors would prefer to emphasize file processing first and COBOL second. It is primarily for such courses that this book has been written.

Organization and Presentation

The material is presented in an order that I believe is logical. In the first chapter, the background environment of computer file processing is examined. It is assumed that students have taken elementary COBOL but have no knowledge of operating systems. The aim is to impart a reasonable understanding of the environment in which a file processing program executes, without going into unnecessary detail. The idea of an access method is introduced here. The second chapter details one important part of the environment of file processing, namely the tape and disk storage media. The chapter gives a comprehensive coverage of these media. A grasp of file processing principles and techniques is impossible without a good background in disk and tape media.

The next three chapters cover sequential file processing in a business environment. There are clear explanations of exactly what the sequential COBOL file processing commands do. There is an introduction to file navigation diagrams for easy communication of just what goes on in more complex file update procedures. COBOL program excerpts illustrate use of essential COBOL. At the ends of the chapters there is enough material for students to understand IBM DD-statements, even where a non-IBM operating system is used.

In Chapter 6 there is thorough coverage of the principles and techniques involved in indexed-sequential file processing. File navigation diagrams are used to communicate file processing procedures, and COBOL excerpts illustrate the essential COBOL. Naturally, emphasis is placed on VSAM. Since VSAM can be used for creating indexed-sequential files with secondary key access, this chapter leads naturally to Chapter 7 on secondary keys.

Chapter 7 emphasizes the principles behind secondary key processing showing how COBOL and VSAM can be used in practice. Without this prior emphasis on principles, students will never learn about the advantages and disadvantages of secondary keys.

In Chapters 8 and 9 there is thorough coverage of hash files. Chapter 8 covers the basic principles in a manner that should be appreciated and understood by business students. Hash files have to be designed for fast access to make the effort worthwhile. After all, if your hash file is slow, time and effort can be saved by using an indexed-sequential file. Properly designed, a hash file is much faster than an indexed file. Chapter 9 shows how these principles can be put into practice. Hash files are illustrated with both COBOL direct and COBOL relative files.

In Chapters 10 and 11 there is introductory coverage of on-line processing with CICS, the most commonly used teleprocessing monitor for on-line processing. Advanced COBOL books rarely cover the use of CICS, which requires a quite different kind of COBOL programming. In Chapter 10, the principles behind using CICS for on-line processing are explained. In Chapter 11 there is an explanation of how file processing with COBOL and CICS is carried out.

Chapters 12 and 13 deal with another important aspect of file processing never covered in advanced COBOL books, that is, the use of the fourth-generation data base language SQL for file processing. This use of SQL for file processing is growing, since it streamlines the COBOL coding process. Chapter 12 explains the principles behind SQL, and Chapter 13 shows how COBOL and SQL are used for file processing in practice.

The student who has studied the chapters of this book will have a much better idea of the possibilities and limitations of file processing than the student who has been restricted to the material in a standard advanced COBOL book. In particular, the student should acquire superior skills in disk/tape media estimates, secondary keys, hash file design and manipulation, on-line processing, and use of SQL file processing.

Supplementary Materials

Features such as secondary keys, and direct and/or relative file access methods for hash files are also available. Fortunately, many computers at universities and colleges have these facilities. Ideally, CICS and SQL facilities should also be available. CICS facilities are usually a problem in an educational institution, unfortunately. This text therefore assumes that many students will not be able to run COBOL CICS programs. However, SQL facilities are becoming more common in college and university settings.

An instructor's manual for *BUSINESS FILE PROCESSING! COBOL, CICS and SQL* is available. It contains helpful material on how to teach the contents of each chapter, together with answers to chapter questions. It also contains many worked examples suitable for use in examinations or practice problems. Transparency masters are included.

Acknowledgements

I am grateful to many people for helping me with the preparation of this book. The most important help came from my students in COBOL and file processing courses. The following people reviewed the manuscript and made many constructive comments: Sue Krimm, Pierce College; David Copenhaver, Westmar College; and Robert P. Burton, Brigham Young University.

Finally, I must thank my editors, Raleigh Wilson and Brete Harrison, for their encouragement, patience, and commitment.

J. Bradley
January, 1988

1 OVERVIEW OF BUSINESS FILE PROCESSING

Business enterprises routinely deal with large quantities of data. Nowadays a significant portion of business data is stored as computer files on magnetic external storage media such as disks and tapes. The details of how business data is organized in such files and how the files are processed by computer are the subjects of this book.

In this chapter we overview business file processing in the contexts of computer file processing technology and the business file processing strategies; these two contexts are intertwined, as will soon become apparent. In the initial section we look at the concept of a computer file. We then look at the ideas behind input and output of data, that is being processed by a computer program. This leads to an overview of operating systems and how they influence file processing. Finally we overview the various business strategies for processing computer files, which involves a discussion of batch, on-line, and interactive processing.

THE COMPUTER FILE CONCEPT

A **computer file** is a collection of items of data permanently recorded on a storage medium such as magnetic disk or tape. We can distinguish at the outset between **document files** and **record files**. Document files are normally used with word processing systems and typically contain some kind of text. (A chapter of this book could be a document file.) Although document files are important in business, because they belong to the specialized field of word processing, they are not the subject of this book. We will be concerned with record files, which we will henceforth refer to simply as files.

A record file is made up of records. Each record normally contains data that describes some entity of the real world, for example, a product, a customer, or an employee. Thus we can have a record file called EMPLOYEE, as illustrated below, where each record contains information about an employee of a firm:

EMP-NUMBER	NAME	SALARY
2345	CODD	21,000
2467	BROWN	32,000
2732	JONES	19,000
3187	SMITH	23,000
3592	JONES	22,500

EMPLOYEE

We can usually imagine a record file as a table (even when it is permanently recorded only on a magnetic medium). In this view each row of the table corresponds to a **record**. Each record is made up of fields. Thus any record from the file EMPLOYEE has an employee number field (EMP-NUMBER), an employee name field (NAME), and a salary field (SALARY). Clearly it is convenient to deal with all the items of data connected with an individual employee as a group; such a group is a record.

Usually one of the fields (or at least a group of fields) in a file has a unique value for each record. In the above example, the EMP-NUMBER field in EMPLOYEE provides the unique value for each record. Such a unique field (or field combination) can be used to identify both a record and the entity described by a record. Thus employee number 2732 identifies a record in EMPLOYEE and also identifies an employee called Jones. Such an identifier field is commonly called a **primary key**, or simply a **key**, for the file. (Notice that in diagrams and displays of computer files it is conventional to underline the primary key field.)

The primary key field is often used for ordering the records in the storage medium. The EMPLOYEE records above are ordered in ascending EMP-NUMBER sequence; they would typically be stored on magnetic tape this way.

The primary key can also permit direct access to a record without needing to scan all preceding records, as is the case with a tape file. Files that permit such direct access require a special organization and must reside on magnetic disk. We shall learn about such files later in the book.

Processing Ideas

Computer files must be processed by computer. Even if you only want to see what is in a file, you must use a computer to process it; in such a case processing consists of reading the file from tape or disk and printing it on a printer or displaying it on a video screen. Generally if you are processing a file, you are either reading data from the file or you are reading it as well as making changes to data in the file. At the same time, an entirely new file may be created as a result of processing one or more older files.

Computer file processing is carried out by a computer program, with a different program necessary for each kind of processing. Such a program is often written by a programmer who works in the company that owns the file. Since the program permits an application of the computer to the work of processing the firm's data, it is often called an **application program**, or sometimes simply a **user program**. An application program is distinct from a **system program**, which performs some fundamental system function for the computer. (A text editor is an example of a system program.)

An application program consists of instructions recorded in the main memory of the computer. The file being processed resides on an external storage device such as a magnetic tape. Records of the file are normally processed one by one. For this to happen, records must first be read from the storage medium into the main memory of the computer. Later, processed records must be written to a file on an external storage medium. In other words records must be input and output for file processing to take place. We overview input/output in the next section.

A note on memory terminology is needed here. **Main memory** (or **internal**, **primary**, or **electronic memory**) is the location in the computer where instructions being executed reside. Data being processed by these instructions must also reside here. No permanent recording can occur in main memory,—a program normally resides in it only when being executed. Constrast this with **auxiliary**, or **external** memory, such as magnetic tape or disk media, where data can be permanently recorded as computer files and where programs can also be permanently recorded (essentially as document files) but not executed.

INPUT/OUTPUT CONCEPTS

Input/output (I/O) concepts are best illustrated by starting with a simple computer, whose main memory can hold (and execute) only one program at a time (see Figure 1.1). Assume that data being input for processing is on magnetic tape. A similar medium could be used for output of data. We have a **central processing unit** (CPU), which actually carries out instructions, and the main memory. The memory holds a program, which is a sequence of instructions that can be carried out by the CPU.

In a separate part of the memory we have a **working-storage area**, which is a collection of memory cells holding data that can be affected

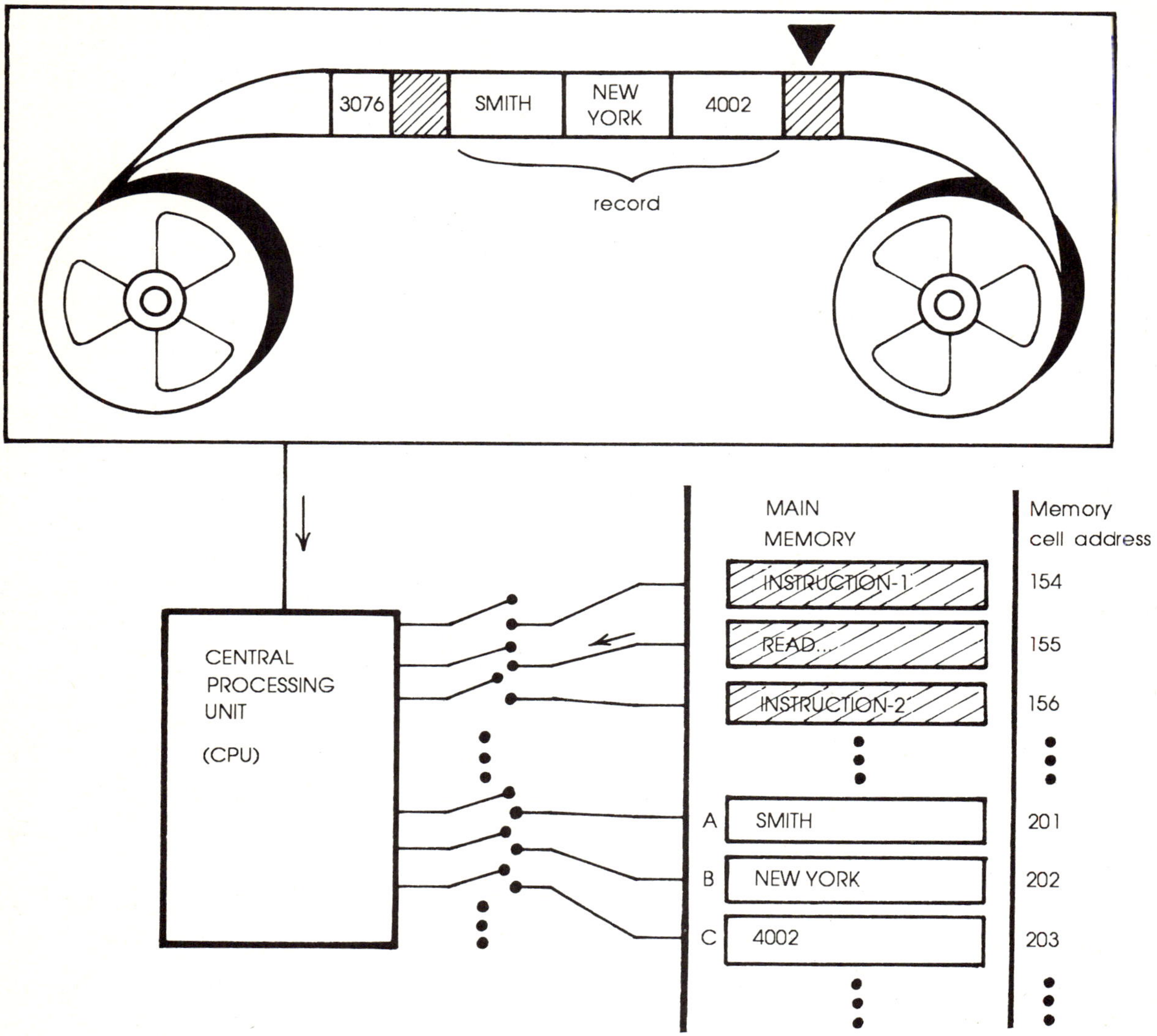

FIGURE 1.1 In a primitive computer a READ instruction, when carried out by the CPU, causes the next group of data items (a record) to be read from the input medium (for example, a magnetic tape), and each item of data (or field value) to be placed in a memory cell (such as A) in main memory (that is, in the working-storage part of main memory). In practice things are never done this way with large computers because the electromechanical nature of the storage device causes the CPU to take far too long to carry out a READ (or WRITE) instruction.

or processed by the execution of one or more instructions from the program. With programs written in COBOL or a similar language, each such memory cell is given a name, such as A, B, or C, as shown in the figure, or even TAX, CUSTOMER-ASSETS, and so on. Such a named memory cell is usually called an **identifier** when COBOL is used for programming, although the term **program variable**, or simply **variable**, is also used and is equally appropriate.

As the program executes, the memory cells containing instructions are electrically connected to the CPU one by one; the CPU is capable of carrying out the instruction in the memory cell to which it is currently connected. This is the essence of the tight relationship between program, or procedure, and the data for the program in the working-storage area. Readers should be clear about exactly what is going on in this simple system, because the systems used in practice with large files normally have several processors, each capable of executing a program in main memory, as we shall see.

Since a computer program processes data in its associated working storage, the next question is how data gets into working storage from outside. In a simple computer system we can have a READ command, which on execution causes the CPU to transmit the next group of items of data (a record) from the input medium to a specified group of memory cells. Thus if we have items of data stored as records on tape in sequence (as shown in Figure 1.1) and if the next group of items following the reading head of the tape drive is SMITH, NEW YORK, 4002, the instruction READ will cause the CPU to transmit SMITH, NEW YORK, 4002 to memory cells 201, 202, and 203. We can use a WRITE instruction to reverse this process and move values in a memory cell (a record) to an external medium.

The Need for an Operating System

The process we have just outlined is simple and quite fundamental. Unfortunately it cannot be used for business file processing in organizations. The problem lies in the execution of the READ (or WRITE) instruction by the CPU.

External storage media reside on electromechanical devices such as disk and tape drives, and even with the fastest of these it normally takes about 10 milliseconds (thousandths of a second) or more to transmit a small quantity of data between main memory and an external storage device. In contrast it takes about a microsecond (0.001 milliseconds) to execute an instruction in main memory that affects data in working storage only. Therefore if there are many read and write operations (and with business file processing there usually are), the CPU will spend most of its time waiting for input and output of data instead of processing it. This is equivalent to a high-priced executive spending 2 seconds at work each day and taking 6 hours to get needed information from the company's library. In the case of the executive, the solution is to hire assistants and develop procedures for them to use in the library. A similar solution is used with computers. Equivalent to the assistants are special input/output processors, or channels; equivalent to the procedures is the multiprogramming operating system.

To recap, a processor executes instructions in a computer system; in a simple system there is just one processor, called the central processing unit. If the central processing unit directly executes READ and WRITE instructions for files on disk or tape, the system becomes too inefficient for use with business files.

THE NONVIRTUAL MULTIPROGRAMMING OPERATING SYSTEM

Although there are many types of operating systems, the best overall classification is into virtual and nonvirtual multiprogramming operating systems. The nonvirtual systems came into use in the mid sixties and were common until the mid seventies. The best known examples are probably IBM's OS/MFT and OS/MVT. Such systems are now obsolete and have been replaced by virtual operating systems, such as IBM's OS/MVS. Nevertheless the virtual operating systems have their foundation in the nonvirtual systems, so that the best way to understand virtual systems is by starting with a study of nonvirtual systems. We shall take IBM's OS/MVT as an example of a nonvirtual system. A great many of the concepts developed for this system are applicable to the widely used virtual system OS/MVS.

The Multiprogramming Concept

In the previous section we saw that a processor executes a program in main memory and that such a program is accompanied by a working-storage area. Because it would take the CPU too long to execute a READ or WRITE instruction, the job of reading and writing data is off-loaded onto one or more special processors, called **I/O processors**, or **channels**. It still takes a long time for an I/O processor to fetch data from an external storage device. The CPU does not wait for the I/O processor to complete an input or output job; instead it executes some other program that is also in main memory. If this program requires input or output of data in turn, the CPU switches to the execution of some other program, and so on.

Thus, to take advantage of off-loading input/output onto separate processors, the main memory must be able to hold a good number of programs so that the CPU can be kept busy. With OS/MVT this is accomplished by dividing the memory into **partitions** of different sizes, each of which is capable of holding a program and associated working storage, as well as some other structures. The partitions vary in size and number to fit the programs currently being executed. The operating system is a large program and resides in a separate part of memory.

Only one program at a time can be executed by the CPU, so that at any instant either a user program in a user partition is executing or the operating system is executing. Suppose that program B is executing. If the next instruction is a READ, execution control passes from program B to the operating system, which starts an I/O processor to read in the required data. Then the operating system switches execution control to some other program, perhaps A, which resumes execution from the point where its execution was interrupted earlier by a READ or WRITE instruction. When a program in a partition has finished execution, the operating system reads in a new program from a lineup of jobs (job stream) on a disk used for this purpose. Thus the operating system controls the execution of programs and input/output of data.

We now look in some detail at what exactly goes on during input and output and how the I/O processors, or channels, enter into the picture. We shall need this insight later when we come to examine different file organizations.

Memory Partition Structure

First we shall look more closely at a memory partition. We saw that it holds a user program and associated working-storage area, as does the memory of a simple computer system. There are additional structures and programs as well. We deal only with the most important of these (see Figure 1.2), namely, the buffer area, the channel program, the access method, and the data control block.

The **buffer area** is reserved for data being transmitted to and from an external storage device. In the section on input/output concepts, we saw that a computer file consists of **records**. A **block** of such records is the unit of transmission between buffer and the external device, so that a buffer must be able to hold at least one transmitted

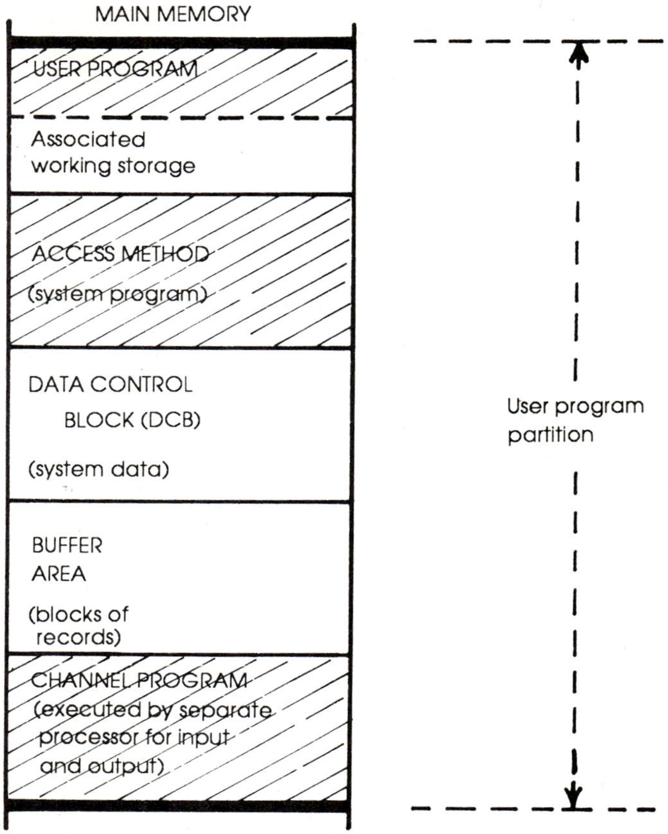

FIGURE 1.2 Some of the more important components of a partition of memory in the earlier versions of the major IBM operating systems. The access method is a large, complex system program that manages all access to a computer file on disk or tape. The data control block is used by the access method and contains technical data about a specific computer file. The buffer area is used to store blocks of records following transmission from an external file or before transmission to the file. The channel program is executed by a separate input/output processor that transmits data between external file and buffer area. The buffer area contains one or more buffers, each capable of holding exactly one data block.

block of records, or **transmitted data block**. A buffer area consists of **buffers**, each capable of holding a single transmitted data block.

The **channel program** is a computer program like any other, except that it is not executed by the CPU: It is executed by the I/O processor, or channel, that delivers a block of records to the buffer (or transmits one from the buffer). An I/O processor can be executing a channel program concurrently with the execution of some other program by the CPU.

The **access method** is a large program constructed by the operating system from an inventory of access method subcomponents. It functions essentially as a subprogram of the user program. It is the access method that brings a record from the buffer to the working-storage area and vice versa. When a block of records must be transmitted to or from a buffer, it is the access method that passes the necessary information to the operating system.

Finally we have a collection of data called the **data control block** (DCB) which contains specifications about the file being processed (for example, record length and block size). The access method uses this data in dealing with the records of the file.

Note that there is an access method, data control block, buffer area, and channel program for *each file* being processed by the user program. Thus in practice the actual user program and associated working-storage area often occupy only a small fraction of the memory space in a partition.

Total System Overview

In Figure 1.3 we show all the relevant parts of the system. We have the CPU and main memory containing the operating system and user program partitions. Program P is processing only one (disk) file and its partition contains one access method, one buffer area, and one channel program. We have a collection of I/O processors as well, each connected to a device (usually disk or tape drive) controller that is in turn connected to an array of disk or tape drives.

Suppose that program P is reading records from a file on a specific disk drive, namely, disk drive X as shown in Figure 1.3. At any given instant there will be records from X in the buffer. Now suppose that the CPU encounters a READ instruction. Execution control goes to the access method, which looks in the buffer for the next record. If it finds it, the record is transferred to the working-storage area and execution control reverts to the user program. This will be the scenario each time a READ statement is encountered by the CPU, until we reach the point where there are no more unprocessed records in the buffer. At this point a READ instruction causes execution control to go to the access method as usual. When access method looks in the buffer and

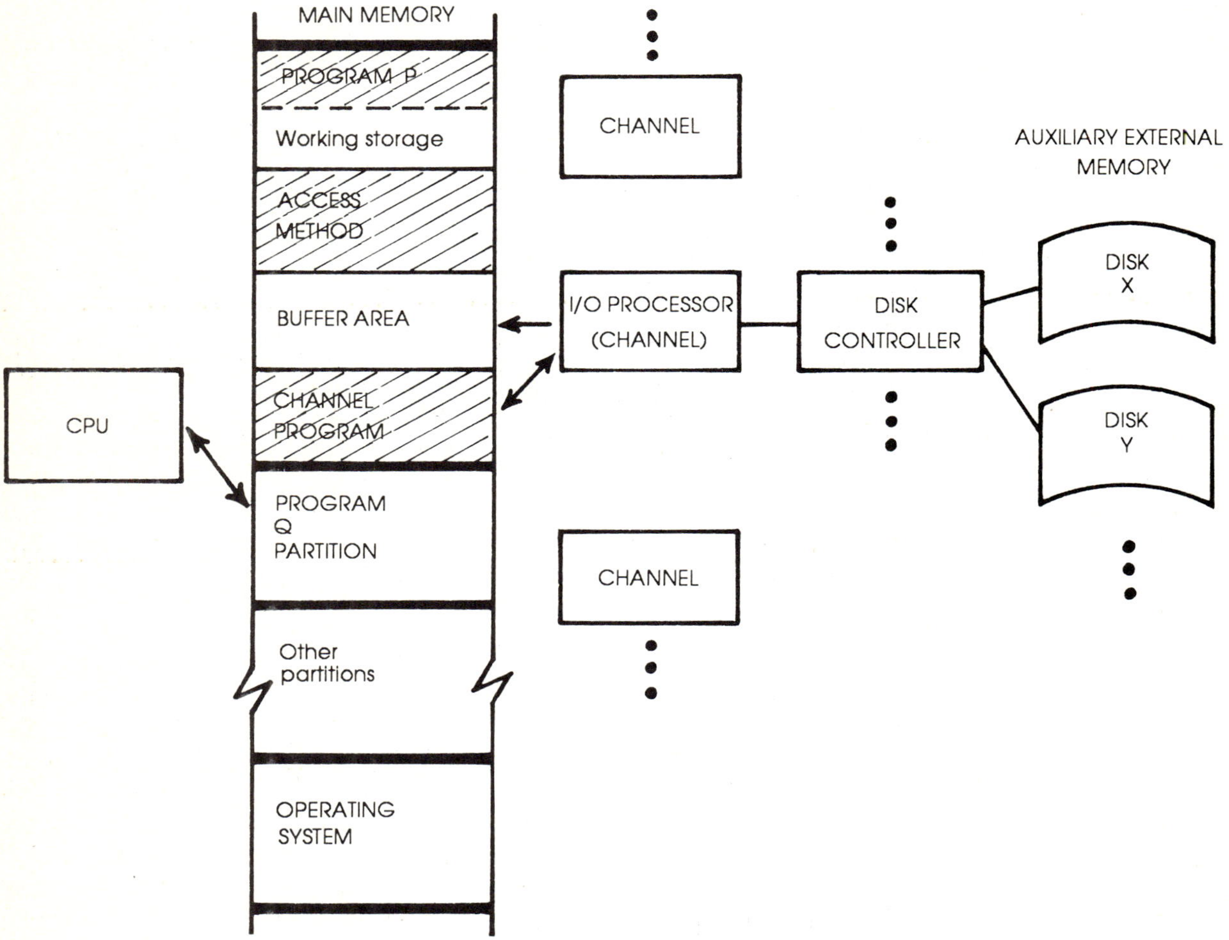

FIGURE 1.3 Illustration of how data is transmitted to a buffer area from an external memory device such as a disk or tape drive. Memory partitions are separated by heavy black lines. A block of records is transmitted from the disk by the I/O processor, or channel, as a result of its execution of the channel program. Channel program commands enable the I/O processor to control the disk controller, which in turn controls the reading of records from the disk. There can be many I/O processors with a large mainframe, all executing concurrently in the service of the end user. When the I/O processor is executing the channel program for user program A, the CPU will be executing some other program, such as a program in a different partition.

does not find the record, it constructs and passes a message to the operating system. The user program partition then shuts down—that is, neither user program nor access method execute—and control passes to the operating system.

The operating system now executes. In its region of memory there is a queue (lineup) of messages from access methods, including the one from the access method for program P. These messages are all requesting input or output of a block of data. The operating system tries to match messages with free I/O processors. When it has done all it can, it passes control back to some partition that is in a position to execute.

Sooner or later the operating system will get control again and our message (from the program P partition) will be matched to a free I/O processor that is connected to the correct disk (disk X). The operating system turns on the I/O processor channel, which begins execution of the channel program in the partition for program P. The I/O processor controls the disk via the disk controller (more about this in chapter 2) and the records are (relatively slowly) transferred as a block to the buffer. Meanwhile the CPU is busy executing some other program in another partition.

When the channel has finished transmitting the required block of records, it interrupts the CPU and control reverts to the operating system once more. The operating system finds another job for the free channel and passes execution control to some other partition that is in a position to execute. Sooner or later the partition for program P will receive permission to execute: and it is the access method that runs first. It takes the next record from the buffer and passes it to the working-storage area for program P. Program P then resumes execution and processes the record in the working-storage area.

When a record is being written, the process above is reversed. Records are passed one by one by the access method to the (ouput) buffer. When the buffer is full, the access method passes a message to the operating system, which sooner or later arranges for a channel to transmit the block of data. In chapter 3 we return to this process and examine it in the light of COBOL READ and WRITE commands.

Move Mode and Locate Mode

The overall method of data transmission between a program's working storage area and external storage described above is only one of two distinct possibilities, and is called **move mode transmission**. It is briefly summarized in Figure 1.4. A block is transmitted to (or from)

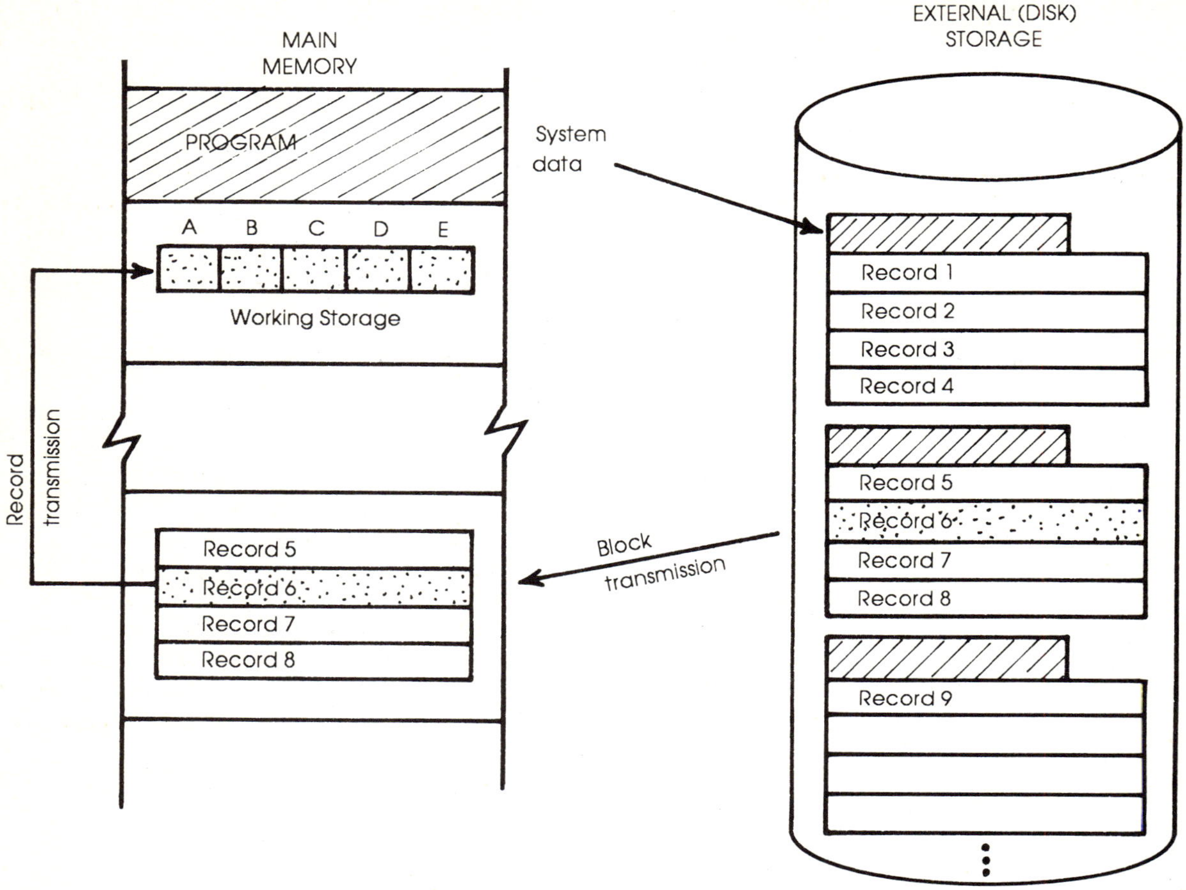

FIGURE 1.4 Illustration of movement of data from external storage to working storage using move mode transmission. The required block is first transmitted to the buffer by the I/O processor executing a channel program. The the access method moves the next record needed by the program to a group of memory cells in working storage (A, B, C, ...) that exactly fit the fields of the record.

the buffer and records are moved one by one to (or from) the working-storage area. It is called *move mode* because it involves a great deal of physical record movement. It is the simplest type of transmission and may be specified in COBOL programs, as we shall see in chapter 3.

The alternative to move mode is **locate mode transmission**. A block of records is transmitted to the buffer as in move mode transmission. However, records are not then transmitted to the working-storage area. Instead the record is processed on location in the buffer; that is, the fields of the record may be processed by instructions (in COBOL) of the application program, as if they were in working storage. Another way to look at this is to regard the buffer space occupied by the record being processed as a temporary extension of working storage. Thus application program instructions can move record fields from the buffer to other working-storage variables and can operate arithmetically on the record fields in the buffer.

COBOL details for locate mode processing are covered in chapter 3. However, because of subtle errors that can arise with COBOL locate mode processing, we cannot recommend it. Its original advantage was that it speeded up processing by eliminating unnecessary movement of data between working storage and buffer. Nowadays the high speed of execution of instructions dealing with movement of data within main memory makes such an advantage dubious.

Double Buffers

In our description of move mode and locate mode transmissions, we always assumed a single buffer for input or for output. Each buffer holds exactly one block of records, so the size of a transmitted block of records and the size of the buffer are exactly the same. In practice a pair of buffers are normally used with a file for either input or for output. This speeds up processing since the channel can be filling (or emptying) one of the buffers of the pair while the records in the other one are being processed by the application program. We return to this subject in chapter 3.

Physical and Logical (Storage) Files

Our study of input and output in a major multiprogramming operating system has now progressed so far that we can introduce the concept of **storage files**. There are two types of storage files, physical and logical. Storage files are simply the conventional files of conventional file processing; we shall normally omit the adjective *storage* and refer simply to physical and locigal files. We hope this does not confuse the reader. A classification of files in Figure 1.5 may help. (As well as storage files, it is possible to have *conceptual* and *external* files. These are important when dealing with files that are *integrated* to form *data bases*. Although we occasionally refer to data bases, the subject is completely beyond the scope of this book.)

A **physical file** is the file as it is physically stored in the recording medium, such as disk or tape. As we shall see, in addition to the

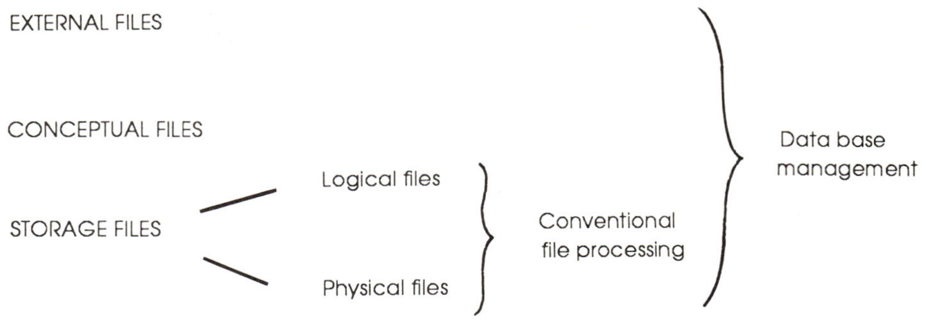

FIGURE 1.5 A classification of files. In this text, we are concerned only with storage files.

records that contain useful data (the **logical records**), additional system data is often stored with each block of records. This is especially true of disks; we shall look at the details in chapter 2. For now, assume that records are stored as shown in Figure 1.6a. Thus the physical file physically exists on a storage medium in the form of magnetized surfaces (assuming magnetic recording media); it can be transported manually and even stolen. With IBM systems such a physical file is often called a **dataset**.

When a block of records is transmitted to a buffer, the attached system data is not transmitted. This means that the transmitted data block is not quite the same as the block of records as physically recorded on disk (Figure 1.6a).

We noted earlier that a buffer contains exactly one transmitted block of records; it is the records in such blocks that are processed by an application program. The collection of records as seen or processed by the applications program is the **logical file** (Figure 1.6a).

The logical file is clearly not the same thing as the physical file, or dataset. For one thing, the logical file does not physically exist, but is abstracted from the physical file, which *does* physically exist. Nevertheless, the concept of a logical file is a very practical one, for it enables us to think about a file without having to visualize the details of exactly how it is stored on disk or tape.

Figure 1.6a applies to records of fixed length. However, where records vary in length, the situation is more complex. With IBM systems, where record lengths vary, each record and the entire block has an additional (4-byte) field to hold record and block lengths. These ad-

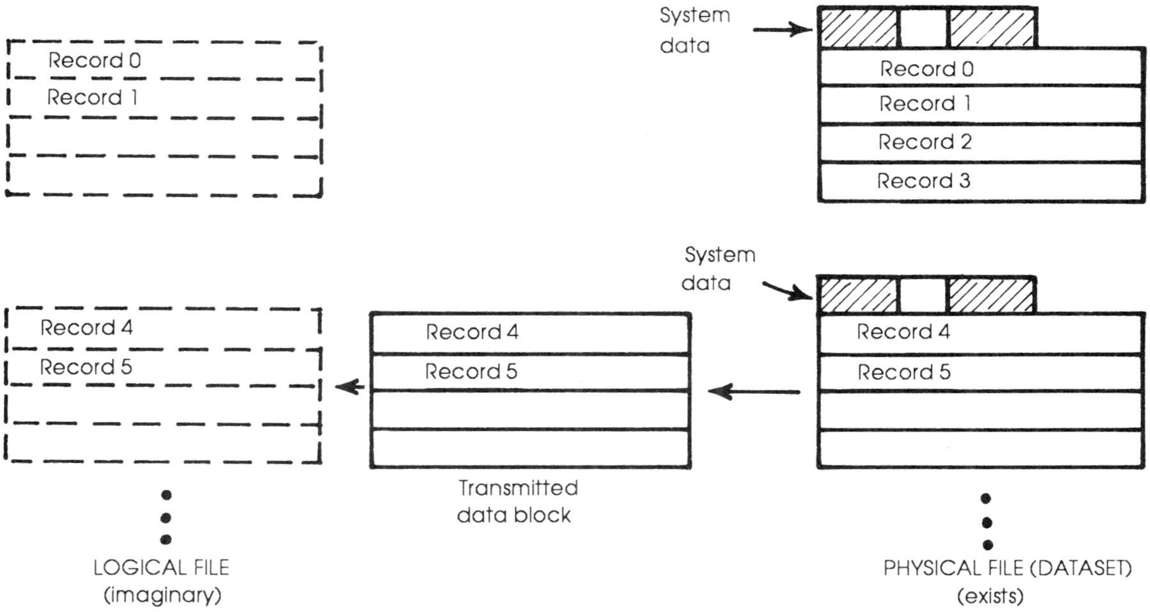

FIGURE 1.6a Logical and physical file concepts for fixed-length records; system data in the physical files can be count and key subblocks (chapter 2).

ditional fields are stored in the physical file, or dataset, and are even transmitted in the transmitted data block to the buffer (Figure 1.6b). However, only the access method (not the application program) makes use of the additional length fields. Since these fields are not seen by the application program, they are not considered part of the logical file. Only the pure records as seen by the application program make up the logical file. The COBOL techniques for dealing with variable length records are covered in chapter 5.

Operating System Command Laguages and JCL

There are many different types of computer files, and for a given type there are many different technical possibilities, such as the number of records in a block (the **blocking factor**) and the record length. Before

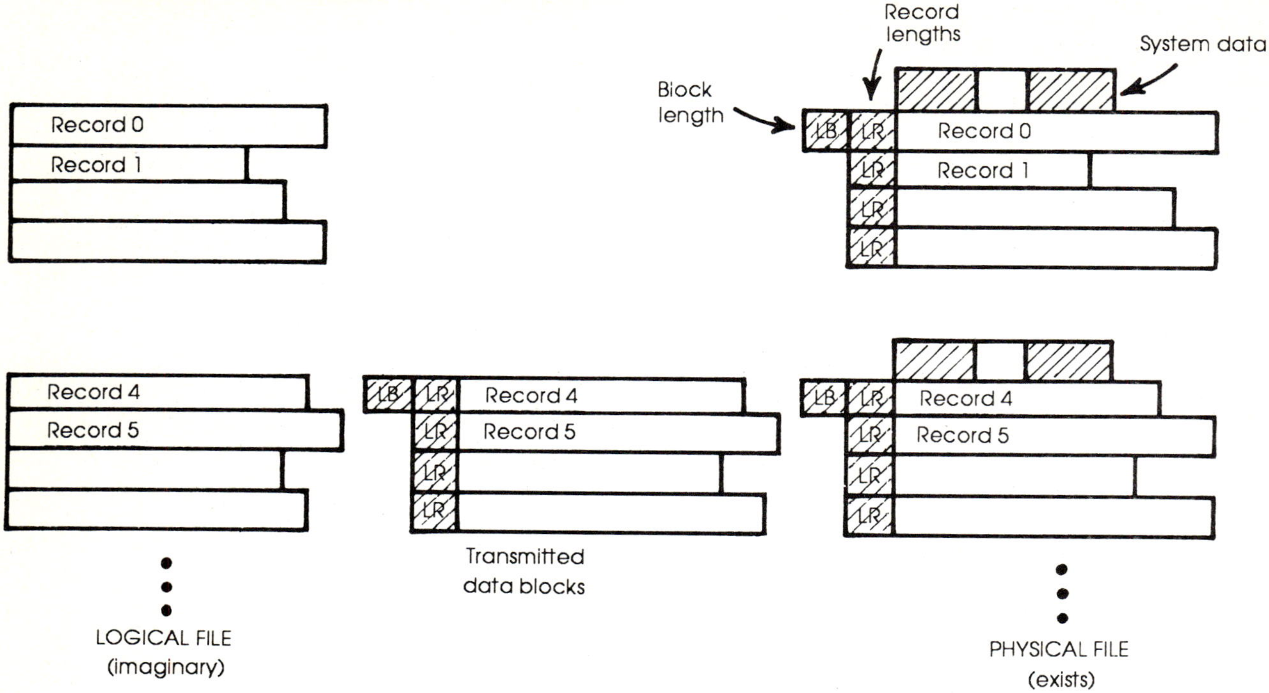

FIGURE 1.6b Logical and physical files with variable length records. In the physical file and the transmitted data block, the records have length of record (LR) and length of block (LB) fields attached.

the operating system can construct an access method, buffers, an I/O processor (channel) program, and a data control block (or the equivalent with non-IBM systems), it must have access to the complete technical specifications for the file.

Some of these specifications required by the operating system may be obtained from the environment and data divisions of the COBOL program that creates the file. Others are obtained from the file label (but only for the case where the file already exists and the processing does not involve its creation.) Finally the operating system obtains the remaining specifications from a specification of the physical file, or dataset specification. This normally accompanies the program that will process (or create) the file, when that program is submitted to the operating system for execution.

Such a dataset specification is called a **dataset definition statement (DD-statement)** with the major IBM operating systems; DD-statements are a part of **job control language (JCL)**. JCL is also used for giving commands to the operating system for compiling, loading, and storing programs and for linking programs to subprograms (**link-editing**).

JCL is complex and is a study in itself. Most of the subject is beyond the scope of this book and is not relevant to file processing. Other non-IBM systems have languages that are the equivalent of IBM JCL; these languages are often called **operating system command languages.** Their syntax is usually quite different fom IBM JCL.

Because IBM JCL is the most widely used operating system command language, and because DD-statements are relevant to computer file processing with IBM systems, we include sufficient material to place them in proper perspective and to enable readers to construct simple DD-statements. The first details appear in chapter 3.

THE VIRTUAL MULTIPROGRAMMING OPERATING SYSTEM

Virtual multiprogramming operating systems began to replace conventional operating systems (that is, the type described in the previous section) in the early 1970s and are now the most common.

A virtual operating system is really a nonvirtual system with an additional powerful facility built in, or superimposed: This is the **demand paging facility**, which we shall soon briefly describe. For now we would like to emphasize that what we learned about nonvirtual operating systems still applies to virtual operating systems; that includes access methods, blocks of records, buffers, data control blocks, channel programs, move mode, locate mode, and the need for either JCL or some other operating system command language. Indeed the JCL DD-statements for many types of files are the same with the major IBM nonvirtual and virtual operating systems. The major virtual IBM operating system is undoubtedly OS/MVS. Another common one, OS/VS-1, is a less powerful version of OS/MVS.

External Page Storage

With a virtual operating system only a small portion of a program is in main memory during execution. Instead of residing in main memory as with nonvirtual operating systems, the equivalent of each complete main memory partition (that is, user program and working-storage area plus all the access methods, data control blocks, buffers, and channel programs) now resides on a special fast system disk. This fast system disk is fast only in terms of other disks, for it is very slow indeed compared to main memory access times. Neverthless the system disk acts as an extension of main memory and is called **external page storage**.

Although it might well have been called external partition storage, the term *page storage* is used because the equivalent of the partitions of nonvirtual operating systems is stored in short portions of data called **pages**, each about 4,000 characters long. Thus the contents of a partition in main memory with a nonvirtual system are the same as the contents of the equivalent of a partition in external page storage with a virtual system, except that external page storage is divided into pages. It is useful to continue to regard external page storage as divided into partitions (see Figure 1.7).

Operation of a Virtual Operating System

A component of the operating system, called the **paging supervisor**, is capable of moving pages (of user program, access method, buffer, and so on) between external page storage and main memory. A program in external page storage cannot execute; that can happen only when the instructions of the program are in main memory. However, the important point is that all of a program's instructions need not be in main memory at the same time: Only a small group of instructions is needed. When this small group has been executed, it can be replaced by the next small group of instructions in the correct sequence.

The small group of instructions is, of course, a page of instructions; at any given instant in the main memory there are many pages from many different user programs and associated access methods, data control blocks, channel programs, and buffers (as in Figure 1.7). In addition at any given instant instructions in only one page in main memory are being executed.

When the instructions in a particular page have been executed, the next page of instructions for the same program is executed, but only if it currently resides in main memory. If it does not, the paging supervisor starts a reserved channel that brings in the page from external page storage and replaces some page that has not been used much recently. While this is going on, some other page, from the equivalent of some other partition, is executed. Thus pages of code from different partitions are executed one after another. In other words execution control switches from one partition to another just as with a nonvirtual operating system. The only major difference is that

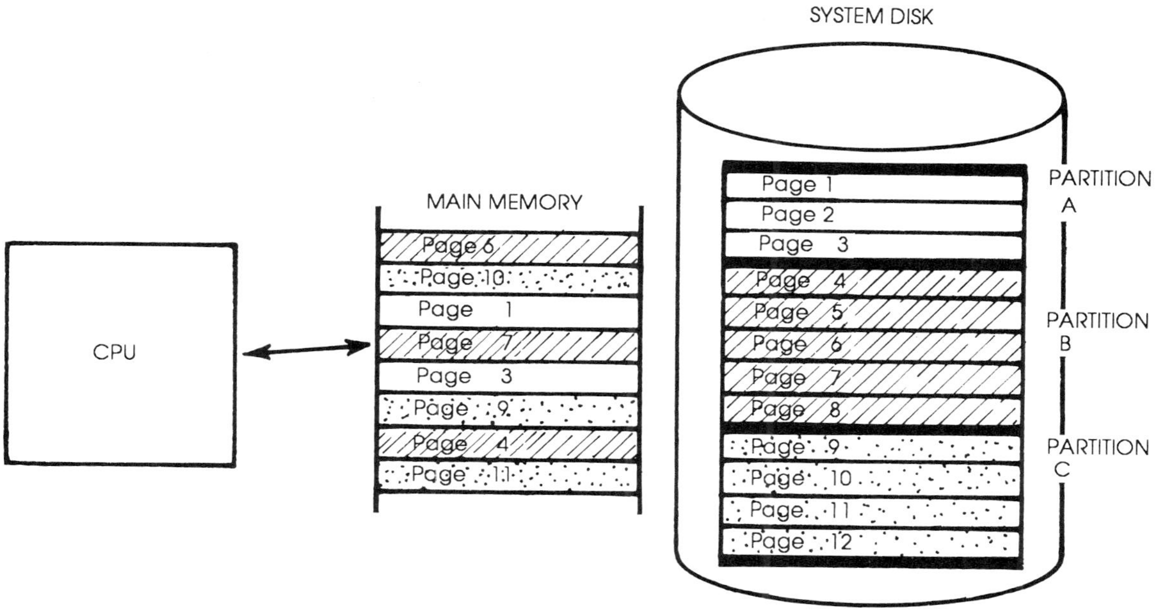

FIGURE 1.7 Principle behind demand paging in a virtual multiprogramming operating system. The application program, working-storage data, and associated access methods and buffer areas within what was a memory partition with a nonvirtual system no longer reside in main memory but on a system disk. The contents of the partitions on the system disk are divided into small pages, with each page containing a portion of a program or data area, or both. Pages are continually copied into main memory, where they can be executed in the case of program pages, or accessed and processed, in the case of data pages. To continue with execution of a program, after the instructions in a page in main memory have been exectued, the operating system will load the next page required into main memory. Remember that the CPU can execute or access only pages in main memory.

in the virtual operation system the partitions are being continually paged in and out of main memory. The method of reading and writing records described for nonvirtual operating systems still applies (with a few minor differences which need not concern us).

Thus the major difference between a virtual and a nonvirtual operating system is the continual paging in and out of memory of the pages of different partitions. This is called *demand paging*, and virtual operating systems are sometimes called **demand-paged operating systems**.

The major advantage of demand paging is that it is always possible to execute an application program, even when the program is too large to fit in memory, since it can be broken up into pages and executed in stages. With a conventional operating system, even normal-sized jobs must often wait a long time before being loading into main memory for execution when there is currently not enough space between any two partitions for the job (even when the total space available between partitions is large enough). This phenomenon is called **fragmentation** of memory.

Thus virtual operating systems perform much better than nonvirtual operating systems and appear to be here to stay. Unfortunately, taking the demand paging facility into account needlessly complicates our perception of operation of a computer system, and worse, it makes effective diagrammatic techniques extremely difficult, if not impossible. Thus demand paging effectively enshrouds the whole topic in mystery, right at the foundation.

The way out of the difficulty is to ignore for the most part that demand paging is taking place and to consider the memory as made up of partitions as described for nonvirtual systems. In most cases no incorrect conclusions will be drawn if this is done.

Therefore, to facilitate future discussions of computer operations and the drawing of diagrams involving main memory, we shall adopt the convention that an application program and accompanying routines and data structures occupy an arbitrarily large partition of main memory. It is to be tacitly understood that such a partition in practice resides in external page storage on a system disk and is paged in and out of memory as required.

BATCH, ON-LINE, AND INTERACTIVE PROCESSING

Business data can be processed in essentially three different overall ways: **Batch, on-line,** and **interactive processing**. On-line processing is by far the most expensive.

Batch Processing

In the beginning of the data processing era, only **batch processing** was used with business data; major commercial operating systems (such as OS/MVT), were designed to facilitate batch processing. In the late 1980s and early 1990s batch processing will probably still dominate. Currently the major commercial operating systems (such as OS/MVS, OS/MVS/XA, OS/VS-1, DOS/VSE from IBM, and GCOS from Honeywell) are still batch-oriented operating systems, although they are also virtual operating systems.

The batch processing concept can best be understood in terms of master file updating. A **master file** contains records of a relatively permanent nature and is of great value to a firm. Examples are a file of employee data or a file of customer data. Master files need to be updated. With batch processing, update information is accumulated in batches over intervals of time and placed in a smaller more transient file called a **transaction file**. Then the transaction and master files are processed, that is, batch processed. A program reads records from the files into buffers and working storage in appropriate order and makes appropriate changes to the master records, or even creates new master records. The result is a new and current version of the master.

Typically many batch jobs like this are being processed concurrently by a batch operating system. A program to carry out a batch updating job (accompanied by necessary job control instructions) is submitted to the operating system from punched cards or an interactive terminal. The operating system places jobs in queues (according to priority) on a reserved (system) disk. When a memory partition becomes free, the operating system loads the next job in the queue into the partition for execution. (But remember that all partitions are actually being demand paged.)

If the system is not very busy, a job submitted may be executed a few minutes later; if it is very busy with complex jobs ahead in the queue, a job may not be executed until the next day. Thus in practice a user who submits a job at a terminal has no further contact with it and simply logs off after submission. Usually the job will cause a message to be printed on the line printer when completed, so that the user will know the result of execution of the job.

Clearly batch processing is very efficient. The multiprogramming operating system keeps the central processor busy processing some job, even when other jobs are held up waiting for data transmission to and from their files. From a business point of view the major disadvantage is the period between updates of a particular master file. Clearly the master is current only immediately after updating and becomes progressively less current as the time for the next update approaches.

Where management requires that master file data be current at all times, batch processing is clearly inadequate, and on-line processing is required. However, a price must be paid for master files that are permanently current.

On-line Processing

On-line processing keeps files permanently current. As soon as update information is available for even a few records it is submitted to the computer system, which executes a program to carry out the necessary updates to the master file. There will typically be more than one file that requires on-line updating, and for any given on-line master file there may be many different updating procedures. This requires the availablity of a collection of on-line updating programs. In addition it is likely that the updating information will come from a large group of different users who are geographically dispersed.

It should now be clear why on-line updating is expensive compared with batch updating. Considerable computer resources must be kept in stand-by alert to respond quickly to any request for an update; in addition expensive communication facilities must be in place to handle the geographic dispersion of persons submitting updates; finally the whole system is much more difficult to implement and thus is expensive in terms of programming effort.

Batch operating systems are extensively used for on-line processing. This is possible because there will be a commercial need for on-line updating of only a minority of master files in an organization, so that most files will still be updated using batch processing. To accommodate on-line updating, a single large partition of the batch operating system, such as OS/MVS, is reserved for on-line processing. This partition is called an **on-line partition**. Other partitions are used in the usual way for batch updating, as described in previous sections.

Although many details of what actually goes on in an on-line partition are covered in chapter 10, Figure 1.8 gives an overview. In the on-line partition there is a perpetual job (that is, a job that never terminates). The major software component in this partition is a complex system called a **teleprocessing monitor**, which is really an operating system within an operating system. The rest of the on-line partition may be taken as divided into subpartitions, each of which is capable of holding an on-line program. (But remember, all of this is demand paged.)

The teleprocessing monitor is connected via a communications network to users at terminals. Users can send messages in predetermined format to the teleprocessing monitor and vice versa. The teleprocessing monitor continually allots a small slice of time to each of its terminals for messages. Typically it will receive a message from a particular terminal asking for a certain update program to execute. Essentially the teleprocessing monitor will load the required program from a library of on-line programs kept on disk. The on-line program is loaded into a subpartition of the on-line partition and executes under the control of the teleprocessing monitor. The user is then free to send further messages to the teleprocessing monitor which are then-passed to the executing on-line program. Conversely the on-line program can send messages to the user via the the teleprocessing monitor. In this way the user sends and receives messages that result in a master file update.

At any given instant within the partition only one on-line program in a single partition can be executing. However, the teleprocessing monitor will switch execution control from one on-line program to another as required. For example, if on-line program A has to wait for a message from a terminal, the monitor will switch execution control to on-line program B, which is in a position to execute. It is for this reason that the teleprocessing monitor is said to function like an operating system within an operating system.

From the point of view of the overall batch operating system, the on-line partition has the highest execution priority; batch jobs in the other partitions are said to be background jobs. Thus if background job A and the on-line partition are competing for permission to execute, the operating system will always give that permission to the on-line partition and let the background job wait. Thus a side effect of an on-line system is a slowdown in the speed of batch updating. Often the management response to this is the installation of a larger CPU (or even an additional CPU) and more memory. In some large installations one CPU handles on-line processing while the other (or others) handle batch processing.

Although we stated earlier that the job in the on-line partition never terminates, in practice it often does. At night the teleprocessing monitor is often shut down, so that important batch jobs get the necessary priority to execute.

One of the most widely used teleprocessing monitors is IBM's CICS (customer information control system, acronym pronounced *kicks)*. It does much of what has been described above and a lot more besides. The essentials of CICS are covered in chapter 10.

FIGURE 1.8 (Next Page) Showing how an on-line system uses a single on-line partition of batch operating system, such as OS/MVS. Other partitions are occupied by conventional batch jobs. Note that all partitions are assumed to be demand paged (not illustrated). The teleprocessing monitor in the on-line partition functions as a self-contained operating system and controls executing of the on-line programs in subpartitions of the on-line partition.

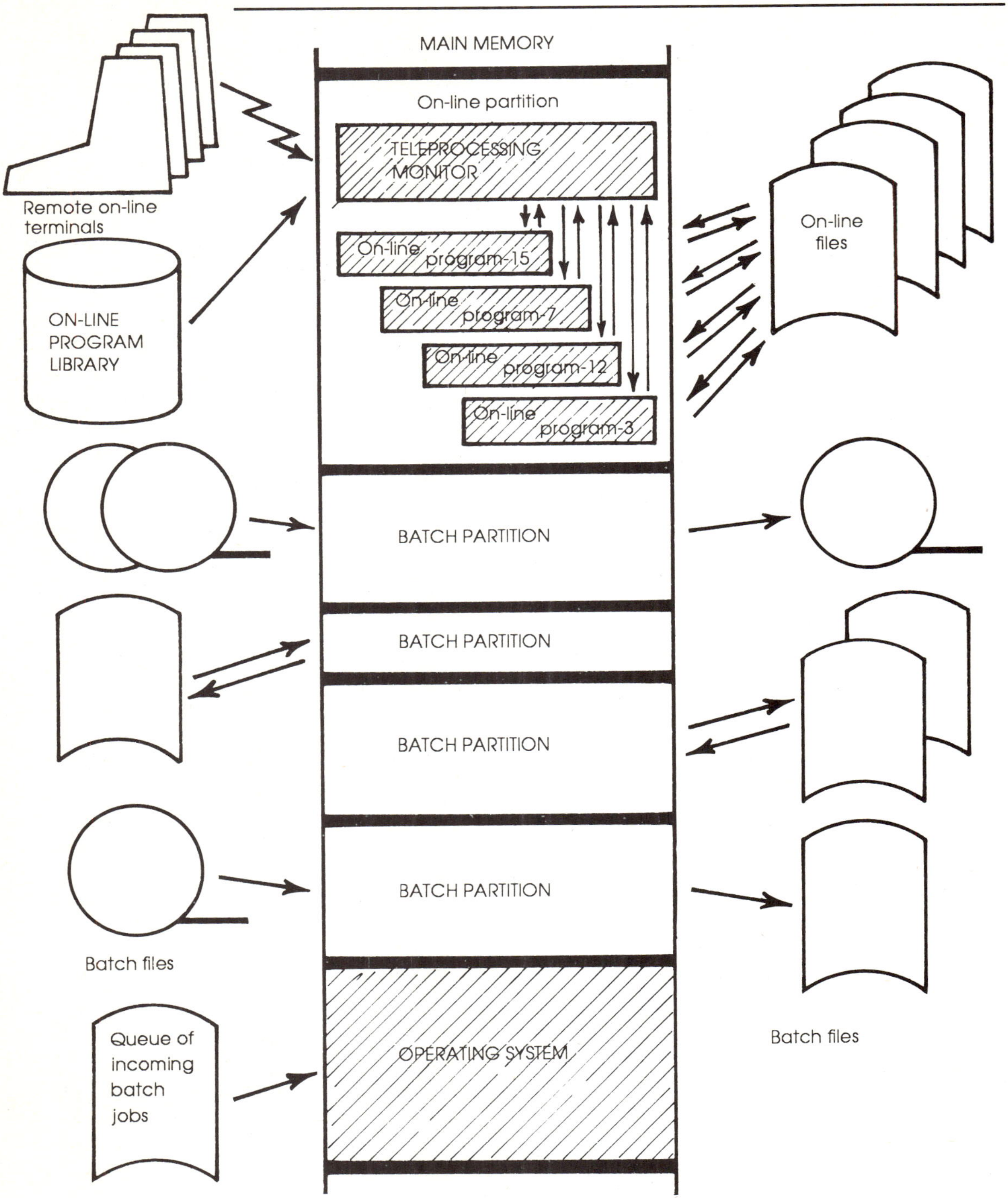
MAIN MEMORY
On-line partition
TELEPROCESSING MONITOR
On-line program-15
On-line program-7
On-line program-12
On-line program-3
BATCH PARTITION
BATCH PARTITION
BATCH PARTITION
BATCH PARTITION
OPERATING SYSTEM
Remote on-line terminals
ON-LINE PROGRAM LIBRARY
Batch files
Queue of incoming batch jobs
On-line files
Batch files

Interactive Processing with a Time-sharing Operating System

Another type of processing, often confused with on-line processing, is **interactive processing**. The confusion arises because strictly speaking on-line processing is a kind of interactive processing, since the remote user is able to communicate with, and thus interact with, an on-line program via messages. However, these messages are in a strict format conforming to the requirements of the teleprocessing monitor and are subject to extensive editing by the system before transmission. Thus writing file processing programs for use with a specific teleprocessing monitor (for example CICS programming) is a special skill (for details see chapter 10).

We also have operating systems that are designed for interactive processing. These are widely used at educational and scientific institutions. Examples are MULTICS from Honeywell, VM/CMS from IBM, and UNIX from Bell Laboratories. Here the memory is effectively divided into a large number of small partitions (as high as three or four hundred). The operating system frequently switches execution control among these partitions (all paged, of course) so that each partition is frequently allowed to execute for a short time slice. In addition each partition can receive input from and direct output to a terminal. This permits a user at a terminal to have his or her program executing in a partition and to interact with it as it executes. In this way we could have a user interacting with a COBOL program as follows: A COBOL ACCEPT command is executed within the program; the execution then stops until the user at the terminal submits the required data; when the COBOL program executes a DISPLAY command the necessary response data is printed on the terminal screen.

Operating systems of this kind are often called time-sharing operating systems because they efficiently share execution time among a large number of users. Most students using this book are likely to have access to such a system. Time-sharing operating systems are ideal for educational establishments, since they permit many students to have inexpensive access to computing resources.

As well as being able to read data from a terminal or output data to a terminal, a program in any of the partitions of an interactive operating system can communicate with external storage devices, particularly disk units, as is possible with a batch operating system. Thus a user at a terminal can give a command to execute a program to carry out a batch update of a master file from a transaction file. Unfortunately the processing is likely to be very slow indeed (all night possibly) if the file is large, because of the number of competing users.

The interactive operating system is designed for the reasonably knowledgeable user with relatively small amounts of data for processing, as is typical of student and scientific processing, but which could be disadvantageous for other processing. A further disadvantage for large scale batch processing is that the number of distinct file organizations supported is likely to be small compared with the big commercial batch operating systems like IBM's OS/MVS.

It is usually also possible to use a time-sharing operating system for keeping a master file current. When we want to update a few records of a particular master, we simply log on and run the required updating program interactively, feeding it the update data as input from the terminal. However, if we have a large number of geographically dispersed users who will need to update a single master file, the time-shared operating system becomes impractical. Besides being very much slower, there is usually no coordination of the updating from the diverse users. With the on-line system using a teleprocessing monitor, the teleprocessing monitor is in overall control; it will coordinate updating and so prevent accidents caused by updating programs that interfere with another'updating of the same file. This aspect of on-line file processing is also covered in chapter 10.

Time Sharing Subsystems with Batch Operating Systems

Just as it is possible to have batch processing with a time-sharing operating system, it is also possible to have interactive processing (as distinct from on-line processing) with a batch operating system. The method involves use of a time-sharing subsystem that is installed in a single partition of the batch operating system. The best known example of this is IBM's TSO (time-sharing-option). This system functions as a perpetual job and time-shares the execution of programs submitted by users at terminals. Meanwhile batch jobs are executed in the other partitions (everything being demand paged, as usual). The facilities provided to the terminal user are much like those of a time-sharing or interactive operating system. In this way the commercial batch operating systems can provide the best of both worlds.

SUMMARY

A computer file consists of records, each of which describes some entity, such as a customer, product, or employee. A record is made up of fields of data, and the field, or combination of fields, that uniquely identifies a record is the primary key field. A computer file resides on magnetic disk or tape. To process a file, an application program in main memory reads records one by one in a part of main memory called working storage.

Reading of records by a program is slow because of the electromechanical nature of the storage devices. Consequently it is more efficient to have many programs executing concurrently in main memory, with reading and writing of records off-loaded to independent input/output (I/O) processors, or channels. Application programs reside in partitions of memory, and overall activity is managed by a multiprogramming operating system.

Records are stored in storage media as blocks of records. When reading records, the I/O processor transfers a block of records to a buffer. An access method then transfers a record from the buffer to the working storage area. For any given application program in a memory partition, the partition will also hold access methods, buffers, and other structures for facilitating reading and writing of records.

Move mode processing requires that a record being processed be moved from buffer to working storage. Locate mode processing permits records to be processed on location in the buffer.

To permit the operating system to construct the access methods and other structures for input/output of the records of any file, exact specifications of the file must be given when the file is created. These can be given partly in the application program that creates the file and partly in operating system command language specifications. Job control language (JCL) is the name given to IBM's operating system command language. A JCL command to specify a file is called a DD-statement (dataset definition), and accompanies the application program.

The file as physically recorded on disk (that is, the physical file), may not be quite the same as the collection of records that the program processes (that is, the logical file). With IBM systems the physical file is called a dataset.

With a virtual operating system, the contents of the partitions of memory are stored on a system disk and broken up into small pages of data. Sufficient numbers of pages to permit programs to execute are held in main memory. There is frequent transfer of pages between main memory and the system disk. This is called paging on demand, or demand paging.

With batch processing, updates to a file are saved; the file is updated perhaps weekly or monthly. With on-line processing, information is used to update the file as soon as the information becomes available.

A teleprocessing monitor resides in a partition (demand paged) of memory and manages a large number of on-line programs that can communicate with a large number of remote terminals. Teleprocessing monitors are used in commerce for building on-line systems that maintain on-line files.

EXERCISES

1. Explain why a READ or WRITE program instruction is not directly executed by the CPU in a mainframe computer.
2. Where is working storage located in a computer and what is its function?
3. Explain the difference between a buffer area and a buffer.
4. In a partition of main memory that contains an application or user program, how many access methods will be needed? How many buffer areas?
5. What does a channel program do?
6. What does an access method do?
7. How does a disk controller work in conjunction with an (I/O) processor?
8. How many data blocks can an input buffer hold?
9. Explain how records in an input buffer are processed with move mode.
10. Explain how data in an input buffer is processed with locate mode processing.
11. Explain the difference between a logical file and a physical file.
12. With variable length transmitted record blocks, explain the nature of any additional fields attached.
13. What is demand paging in a virtual operating system? Explain how it eliminates memory fragmentation.
14. What does a teleprocessing monitor do? What is an on-line partition?

2 TAPE AND DISK STORAGE MEDIA

Computer files are stored on magnetic tape and disk; an understanding of these storage media is a prerequisite for understanding not only conventional file processing, but also data base technology. In this chapter we cover the physical characteristics of both tapes and disks. We look in particular at the different ways in which data can be stored or formatted on these media and, at the (amount of) time required to read and write records under different circumstances. We deal with tape media first.

OVERVIEW OF TAPE STORAGE MEDIA

Magnetic tape is still probably the most widely used medium for storing computer readable data with large computers; it appears unlikely that this situation will change much in years to come. A standard reel of tape is cheap (less than $20) and, with careful management, such a reel can hold as much data as half a million punched cards; this is the equivalent of about 10,000 pages of text, or twenty good-sized books. Furthermore a reel of tape is compact and inexpensive to store on racks in tape libraries. As a result, most larger business organizations have tape libraries holding thousands of reels of tape.

Care must be taken with tapes. Because data is recorded magnetically on the tape, it may easily be destroyed by a magnet. Very tiny magnets, in the form of magnetically charged dust worn from tapes, are a particular menace, for they stick to the tape and cause errors when the tape is being read. In addition a single crinkle can render a tape worthless. Crinkles are avoided by careful handling; the dust problem is minimized by simple cleanliness or more recently by the use of newer types of data recording that are less sensitive to magnetic dust.

The major disadvantage of tapes is that they can only be read sequentially, much like the scrolls of the ancient world. This has meant that tape files are not used to form large data bases (collections of integrated and cross-referenced files), which have a basic need for direct access, so that cross references may be followed. However, even with data base technology there is a need for tape files, since tapes are ideal

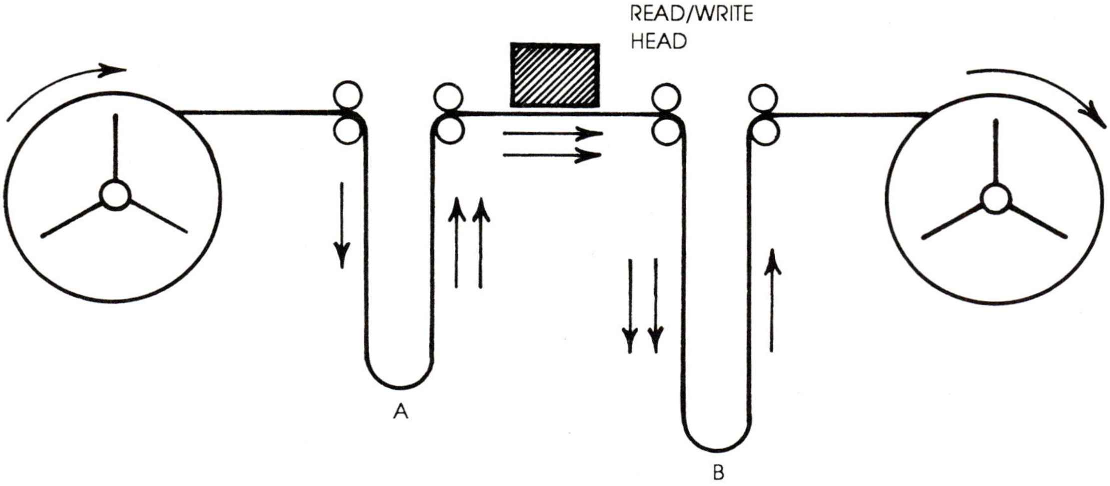

FIGURE 2.1 Schematic of a tape drive. For electrical and magnetic reasons, before date can be read from the tape, the tape must be moving at high speed. To reduce the time required to accelerate the tape to this speed, loops of tape are used as at A and B. The light-weight tape in the loops is first accelerated, with the heavier reels catching up later.

for archiving back-up copies of direct access data base files, in case something happens to the data base. Thus tape files are pervasive—it is important to have good understanding of them.

Physical Characteristics

Tapes are read and written using **tape drives**, (most readers will have seen a picture of one). A tape drive cannot be connected directly to the input/output (I/O) processor (or channel) with mainframe computers, but is attached to a **tape-drive controller**. This controller is then attached to the I/O processor (see also chapter 1). The controller responds to instructions executed by the I/O processor by carrying out the operations necessary to control the tape drive.

Tape drives are sensitive and complex devices—a great deal of fine control is needed to ensure satisfactory operation. The control hardware could be integrated into the tape drive, thus eliminating the need for a separate controller. But controller hardware is expensive, so it is cheaper to have a separate controller that can be used to con-

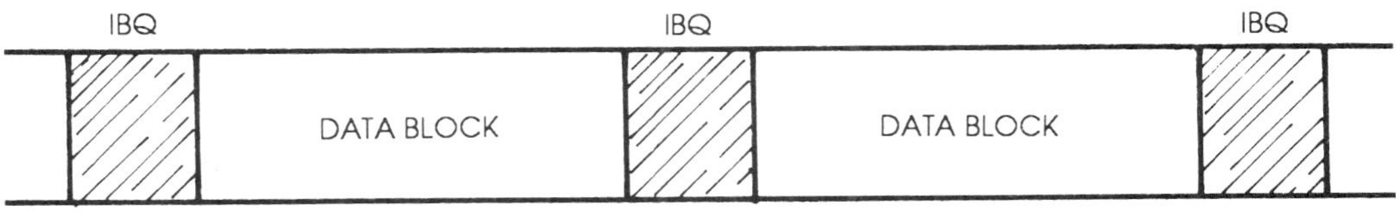

FIGURE 2.2. A tape has gaps (interblock gaps, or IGBs) between blocks of useful data. These gaps are simply areas in which no data is recorded and are needed for the read/write head to have room to accelerate, decelerate, and stop between reading or writing blocks of data. The gaps are quite large and can significantly affect the amount of data a tape can hold.

trol several tape drives. With a mainframe computer, a controller and tape drive can cost the best part of $100,000.

Readers who have watched a tape drive in operation will have noticed that the reels are stopped a great deal of the time, moving only in short jerks. A schematic of a tape drive is shown in Figure 2.1. When data is not being read the tape is stopped. For data to be read, the tape must first accelerate to a fairly high speed. Because the tape reels are heavy and cannot be accelerated quickly, the loose loops of tape (at A and B in Figure 2.1) move first, with the heavier reels catching up later.

It should be understood that the tape can be read only when it is moving quickly, for fundamental electrical reasons that are essentially the same as the reasons why a dynamo on a bicycle will give light only when the bicycle is moving. Anyway we have the following sequence: Initially the tape is stopped, with no reading possible; then it is accelerating, with still no reading possible; then it is moving at uniform speed and is being read; then it is slowing down with no reading possible; and finally it is stopped.

This means that there have to be extensive portions of the tape without any data recorded on them, so that the read/write mechanism is over these regions when the tape is accelerating, decelerating or simply stopped. Such regions are basic to magnetic tape and are called **interblock gaps** (IBGs); they are used to separate blocks of data on the tape, (see Figure 2.2).

IGBs give rise to many of the technical difficulties associated with laying out data on tapes. The gaps must be quite large and, with commonly used tapes, could otherwise contain 960 bytes of data. Thus a tape with many gaps will have a lot of space that cannot be used for data. We look at this in more detail in the next section, but for readers who prefer to skip the technicalities, the basic aim is to make the

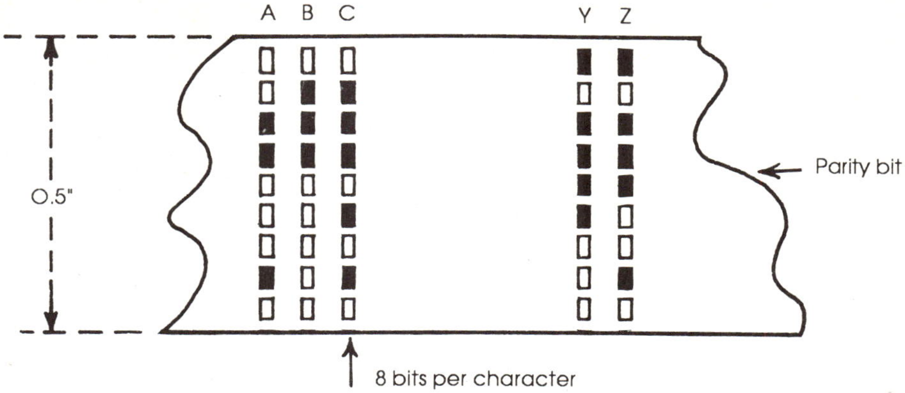

FIGURE 2.3. One byte, or character, of data is stored transverse to a tape. The 8 bits for each character are supplemented by an additional parity bit, which ensures that there is always an odd number of 1-bits (black) for each character and thus facilitates error detection. The recording density is the number of characters that can be stored per inch of tape. The tape illustrated above is a standard 9-track tape.

blocks of data sufficiently large so that the gaps take up only a small percentage of the tape. This also permits the tape to be read faster, as we shall see in a later section.

HOW MUCH DATA CAN GO ON A TAPE?

A common problem with tapes is figuring how much data a tape can hold under different circumstances; in this section we shall see how to make such estimations easily.

First we must look at exactly how data is stored on a tape. A short section of tape is illustrated in Figure 2.3. A byte (or character) of data is stored transverse to the tape using an 8-bit code. (With earlier tapes a 6-bit code was used.) An additional bit (the **parity bit**) is used for error checking by the tape drive. Such a tape, which is standard, is said to have 9 **tracks**.

When data is written on the tape a 1 or a 0 is recorded for each bit making up the 8 bits of a character. The **parity bit** is then recorded to make the total number of 1-bits an odd number. Later if a piece of magnetic dust causes a 1 to be mistaken for a 0 (or vice versa), the number of 1-bits will no longer be an odd number and the tape drive will register a **read, or parity, error**. Most drives will automatically retrace and reread several times (with the aim of removing the offending dust particle) before an error message is delivered to the program responsible for the reading. Generally the program must contain procedures to handle such an emergency (see chapter 3). A simpler way of looking at this is to assume that a 9-bit code is being used, where every character contains an odd number of 1-bits!

There are two types of codes in use for the characters on the tape. These are the Extended Binary Interchange Code **(EBCDIC code)** from IBM and the American National Standard Code **(ASCII code)**. As might be expected, the EBCDIC code is used on IBM mainframes and IBM look-alikes, which together constitute the majority of mainframes, while the remaining mainframes use the ASCII code. The only practical point here is that the user must know the code used to store data on a tape to be able to read the data. With the major IBM operating systems the type of code to be used can be specified in the job control language (JCL) specifications for the file.

Except for the need to incorporate procedures in application programs to handle parity errors when they occur, users may conveniently forget about how characters are actually stored on tape. However, they must be aware of what is called the **recording density** of the characters on the tape and how much space is taken up by gaps. These are the basic storage parameters, which we now look at in more detail.

The Basic Storage Parameters

The number of characters that can be stored along an inch of tape is called the **recording density**. Often a given tape drive model will permit several recording densities, one of which is standard while the others are optional. In the table below, we have the three most common densities and associated IGB sizes for IBM tape drives.

DENSITY *(bytes per inch)*	GAP *(inches)*	GAP *(bytes)*	TAPE LENGTH *(feet)*	NOMINAL CAPACITY *(megabytes)*
800	0.6	480	2,400	23
1,600	0.6	960	2,400	46
6,250	0.3	1,875	2,400	180

These parameters apply to many of the models of the widely used family of IBM 3420 tape drives and plug compatible units. Note that the density is commonly specified in either bytes per inch (bpi) or sometimes bits per inch (bpi). Both specifications are identical, since 1,600 bytes on an inch of tape means 1,600 bits along an inch of a track of a tape! Probably the most common type of recording in use involves 1,600 bpi and a gap of 0.6 inches, or 960 (wasted) bytes.

Tape lengths of 2,400 feet are standard in file processing. Shorter tape lengths are available, but these are more likely to be used for holding programs.

We are now in a position to show how to calculate tape capacities. We also include some less precise graphical methods, since in many cases an estimate accurate to within a few percent is all that is required. We give graphical results for the more common 1,600-bpi tapes, but illustrate the method of calculation underlying the charts using the 6,250-bpi tapes. This should enable readers to make estimates easily with 1,600-bpi tapes and understand how to do the calculations when an exact answer is required.

Efficiency of Tape Utilization

Suppose that we have a 6,250-bpi tape that is full of 2,000-byte blocks; we want to know (a) what percentage of the tape contains useful data, and (b) how much useful data is on the tape. The method is simple and is based on the observation that every block on the tape must be accompanied by a gap of 1,875 bytes (see Figure 2.2). This means that 2,000 bytes of useful data take up 3,875 bytes of space on the tape (2,000 + 1,875). This is true everywhere on the tape, so that the percentage of space occupied by the data blocks must be 100*2,000/3,875 or 51 percent. This answers the first part of our problem.

To determine exactly how much data is on the tape (the second part of our problem), we need to know how many blocks are on the tape. In theory the tape can hold 12*2,400*6,250 or 180,000,000 bytes of data. This is the **nominal capacity** of the tape. Because each block on the tape actually takes up (2,000 + 1,875) bytes, the total number of blocks on the tape must be close to *180,000,000*/3,875, or 46,451.6 blocks. However, there cannot be only *part* of a block on the tape, so the exact answer is 46,451 blocks. This means 46,451*2,000 or 92,902,000 bytes, which is also about 51 percent of the nominal capacity. This is what we would expect, given the answer to the first part of our problem.

In Figure 2.4 we have a curve that may be interpreted either as the percentage efficiency of tape utilization plotted against data block

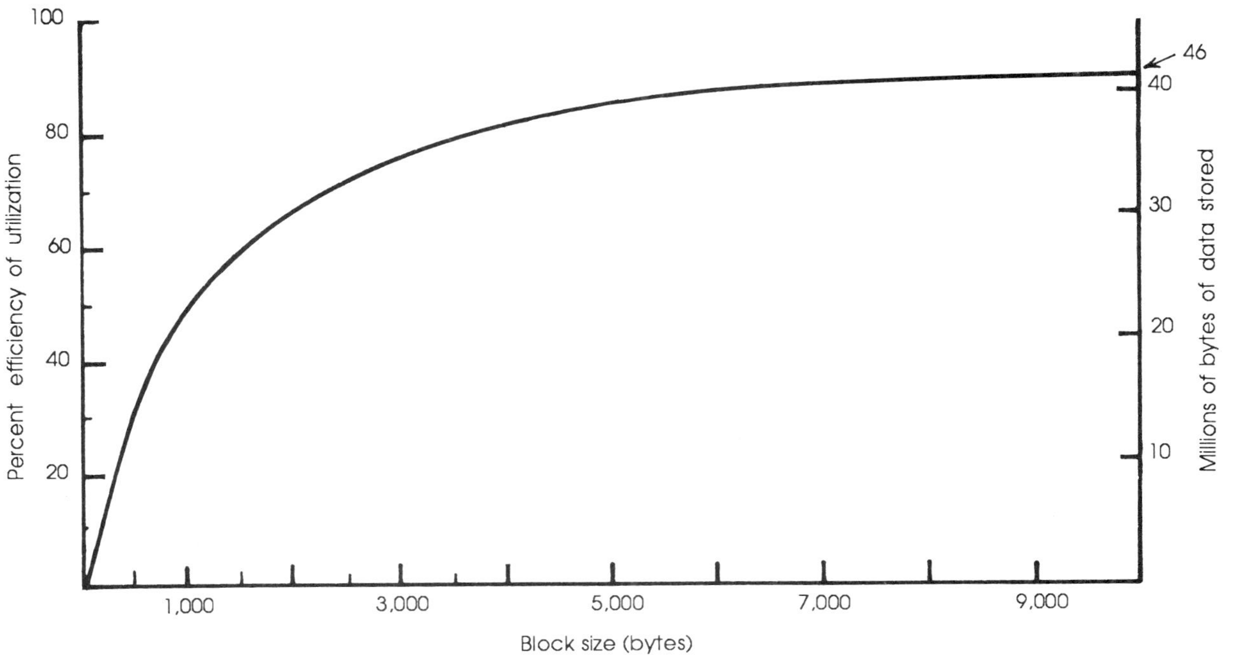

FIGURE 2.4. The curve gives the percentage of the space on a full 1,600-bpi tape that is actually occupied by useful data versus the block size. It also gives the total useful data on the tape (right axis) versus block size for a full 1,600-bpi tape.

size, or as the total number of bytes on the tape plotted against block size (for the case of the commonly used 1600-bpi tape). Thus we see that a block size of 2,000 bytes will result in about 66 percent of the tape containing the useful data, with the remaining space used for IGBs. The curve was derived using the calculation method outlined above. The curve in Figure 2.5 gives the number of blocks that can be placed on a 1,600-bpi tape versus the block size.

Selecting Block Size

It is clear that we must always choose the largest possible block size to reduce wasted space by interblock gaps. Later we shall see that too many gaps also slow down reading of the tape.

In general, however, we cannot make the block size arbitrarily large, for two reasons. First, the block size equals the buffer size and

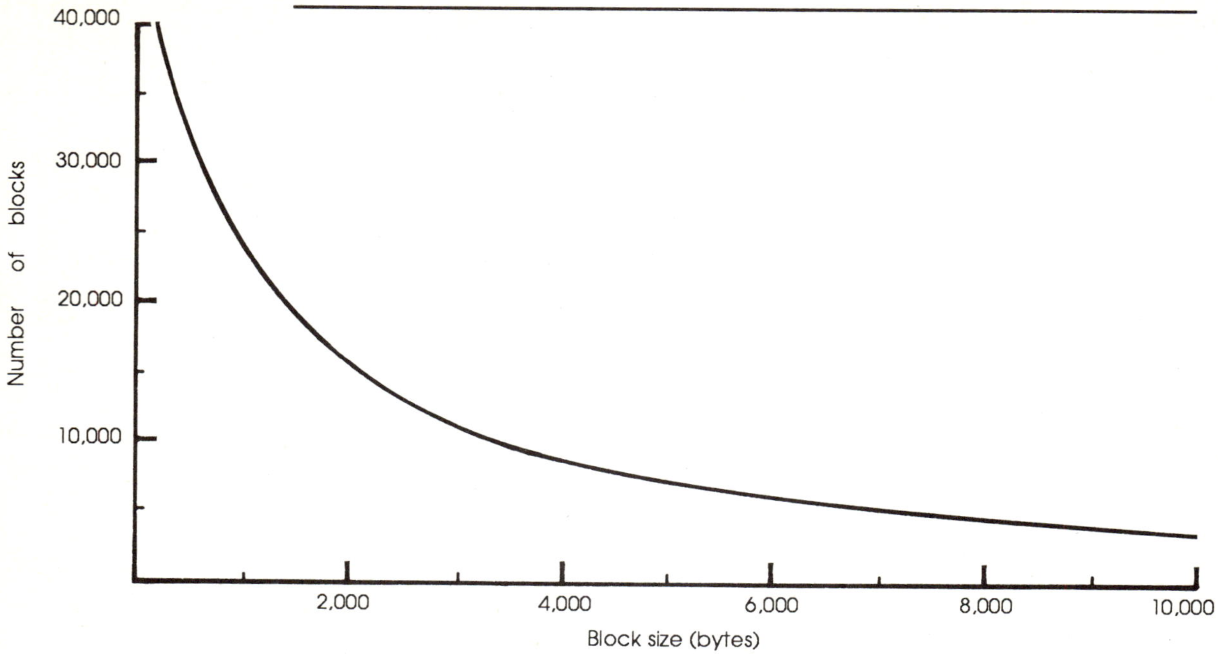

FIGURE 2.5. Number of data blocks that can be placed on a full 1,600-bpi tape versus block size.

thus large block sizes mean that the memory space taken up by application programs and associated data areas will increase; which further means that either we have fewer programs executing concurrently or we have an increase in the amount of paging with a virtual operating system. Thus system performance decreases. Second, a larger block takes longer to read; this increases the time during which channels are tied up and not available for input/output for other programs. Thus in this way system performance also degrades.

Generally block sizes between 1,500 and 4,500 bytes are used with 1,600-bpi tapes, which gives utilization efficiencies between about 60 percent and 83 percent, (as can be seen in Figure 2.4). With 6,250-bpi tapes, somewhat higher block sizes are often used.

Blocking Factors

In practice we often must know how many records we can get on a tape. Clearly this number depends on the size of the records and the

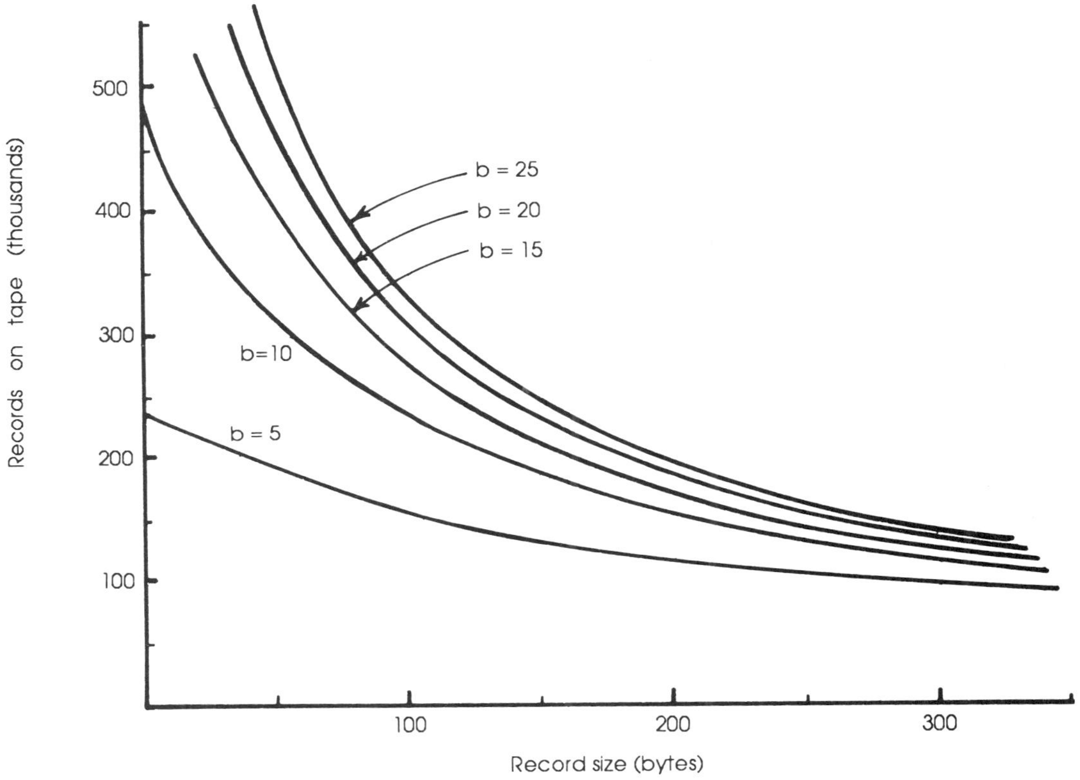

FIGURE 2.6. Illustrating the relationship between the number of records on a completely filled 1,600-bpi, 2,400-foot reel of tape and the record size, for different blocking factors (b values on curves). Note that with small record sizes the number of records that the reel can hold increases markedly with blocking factor.

number of records in a block, that is, the blocking factor. The most common tape files contain fixed length blocks each containing a fixed number of fixed length records. This is known as **fixed blocked (FB) format**.

With FB format a common problem is calculating how many records of a given size we can get on a tape using a certain blocking factor. To be specific suppose that we have 100-byte records with a blocking factor of 20 and need to know the number of such records that we can place on a 6,250-bpi tape.

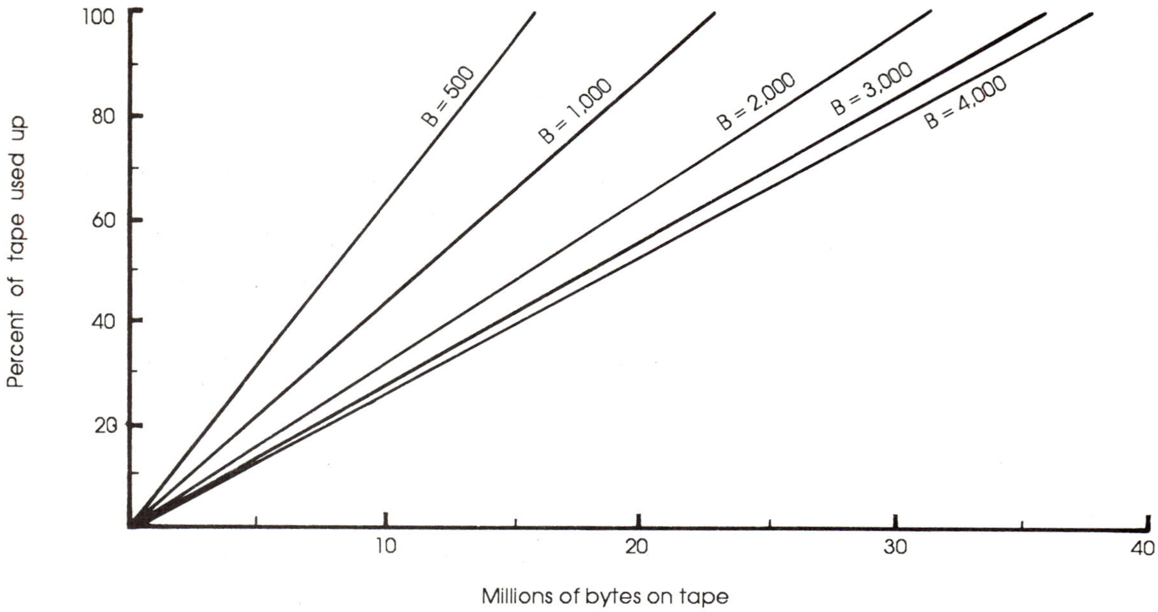

FIGURE 2.7. Showing what percentage of a tape is occupied by a file with a given number of bytes, for different block sizes. That part of the tape not used could contain a second file. The symbol B is used for block size. Tape density is 1,600 bpi.

First we derive the block size, which is 20*100, or 2,000 bytes. Then we use this block size to get the number of blocks that can fit on the tape. We did this calculation earlier; the result was 46,451 blocks. Since each block has 20 records the total records in the file will be 929,020 records, which is quite a lot.

The results of similar calculations with 1,600-bpi tapes are displayed graphically in Figure 2.6. We see that a 1,600-bpi tape can hold about 315,000 records, when a record's size is 100 bytes and the blocking factor is 20.

Partially Full Tapes

A reel of tape, or **volume**, can hold several different files when the files are small, but a single file can require many reels (volumes) if the file is large. Frequently we would like to know what percentage of a tape is needed for a given file for a given block size. To be specific, suppose that we have 20 million bytes of data, and we want to know what percentage of a 6,250-bpi tape is occupied by the complete file when the block size is 2,000 bytes.

First we must calculate how many bytes are taken up on the tape. Each block takes up (2,000 + 1,875) bytes when we include the gap, that is, 3,875 bytes. But we have 20 million bytes of data, that is, 20,000,000/2,000 blocks of data, or 10,000 blocks. That means 10,000*3,875 bytes taken up on the tape, or 38,750,000 bytes. But the tape nominal capacity is 12*2,400*6,250 bytes or 180,000,000 bytes. This means that the file occupies 100*38,750/180,000 percent of the tape, or about 21 percent.

If the space required had exceeded 100 percent, we would have needed more than one reel (volume). We carried out similar calculations for a 1,600-bpi tape and used the results to plot the curves in Figure 2.7. Here we show the percentage of a partially full tape needed to hold a given number of bytes for different block sizes. The curves may be extrapolated to cover the case where more than one reel will be required (that is, the percentage of tape required exceeds 100).

Variable Length Records

Occasionally the records of a file have varying length. Modern practice is to avoid such records if at all possible, since they unnecessarily complicate file processing, especially information retrieval involving multiple files. Because data base processing is one type of multiple file processing, variable length record files are not recommended for-data bases, although there are currently many older data bases that contain them. This short section deals with the details of tape capacities with variable length records; readers are advised to skip it on their first reading of this text.

With IBM mainframes when we construct a variable length record file, each record written out on tape has an additional 4-byte field attached to carry the length of the record, so that the access method can distinguish one record from another on retrieval. In addition there is a further 4-byte field attached to the block to carry the length of the block, since the block size will also vary.

This type of format is called **variable blocked (VB) format** (see Figure 2.8). Notice that between each block is the standard interblock gap, and that the total block size is the sum of the record sizes plus 4n plus 4, where n is the number of records to a block.

With IBM VB format, in the JCL for the program that creates the file, the programmer must specify:

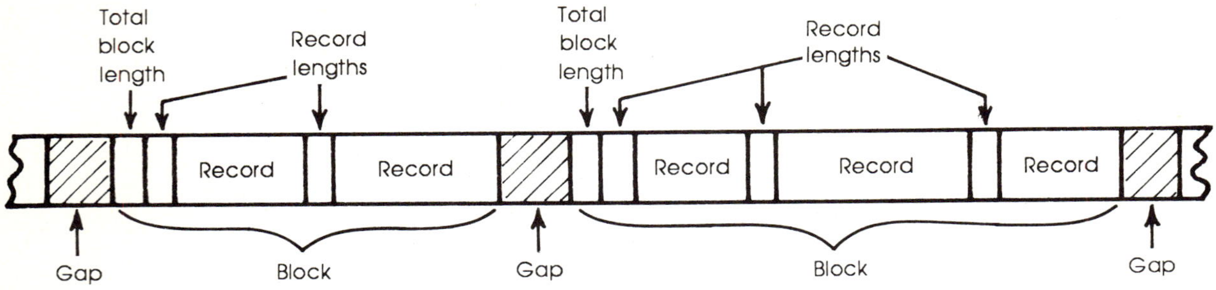

FIGURE 2.8. Variable blocked format (VB format) on tape. Attached to each record is a 4-byte field to hold the length. An additional 4-byte field is attached to the beginning of the block to hold the total block length. There has to be a maximum block size specified for the file and a maximum record size.

a. The maximum block size that will be allowed

b. The maximum record size that can occur

A little thought will show that these specifications imply a minimum block size as well, so that block sizes on the tape will fluctuate between a minimum and a maximum.

We can illustrate this with an example. Suppose that the maximum allowed block size is 3,000 bytes and the maximum record size is 100 bytes. Now suppose that as the file is being created, records are being placed in the buffer one by one to form the next block, and that the total bytes so far placed in the buffer (including the extra 4 bytes for the block size and the extra 4 bytes for each record length) is 2,900.

This size ensures the possibility of the block always being able to hold one more record, for even if the largest possible record happens to come next (100 bytes), we can still fit it in. But if there had been 2,901 bytes already in the potential block, we have the possibility that the next record will be the largest possible and will not be able to fit into this block. In that case 2,901 would be the minimum block size, given by the maximum block size minus the maximum record size plus one.

Note that the maximum block size specification includes the 4-byte block-length field. Furthermore the maximum record-length specification includes the 4-byte record-length field.

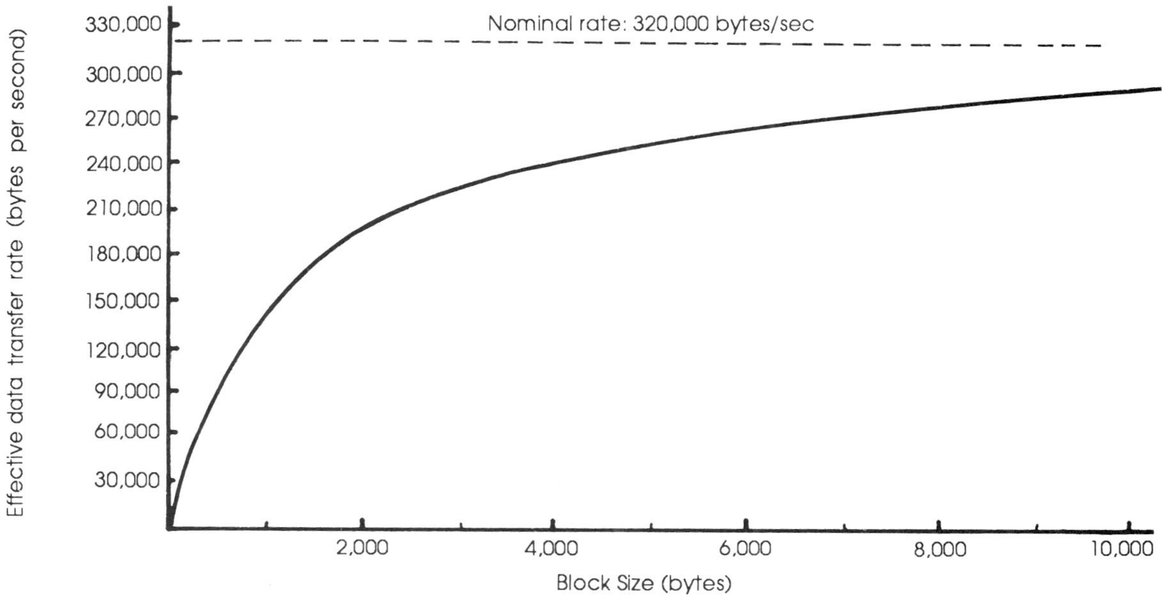

FIGURE 2.9. Effective data transmission rate as a function of block size. The tape has a density of 1,600-bpi and a gap size of 960 bytes. It is assumed that 4 milliseconds elapse, due to time spent by the read/write head in the inter-block gap, before actual data transmission can begin. The tape speed is assumed to be 200 inches per second, giving a nominal transmission rate of 320,000 bytes per second, the nominal transmission rate is 1.5 megabytes per second.

When making estimates of tape capacity with variable length records, it is reasonably accurate to use the average block size, which is taken as the average of the maximum and minimum allowed block sizes. We can then apply the techniques used previously for fixed length blocks.

As an example of this, suppose that we have the VB format file with a 3,000-byte maximum block size and a 100-byte maximum record size. Note that these maximums include all necessary 4-byte length fields. As we have already seen, these specifications imply a 2,901-byte minimum block size. Let us further assume that we want the number of blocks that can fit on a 1,600-bpi tape. The average block size will be (3,000 +2,901)/2, which we can take as 2,951.

Tape Labels

When a file is formatted on magnetic tape, in addition to blocks and interblock gaps, at the beginning of the file there is a **header label** and at the end a **file trailer label**. These labels contain information about the file, including the physical file name, and are used by the operating system for checking purposes and for constructing the data control block (see chapter 1) used by the access method.

In addition to file labels, there is also a **volume label** at the beginning of every reel of tape. This identifies the reel and contains the volume serial number, which is also normally printed on the outside of the reel. The volume and file labels are magnetically recorded.

As far as space is concerned, labels take up a negligible amount and may be neglected when carrying out space calculations of the type described above.

HOW FAST ARE TAPE FILES?

How fast a tape file may be read or written depends on the speed of the tape and the size of the blocks. We mentioned earlier that for physical reasons the tape must move at a constant speed for data to be read or written. Thus if this constant speed is 100 inches per second and data is stored on the tape at a density of 1,600 bytes per inch, clearly the rate at which data can be read (or written) is 1,600*100 or 160,000 bytes per second. This would be the **nominal data transmission rate** for the file and is usually quoted by the manufacturer. Unfortunately the nominal data transmission rate is never achieved in practice because it takes time for the tape to accelerate to the standard tape speed; during this time no data is transmitted.

Typical tape speeds vary from 75 inches per second to 200 inches per second, with 200 inches per second becoming common. A speed of about 100 inches per second is also common.

Suppose now that a block of data is to be read. Initially the tape is stopped with the read/write head in an interblock gap. First the tape accelerates until it has reached the standard speed. Things are arranged so that it reaches this speed just as the data in the block comes under the read/write head. From there until the end of the block the speed is constant; finally the speed decreases from the standard speed (assumed to be 200 inches per second) until it reaches 0, and the tape is stopped once more with the read/write head over the gap.

Now suppose that the block is 2,000 bytes long and that the tape has an interblock gap of 0.6 inches with a recording density of 1,600-bpi. We would like to know the actual rate of data transmission for reading this block, assuming a tape speed of 200 inches per second.

It is clear that the nominal rate of transmission is 1,600*200 or 320,000 bytes per second, which looks impressive. When the read/write head is over the data block this is the rate of transmission being used, so that the time required for the actual transmission must be 2,000/320,000 seconds, that is 0.00625 seconds, or more simply 6.25 milliseconds. (With disk and tape timing calculations it is common to use milliseconds, since the time required to read and write blocks is always of the order of milliseconds).

However, there is the additional delay in getting the tape up to standard speed. The tape must move through half a gap before the block is reached. Recall that a gap will have 960 bytes, so that half a gap is 480 bytes (with a standard 1,600-bpi tape). On average the tape will be moving at half the standard speed while in the gap, that is, the average of the initial speed of 0 and the final speed of 200 inches per second, which is still 100 inches per second. This means that the effective transmission rate for the 480 bytes of gap is 1,600*100 bytes per second or 160,000 bytes. Hence the average time taken to read the half gap is 480/160,000 seconds or 3 milliseconds. Some additional time elapses before the tape responds to a signal from the controller to accelerate, so that about 4 milliseconds elapse before data is actually transmitted.

Thus the time to read the block is 4 + 6.25 milliseconds or about 10 milliseconds. Readers should appreciate the significance of a figure of this magnitude. Ten milliseconds may not sound very large—certainly not on the human scale of events—but from the machine viewpoint it is a long time. The time taken by the central processing unit (CPU) to execute an instruction in main memory is of the order of microseconds in mainframe computers and a lot less in supercomputers. Thus a mainframe computer could execute tens of thousands of instructions in the time it takes to read a 2,000-byte block from a tape. Similar but often worse figures apply to disks, and it is this relatively long time to obtain data from a tape or disk that is responsible for so many of the methods—and indeed problems—that occur in the field of file processing.

In practice if it takes 10 milliseconds to read a 2,000-byte block, the actual or effective transmission rate must in this case be 2,000/10 bytes per millisecond or 200,000 bytes per second. This is a lot less than the manufacturer's nominal transmission rate of 320,000 bytes per second.

We have repeated this calculation for different block sizes, with the results shown in Figure 2.9. It is clear that it will be difficult to even come close to the nominal data transmission rate in practice, but that it is best to keep the block size as high as possible. Note that with a 6,250-bpi tape and a tape speed of 200 feet per second (available on IBM 3420 Model 8), the nominal data transmission rate is 1.5 megabytes per second.

Elapsed Time To Process a Complete Tape

It is difficult to estimate the time required to process a complete tape of data, notwithstanding the analysis above. As mentioned earlier, the tape moves in fits and starts. When the tape is stopped, it is likely that the operating system has switched control to some other program that is not engaged in processing the tape in question; only some time later does the program responsible for the tape get permission to continue execution, thus eventually causing another block to be read from the tape.

Thus a significant amount of time is spent with the tape stopped; this time will vary widely depending on type and number of other programs being executed concurrently. To get some idea of the magnitudes involved, assume 2,000-byte blocks on a 1,600-bpi tape with 960-byte gaps and a tape speed of 200 inches per second. Also assume that the average time the tape spends stopped between reading of consecutive blocks is one tenth of a second or 100 milliseconds; in many cases in practice this figure could be too low.

Consulting Figure 2.6 we see that we have about 15,000 blocks on the tape. Earlier we saw that it takes about 10 milliseconds to read a block. But the tape stops for 100 milliseconds between blocks, so the total elapsed time to process a block would be 110 milliseconds. This means that the total elapsed time to process the tape would be 15,000*0.110 seconds or about half an hour. Note that this is only a typical time; it could be somewhat better or much worse.

Some readers may object that since the time that elapses between reading blocks is often very large compared with the time to read a block, it makes no sense to try to make the time to read a block as short as possible. From the individual programmer's point of view this may make sense, but from installation management's point of view it does not. The time between reading of blocks is determined largely by the time taken by other programs to carry out their tasks. Thus if all files being used by all the programs have block sizes as large as possible and have high effective data transmission rates as a result, the amount of data processed by the installation will be maximized and the organization will get more work out of its computer.

ERROR PREVENTION AND RECORDING MODES

Earlier we saw that every byte on a tape is accompanied by a parity bit to help detect errors. Errors are usually caused by magnetically charged dust that is abraded from the tape and which then clings to the tape surface. The conventional mode of recording data on tape renders the tape especially susceptible to errors caused by magnetic dust. Referring back to Figure 2.3, with conventional recording the tape is magnetized only where a 1-bit is recorded and not magnetized where there is a 0-bit. Thus a piece of magnetic dust clinging to a spot where there should be a 0 can be mistaken for a 1-bit; another piece clinging to a magnetized spot where there is a 1-bit recorded can effectively neutralize the recorded magnetization so that the spot is interpreted as a 0-bit.

This conventional recording of data is known as **NRZI recording mode** (short for *nonreturn to zero on ones*) and is the least expensive. A more expnsive recording mode has come into wide use in recent years in an effort to counteract the dust problem. This is called **PE recording mode** (for phase-encoded). The basic idea is that both 1-bits and 0-bits are represented on tape by a local magnetization of different intensities. In addition both bit types are allowed a range of magnetization. Thus if a magnetic dust particle is clinging where a 1-bit is recorded, as long as the additional magnetization from the dust particle does not take the total magnetization outside the allowed range for a 1-bit, then a 1-bit will still be recognized.

Many modern tape drives are capable of handling tapes either in PE or NRZI recording mode. If we take the well-known family of IBM 3420 tape drives, some permit only PE mode, some only NRZI mode, and some permit both.

TAPE LIBRARY MANAGEMENT

A tape library can be a valuable investment that is worth managing well. In a large business organization there can easily be 10,000 volumes in the tape library. In such a library the value of the empty reels alone could exceed $150,000. When we include the cost to the organization of replacing essential data on those tapes should they ever be destroyed, their value must be appraised in the many millions of dollars. There are three major aspects to the management of a tape library: The physical care of the tapes, the inventory management system, and the security system.

Physical Care of Tapes

To minimize the possibility of mechanical damage, tape reels should be stored in an upright position and never one on top of another. Tape racks that resemble book shelves in book libraries are widely used for this purpose. A wide range of storage temperatures, from well below freezing to as high as 120°F (49°C), is allowable. Nevertheless tapes should be used only within much stricter limits, between about 60°F (15°C) and 95°F (35°C) and between about 10 percent and 75 percent humidity.

Because of the magnetic dust problem, tapes should be cleaned regularly, at least once between every fifteen mounts and preferably more often. Following a sequence of mounts the tension (stretching force) on the tape becomes unequal along the tape and can result in damage. During tape cleaning the tape should be rewound to equalize tension everywhere on the tape. In addition all tapes should be wound and rewound annually.

If a tape persists in giving more than one or two errors per week, it probably pays to discard the tape (after copying its contents), since the lost productivity at the installation due to the persistent errors will invariably exceed the cost of a new reel. If such a policy is enforced it is likely that the tapes at the installation will be just as reliable as the disks.

Inventory Management System

The heart of any tape file inventory management system is a tape file index, which functions much like the index of a book library. The tape-file index can be a manual card index with a card for each file on a volume, or it can be a direct access computer file in which each record describes a file on a volume.

Because of the continued need to update the tape-file index, it is best to implement it as a computer file. The file can be edited directly on a terminal in the tape library. The terminal can be connected to the installation's mainframe computer, although nowadays is is probably a lot simpler, and even more secure, to use a personal computer to hold the tape-file index. The power of a personal computer, such as the IMB PC XT, is more than sufficient for the task.

The fields of a record of the tape-file index are typically as follows:

Volume Serial Number

Volume Type: Whether or not it is a multifile volume

Dataset Name: Unique file identifier

File Sequence Number: Sequence number applicable in the case where the file extends over several volumes

Relative File Position: The order in which the file appears on the volume, if applicable

Recording Density: 800, 1,600 or 6,250 bytes per inch

Recording Mode: PE or NRZI mode

Record Format: FB, VB, F (fixed length, unity blocking factor), or V (variable length, unity blocking factor), and some other possibilities

Record Length: Maximum record length in the case of VB or V record format, otherwise fixed record length

Block Length: Maximum block length in the case of VB or V format, otherwise fixed block length

Total Blocks: Total number of blocks in the file on this volume.

Recording Code: EBCDIC or ASCII

Total Mounts: Mounts since last cleaning

Creation: Date of file creation

Retention: Date at which file is no longer needed

Catalogue: Whether or not the file is catalogued in the system catalogue

Dataset Type: Whether the dataset contains a file of data that is processed or a computer program

Rack Location: Identification of the rack that stores the volume

Owner: Person or group responsible for the file contents, if applicable

Loan Status: Location of file when not in library

Because a single volume can contain many files, or datasets, and because a single dataset can occupy more than one volume, there may be several records in the index with the same volume serial number and several records with the same dataset name. This means that the primary key to the file is the combined volume serial number and dataset name fields, since only the pair is necessarily unique. Nevertheless the file is best organized in such a manner that all records with either the same volume number or with the same dataset number are directly retrievable.

Security

A great deal of attention has been paid to the security of on-line data bases. However, the security of the contents of tape libraries is equally as important. Tape libraries can contain important and valuable data, the loss of which could do great harm. It should always be remembered that most data base storage files on disk have **back-up files** on tape. Although the back-up files may not always be as current as the original data base files, they will normally still contain a great deal of current and valuable information. We can say that tapes are secure when they are protected from:

a. accidental or malicious damage

b. theft

c. unauthorized disclosure of content

To minimize accidental physical damage, tape libraries should be housed in parts of buildings that can withstand hazards such as fire, flood, earthquake, and even acts of war. Where this is not possible, it is prudent to replicate the library in another location.

Malicious physical damage is usually the result of someone tampering with the tapes; for example, passing the tapes close to a strong magnet is sufficient to ruin them. The usual remedy is severely limiting physical access to the tapes. This also reduces the risk of theft, or even of substitution, of tape reels.

Accidental modification of tape contents is normally prevented by the need to insert a plastic **write-ring** into a groove on the back side of the reel when the reel is mounted. The tape can be written on only when the ring is in place. (The write-ring activates a switch immediately behind the mounted reel.) The operator must be told to insert the ring, as this cannot be specified in the JCL specifications that accompany a job submitted for execution. The operating system will ask the operator to mount volumes specified in the JCL, but will not give the operator any information about necessary write-rings.

Unauthorized disclosure of tape contents is much harder to prevent, especially if jobs involving tape reels are submitted via a remote terminal. The user at the terminal normally has to identify himself or herself to the operator before the operator will agree to mount the requested volumes. Unfortunately a clever intruder can always break into the system and learn enough about required identifiers and passwords to masquerade as an authorized user. The only solution here is a good overall computer security system. It helps if the index file for the tape library is on a disk attached to a personal computer that is not attached to the mainframe in such a way that it can be activated from remote terminals. This at least will make it impossible for an intruder to browse in the tape library index before selecting his or her quarry.

CARTRIDGE TAPE DRIVES FOR MAINFRAME COMPUTERS

In 1984 IBM announced the IBM 3480 series of tape drives for high capacity tapes with high nominal transmission rates. The drives became available in 1985 and are designed to eventually replace the 3420 series of tape drives that use the conventional 2,400-foot, 1,600-bpi and 6,250-bpi tapes described in this chapter. Nevertheless it is not expected that this will happen overnight, and 1,600-bpi and 6,250-bpi tapes should be in wide use for a long time to come.

Instead of the standard 9 1/2 inch-diameter reel the new cartridge is about half that diameter, thus permitting the more compact archival of tapes. The nominal data transmission rate is 3 megabytes per second, compared with 320,000 bytes per second for a 1,600-bpi tape and 1.5 megabytes per second for a 6,250-bpi tape (at 200 inches per second on an IBM 3420 tape drive). This is a significant improvement.

The nominal storage capacity of the new cartridge tape is 200 megabytes, compared with 46 and 180 megabytes for the 1,600-bpi and 6,250-bpi tapes, respectively. This is only a marginal improvement over the 6,250-bpi tape. Although the recording density on the cartridge tape is much greater than before (at 38,000 bpi), a much shorter tape results in the relatively low data carrying capacity.

An IBM 3380 disk (see Appendix 1) can hold up to 1,250 megabytes. In commerce, back-up tapes for disk files are a way of life; it takes seven or eight 6,250-bpi reels to hold the contents of an IBM 3380 disk spindle. Thus dumping the contents of such a disk onto tape reels is a lengthy operation. Because of the need for tape reels with a nominal capacity matching those of the current high capacity disk drives, we can expect that in the future new (possibly longer) cartridge tapes will become available.

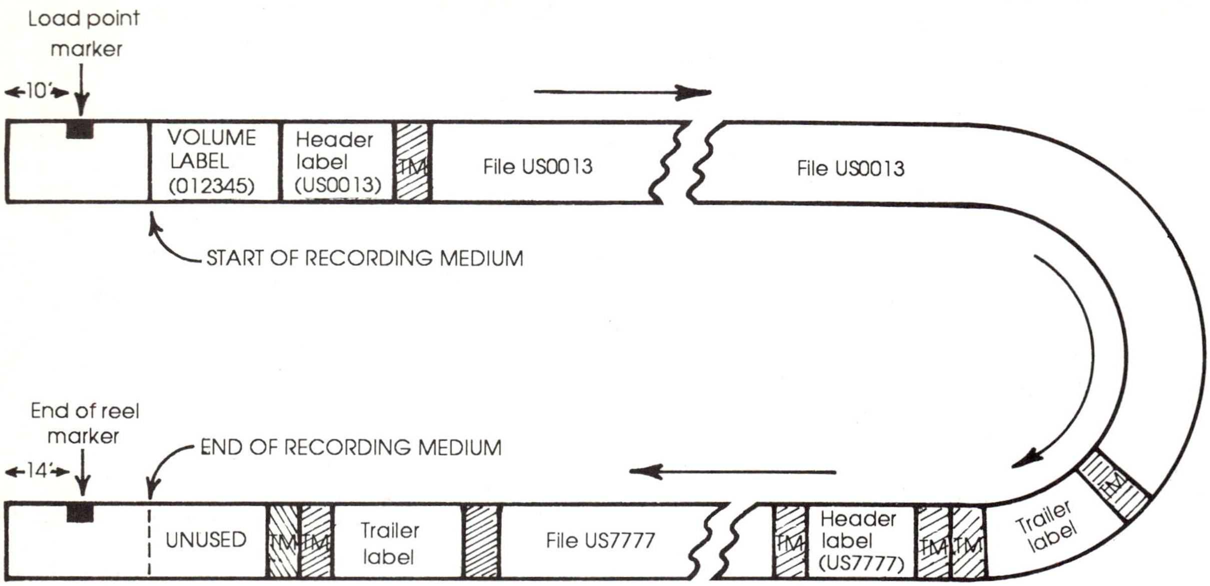

FIGURE 2.10a. Format of a reel with multiple files. The volume label essentially identifies the reel, when the header label identifies a file. The file trailer label contains a count of the number of blocks in the file. TM denotes a magnetic tape mark, used by the system to separate labels and data.

COMPLETE TAPE FILE FORMATTING

In this section, we look at how a complete file (or dataset) is formatted on tape. This formatting applies to IBM systems and can be skipped on your first reading of this text.

There are two distinct possibilities to be considered: Either a file is small enough to fit on a single reel (volume) or it is so large that it requires several reels (volumes). We look first at the case of a file on a single reel.

The overall situation is depicted in Figure 2.10a, which shows a tape that is large enough to contain two distinct files, with some space left over at the end. The first file on the tape has a name (dataset name) and is called US0013. Such a name must be unique to the installation and, as mentioned earlier, will actually be recorded at the beginning of the physical file or dataset in a *file header label*. The *volume*

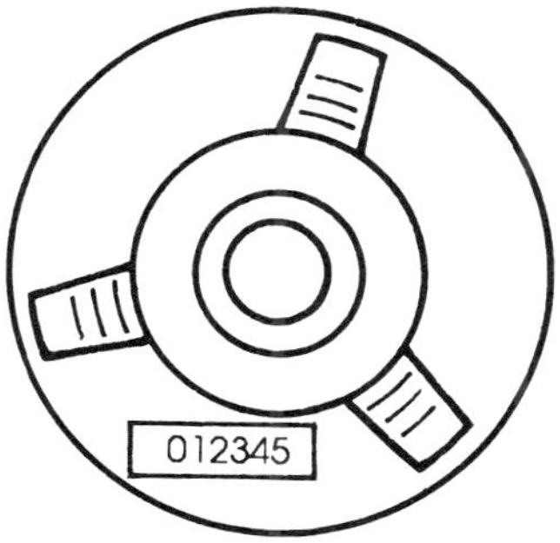

FIGURE 2.10b. At the least, the volume serial number identifying the volume will also be written on a label exterior to the file.

label at the beginning of the volume will contain at least a unique serial number identifying the reel. Typically also this **volume serial number** will be written on the exterior of the tape by the person looking after the installation's tape library (as in Figure 2.10b).

Volume and file header labels have a standard format at most installations and are used to eliminate the possibility of the wrong tape being mounted. For example, when a file is to be processed by a program, in the accompanying JCL specification for the file there is usually a specification of both the serial number of the volume (or reel) on which the file resides as well as a specification of the file (or dataset) name. When the application program executes, the operating system displays on the operator's console a request to mount the required reel. When this has been done, the system first reads the volume label to check that the correct volume has been mounted; then it checks the file header label to check that the correct file is on the volume. If the file does not come first in the volume, the **relative position of the file** (second, third, and so on) must be specified in the accompanying JCL, so that the operating system can cause the tape to be positioned at the beginning of the required file header label. A reel with many files is called a **multiple file volume.**

Note that **multiple file volumes** are rarely used with files that are frequently updated. To update a tape file we construct a new file on another tape, as covered in later chapters, so that multiple file volumes would simply be too awkward to justify.

As discussed earlier, at the end of each file there is a *file trailer label.* This is also used for checking purposes. Essentially it contains the total number of blocks in the file; this figure is recorded there when the file is created. When the file is read the operating system counts

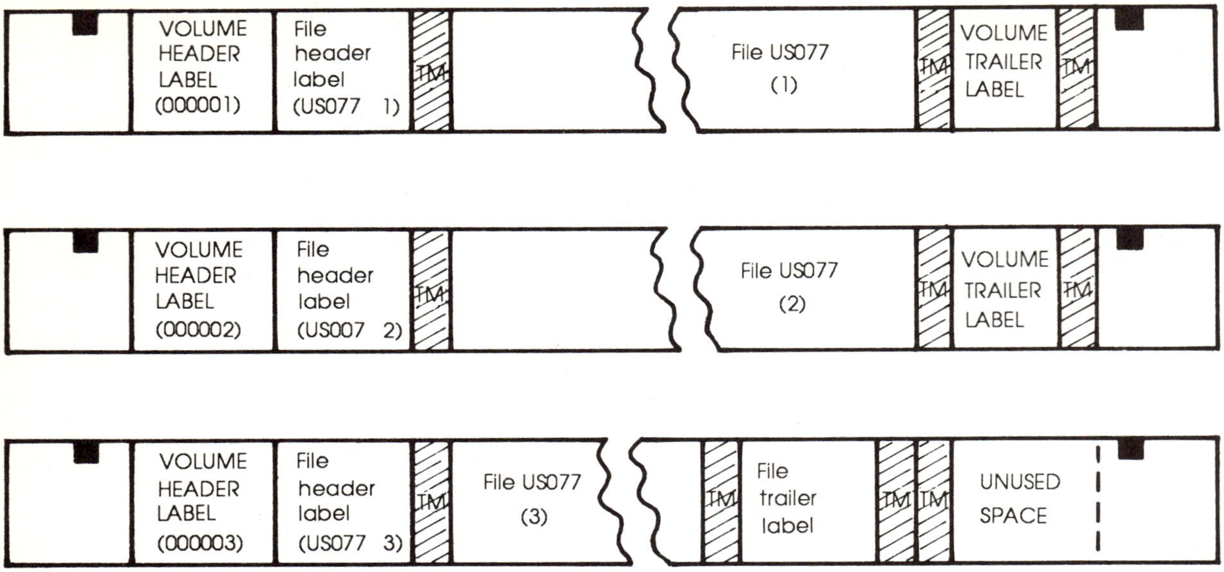

FIGURE 2.11. Format of a multivolume file.

the number of blocks read and at the end compares with the number recorded in the trailer label. If they do not match, an error message is generated, indicating a failure on the tape drive.

When a new file is created on a new reel, a volume serial number need not be specified in the JCL. When not specified the operating system generates a serial number and records it in the volume label, at the same time informing the operator at the consol of its action. Either the operator or the tape librarian will then write this number on the exterior of the tape.

Volume labels can also be created by a **utility program**, before a reel is used. With such a preformatted reel, the volume serial number is specified in the JCL accompanying the application program that initially loads the file.

Markers are used to delineate the various portions of a reel. Between labels and files the system records a special **magnetic tape mark**. In addition about 10 feet from the beginning of the reel there is a **metal load point marker** to indicate that the recording medium is about to begin; another metal marker occurs about 14 feet from the end to indicate the end of the recording medium. This allows enough tape for threading and demounting. Two consecutive tape marks signify the end of a file, or dataset (Figure 2.10a). Even when there are several files on a single reel, the space taken up by labels and tape marks rarely exceeds 1,000 bytes and can thus be neglected when estimating available space on the tape.

The complete file format for the case where the file occupies several volumes (the multivolume file as opposed to a multifile volume) is illustrated in Figure 2.11, where a file (file identifier, or dataset name, US077) is shown as occupying three volumes. Each volume has its own volume label containing the serial number of the volume and other information. Each volume except the last has a volume trailer label containing the number of blocks on the volume. There is a file header label at the start of each volume, which contains the file identifier and the file sequence number, so that the system can check that the different volumes of the file are mounted in the correct sequence. The last volume has a file trailer label.

Do-It-Yourself Labels

Standard file labels are used at most installations. The major IBM operating systems allow for nonstandard labels as well, and there is a substantial manual on the subject. However, a simple method of creating an additional nonstandard label involves placing label information in the first few records of the file. Thus processing programs would treat these initial label records differently from the other normal records.

OVERVIEW OF DISK STORAGE MEDIA

Records on magnetic tape can only be accessed in sequential order. In contrast records on a magnetic disk may be accessed both sequentially and directly. This advantage of disk storage media is not without certain costs. A disk pack, the disk media equivalent of a reel of tape (volume), is relatively expensive. In addition sequential processing of disk files is often slower than tape file processing.

There are some other practical inconveniences as well. For example, dropping a reel of tape will probably not seriously damage it; dropping a much heavier and bulkier disk pack may well ruin it, since it is precision engineered and normally spins at speeds of up to 3,000 revolutions per minute.

A more serious problem is dust on the disk recording surface. The separation between read/write head and disk surface is nowadays much smaller than the diameter of a typical dust particle. This

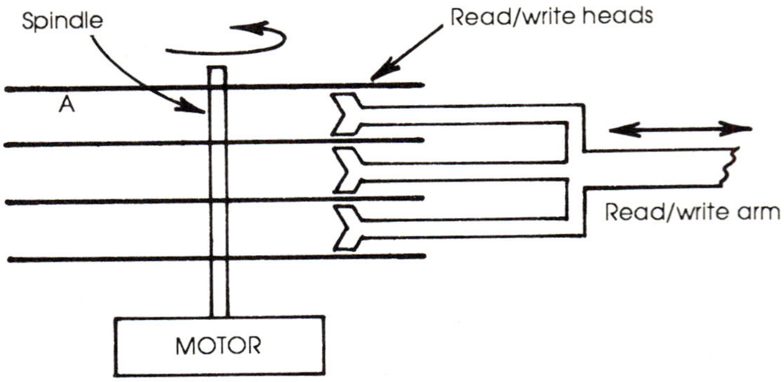

FIGURE 2.12a **Computer disk schematics: Disk drive assembly. Note that the disk rotates continuously when the drive is switched on. The read/write arm moves in response to channel program commands.**

together with the high rotation speed of disks means that a collision with a dust particle can cause the head to *crash* and damage the recording surface. As we shall see later, recent developments have minimized this problem.

Nevertheless for applications requiring direct access to records, magnetic disks are used almost universally; currently there is no technology on the horizon that could replace magnetic disk technology in commerce on any significant scale. Indeed, if current trends continue we can look forward to continual improvements in disk technology. Disks are thus important; in the remaining sections of this chapter we look at this storage medium in some detail.

We begin with an examination of the physical characteristics of disk packs and disk drives. First we look at how disks are connected to the input/output (I/O) processor. Then we look at the structure of disk drives, followed by a look at the different kinds of disks that are commonly used; finally we introduce the all-important cylinder concept. In later sections we look at how much data can be stored on disk and how much time it takes to read and write records.

Disk Controllers

Disk drives are high-precision electromechanical devices and require a great deal of fine control for successful operation. This means that we must have control electronics to physically carry out the instructions executed by the (I/O) processor, or channel. Because control

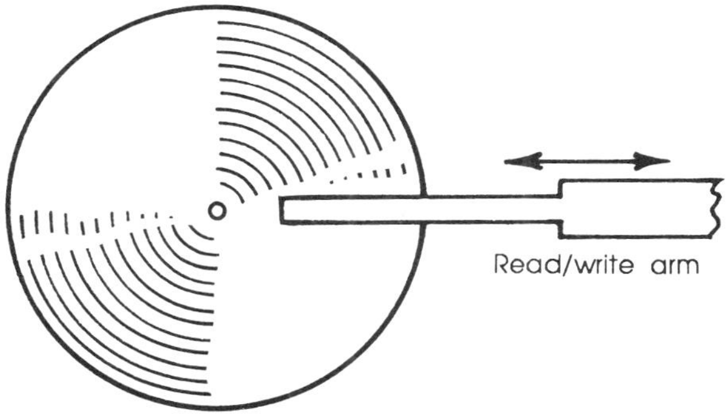

FIGURE 2.12b Computer disk schematics: View of a disk surface. There may be hundreds of concentric magnetically recorded data tracks on a disk's surface. The read/write arm can move in and out and thus access any track. Regardless of radius, each track has the same data capacity.

electronics is expensive, it is shared among what has come to be called a **string** of disk drives and comes as a separate unit, called a disk controller. Depending on the number, type, and configuration of the disk drives, more than one controller may be needed.

Structure of Disk Drives

A **disk pack** consists of a set of metal disks mounted on a single **spindle** (see Figure 2.12a). It rotates continuously when the disk drive is turned on. This should be contrasted with tapes, which move only when a block of data is being transmitted. Each disk contains two recording surfaces, consisting of concentric recording tracks (see Figure 2.12b). For each surface there will be at least one read/write head mounted on a mobile arm that can move the head from one track to another, under the control of the disk controller. These arms are arranged into a comb, the whole of which can move in and out, so thatif one head on the comb is over the nth track on its disk surface, the other heads will be over the nth tracks of their respective surfaces.

This physical arrangement leads directly to the **cylinder concept**, which we shall discuss shortly. This ability of the read/write heads to move from one set of tracks to another permits direct access of recorded data. An appropriate movement of the comb, that is, a **seek operation**, will permit any track to be selected for reading or writing. Unfortunately, for mechanical reasons a seek is a relatively slow operation, typically taking about 25 millisceonds, so that direct access with disks is slow.

Not all the surfaces of the set of disks on a spindle are used for recording data. The outer top and bottom surfaces are merely protective; another surface, typically the top inner surface (surface A in Figure 2.12a) is used for controlling the movement of the read/write arms and contains prerecorded tracks for this purpose. Note that all data tracks have the same nominal data capacity regardless of track radius.

Types of Disks

Many different types of disk are available commercially, often with only minor structural differences. However, we can distinguish between three major types of disk: (a) **fixed head disks**, (b) **mobile head removable disks**, and (c) **mobile sealed-head nonremovable disks**.

Fixed head disks have a read/write head for each track or for each small group of tracks. This eliminates the **seek time**, that is, the time required for a read/write arm to move to a required track. Such disks are very expensive and are not normally used for holding large files. They are used with operating systems for holding pages in external page storage.

Mobile head disks are commonly used in business. They typically have one mobile set of arms, or **actuator**, per disk pack, although they may have two. In addition the disk pack can be removed from the drive and stored in a disk pack library. A good example is the IBM 3330 disk drive.

In recent years very large capacity disks **(mobile sealed-head nonremovable disks)** have come into common use. Here *the whole disk pack and mobile arm arrangement is sealed and cannot be removed,* since the high density of tracks on a disk surface makes disk pack removability difficult to engineer. A very widely used disk of this type is the IBM 3350, which appeared in the last half of the 1970s. An even higher capacity disk of this type is the IBM 3380, which appeared in the early 1980s. It has two actuators per drive and two drives per unit, all sealed. The IBM 3380 is an example of what has come to be known as **Winchester disk technology**.

Winchester disk technology is much more reliable than earlier disk technology. A significant problem with disks has always been dust on disk tracks, since (as mentioned earlier) the separation between head and track is less than the diameter of a typical dust particle. A collision between a dust particle can cause the head to *crash,* that is, it will scour the surface of the disk. Sealing the pack in a dust-free environment will help, but cannot completely solve the problem of avoid-

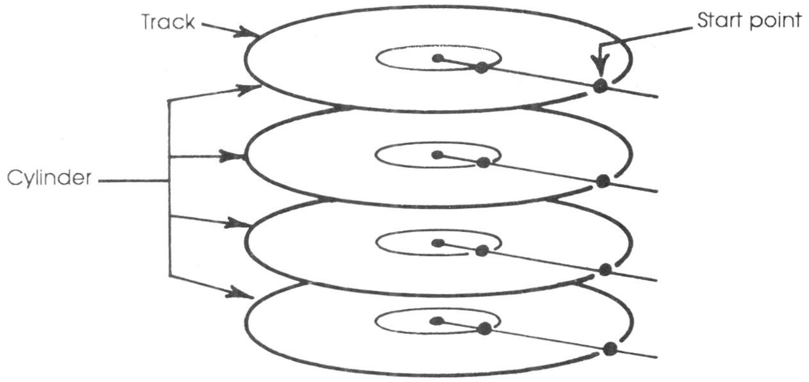

FIGURE 2.13. The cylinder concept. All tracks of the same radius form a cylinder of tracks, the data on which can be read without motion of the read/write arm assembly. There are as many cylinders on a disk pack as there are tracks on a surface. Note that each track of a cylinder has a well-defined starting point.

ing damage to the tracks due to scouring by the heads. The problem is that when the disk drive is turned off, the head is physically in contact with a track. When the drive is turned on and as the disk picks up speed, the head takes off just like an aircraft lifted by aerodynamic forces. The reverse happens when the disk is shut down. Unfortunately during head take-off and landing, the head is in contact with the track and scouring of the oxide coating results, eventually resulting in damage.

Winchester disks have a special landing and take-off track that does not store data. In addition since the head flies close to the track because of the high density of tracks, the oxide coating is reinforced so that damage due to a crash is either minimized or prevented. Thin-film microcircuit technology is used to make the sensitive surface of the read/write head as well, to enable it to handle the high density of tracks. The result is that a single drive of an IBM 3380 can hold about 1,250 million bytes. (Compare this with a 2,400-foot reel of 1,600-bpi tape, which can hold about 46 million bytes.)

The Cylinder Concept

An understanding of the **cylinder concept** is basic to an understanding of disk files (see Figure 2.13). Each track has an electrically

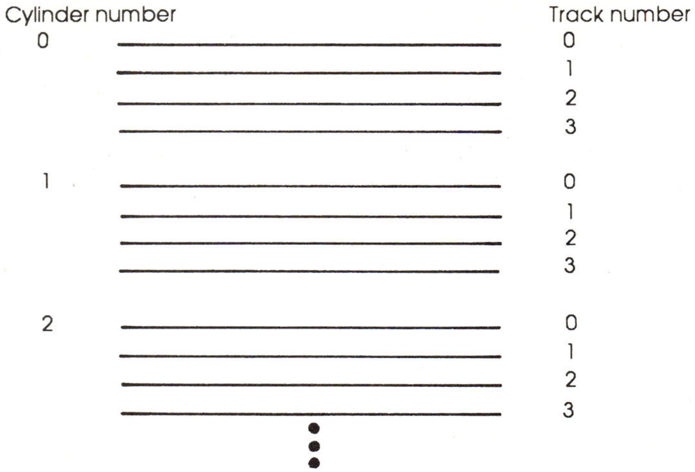

FIGURE 2.14. For data storage purposes a disk should be regarded as a succession of cylinders (starting at cylinder 0), each containing a fixed number of tracks. A sequential file is written out onto a disk cylinder by cylinder in ascending cylinder number order, as shown. Each track can hold the same amount of data regardless of whether the track has a small radius or a large radius.

defined start and end point. In addition all tracks of the same radius are accessible without the need for motion of the set of read/write arms, that is, without the need for a seek. Such a set of tracks is called a **cylinder**. The outer cylinder is cylinder 0 and the inner cylinder is cylinder n, n being the number of tracks per surface. Thus each cylinder contains a set of tracks; it is convenient to imagine a disk as consisting of a set of cylinders, starting with cylinder 0. In this view each cylinder contains a fixed number of tracks (see Figure 2.14). Thus we can identify a desired track by means of the cylinder number and track number within the cylinder.

As we shall see later, when a sequential file is stored on disk, it is stored in cylinder/track order—that is, cylinder 0 is filled first, then cylinder 2, and so on. Of course nowadays disks have such large capacity that many files are commonly stored on one disk. Thus a file could start at cylinder 75 and extend as far as cylinder 98. With IBM systems the quantity of cylinders needed may be used to specify the size of a file in Job Control Language specifications.

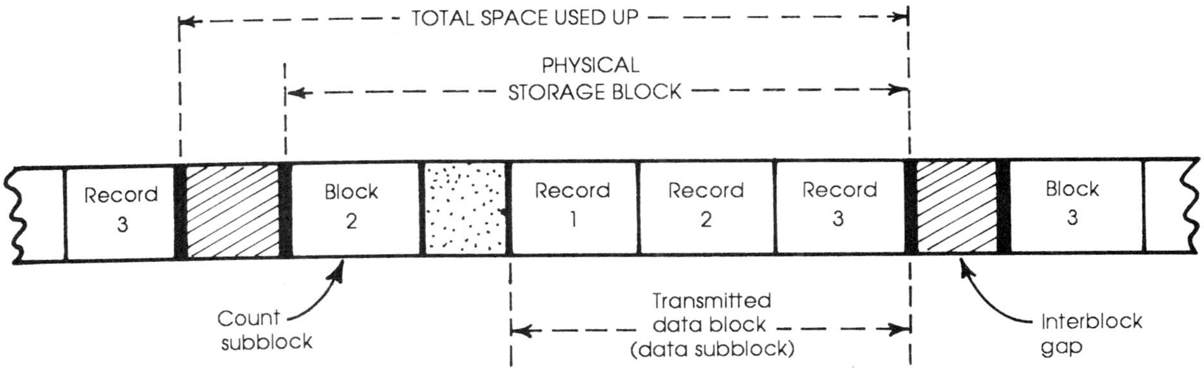

FIGURE 2.15. IBM's count-data format. In each physical block on a track there is first a count subblock to identify the block (among other things) followed by an intersubblock gap, followed by a (data) subblock that holds the block of records transmitted from the buffer for storage. The additional space taken up by the interblock gap, intersubblock gap, and count subblock is sometimes called the count-data factor. For an IBM 3350 disk it amounts to 185 bytes exactly. The records above are all the same length so that they are also in fixed block (FB) format. For variable length blocked records (VB format).

HOW MUCH DATA CAN BE STORED ON A DISK?

The amount of data that can be stored on a disk depends upon how data is formatted on the disk. There are two main ways this is done. First there is the **software formatting** method, used with most IBM disks and IBM disk look-alikes. This is probably the most commonly used method, and we shall study it in some detail. Then we shall look briefly at the other method of formatting a disk, known as **sector formatting**.

Software Formatting

With software formatting each track contains an integer number of physical blocks of data. The first two blocks are always system blocks, so that the space taken up by them is not available to the user; we can conveniently forget about this space. The space available to the user is the **nominal track capacity**. All tracks have the same nominal capacity.

There are two types of software formatting for the physical data blocks of user data on a disk track: **Count-data format** and **count-key data format**. It is important to have an understanding of them, and we take them in turn.

Count-Data Format

Count-data format is the simpler of the two methods of software formatting (see Figure 2.15). The physical data block contains two subblocks: A **data subblock** containing the user's data that was transmitted from the buffer, and a system subblock called the **count subblock**, which essentially contains a number that identifies the block. Thus on a track we will have block 1, block 2, and so on.

The reader may wonder why it is necessary to count the blocks using count subblocks, which clearly waste space. After all, if we suppose that the computer needed to retrieve block number 6, it could easily do so by counting blocks from the start of the track until block 6 is reached. However, when the read/write head reaches the rotating track it will read the blocks starting at some arbitrary point on the track. If each block contains its block number then the controller will not have to wait for the start of the track to begin counting. Hence the count subblock. It has some other uses too but these need not concern the business user.

The data subblock contains the user's data, that is, the block of data originally transmitted from a buffer to the disk. Thus for most purposes it is accurate to say that the data subblock contains the *transmitted data block*.

Let us suppose that the transmitted data block contains B bytes. Then on the track the complete block will take up additional bytes to allow for the count subblock, the gap between the subblock, and the gap between two blocks. Let us call the total of this additional space c. Then we can say that (c + B) is the space taken up on a track by a block. The value of c is fixed for a given make of disk. For the commonly used IBM 3350 disk, c is 185, which means that the additional space required is not very great. Note that c is sometimes called the **count-data factor** for the disk.

It is now a simple matter to compute how many blocks a track can hold. We simply divide (c + B) into the nominal capacity of a track. For the IBM 3350 disk the nominal capacity is 19,254 bytes. Thus if we transmit 2,000-byte blocks (that is, B = 2,000) to the disk, the number per track will be:

19,254/(185 + 2,000) or 8.81

But since we can only have an integer number of blocks,the answer must be rounded down to 8. Thus the general formula for the number of blocks per track is:

$$\lfloor S/(c + B) \rfloor$$

S is the nominal capacity of a track; $\lfloor\rfloor$ indicates rounding down to the nearest integer.

To determine how many blocks in a cylinder, we simply multiply by the number of tracks in a cylinder. For example, an IBM 3350 disk has 30 tracks per cylinder; therefore the cylinder can hold 8*30 or 240 2,000-byte transmitted data blocks, using the result above for the number of blocks per track. There are 555 cylinders per drive on an IBM 3350 disk, so that the entire disk could hold 555*30*8 2,000-byte transmitted data blocks, or 133,200 blocks. This means that there are 133,200*2,000 bytes for the disk or about 266 million bytes. This should be compared with the nominal capacity of the disk, which is 19,254*30*555 or about 320 million bytes.

TRACK CAPACITY: IBM 3350 DISK

Count-data blocks: Bytes in a data subblock (B)		Count-key data blocks: Bytes in key and data subblock (k + B)		Blocks per track (n)
Min.	Max	Min	Max	
9443	19069	9361	18987	1
6234	9442	6152	9360	2
4629	6233	4547	6151	3
3666	4628	3584	4546	4
3025	3665	2943	3583	5
2566	3042	2484	2942	6
2222	2565	2140	2483	7
1955	2221	1873	2139	8
1741	1954	1659	1872	9
1566	1740	1484	1658	10
1420	1565	1338	1483	11
1297	119	1215	1337	12
1191	1296	1109	1214	13

FIGURE 2.16 Track capacities for an IBM 3350 disk. A similar table is given in Appendix 1 for the IBM 3380 disk. See the text for instruction on using the table.

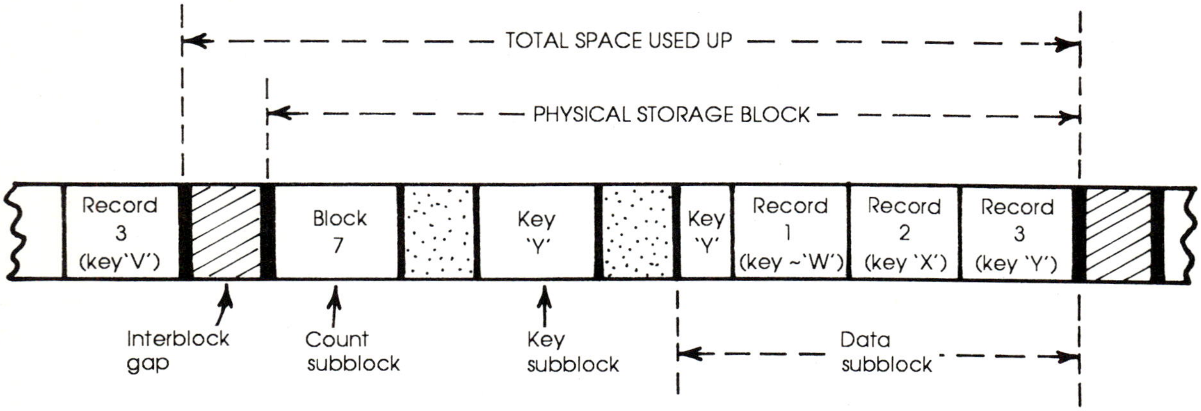

FIGURE 2.17 IBM's count-key data format for the case of fixed length records, where record keys are embedded within the records. The major difference between this and count-data format is the key subblock, which contains the key of the last record of the block (key 'Y' in this case). Another minor difference is that the data subblock or transmitted data block also contains the key of the last record redundantly at the beginning of the subblock. Records in the data subblock are in ascending primary key order.

A great deal of the calcuation effort required for figuring how many blocks can fit on a track can be avoided by the use of a track capacity table; readers should learn how to use one. An example is given in Figure 2.16 for the IBM 3350 disk. The principle behind the table is simple.

Suppose there are to be 5 blocks on a track. Then we can have a minimum block size that will result in 5 blocks, for the case where what is left over at the end of the track is slightly less than the space required to take another block. From the table this block size (transmitted block size, B) is 3,025 bytes. Conversely there must also be a maximum block size where there is no space or almost no space left at the end of the track. From the table this will be 3,665 bytes. It follows that when the block size is between 3,025 and 3,665 bytes, the track will hold 5 blocks.

It is a simple matter to use the table to find out how many 2,000-byte transmitted blocks we can have on a track. We search the table to find a row where the minimum block size is less than 2,000 and the maximum is greater than 2,000. This is the eighth row, giving us 8 blocks per track, exactly as we computed earlier.

The methods outlined above apply to most IBM disks, with the exception of the big Winchester disk (the IBM 3380). With this disk there is a minor variation in the method used because of some additional system data per block (the details are given in Appendix 1). There are slight modifications to the structure of the track capacity table for the IBM 3380 disk as well (also explained in Appendix 1).

Count-Key Data Format

With **count-key** data format there is an additional subblock, called the **key subblock** (see Figure 2.17). The key subblock contains the key of the last record in the data subblock or transmitted data block. This format is used with some direct access files (notably indexed-sequential files, see chapter 6).

To calculate the space taken up on a track by a count-key data block, it must be understood that not only will B (the transmitted data block size, or data subblock size) vary with the application, but the key subblock will also vary, depending on the size of the key. The remaining space taken up by two intersubblock gaps, the interblock gap, and the count subblock (refer to Figure 2.17) will be constant. Thus the expression for the space taken up must be (r + (k+B)), where r is a constant for a given type of disk, often called the **count-key data factor**, and k is the key length. (An additional complication is that the key of the last record also redundantly appears at the beginning of the transmitted data block [for reasons that are not relevant], although the few additional bytes involved can often be neglected in calculations.)

Suppose now that we have a file with record length 100 bytes, blocking factor 20, and record key length 6 bytes, and that the file is stored on an IBM 3350 disk in count-key data format. The count-data factor r for an IBM 3350 disk is 267 bytes. To find out how many blocks a track can hold, we first calculate the size of B, the transmitted data block. This is approximately 100*20, but more accurately 100*20 + 6; or 2,006 bytes, when we take into account the key length at the beginning of the transmitted data block. Applying the formula (r + (k+B)), the space taken up by a block must be 267 + (6 + 2,006) or 2,279 bytes. Recalling that the nominal space on a track of an IBM 3350 disk is 19,254 bytes, the number of blocks we can have is:

19,254/2,279 or 8.45

However, since we can only have an integer number of blocks the answer must be 8 blocks. The general formula is:

$$\lfloor S/(r + (k + B)) \rfloor$$

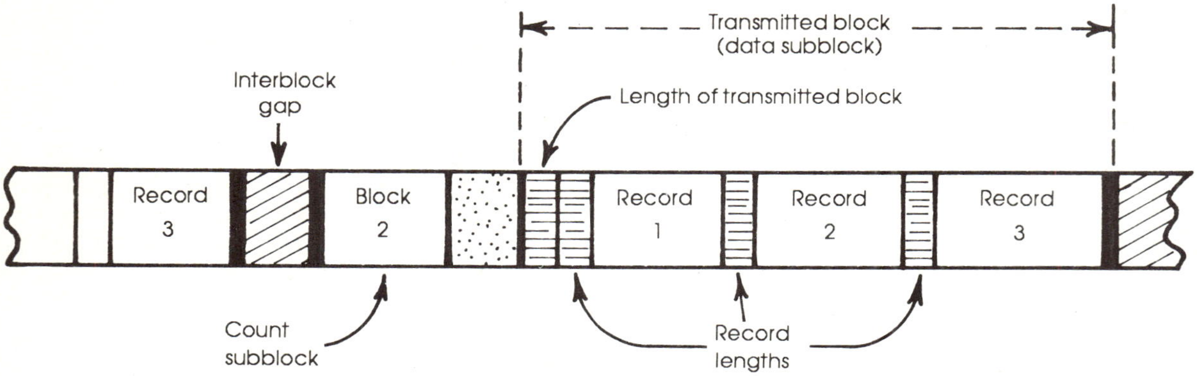

FIGURE 2.18 IBM's count-data format for the case of variable length records. To each record is added a 4-byte field to contain the record length. A 4-byte field is also added to the data subblock to contain its length. Thus if the 3 records above had lengths 50, 80, and 60, the total length of the data subblock would be (50 + 80 + 60 + 3*4 + 4) or 206 bytes. The total space taken up on the track would be 185 + 206 or 391 bytes, since 185 is the count-data factor.

As with count-data format we can use a capacity table to determine how many blocks will fit on a track given the size of the data subblock (B) and the key length. This time we deal with maximum and minimum values of (k+B). Thus if B is 2,520 bytes and the key length is 6 bytes, then (k+B) is 2,526 bytes. Referring to the table in Figure 2.16 for the IBM 3350 disk, we see that 2,526 is between that minimum (2,484 bytes) and maximum (2,942 bytes) for which the number of blocks per track is 6. Thus k+B equal to 2,526 means 6 blocks per track.

We can do similar calculations for most IBM disks and use similar capacity tables. However, some modifications are required for the case of the IBM 3380 disk, (explained in Appendix 1, which also includes specifications for both the IBM 3350 and IBM 3380 disks).

Variable Length Records

As with blocks of variable length records on tape, in the JCL there must be a specification of the maximum length of a block and the maximum length of a record. As we saw earlier, in effect this means that we are also specifying a minimum size for each block. Attached to

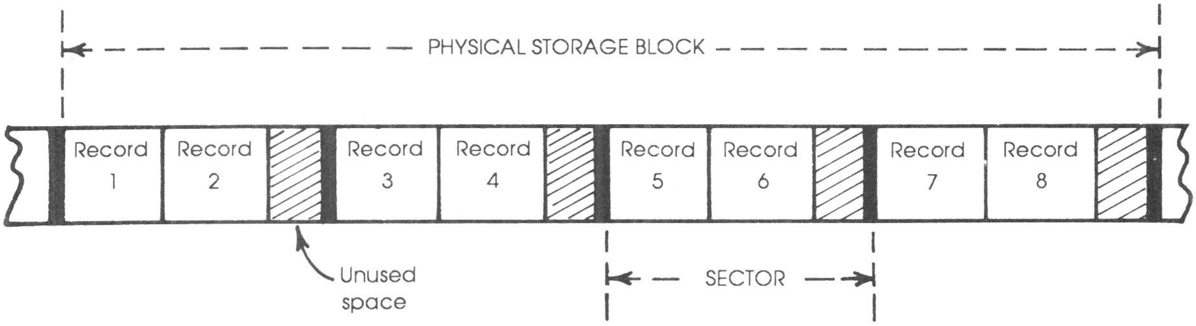

FIGURE 2.19 Sectors tend to be small and often a number of them are needed to contain a block of data. Typically each sector contains an integer number of records so that there can be unused space at the end of each sector within a block. IBM's FBA (fixed block architecture) formatting is a type of sector formatting similar in principle to that illustrated, although it has many more complex features. The IBM sector size is 512 bytes; FBA formatting is used with IBM 3310 and 3370 disks.

each record on a track will be a 4-byte field indicating the record length; attached to the beginning of this collection of records is another 4-byte field giving the total length of the data subblock (see Figure 2.18). Thus the data subblock has the same format as the corresponding data block on a tape. The formula c+B for the space taken up by a block still holds, although now we should take an average for the value of B when determining the number of blocks per track. The average value for B will be halfway between the maximum and minimum allowed values, as explained with tapes.

With count-key data format the 4-byte record and block-length fields are placed in the data subblock, much as in the case of count-data format. However, the details can be tricky, and readers are referred to the manuals. There is also a little more to count-key data format than we covered in the previous section; the additional details are covered in Appendix 1.

Sector Formatting

With **sector formatting** each track of the disk is divided into fixed length **sectors**. There is an electronically detectable mark at the beginning of each sector, so that a sector is directly accessible. A block of data will begin at the start of some sector, as shown in Figure 2.19, so that the block may be indentified, or addressed, by its cylinder number, track number, and sector number. The number of sectors per track is the same for all tracks for geometrical reasons: There will typically be 4 sectors per track for small capacity disk tracks; and typically 8 or 16 sectors per track for larger capacity tracks.

A sector usually has quite a small capacity, often 512 bytes, and is thus too small to contain a data block in many cases. In such cases the block will take up as many sectors as necessary, (as illustrated in Figure 2.19); in other words a block can span many sectors. However, records do not usually span sectors; there will be an integer number of records in each sector, with the possibility of some wasted space at the end of each sector. Note that some IBM disks use a more complex but basically similar type of sector formatting, called *FBA formatting* (see Reference 1).

Recording Density and Recording Mode

The number of bytes (or bits) per inch of track has little meaning when dealing with disks, in contrast to the situation with tapes where the number of bytes per inch of tape is very important. The density of recording varies on a disk, so that the data is more densely recorded on an inner track than on an outer one. Thus all tracks can hold the same number of data blocks. Note also that a byte, or character, of data is recorded along a track as shown in Figure 2.20. Contrast this with tapes, where a byte is stored transverse to the tape. A parity (or error-checking) bit is not usually included in a byte recorded on a disk track. With IBM count-key and count-data formats, error checking is performed by parity or cyclic-check bits in the count subblocks.

Disk File Labels and Volume Table of Contents

We saw that with tapes there is a volume label for each reel and a header and trailer label for each physical file or dataset. With disks the situation is somewhat different. Each disk pack does have a

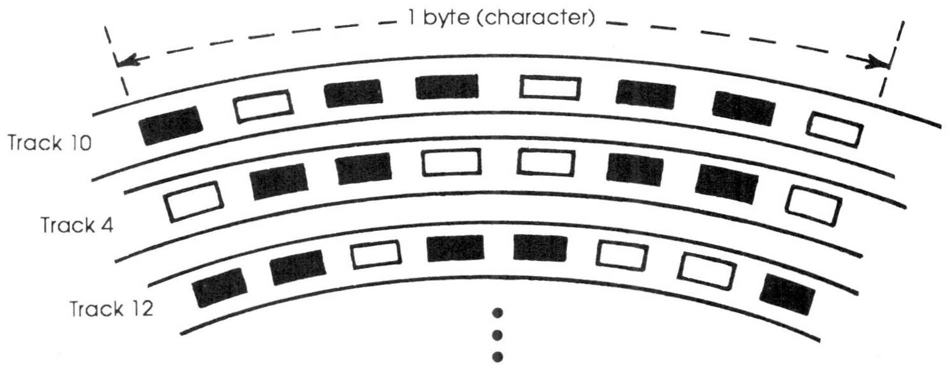

FIGURE 2.20 Data is recorded in bits along a track with 8 bits per character of data and is not recorded transverse to a track. A parity, or 9th bit, is not recorded. There is instead a cyclic-check bit in the count subblock of each block (with IBM software formatting). Data will begin at the start of some sector, as shown in Figure 2.19, so that the block may be identified, or addressed, by its cylinder number, track number, and sector number. The number of sectors per track is the same for all tracks for geometrical reasons: There will typically be 4 sectors per track for small capacity disk tracks; and typically 8 or 16 sectors per track for larger capacity tracks.

volume serial number, and each dataset on disk is identified by a dataset name. However, this information, along with information needed for the data control block (such as block size, record format, and so on) is not stored in labels. Instead there is a directly accessible **volume table of contents (VTOC)** that contains all necessary technical information about each dataset stored on the volume.

VTOC occupies a single cylinder and is accessed by the operating system several times when a dataset is processed. Before the file is processed, the volume serial number is checked; this is recorded in the VTOC. Also the dataset name is checked, and information necessary for the construction of the appropriate data control block (see chapter 1) may be retrieved. At the end of processing, the total number of blocks read may be checked against the number listed in the VTOC entry for that dataset. The VTOC is usually located in the middle of the disk. This reduces the distance the arms have to travel to get to the average dataset.

HOW LONG DOES IT TAKE TO ACCESS A DISK

The time it takes to access a disk depends upon how the file involved is being processed. In general we have sequential access and direct access; the time required to read or write a block of data is quite different for each case.

Sequential Disk Access

With sequential disk access the data is read or written in cylinder number order. We shall consider the times involved for reading. An exactly equivalent analysis applies to writing.

When the blocks on a cylinder are being read sequentially, the read/write arm assembly is not moving, so that no seek is involved. Note that the blocks will be recorded in sequence along a track (see Figure 2.14). When a block has been read, the track continues to rotate. Thus when the time comes to read the next block, the read/write head must wait until the required block passes by. Sometimes it will have to wait almost a full revolution and sometimes almost no time at all—on average it will have to wait half a revolution. This wasted time is called the **rotational delay** or the **latency**. For an IBM 3380 disk the time for a single revolution (R) is 16.7 milliseconds, so that the rotational delay is R/2 or close to 8.3 milliseconds, which is rather a long time.

Once the read/write head is adjacent to the required block, further time is expended in actually reading the block. For all practical purposes we can take this time as B/s, where B is the data subblock or transmitted data block length in bytes, and s is the nominal rate of data transmission for the disk in bytes per second. For an IBM 3380 disk s is 3 million bytes per second, so that the time required to transmit a 2,000- byte block would be 2,000/3,000.000 seconds or 0.66 milliseconds. Taking the rotational delay into account, the total time is 0.66 + 8.3 or about 9 milliseconds. Thus the time to read a disk sequentially is dominated by the rotational delay. The general formula for the time to read a block is therefore:

R/2 + (B/s)*1,000 milliseconds

Continuing the case of reading a 2,000-byte block by sequential access, if the time required to read the block is actually 9 milliseconds, then the actual rate of data transmission must be 2,000/0.009 bytes per second, or about 220,000 bytes per second, which is very much less than the nominal rate of 3 million bytes per second. The moral is that quoted nominal rates of data transmission for disks are largely irrelevant in a practical data processing situation.

Direct Disk Access

When a block of data is read by direct access, the read/write arm assembly has to move to select the correct cylinder. The time required for this movement is the **seek time** and is quite long. The time varies, depending on how many tracks the head must move over; in practice we use an average figure. For the IBM 3380 the seek time (P) is 16 milliseconds on average, which is a very long time by computer standards.

Once the read/write head selects the correct track, the average rotational delay (R/2) elapses before the correct block is found. Then we have the time (B/s)*1,000 to actually transmit the block, as was explained for sequential processing. Hence a formula for the total time to read a block from a disk is as follows:

$$P + R/2 + 1{,}000*(B/s) \text{ milliseconds}$$

For a 2,000-byte transmitted data block this time comes to 25 milliseconds. Readers should compare this with a typical time of about 10 milliseconds to read a 2,000-byte block from a 1,600-bpi tape moving at 200 feet per second, as explained in chapter 2. The corresponding figure for the IBM 3350 disk is 35 milliseconds.

Consequences of Long Access Times for Data on Disk

Disk storage is widely used largely because it permits direct access to large quantities of data. Because of this convenience the relatively long times to access disks, particularly with direct access, are tolerated. It is not likely that these times will be reduced much by technological advances in the near future. We are dealing with electromechanical technology, and it is a wonder that disk suppliers have been able to reduce access times to their current levels. Thus data stored on disks is time consuming to access directly; when we take into consideration the large quantities of data that can be stored on a disk, processing times can be very long indeed.

It follows that much of file system design involves selection of strategies to minimize the processing time required. This is also true of tape file processing, even though tapes are generally faster than direct access disk file processing. Thus timing considerations dominate file processing. This domination extends into data base processing as well, since a data base after all is a collection of (integrated) files, which are usually direct access files. Considerations of file processing times will therefore play a significant part in the remainder of this book.

SUMMARY

Computer files are commonly stored on magnetic disks and tape. With tape files only sequential access is possible; with disk files both sequential and direct access are possible.

Records are stored on tapes in blocks, with each block separated by an interblock gap (IGB) that can be quite large. The gap is a space on the tape that holds no data and is used as a place for the tape to stop adjacent to the read/write heads of the tape drive.

Because of the size of the IGB, blocks should be kept large to minimize the percentage of space taken up by the gaps. When doing calculations for how many blocks a tape can hold, a block should be regarded as taking up a space equal to the block size plus the interblock gap.

A tape moves from one gap to the next as it is being read. The time to read a block is thus the time taken to accelerate adjacent to the gaps, plus the time to actually transmit the block.

When managing tapes, physical care must be taken to avoid magnetic dust particles and crinkles. There should also be a tape inventory management system and a security system.

Each tape bears a volume label; a tape also includes a file header and trailer label for each file on the tape. We can have both multifile volumes and multivolume files. A volume is a term for either a tape or a disk pack.

A disk pack is made up of metal platters on a single spindle and rotates at constant speed when in use. Each side of a platter has many concentric circular tracks that can hold the same quantity of data. A mobile comb-like arrangement of read/write heads (the read/write arm) permits the data on any track to be read by direct access.

The collection of tracks of the same radius is called a cylinder. All the records on a cylinder can be read or written without needing to move the read/write arm. Records placed on a disk in sequential order are written out in acending track and cylinder order.

A disk can be formatted either by physically defined sectors on each track (hardware formatting) or by software formatting. Common

IBM-originated software formats are count-data formats and count-key data formats.

To compute how much space on a disk a file will take, you begin by computing how many blocks can be on a track. By dividing the number of blocks per file by the number of blocks per track, you will get the number of tracks required, from which the number of cylinders may be deduced. To determine the number of blocks per track, you divide the track capacity by the space taken up by a block (or you can look it up in a table). The space taken up by a block is the blocking factor multiplied by the record length plus additional data that depends on the type of formatting.

The time to access a block on a track is equal to rotational delay, plus actual data transmission time when using sequential access. When using direct access, access time is the sum of seek time, rotational delay, and transmission time. Disk access times are very long for even the fastest disks.

EXERCISES

1. Explain the need for interblock gaps (IGBs) on a tape file.
2. On a 1,600-bpi tape with an IBG of 960 bytes, we have a file with 100-byte records at a blocking factor of 30. Compute the length of tape in inches required for 60,000 records.
3. With a 6,250-bpi tape with an IBG of 1,875 bytes, we have a file with 100,000 200-byte records with a blocking factor of 20. (a.) What percentage of the space taken up by the file is wasted in interblock gaps? (b.) What percentage of the tape is taken up by the file? (c.) If the file were extended to fill the tape, how many records would it have?
4. With a 6,250-bpi tape with an IBG of 1,875 bytes, we have 150-byte records with a blocking factor of 30. Assuming that the tape is read at a speed of 100 inches per second, what is the time required to read a block?
5. We have a variable length record file on a 1,600-bpi tape with an IBG of 960 bytes. The maximum block size (including length fields) is 3,000 bytes; the maximum record length (including length field) is 400 bytes. What is the average block size? How much data (in bytes) would be in a file that took up the entire tape?
6. A file with 100,000 records, each 100-bytes long with a blocking factor of 30, resides on an IBM 3350 disk. The record key is

20 bytes long. Use the track capacity table to determine the number of cylinders required for (a) count-data format and (b) count-key data format.

7. With an IBM 3350 disk, compute the number of blocks that can go on a track using data from Appendix 1, if the records are 150 bytes long and the blocking factor is 20. Assume (a) count-data format and (b) count-key data format.
8. With an IBM 3350 disk, we have a file with 200-byte records and a blocking factor of 25. Count-data format is used. Using data from Appendix 1, compute the time to read a block (a) by sequential access and (b) by direct access.
9. A file with 300,000 records each 100 bytes long with a blocking factor of 40 is stored in count-data format on an IBM 3350 disk. The file is reorganized and stored on the same disk in count-key data format, with key length 20 bytes. Use the data in Appendix 1 to compute how many extra cylinders will be required.
10. Repeat question 6 for the IBM 3380 disk. Necessary parameters are in Appendix 1.
11. Repeat question 7 for the IBM 3380 disk.
12. Repeat question 9 for the IBM 3380 disk.

References

Bohl, M. Introduction to IBM Direct Access Storage Devices, SRA, Palo Alto, 1981.

3 SEQUENTIAL FILE PRINCIPLES AND CREATION

Sequential files are the most common kind of file and are widely used in commerce. Typically sequential files are created and manipulated using COBOL programs; therefore we begin this chapter by looking at COBOL's the sequential file processing facilities. We shall look at what actually goes on during execution of a sequential file processing program. This will help the reader to place the many COBOL file processing details in perspective; the reader will also be able to appreciate the power of the sequential file processing facilities available in COBOL.

We then look at some of the methods for specifying file processing programs in business. These methods include input/output (IPO) charts, hierarchy diagrams, outline flow charts, and file navigation diagrams.

After that we examine a fairly comprehensive business example of the creation of a sequential file using COBOL. We conclude with coverage of how to handle input/output (I/O) errors with COBOL, and with brief coverage of the IBM job control language (JCL) needed for running file processing programs on IBM mainframe computers.

Be aware that this is not a COBOL textbook in the conventional sense. We shall place COBOL file processing in the broader perspective of both business computer systems and the underlying theory of computer files. For this reason we usually present only COBOL program excerpts that illustrate the essentials of the files and file processing techniques required for a given task. It is assumed that readers with an elementary knowledge of COBOL will be able to fill in extraneous details, such as code, for report formats. Inclusion of such detail in this book would serve only to obsure the file processing principles that are our major focus. Such peripheral (but necessary) COBOL coding techniques can be found in any standard COBOL text.

PROCESSING AND PRINCIPLES FOR COBOL SEQUENTIAL FILES

In general COBOL file processing causes records in files to move from external storage devices (tapes and disks) to internal (or electronic) memory and vice versa, under the influence of COBOL file processing commands. A good way to gain an understanding of COBOL file processing facilities and commands is to examine them in the light of physical movement of records during file processing. In particular this is the best way to gain an understanding, in COBOL terms, of the difference between **move mode** and **locate mode** processing.

Record Movements during Sequential File Processing

Figure 3.1 depicts movement of records during execution of a simple COBOL program. This program creates a new tape file, OUTTAPE, from records read from another tape file, INTAPE. INTAPE and OUTTAPE records are not equal in size, but we may assume for the sake of the illustration that one OUTTAPE record is created and output for each INTAPE record read. Furthermore, although the two files are tape files, the discussion would not be different if the files were on disk.

Figure 3.1 shows an internal memory partition that contains the file processing program along with associated structures (we are assuming a multiprogramming operating system). Among these associated structures are the buffer areas for the two files. Knowing what goes on in these buffer areas is vital for understanding COBOL file processing commands. The buffer area for INTAPE is called an **input buffer**; that for OUTTAPE is called an **output buffer**. For simplicity we have shown each buffer area as containing exactly one buffer. A buffer area can contain (be made up of) many buffers. Each buffer can hold a block of records, which is the unit of transmission between internal memory and external storage. (Note that with virtual operating systems an internal memory partition like that in Figure 3.1 would be continually demandpaged to and from a system disk. Readers can conveniently forget about this complication.)

Once the block of records currently residing in the input buffer has been processed, a new READ command execution causes a new block to be transmitted from INTAPE to the input buffer and at the same time causes the first record of this new block to be transferred to a working-storage record structure called INREC. However, if all the records in the block currently in the input buffer were not processed,a

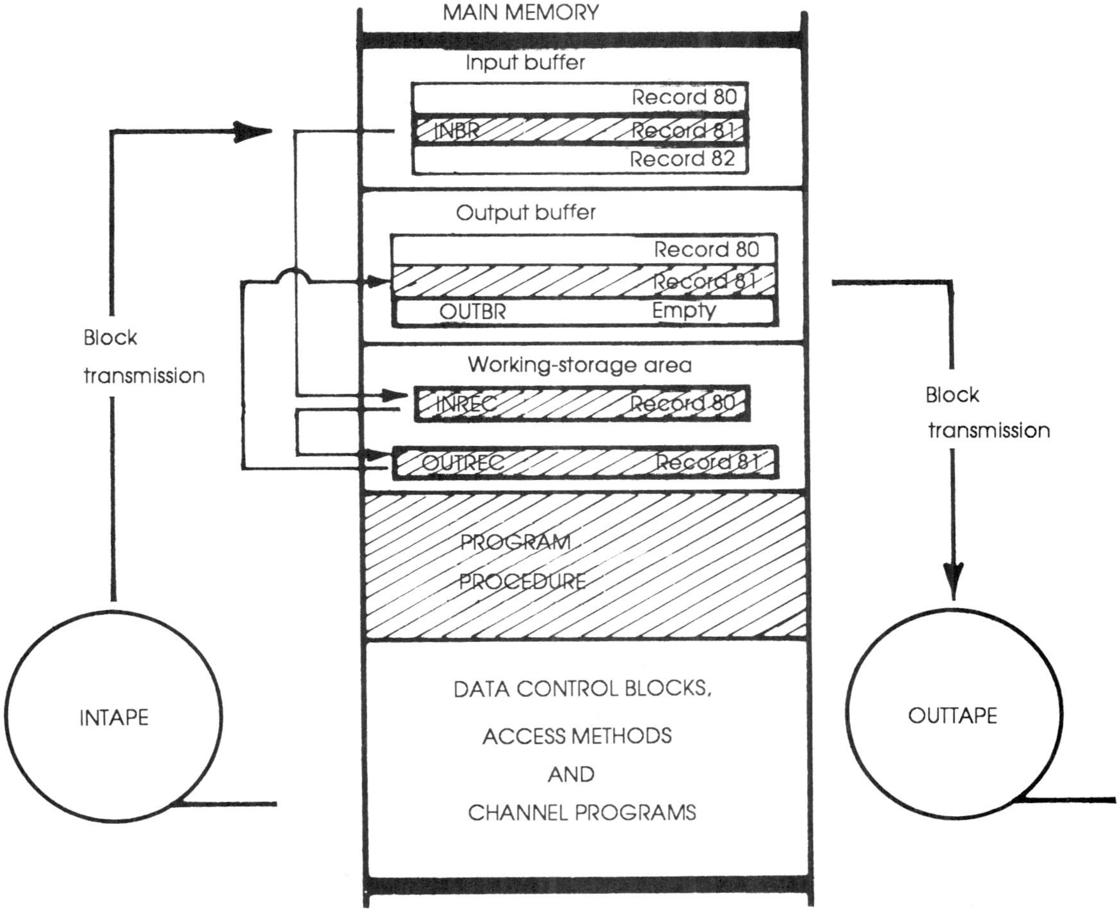

FIGURE 3.1 Illustration of the movement of records during file processing. We can imagine the processing to consist of creating a new record in the output file OUTTAPE for each record in the input file INTAPE. It is important to understand that the COBOL buffer records INBR and OUTBR are mobile within their buffers. A typical READ instruction moves INBR coincident with the next record, which is then moved to the working-storage record INREC. A WRITE instruction reverses this with OUTREC and OUTBR.

READ command execution would not cause a new block to be transmitted to the input buffer; instead only the next record in line to be processed would be transferred to the working-storage structure INREC.

With output the situation is reversed. A WRITE command execution causes the record currently in the working storage OUTREC to move to the next empty record slot in the output buffer. If the transfer of this record to the output buffer actually fills the buffer, the entire block of records in the buffer is also transmitted to the tape file OUTTAPE.

If you look carefully at Figure 3.1 you will notice that the record slot in the input buffer from which the current record is transferred to the working-storage structure INREC has a name, INBR. Similarly the record slot in the output buffer to which the record currently in the working-storage structure OUTREC is transferred also has a name, OUTBR.

Both INBR and OUTBR are buffer record structures, which are physically mobile within their respective buffers. For example, a READ command execution causes INBR to move forward coincident with the next record to be processed, that is, the record transferred to INREC. Conversely, when a record in OUTREC is written by a WRITE command execution, the record is moved to the current OUTREC structure, which then immediately moves forward to the next empty record slot in the buffer and awaits a new record from the next WRITE execution.

These movements have an important programming consequence. Following a READ execution, both buffer structure INBR and working-storage structure INREC are holding the same record. But following a WRITE execution, OUTBR does not hold the same record as OUTREC. This is illustrated in detail in Figures 3.2 and 3.3, which show buffer contents following reading and writing a series of blocked records, such as A, B, and C.

Note that Figure 3.1 applies to record files where blocking is possible, such as tape and disk files. With COBOL a single punched card is a record of a file of cards, and a single line on a line-printer is a record of a printer file. Card and printer files cannot be blocked; therefore the corresponding buffers contain only one record. With IBM systems, card readers and printers are called **unit record (U-R) devices**.

Double Buffers

Although Figure 3.1 shows only single input and output buffers, it is standard practice to use double buffers (the default with almost all operating systems). Nevertheless the essential movement of records described above is not altered if we have two input buffers and two output buffers for processing. With the extra input buffer, when all the records of the other buffer have been processed (following a succession of READ commands), execution of a further READ command allows the mobile buffer structure INBR to move immediately to the first record of the buffer that has not been processed. This means that the operating system does not have to give execution control to some other memory partition while it is allowing the channel, or input/output (I/O) processor, to transmit a new block from INFILE to replace the block in the buffer that has already been processed. Instead the next record can be moved from INBR to INREC while the channel is concurrently filling up the other buffer. In this way performance is improved by the use of double buffers. Double output buffers have a similar effect. Most operating systems provide double buffers by default.

The COBOL READ Command with Sequential Files

Refer again to both Figures 3.1 and 3.2. Imagine that we are reading the blocked records A, B, C, and so on into internal memory from the tape file INTAPE. As before, the mobile buffer record structure is INBR and the working-storage structure is INREC. In Figure 3.2 the blocking factor is 3.

In any COBOL program, before the records of a file can be read or written the file must be opened, using an OPEN command. To read records we open for input (INPUT) processing with the OPEN command:

```
OPEN INPUT INTAPE.
```

This command allows only reading of records. If we subsequently want to write records into the file, it must first be closed (with a CLOSE command) and then reopened for update (UPDATE) operations.

The practical effects of the OPEN INPUT command are twofold:

a. It causes the file header label to be checked, if there is one.
b. It causes the first block of records in the file to be transmitted to the input buffer (Figure 3.2); or, in the case of double buffers, the first two blocks are transmitted.

However, neither the buffer record (INBR) nor the working-storage record (INREC) as yet contains a record. They need the execution of the first READ command in order to get a record.

The read command has the format:

```
READ INFILE INTO INREC,
      AT END imperative statement.
```

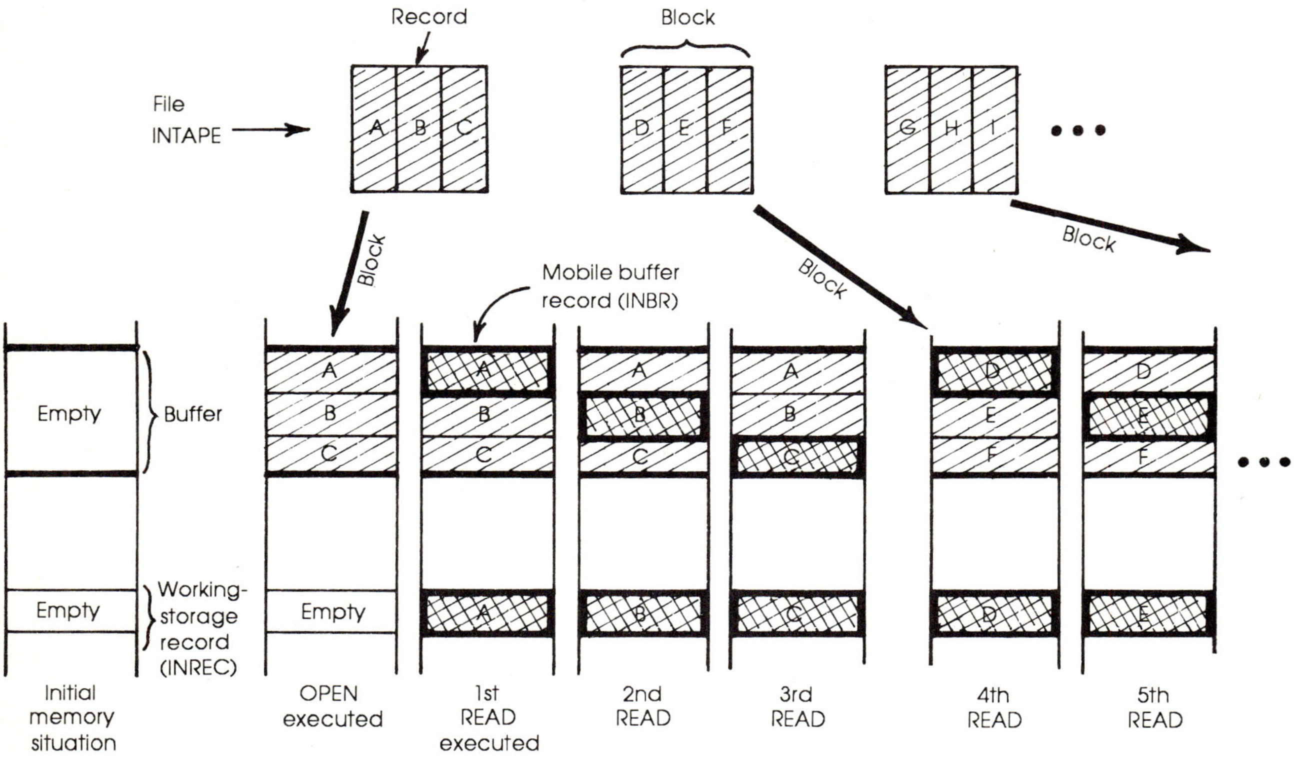

FIGURE 3.2 Details of what goes on in the buffer and working storage as a sequential file is read. OPEN causes the first block to move to the buffer, but data is not available as either the buffer record or the working-storage record. As each READ is executed the mobile buffer record structure (INBR) moves coincident with the next record and a copy is moved to the working-storage structure. The blocking factor above is assumed to be 3. When the 4th READ is executed a new block is moved to the buffer and the first record copied into the working-storage structure (INREC). See also Figure 3.1.

The first time this READ command is executed the buffer record INBR positions itself with the first record in the buffer; the contents of INBR are also moved to the working-storage structure INREC. From now on each execution of READ causes INBR to move to the next record in the buffer, and the contents of INBR to move to INREC. When a READ has moved the last record in the buffer from INBR to INREC, a further READ causes the next block in INTAPE to be transmitted to the buffer, and INBR to be positioned at the first record of this new block (Figure 3.2). Although the figure shows a single buffer, this process is not materially affected by double buffers.

When the last record of the file has been read from the buffer, a further READ command execution causes the COBOL imperative statement following AT END to be executed. This causes the program to take action appropriate to reaching the end of the input file.

To close the file we issue:

```
CLOSE INTAPE.
```

In the case of a tape file this causes the reel to be rewound automatically, unless we had originally specified in the OPEN statement that it was not to be rewound. Such a rewind-inhibiting OPEN would be:

```
OPEN INPUT INTAPE NO REWIND.
```

At the most, rewinding takes only a few minutes with commonly used tape drives.

The COBOL WRITE Command with Sequential Files

Refer to both Figures 3.1 and 3.3; this time imagine that we are writing out the file OUTTAPE. The blocked records being written are A, B, C, and so on, with blocking factor 3 (as shown in Figure 3.3). The output buffer record structure is OUTBR and the working-storage record is OUTREC.

Before we can write records into a file, the file must be opened for output (OUTPUT) as follows:

```
OPEN OUTPUT OUTTAPE.
```

The effect is twofold:

a. It causes the header label to be written.
b. It causes the buffer record structure OUTBR to be positioned at the start of the empty buffer, awaiting arrival of the first record.

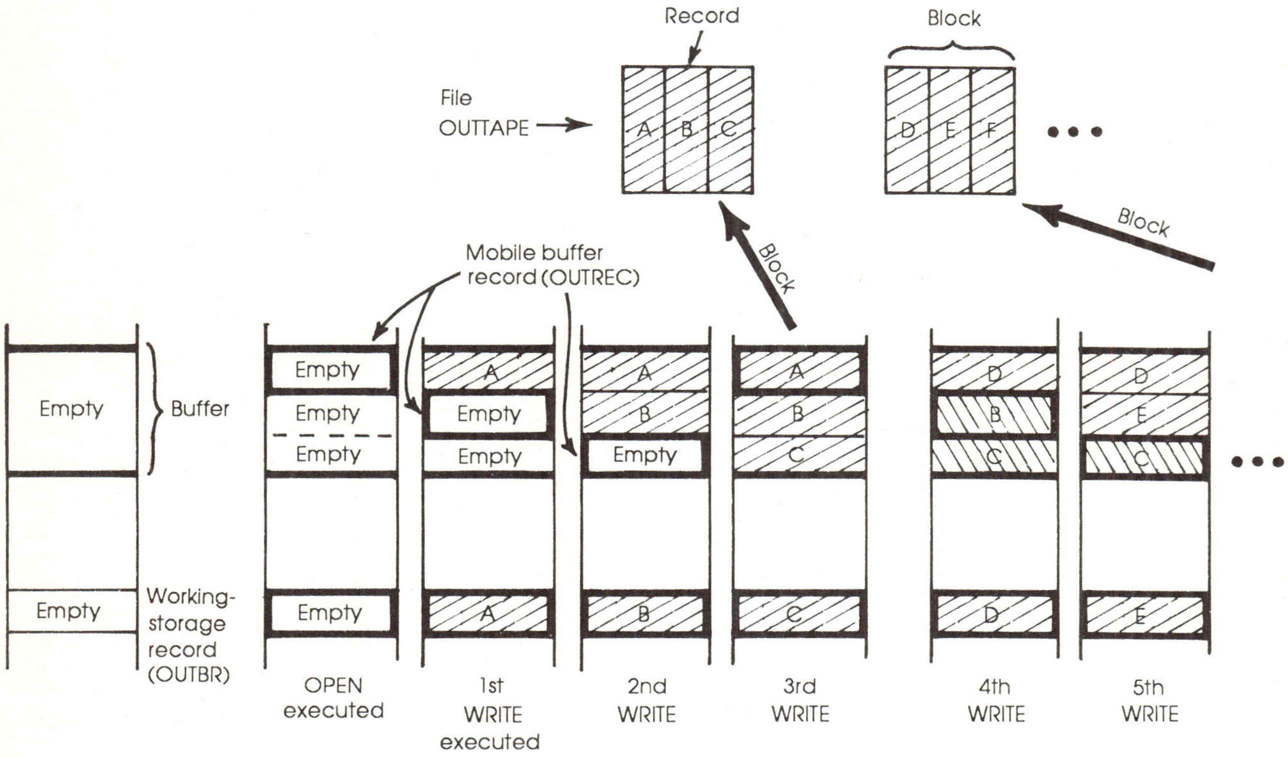

FIGURE 3.3 Details of what goes on in buffer and working storage when a sequential file is written. Observe that the situation is more complex than with file reading (Figure 3.2). The mobile buffer record (OUTBR) occupies the next available space in the buffer at all times, awaiting the next record from the working-storage structure (OUTREC). A WRITE causes the record in OUTREC to move to OUTBR, which then shifts to the next vacant buffer slot. At the end of the 3rd WRITE (with blocking factor 3), record C has moved to the last buffer slot, the block has been copied to the tape, and OUTBR has moved to the first vacant slot which actually contains record A!

It is a WRITE command execution that causes the first record to move to the output buffer. The format of the WRITE command is:

```
WRITE OUTBR FROM OUTREC.
```

Notice that the file involved is not mentioned in the command. When this command is executed two things happen. First the record in the working-storage structure OUTREC moves to OUTBR in the output buffer. Second the mobile OUTBR record structure moves to the next vacant record slot in the buffer, ready for the next record (Figure 3.3). When a WRITE transfers a record to the buffer that fills it, then, in addition, the buffer contents (a block of records) are transmitted to the file OUTTAPE, and OUTBR moves to the start of the buffer to await the next record.

Notice that transmission of the buffer contents to the file does not cause deletion of the buffer contents. This can be a source of error, for it normally means that following a WRITE the contents of OUTREC will not be the same as the contents of OUTBR. Why this is so should be clear from Figure 3.3. In contrast, following a READ (Figure 3.2), the contents of INREC are the same as those of INBR. Thus it is thus tricky to use OUTBR in a program. (As before,, although Figures 3.1 and 3.3 depict a single output buffer, the operation of WRITE is not affected significantly by the use of double buffers).

When the last record has been written to OUTTAPE, a CLOSE OUTTAPE command is issued. This causes the contents of the buffer (probably not completely full) to be transmitted to the file and also closes the file.

The above discussion tacitly assumes creation of a new file. Occasionally we need to extend an existing file by adding records at the end. This can be done with any file on disk, provided there is still some space left on the disk. But with a tape file it can be done only with the last file on a reel, assuming there is still space left on the reel. To write out records to the end of the file we open the file with:

```
OPEN EXTEND OUTTAPE.
```

The WRITE statement can then be used as described above.

In all cases we close the file with the usual CLOSE command. Rewind/no rewind conditions for tape files are as for reading a file.

The COBOL REWRITE Command with Sequential Files

The REWRITE command can be used only with files on disk. Suppose that the file is called MASTER, the buffer record structure is BR, and the working-storage record structure is WSR. The file would be opened for both input and output operations, as follows:

```
OPEN I-O MASTER.
```

We can now issue both READ and REWRITE commands. Typically a record will be read into WSR, a field will be changed, and the updated record will be written back to the disk file, where the original record will be overwritten by the updated version. If we assume that a field of the record is SALARY, then the SALARY field in the next record of the file MASTER could be updated as follows (note that the file name is not used in the REWRITE command):

```
READ MASTER INTO WSR, AT END ...
COMPUTE SALARY IN WSR = SALARY IN WSR + 1000.
REWRITE BR FROM WSR.
```

When REWRITE is executed the record in WSR is moved to replace the record in BR. As records from MASTER are read in, it is possible that most of them will not need updating and thus rewriting to the disk. Nevertheless once the buffer records have all been read by READ commands, the entire buffer contents will be used to overwrite the corresponding block on disk if any of those buffer records were replaced using a REWRITE command. To close the file we use CLOSE as before.

Move and Locate Mode Processing

The use of READ, WRITE, and REWRITE commands described above involves **move mode processing**. In move mode processing, blocks of records move between buffers and external storage, and records being processed move between buffer and working storage.

Locate mode processing is an alternative to move mode processing. Here blocks move between buffer and external storage, as with move mode. The difference is that records are not moved from buffer to working storage; instead records are processed within the buffer, that is, within either the input buffer or within the output buffer. Processing within the input buffer is illustrated in Figure 3.4, where we are reading in the file INFILE and writing out the file OUTFILE. We can imagine the processing as simply making a copy of INFILE.

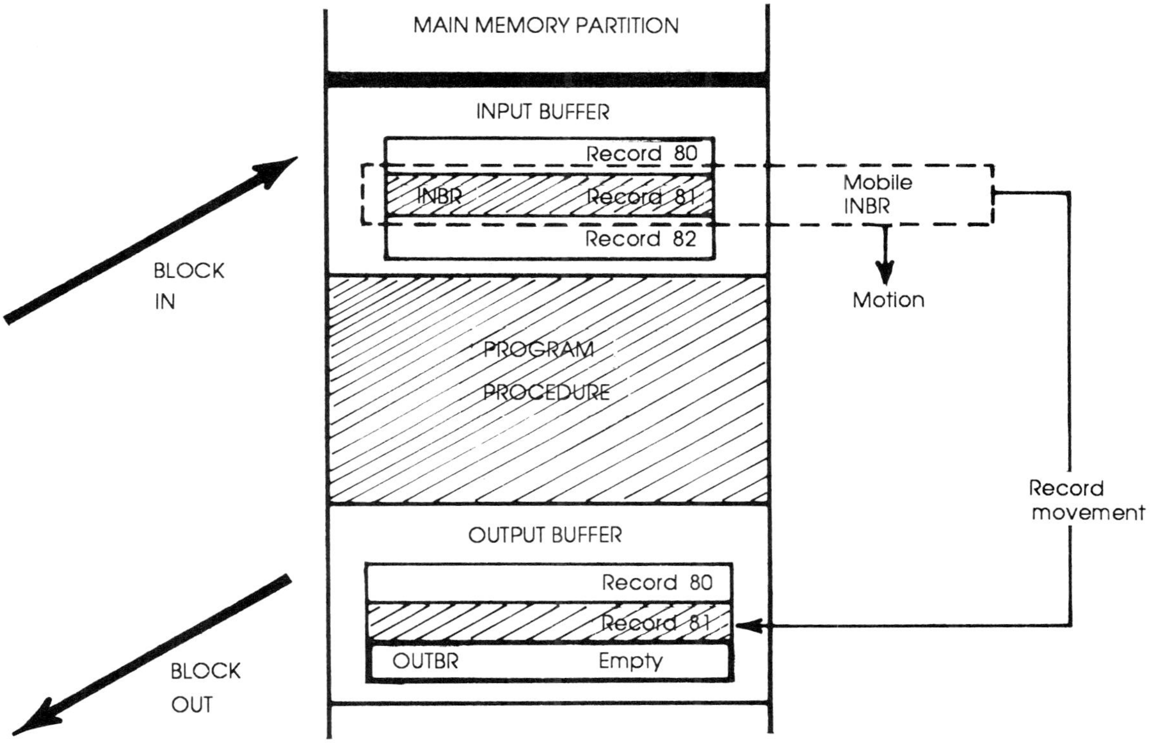

FIGURE 3.4 Locate mode processing the input buffer. Incoming records are processed in the input buffer in the mobile input buffer structure INBR, instead of in working storage. Following processing directly in INBR, the record is written directly into the output buffer structure OUTBR, which then moves to the next empty buffer slot. Locate mode processing in the output buffer is also possible.

To read the next record, the command:

```
READ INFILE, AT END ...
```

is executed. This causes the mobile input buffer record structure to move coincident with the next record in the buffer. The program can now do any necessary processing with the contents of INBR (perhaps some editing or validity checking). The record is then output directly to the output buffer as follows:

```
WRITE OUTBR FROM INBR.
```

This causes the record in INBR to be copied to the next empty output buffer record slot.

When the output buffer is full, the entire block is transmitted to the storage file. Similarly when the last record of the input buffer has been processed, a new READ causes a new block to be transmitted from the input file to the input buffer.

READ and WRITE Statements Revisited

Locate mode processing is possible because essentially the following READ command for move mode processing

```
READ INTAPE INTO INREC, AT END ...
```

is the equivalent of the pair of following COBOL statements:

```
READ INFILE, AT END ...
MOVE INBR TO INREC.
```

In a similar manner, the WRITE statement for move mode processing is equivalent to the following:

```
MOVE OUTREC TO OUTBR.
WRITE OUTBR.
```

This enables us to do locate mode processing with the record being processed in the output buffer. Readers are invited to try this as an exercise.

It is clear that locate mode processing is somewhat more efficient, since movement of records in internal memory is reduced. Nevertheless unless the records involved are very large, the saving is not all that significant. In commerce, quite large records often occur in files, so that locate mode processing is common. Readers are cautioned, however, that very subtle errors can occur when locate mode processing is used, mainly because of the mobility of the buffer record structure (INBR or OUTBR) in the buffer. For this reason we shall largely concentrate on the simpler move mode processing.

Records and Files with a COBOL Program

As readers probably know, a COBOL program has four major divisions, namely, identification, environment, data, and procedure (see Figure 3.5). The identification division is where the program is named and is of little fundamental importance. In contrast the environment and data

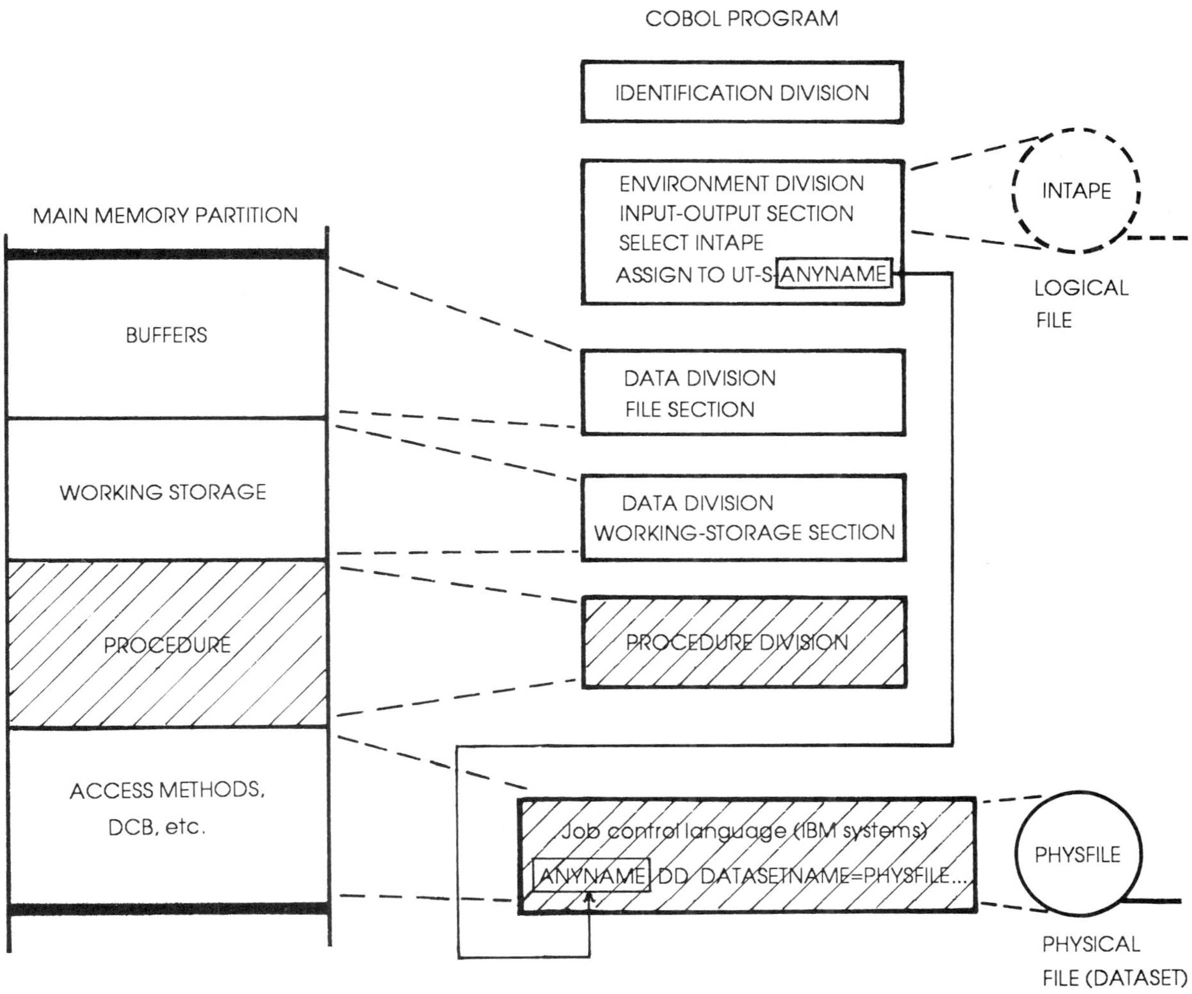

FIGURE 3.5 This diagram shows how the different parts of a COBOL program relate to the layout of data structures and instructions in an operating system partition. It also illustrates file naming conventions with IBM systems.

divisions are very important: Within these divisions we specify the files and record structures used in the processing.

In the input-output section of the environment division we specify:

a. The logical file name

b. The physical file specification (or at least a reference to a specification for the physical file)

An example follows:

```
SELECT INTAPE
       ASSIGN TO UT-S-ANYNAME.
```

This is used with IBM System 370 operating systems. INTAPE is the logical file name, that is, the name of the file of records as seen by the program in the working-storage area. (The logical file is an imaginary file consisting only of the records, and not blocks of records, that can fit into working storage).

The physical file (or dataset) has blocked records; in the case of disks these may contain some additional system data that is not read into working storage. In the SELECT statement above, ANYNAME is not the name of the physical file but the name of the non-COBOL dataset specification required with IBM systems. ANYNAME is called a **ddname**, and the dataset specification is called a **DD-statement**. The DD-statement is normally placed at the end of the program, as illustrated in Figure 3.5. In the incomplete DD-statement below, the name of the dataset is PHYSFILE, the file is on a 2400-type tape drive, and the volume serial number for the reel is 007. (Later we give a more complete example of a DD-statement.)

```
//ANYNAME  DD  DATASETNAME=PHYSFILE,UNIT=2400,VOL=SER=007,..
```

In addition to a reference to a physical file specification, many of the physical file specifications can be placed directly in the input-output section of the environment division.

In the file section of the data division (Figure 3.5), we specify the buffer record structures (such as INBR and OUTBR). These structures are mobile within their buffers.

In the working-storage section of the data division we have the specifications for the working-storage record structures (such as INREC and OUTREC). These structures hold records being processed during move mode processing.

Actual file processing instructions are placed in the procedure division. To use an analogy, the file and record specifications in the environment and data divisions list the cast of characters, whereas the procedure division contains the plot.

COBOL File Names

Within a COBOL program we use the **logical file name**. This has nothing to do with the physical file, or dataset, name that is encoded in the file label (and also specified in the JCL DD-statement specifying a dataset). For example, the logical file name for the input file in Figure 3.1 was taken as INTAPE. This meant that within the procedure division we could use this name with READ statements, such as:

```
READ INTAPE INTO INREC, AT END ...
```

It is this logical file name that is specified after SELECT in the input-output section of the environment division.

The logical file name is arbitrary. The physical file name (dataset) name is not arbitrary and is physically encoded in the file label. With IBM systems it is the DD-statement that connects the arbitrary logical file name with the permanent dataset name. This means that we could have two different versions of the same program, which differ only in the logical file names. If connected via identical DD-statements to identical datasets, the processing carried out by the programs would also be identical.

SPECIFICATION OF COMPUTER FILE PROCESSING

Business enterprises normally carry out a wide variety of file processing activities, as we saw in chapter 1. The first stage in arranging for such processing is deciding what is required. It is the job of a systems analyst, and not a COBOL programmer, to decide just what processing is required in any given situation. In this section we look at the ways in which a systems analyst communicates what processing is required to a programmer, so that the programmer can code a program to meet these requirements. We begin with an outline of an example that involves creation of a computer file.

A Typical Business File Processing Example

This example involves creation of a file called SHIPPED-ITEMS. Although this file can be used in later processing to generate invoices, we will not cover that here. The following should place the SHIPPED-ITEMS file in context.

When a firm (vendor) sells items to another firm (purchaser), the purchaser receives not only the items ordered but the following important documents as well:

a. The bill of lading

b. The invoice

c. The monthly statement

The bill of lading (or packing slip) simply accompanies the goods shipped to the purchaser. It lists the goods shipped; the purchaser will check the list to see that it matches the physical goods received.

Historially, the bill of lading goes back to times when shipment of goods was subject to great hazard, not the least of which was a dishonest carrier. For example, if an Arab merchant had to ship ten bags of dates across the desert by camel train and feared theft of some of the bags, he would also send ten shells (or other items) in a sealed container: The shells would be the bill of lading. On arrival, the purchaser would simply check that the number of shells matched the number of bags.

A typical bill of lading is illustrated in Figure 3.6. Each bill has a unique identification number (bill of lading number), gives some minimal information about the customer, and contains the address of the consignee (place to which the goods are shipped). It also contains line items, each of which describes the type of item shipped, such as 100 transistors or 200 staplers. Since a shipment typically involves a number of different types of items, a bill of lading typically has several line items. Also it often contains an estimate of the value of the shipment, although an exact statement of value is reserved for the invoice.

The vendor normally sends an invoice to the purchaser as soon as possible after shipment, usually within a few days. The invoice is essentially a bill for payment and lists items delivered, together with unit prices, freight costs, and taxes. The bottom line is what the purchaser must pay.

Usually the invoice is not sent with the goods because of the time required for invoice preparation. It is good business practice to ship as soon as possible, because the customer may find another supplier if the vendor is tardy. Thus there is usually not enough time to prepare the invoice before the goods are shipped. Nevertheless to ensure prompt payment by the purchaser, the vendor attempts to mail the invoice as quickly as possible: This is the reason that computer preparation of invoices is common in business.

```
BILL OF LADING DATA ITEMS

Consignee Name:           Snowcap Electronics
Consignee Address:        10, Transformer Road, Denver,
                          CO, 91752
Customer Number:          23677
Bill of Lading Number:    45678
Line-item-1
Number of Pieces: 100
Description:      Transistors
Item Code:        234-24
Line-item-2
Number of pieces: 300
Description:      Resistors
Item Code:        092-46
Estimated Value:                 185.00
```

FIGURE 3.6 Illustration of the data items or fields that are filled out on a standard bill of lading or (packing slip) form. This can be done by a computer although it is still probably more commonly done manually in part by sales, warehouse, and shipping personnel.

Typically a purchaser receives many shipments and invoices from a vendor each month and makes many payments. At the end of each month the vendor sends the purchaser a monthly statement, which typically details what the customer owes on each invoice and the total amount owing.

The computer system required for preparing the monthly statement is often different from that used to prepare the invoices, especially in a batch system. Nevertheless files generated by the invoice preparation system—in particular the file containing the total owing on each outstanding invoice generated in a recent period (called the accounts receivable summary file)—are needed in the monthly statement generation system.

In batch processing for ultimately generating invoices and monthly statements, the initial data entry begins with the bills of lading issued each day by the shipping department. The bills are batched each day and sent to the data entry department. In the old days of punched cards, a card was punched for each line item on a bill; that meant that for each bill of lading there was group of cards.

Nowadays this data is keyed directly into a disk file (or tape file), with the format of each record similar to that for punched cards; that is, a byte of space for each character of data. In addition, as with the card file of former years, there will be a group of records for each bill of lading, with a record of the group corresponding to a line item (see Figure 3.6). Let us give this file the logical name BOLDATA.

From this bill of lading (BOL) data on disk an initial file is generated using an edit and load program. This initial file can be on tape or disk, but for purposes of illustration we shall assume a tape file with logical name SHIPPED-ITEMS.

The edit and load program is very important. Although in principle this program involves little more than the copying of the file BOLDATA to form the file SHIPPED-ITEMS, the processing marks the entry point of data into the computer system. It is thus the place where extensive editing and checking must be carried out to ensure the accuracy, consistency, and reasonableness of the new data. This is called **validity checking**. Therefore the bulk of the code in the edit and load program is used for validity checking the incoming data in the file BOLDATA. During processing, BOLDATA records containing invalid, unreasonable, or otherwise doubtful data are rejected; rejected record contents are printed in an edit report, together with an explanation of the reason for rejection.

The initial processing of BOLDATA is a sort on bill of lading number, before actual submission to the edit and load program. This ensures that all line items belonging to the same bill of lading are grouped together. This permits the edit and load program to reject the entire group of records for a given bill of lading, if a single line-item record from the group has defective data.

The data for rejected records listed in the edit report output by the program is later manually compared with the actual bills of lading involved; any corrected records may be re-entered in a later version of BOLDATA. If that does not solve the problem, the bills of lading are returned to shipping for clarification.

Before looking at the specification of the edit and load program and to keep things in a business context, we will look at the later processing applied to SHIPPED-ITEMS. Customer names and addresses are not in the records of SHIPPED-ITEMS, only the address of the consignee. A new file, SI2, is created by attaching customer names and addresses (held in a master file CUSTOMER) to the records of SHIPPED-ITEMS. Then a further new file, SI3, is created by adding prices of items to the records of SI2 (price information is taken from a master file on product prices).

From the data in SI3 the invoices are generated. In addition SI3 is used to update the accounts receivable summary file, which shows the amount owing on each outstanding invoice generated in a recent period. (This should not be confused with the accounts receivable

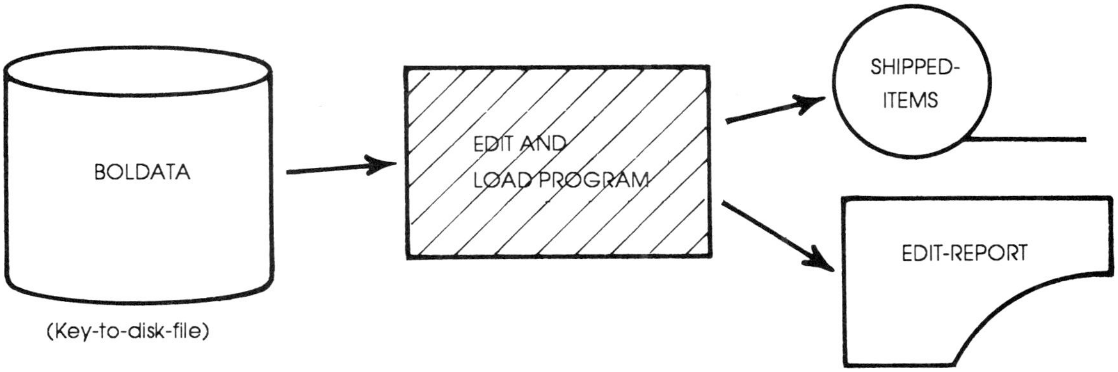

FIGURE 3.7 **System diagram for loading the file SHIPPED-ITEMS from records keyed into the disk file BOLDATA (bill of lading data). Extensive checking of the data in the records in BOLDATA is necessary, since the records in SHIPPED-ITEMS represent the initial entry point of data into a system that ultimately generates invoices, monthly statements, and accounts receivable records. The fields of BOLDATA and SHIPPED-ITEMS are illustrated in Figure 3.8.**

master file, which lists the amount owing by all customers and all invoices outstanding.)

A system diagram for the processing of the original file BOLDATA to generate the file SHIPPED-ITEMS is shown in Figure 3.7. Both BOLDATA and SHIPPED-ITEMS have the same fields; the field layout is shown in Figure 3.8. We can now use the problem of specifying the processing to illustrate file processing specification techniques.

The overall processing is specified by a systems analyst, who prepares a program specification. Using this program specification, a programmer in turn prepares the following (after which he or she codes the program):

a. A hierarchy diagram, and possibly a flow chart
b. An input/output diagram
c. Possibly a file navigation diagram

The Program Specification

Normally a systems analyst designs the overall processing system, such as the system for generation of invoices described in the previous section. This gives the systems analyst a bird's-eye view of the entire

CUSTNUMBER	BILLNUMB	ITEMCODE	ITEMQUANTITY	ITEMDESCRIPTION
23677	45678	234-24	100	LASER
23677	45678	092-46	300	GYROSCOPE
13982	45687	091-23	800	TURBINE BLADE
.				
.				
.				BOLDATA
SHIPPED-ITEMS				

FIGURE 3.8 Fields and sample data for the files BOLDATA and SHIPPED-ITEMS. For conventions applying to field values and formats, see the programming specifications in Figure 3.9.

system and permits understanding of exactly what processing is required at each step, such as the initial processing step of generating the file SHIPPED-ITEMS from the disk file BOLDATA. The nature of the processing is communicated to the programmer in an important document called a **program specification**.

There is an example of a program specification for generating SHIPPED-ITEMS in Figure 3.9. The details listed are merely typical and for the most part do not concern us, since they involve the specifics of what has to be checked for each field of a BOLDATA record. One point is worth noting however, since it will have a pronounced effect on the nature of the processing and organization of the program: This is the requirement to reject all BOLDATA records with the same bill of lading number as a record with a field that has failed any of the checks. The reason for this is explained in the specifications.

PROGRAMMING SPECIFICATIONS

DATE: 15 October
PROGRAM: Edit and Loading Program for SHIPPED-ITEMS
TO PROGRAMMER: Paul Prodigal
FROM SYSTEMS ANALYST: Ann Analing

This program will edit and load a tape file from data in a disk file that has been keyed in; both files have the same record format with the fields Customer Number, Bill of Lading Number, Item Code, Item Quantity, and Item Description. An edit or exeception report will be output as well. Both files are in ascending Bill of Lading Number order; duplidate Bill of Lading Numbers will be common.

The following checks should be carried out:

1. The Customer Number is numeric. The number of digits is 5. The sum of the digits has a units digit equal to the 3rd digit of the customer number.
2. The Bill of Lading Number is numeric. Number of digits is 5. The sum of the digits plus 8 has a units digit equal to the last digit of the bill of lading number.
3. The Item Code is alphanumeric. Number of characters is 6. If first character 0, 1, or 2, then the 4th character is a dash; otherwise it is A, B, or C. The last two characters are numeric.
4. The Item Quantity is numeric. It must exceed 99 and must be less than 10,001.
5. The Item Description is alphanumeric and must not exceed 40 characters. Up to 5 words are allowed, each separated by exactly one blank. Accuracy of item description will be checked in a later processing stage.

When a record with a given bill of lading number is rejected, all records with that bill of lading number must be rejected. This is important, since otherwise and invoice for only part of a shipment could be generated in later processing stages. When a field of a record fails a check, details of the nature of the failure should be output on an edit report. A bill of lading has at most 18 lines of data, for each of which a record will have been keyed into the disk file.

FIGURE 3.9 **Programming specifications for the program to load the tape file from disk data for the system in Figure 3.7.**

Hierarchical Program Structure Design

The days when a commercial program for use in routine processing was written as a private work of art are long gone. Commercial programs have a long life, represent a substantial investment, and must be maintained. To reduce the heavy cost of maintenance, commercial programs are structured into independent modules. When taken together these modules give the program a hierarchical structure. A **hierachy diagram** specifies this modular structure—therefore it not only specifies the structure of the program but also forces the programmer to give the program a hierarchical structure. (Note that if the structure is not hierarchical, it must have the form of a network, which is much more complex. Thus a hierarchical structure diagram forces simpler program structure.)

Each module of the hierarchical structure is coded as a COBOL paragraph. In addition (as far as possible) each module carries out a single task, such as outputting the headings of an edit report.

The independence of the modules means that a later maintenance programmer can inspect the hierarchical structure diagram to determine where in the organization a targeted task is performed. The programmer can then make changes to the module involved without having to worry that these changes will affect other modules.

Preparation of the hierarchy diagram of program structure is a programmer responsibility. A great deal of thought and much trial and error goes into it; it can be constructed only by someone who has both studied the program specification and is thoroughly familiar with COBOL. The systems analyst involved in the project will probably want to review the diagram, however. In Figure 3.10 we have an example of a hierarchy diagram for the generation of the file SHIPPED-ITEMS, according to the processing specified in Figure 3.9.

The modules for the major programming tasks are shown at the second level down. The second-level tasks clearly include writing out the headings for the edit report and processing the records with the same bill of lading number. The task of validating BOLDATA records can be broken down into smaller tasks involving the individual BOLDATA fields, as shown in the diagram.

The hierarchy diagram is often supplemented by a **flow chart** of the processing, which shows the sequence in which the major tasks are carried out.

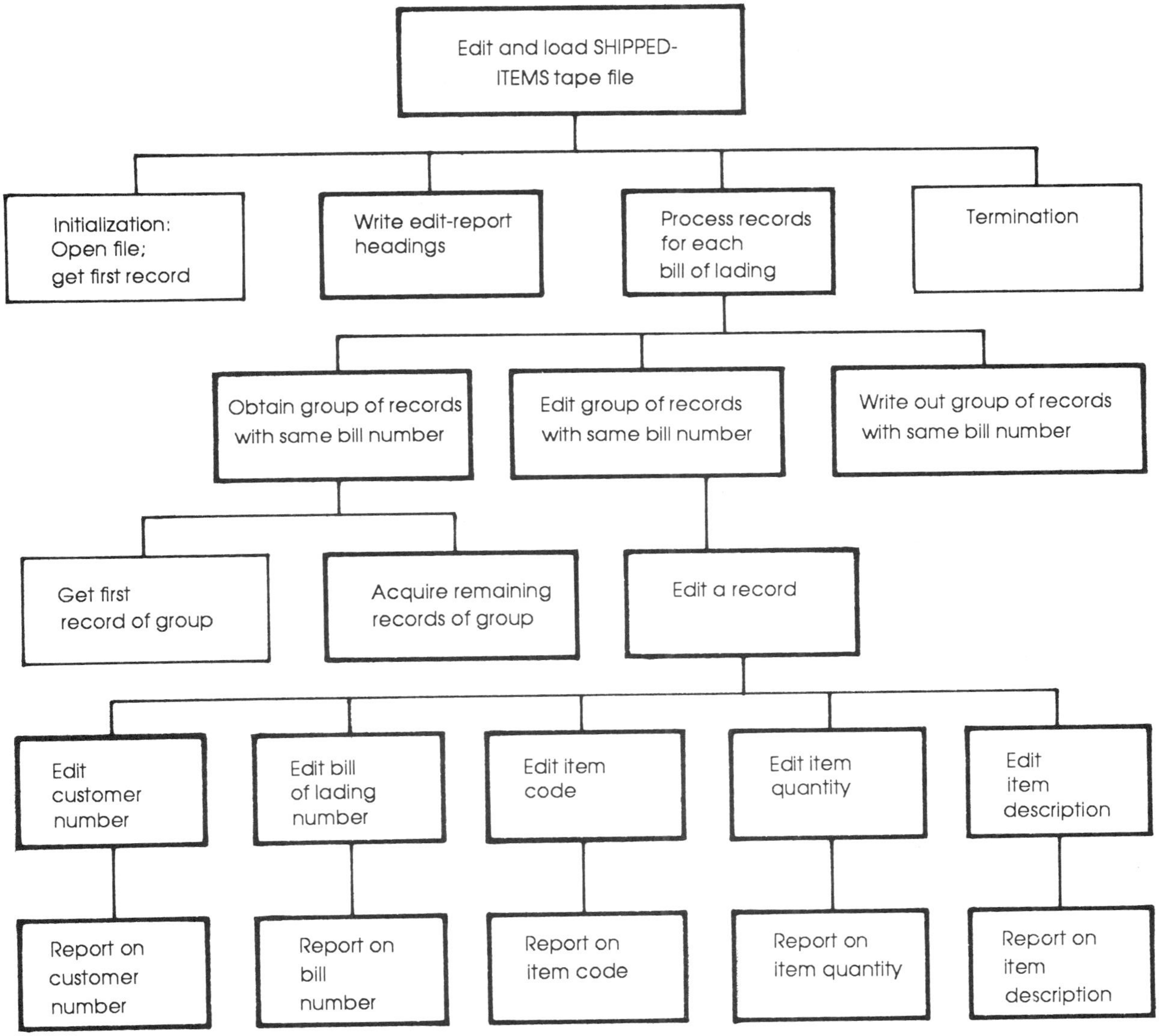

FIGURE 3.10 Possible hierarchy diagram for the structure of the program to load the tape file described in Figure 3.7. The program is divided into modules, each with a high degree of independence. A heavy box indicates a module, whereas a light box indicates that the code involved is contained within the module above. While the program essentially only copies data from a disk file onto tape, it is complicated because of the need for editing of the data in the disk file. The data on the disk is new data, entering the system for the first time, and must be carefully checked. For each module in the hierarchy, the programmer normally will draw up an input/output (IPO) diagram (see Figure 3.11). It is the programmer who draws the hierarchy diagram.

Input/Output (IPO) Charts

For each independent module of the hierarchy diagram the programmer will normally complete an **input/output (IPO) chart** before coding of the module begins. The diagram lists the type of data input to and output from the module. It also lists the processing that is carried out by the module and the tasks initiated by the module (and thus actually carried out by subsidiary modules of the hierarchy). In Figure 3.11 we have an example of the IPO chart for the module that edits a BOLDATA record (see also Figure 3.10).

File Navigation Diagrams

File navigation diagrams originated in data base processing and can be used in ordinary file processing. The diagram shows a typical sample of the records of the file or files used in the processing. It also shows the pathway taken by the program in reading or writing the records; thus it shows the exact sequence of records read and written.

INPUT/OUTPUT CHART

PROGRAM: Loading program for SHIPPED-ITEMS		PROGRAMMER: Paul Prodigal
MODULE Edit disk record	FUNCTION Edits a disk record	OUTPUT 19 October
INPUT Disk Record	PROCESSING 1. Edit customer number 2. Edit bill of lading number 3. Edit item code 4. Edit item quantity 5. Edit item description	OUTPUT 1. Edited record 2. Edit-report entries 3. Valid or invalid record message to parent module

FIGURE 3.11 Input/output (IPO) chart for the module that edits a BOLDATA record. For each module in the hierarchy diagram (Figure 3.10) there has to be a specification of (a) the input data to the module, (b) the processing carried out by the module, and (c) the data output from the module. Coding should begin only when all the IPO charts are complete.

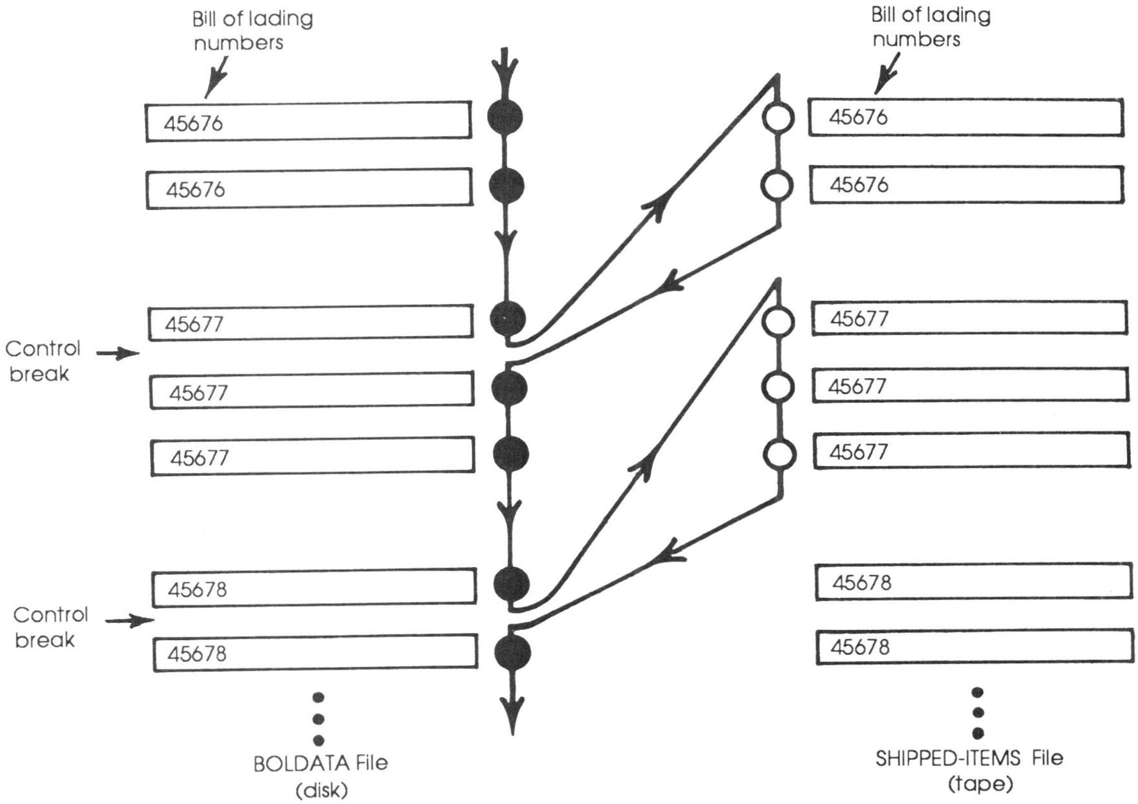

FIGURE 3.12 File navigational diagram for the procedure to edit and load the tape file containing shipped items data. The processing is straightforward; the diagram is merely an example of a file navigational diagram. Nevertheless even with this simple processing, where groups of cards with the same bill of lading number are processed, the diagram clearly shows something that is not easily discernible from either the hierarchy diagram (Figure 3.10), the outline program flow chart, or the program: namely, that before the records of a group can be written, the first record of the next group must read. This is the only way the program can determine that the end of the group has been reached! File navigational diagrams are most useful when the file processing is complex. This type of processing is called control break processing, since a change in the value of a bill number signals a break in current processing, that is, the scanning of the disk records.

File naviagtion diagrams can be used to show either the typical overall processing or simply the processing undertaken in specific circumstances, such as with records at the end of files. However, when the processing is complex, a diagram for the overall processing can be very difficult to draw. Nevertheless a diagram for a particular instance of the processing can be highly communicative. The first example of a file navigation diagram (for the processing of the file BOLDATA to generate the file SHIPPED-ITEMS) is shown in Figure 3.12.

COBOL PROGRAM FOR EDITING AND LOADING A SEQUENTIAL FILE

In this section we look at some of the file processing essentials of a COBOL program to edit and load the tape file SHIPPED-ITEMS, using source data originally keyed into the disk file BOLDATA. We shall use the program structure outlined in the hierarchy diagram in Figure 3.10, but we shall spare the reader the details of the editing modules. The required programming details have little to do with file processing, are common to all programming languages, and should present no problem to readers familiar with COBOL. Readers not familiar with COBOL may need to consult a COBOL programming text.

(Readers are reminded that in this book we do not attempt a detailed exposition on COBOL programming. Instead we attempt to place all important aspects of file processing, including the COBOL programming aspect, in a realistic business perspective. Some COBOL programming detail is therefore unavoidable, but we attempt to emphasize those COBOL details that are directly relevant to computer file processing.)

Identification, Environment, and Data Division Specifications

In a COBOL program all the files, record structures (group items), and identifiers (variables) involved in the processing are specified in the environment and data divisions of the program, as we have seen. If we include the initial identification division, these specifications could be as follows:

```
IDENTIFICATION DIVISION.
PROGRAM ID. EDIT-LOAD.

ENVIRONMENT DIVISION.

CONFIGURATION SECTION.
      SOURCE COMPUTER. IBM-370.
```

```
       OBJECT COMPUTER. IBM-370.

 INPUT-OUTPUT SECTION.
 FILE CONTROL.

       SELECT BOLDATA ASSIGN TO UT-S-DDBOL.
       SELECT SHIPPED-ITEMS ASSIGN TO UT-S-DDSHIP.
       SELECT EDIT-REPORT ASSIGN TP UR-S-SYSPRINT.

 DATA DIVISION.
 FILE SECTION.

 FD    BOLDATA
       LABEL RECORDS ARE STANDARD
       RECORD CONTAINS 51 CHARACTERS
       BLOCK CONTAINS 40 RECORDS
       DATA RECORD IS BOLBUFREC.

 01    BOLBUFREC PIC X(51).

* BOLBUFREC is the buffer record structure for the logical
* file BOLDATA.

 FD    SHIPPED-ITEMS
       LABEL RECORDS ARE STANDARD
       RECORD CONTAINS 51 CHARACTERS
       BLOCK CONTAINS 60 RECORDS
       DATA RECORD IS SHIPBUFREC.

 01 SHIPBUFREC PIC X(51).

* SHIPBUFREC is the buffer record structure for the logical
* file SHIPPED-ITEMS.

 FD    EDIT-REPORT
       LABEL RECORDS ARE OMITTED
       RECORD CONTAINS 133 CHARACTERS
       DATA RECORD IS EDITBUFREC.

 01 EDITBUFREC PIC X(133).

* File EDIT-REPORT is a printer file with unblocked
records.
* However, it can still use a buffer record structure like
* EDITBUFREC.

 WORKING-STORAGE SECTION.

 01 BOLREC.
       02  CUSTNUMB           PIC 9(5).
       02  BILLNUMB           PIC 9(5).
       02  ITEMCODE           PIC X(5).
       02  ITEMQUANTITY       PIC 9(5).
```

```
            02  ITEMDESCRIPTION    PIC X(30).

      * BOLREC is the working-storage structure for the
      * input file BOLDATA.

        01 SHIPREC.
            02  CUSTNUMB           PIC 9(5).
            02  BILLNUMB           PIC 9(5).
            02  ITEMCODE           PIC X(5).
            02  ITEMQUANTITY       PIC 9(5).
            02  ITEMDESCRIPTION    PIC X(30).

      * SHIPREC is the working-storage structure for the
      * output file SHIPREC.

        01 EDITREC.
            02 ...
```

In the ASSIGN clauses we have specified the disk file BOLDATA and the tape file SHIPPED-ITEMS as sequential files (actually as *utility sequential*, or UT-S files). These files contain blocked records. The printer file EDIT-REPORT is defined as *unit record sequential*, or UR-S file, and may not contain blocked records.

The ddnames are DDBOL, DDSHIP, and SYSPRINT. As we have seen, these refer to DD-statements written in IBM JCL that will accompanies the program when submitted for execution.

In the file section of the data division there is essentially a specification of the buffers and mobile buffer record structure for each of the three files. There cannot be a label with the printer file, and a record must be 133 bytes long (the number of characters that fit on a printer line).

For each file we specified a mobile buffer record structure; these are BOLBUFREC, SHIPBUFREC, and EDITBUFREC. If we wanted we could have specified the individual fields for these three buffer records. However, we intend to restrict processing to data in the working-storage structures, so that the fields in the buffer records will never be referenced in the program and therefore need not be specified. The lengths of the buffer records must equal those of the corresponding working-storage records.

In the working-storage section we have specified the working-storage record structures for each of the three files. In the procedure division (next section), we have not included the details of the checking of each field of incoming BOLDATA records; therefore we have omitted the details of the fields of the EDIT-REPORT file in the EDITREC working-storage structure. Readers are invited to fill in the details as a programming exercise if they have the inclination.

Readers may have noticed that in the file section of the data division we have specified the number of records per block (blocking factor) for both the files BOLDATA and SHIPPED-ITEMS. The blocking factors that we use are arbitrary but reasonable. With IBM systems we can also specify the block size in the DD-statement. However, if we do we must specify BLOCK CONTAINS 0 RECORDS in the file section. The IBM COBOL compiler requires this detail.

Some additional working-storage identifiers (or variables) are needed for the processing. These are:

```
01 RECORDS-WITH-SAME-BILLNUMB.
      05 LINE-DATA OCCURS 18 TIMES.
              10 CUSTNUMB               PIC 9(5).
              10 BILLNUMB               PIC 9(5).
              10 ITEMCODE               PIC X(6).
              10 ITEMQUAN               PIC 9(5).
              10 ITEMDESCRIPTION        PIC X(30).
77 VALID-BILL                           PIC X(3).
77 MORE-RECORDS                         PIC X(3).
77 TOTAL                                PIC 99.
77 COUNTA                               PIC 99.
77 COUNTB                               PIC 99.
```

If we look back at the hierachy diagram in Figure 3.9 we see that in processing we first read a group of records with the same bill of lading number. This means that we have read all the line items for a particular bill of lading. It is only after all the records for a particular bill have been read that they are checked for valid fields. Thus we need somewhere to put a group of records for a particular bill of lading. We use the structure RECORDS-WITH-SAME-BILLNUMB for this purpose. It can hold up to 18 records; we assume that 18 is the largest possible number of line items for a bill of lading. The identifier TOTAL is used to keep track of the number of records with the same bill number; COUNTA and COUNTB are used for scanning through the group of records for a given bill number.

The Procedure Division

The structure of the procedure below for processing the input file BOLDATA to generate the output file SHIPPED-ITEMS follows that given in the hierarchy diagram earlier in Figure 3.10:

```
PROCEDURE DIVISION.
EDIT-AND-LOAD-SHIPPED-ITEMS.
      OPEN INPUT BOLDATA.
      OPEN OUTPUT SHIPPED-ITEMS.
      OPEN OUTPUT EDIT-REPORT.
      READ BOLDATA INTO BOLREC,
             AT END DISPLAY "NO INPUT RECORDS",
                      STOP RUN.
```

```
           MOVE "YES" TO MORE-RECORDS.
           PERFORM WRITE-EDIT-REPORT-HEADINGS.
     * Writes the headings for the edit report on the reason
     * for rejecting BOLDATA records.
           PERFORM PROCESS-BILL-OF-LADING
                           UNTIL MORE-RECORDS = "NO".
     * Carries out the core of the processing for the records
     * for each bill of lading.
           CLOSE BOLDATA.
           CLOSE SHIPPED-ITEMS.
           CLOSE EDIT-REPORT.
           STOP RUN.

     * * * * * * * * * * * * * * * * * * * * * * * * * * * * *
     * This module writes the edit report headings. Details
     * are not important from a file processing viewpoint.
     * The module can be trivially simple if desired.
     * * * * * * * * * * * * * * * * * * * * * * * * * * * * *

      WRITE-EDIT-REPORT-HEADINGS.
           ...

     * * * * * * * * * * * * * * * * * * * * * * * * * * * * *
     * This module is responsible for processing the records
     * for each bill of lading.
     * * * * * * * * * * * * * * * * * * * * * * * * * * * * *

      PROCESS-BILL-OF-LADING.
           PERFORM OBTAIN-GROUP-FOR-SAME-BILL.
     * Places all the next set of records with the same bill
     * number in the structure RECORDS-WITH-SAME-BILLNUMB.
           MOVE "YES" TO VALID-BILL.
           COMPUTE COUNTA = 0.
           PERFORM EDIT-RECORDS-IN-GROUP
                   UNTIL COUNTA = TOTAL.
     * Records belonging to the current bill of lading are
     * checked for validity. TOTAL gives the number of records
     * belonging to the current bill of lading.
           COMPUTE COUNTB = 0.
           IF VALID-BILL = "YES" THEN
                   PERFORM WRITE-RECORDS-FOR-VALID-BILL
                           UNTIL COUNTB = TOTAL.
     * If all of the records for the current bill are found to
     * be valid they are all written out to SHIPPED-ITEMS.

     * * * * * * * * * * * * * * * * * * * * * * * * * * * * *
     * This module places all the next set of records with
     * the same bill of lading number in the structure
     * RECORDS-WITH-SAME-BILL-NUMBER.
     * * * * * * * * * * * * * * * * * * * * * * * * * * * * *

      OBTAIN-GROUP-FOR-SAME-BILL.
           MOVE BOLREC TO LINE-DATA(1).
```

```
        COMPUTE TOTAL = 1.
        IF MORE-RECORDS = "YES" THEN
                PERFORM ACQUIRE-REMAINING-GROUP-RECORDS
                UNTIL BILLNUMB IN BOLREC
                        NOT = BILLNUMB IN LINE-DATA(1)
                        OR MORE-RECORDS = "NO".
* Gets rest of records for the current bill number.

* * * * * * * * * * * * * * * * * * * * * * * * * * * * *
* This module writes all the records for a valid bill
* of lading into the file SHIPPED-ITEMS.
* * * * * * * * * * * * * * * * * * * * * * * * * * * * *

  WRITE-RECORDS-FOR-VALID-BILL.
        COMPUTE COUNTB = COUNTB + 1.
        MOVE LINE-DATA(COUNTB) TO SHIPREC.
        WRITE SHIPBUFREC FROM SHIPREC.

* * * * * * * * * * * * * * * * * * * * * * * * * * * * *
* This module acquires the records (other than the first)
* for the current bill of lading number.
* * * * * * * * * * * * * * * * * * * * * * * * * * * * *

  ACQUIRE-REMAINING-GROUP-RECORDS.
        READ BOLDATA INTO BOLREC,
                AT END MOVE "NO" TO MORE-RECORDS.
        IF BILLNUMB IN BOLREC = BILLNUMB IN LINE-ITEM(1)
                        AND MORE-RECORDS = "YES"
                THEN COMPUTE TOTAL = TOTAL + 1,
                     MOVE BOLREC TO LINE-ITEM(TOTAL).

* * * * * * * * * * * * * * * * * * * * * * * * * * * * *
* This module carries out checking of the records
* currently
* in RECORDS-WITH-SAME-BILL-NUMB, that is, belonging to a
* single bill of lading. The details are not relevant to
* file processing as such. Requirements are given in the
* program specification in Figure 3.9. Readers are invited to
* complete this module and associated subsidiary modules as
* a programming exercise.
* * * * * * * * * * * * * * * * * * * * * * * * * * * * *

  EDIT-RECORDS-IN-GROUP.
        ...
        IF (errors found) THEN MOVE "NO" TO VALID-BILL.
```

The structure and logic for the above procedure can also be found in the hierarchy diagram in Figure 3.10.

In the procedure above the actual file manipulation is not very complex. However, with more complex file processing of the type often found in business file processing, even with the help of hierarchy diagrams and flow charts, it can be a time-consuming business to get a grasp of the essentials. It is in such cases that file navigation diagrams are useful for communicating the file processing essentials.

Use of a File Navigation Diagram

A file navigation diagram for the procedure above is illustrated in Figure 3.12. It shows the sequence of readings and writings involving the files BOLDATA and SHIPPED-ITEMS. The line with the arrows shows the sequence of records read and written. A black circle indicates the reading of a record, and an open circle the writing of a record.

The diagram shows clearly that in processing we not only read a group of records of the same bill of lading number before outputting the SHIPPED-ITEMS records, we also read the first record of the next group. The procedure does this because it is not possible to tell that a group has ended until a record has been read with a different bill of lading number.

In the procedure above successive input BOLDATA records are read until a record is read for which the bill of lading number does not equal a control number for that group. The control number is the value of BILLNUMB in LINE-ITEM(1). Thus the control number serves as a process **control break**, since we break the process or scanning sequence one record past each group with the same bill number. This is clearly brought out by the file navigation diagram. Control breaks are common in file processing, because records frequently have to be grouped for checking, summary computations, and other tasks.

Robust File Processing Programs

The procedure above is by no means perfect. A major fault is that it does not take into account everything that can go wrong. The more a program can withstand invalid input data the more robust (or *idiot-proof*) it is said to be. Unfortunately, robust programs are expensive, since making allowances for things going wrong increases both the length and complexity of the program.

There are many ways in which the above program could go wrong. For example, suppose that the data entry person makes an error in entering the bill of lading number on a BOLDATA record being keyed, and suppose that by chance the incorrect bill number is one that can pass the validity checking in the EDIT-RECORDS-IN-GROUP module. What will happen?

A little thought shows that we could get two invoices generated by the entire system where only one shipment was made. The customer would be billed for the correct amount (if you add the amounts in each invoice), but one of the invoices would refer to a nonexistent shipment. To prevent such an error the BOLDATA records keyed for a given bill of lading can be numbered in sequence by the data entry person. The procedure can then be designed to check that the bill number does not change before expiry of a sequence of records for a given bill number. The processing for this type of error prevention is more complicated that you might think; readers are invited to incorporate it in the above procedure as an exercise.

INPUT/OUTPUT (I/O) ERROR HANDLING WITH COBOL

As we saw in chapter 2, errors can occur in the reading and writing of records, particularly with magnetic tape files, because of interference from magnetic dust particles clinging to the tape. Thus there must be code in every commercial program that processes tapes (and disks) to permit proper action to be taken in the case of an input/output (I/O) error.

The COBOL code for the action to be taken on I/O errors is placed in what are called **declaratives** sections right at the beginning of the procedure division. Consider again the files BOLDATA and SHIPPED-ITEMS. It is possible that the action routines for these files in the case of an I/O error could differ from one another. We can code these routines as follows:

```
   PROCEDURE DIVISION.
** The following gives the action to be taken in case of
** an I/O error with any of the files involved in the
** processing.
   DECLARATIVES.
** File BOLDATA I/O error:
   BOLDATA-SECTION.
         USE AFTER ERROR PROCEDURE ON BOLDATA.
   ERROR-ROUTINE-BOLDATA.
         DISPLAY "I/O ERROR ON BOLDATA".
         DISPLAY "MOST RECENT RECORD READ:", BOLREC.
         READ FILE BOLDATA INTO BOLREC,
            AT END MOVE "NO" TO MORE-RECORDS.

** File SHIPPED-ITEMS I/O error:
   SHIPPED-ITEMS-SECTION.
         USE AFTER ERROR PROCEDURE ON SHIPPED-ITEMS.
   ERROR-ROUTINE-SHIPPED-ITEMS.
         DISPLAY "I/O ERROR ...".
         ...

   END DECLARATIVES.
```

For example, if an I/O error occurs while a READ instruction is applied to the file BOLDATA, the paragraph ERROR-ROUTINE-BOLDATA will be executed. This causes the news of the I/O failure to be printed and an attempt at reading the next record. Once ERROR-ROUTINE-BOLDATA had been executed, the main procedure resumes execution from the point where the error occurred. Had the error paragraph not been coded in the declaratives section the program would simply have stopped.

IBM DD-STATEMENTS

Readers should note that this section is relevant only where there is either an interest in, or a need to use, the widely used operating system OS/MVS and similar systems. Otherwise, readers may skip this section.

Earlier we created the tape file SHIPPED-ITEMS,and in the environment division specified the file as follows:

```
SELECT SHIPPED-ITEMS
       ASSIGN TO UT-S-DDSHIP.
```

DDSHIP refers to the DD-statement that specifies the physical file (dataset). This DD-statement will be added to the end of the program and used by the operating system. An example is as follows:

```
//DDSHIP  DD   DSN=SHIP1,UNIT=TAPE,VOL=SER=007,
//       DCB=(LRECL=51,BLKSIZE=3060,RECFM=FB),
//       DISP=(NEW,KEEP)
```

Here the dataset name (DSN) is SHIP1: this name will be recorded on the dataset label. UNIT=TAPE specifies that the file will be created using a tape drive. We could, if desired, specify a particular type of drive, such as UNIT=3420. With VOL=SER=007 we are specifying the number of the volume (or reel); this information should have been recorded earlier on the volume label, as described in chapter 2. The operator or tape librarian should also have manually written this volume-serial number on the outside of the reel (see Figure 2.13b).

Next comes a group of parameters known as data control block (DCB) parameters. The logical record length (LRECL) is 51 bytes; the data block size (BLKSIZE) is 51 * 60 or 3,060 bytes (for a blocking factor of 60). We also specify that the record format (RECFM) is fixed-length blocked (FB) records.

(Note that if you specify the block size in the DD-statement, you have to specify BLOCK CONTAINS 0 RECORDS in the data division.

Note also that the BLKSIZE parameter is the size in bytes of the block as transmitted to the buffer and certainly does not include the size of the interblock gap on the tape.)

The last item in the DD-statement above is the disposition (DISP) specification, which usually has two parameters. The first one specifies the current status of the dataset; here we specify NEW since the file is being created. The second specifies what is to be done with the dataset after it has been processed; here we specify KEEP. (The dataset would be deleted if we specify DELETE here.)

Finally we should note that there are no blanks in DD-statements, except before and after DD. It is easy to get DD-statements wrong, and experimentation is often required. Application programmers, and even system analysts, who work with IBM systems are expected to have a working knowledge of IBM JCL; the construction of DD-statements is the most common task.

The DD-statement for a printer file is standard, even including the ddname (SYSPRINT), which must match that given in the SELECT clause. For example, in the case of the edit report file EDIT-REPORT, we had the SELECT clause:

```
SELECT EDIT-REPORT
       ASSIGN TO UR-S-SYSPRINT.
```

Therefore, the DD-statement would be:

```
//SYSPRINT DD SYSOUT=A
```

The DD-statement for a file being created, such as SHIPPED-ITEMS above, is usually much more complex than that for a file that already exists, for which most of the required parameters are available to the operating system from the dataset label. For the existing file BOLDATA on disk the SELECT clause was:

```
SELECT BOLDATA
       ASSIGN TO UT-S-DDBOL.
```

The corresponding DD-statement could have been:

```
//DDBOL DD DSN=BOL1,UNIT=DISK,DISP=(OLD,KEEP)
```

When we must specify a new dataset on disk, the lengthy DD-statement required includes a specification of the disk space needed by the new dataset (the SPACE parameter). An example of this is given later at the end of Chapter 4.

SUMMARY

When processing a sequential file, it must first be opened with an OPEN command. If records are to be read the file must be opened for input; if records are to be written it must be opened for output; if records are to be read and then rewritten (disk only), the file must be opened for input/output (I-O in COBOL).

A READ command places a buffer record structure coincident with the next record in the input buffer and moves its contents to working storage. When the last record of the buffer has been moved to working storage, the next READ also moves the next block from the storage device to the buffer. A WRITE command moves the contents of a working-storage structure to the next empty record slot in the output buffer; the WRITE command that fills the buffer also moves the buffer contents to the storage device.

A REWRITE command moves a record recently read from working storage to its place in the buffer. At the end of reading all the records in that buffer, if a REWRITE has been used with any of them, the entire buffer is rewritten back to disk.

In a COBOL program a file has a logical name, used with all COBOL commands. The file also has a physical (or dataset) name, which is recorded on the storage medium. With the main IBM batch operating systems, a physical file is specified by means of a DD-statement that accompanies a program that uses the file.

In generating a new program to create or process a file for business purposes, a systems analyst first prepares program specifications that are passed to a programmer. The programmer prepares a hierarchical diagram of the processing, an input/output diagram, and possibly a file naviagation diagram, before coding the program.

In any program that processes files, there must be code to handle input/output errors. With COBOL such code is placed in the declaratives section of the procedure division.

EXERCISES

1. Complete the details of the program EDIT-LOAD in this chapter.

2. Alter the program EDIT-LOAD as follows: BOLDATA records at data entry are numbered in sequence for a given bill of lading; the program should check that all the records for a given bill are dealt with even where an incorrect bill number is entered that passes the validity check.
3. Draw up a file navigation for the essentials of the processing for exercise 2.
4. Write a program specification for creation of a file, CUSTOMER, that contains data about customer numbers, customer names, and customer addresses. The specification should contain details of validity checking for the data. Assume that the data was originally keyed into a disk file, KEYCUST.
5. Draw up a hierarchy diagram, a flow chart, input/output diagrams, and a file navigation diagram for the creation of the file CUSTOMER (exercise 4).
6. Write the COBOL program for creating the file CUSTOMER (exercises 4 and 5).
7. Write a program specification for creation of the file PRODUCT. A record of the file contains information about a product that can be shipped (to a customer). Fields should at least give product number, product name, product description, and unit and quantity prices. The specification should contain details of validity checking for the data. Assume that data was originally keyed into a disk file, KEYPROD.
8. Draw up a hierarchy diagram, a flow chart, input/output diagrams, and a file navigation diagram for the creation of the file PRODUCT (exercise 7).
9. Write the COBOL program for creating the file PRODUCT (exercises 7 and 8).
10. Write the program specification for creation of a new file, SHIPPED-ITEMS2, by adding customer data from a CUSTOMER file (exercise 4) to the file SHIPPED-ITEMS (exercise 1).
11. Draw up the hierarchy diagram, flow chart, input/output diagrams, and file navigation diagram for creation of the file SHIPPED-ITEMS2 (exercise 10).
12. Write the COBOL program for creating SHIPPED-ITEMS2 (exercises 10 and 11).
13. Write the program specification for creation of a new file, SHIPPED-ITEMS3, by adding price data to the records of SHIPPED-ITEMS2 (exercise 10) for products (items) taken from the file PRODUCT (exercise 7).

14. Draw up the hierarchy diagram, flow chart, input/output diagrams, and file navigation diagrams for creation of the file SHIPPED-ITEMS3 (exercise 13).
15. Write the COBOL program for creation of SHIPPED-ITEMS3 (exercises 13 and 14).
16. Prepare the program specification, draw up all necessary diagrams, and write the program for generating invoices from the file SHIPPED-ITEMS3 (exercises 13, 14 and 15).

4 SEQUENTIAL FILE PROCESSING

In this chapter we look at the different ways in which sequential files may be processed. It is probably true to state that the bulk of commercial file processing involves sequential files. Generally the processing involves either updating of existing files or information retrieval. We attempt to exclude from consideration processing that involves creation of new files, as we have already covered that in the previous chapter. Nevertheless, a great deal of sequential file updating can be argued to be merely another form of file creation.

Sequential files can be either on tape or disk; although this makes no difference to programs for initial creation of files, it can make a very substantial difference when it comes to certain types of updating. Accordingly we begin with a general discussion of tape versus disk processing of sequential files. We then give some examples demonstrating the variety of updating that occurs in commerce. Finally we look at information retrieval.

DISK VERSUS TAPE FILE PROCESSING

Sequential files are created, kept (archived) somewhere, updated at intervals, and used for information retrieval that typically involves generation of reports and business documents (such as invoices, as described in chapter 3).

As far as initial creation is concerned it makes no difference to the file creation program (and only minor differences to DD-statements or equivalent) whether tapes or disks are used.

As far as keeping, or archiving, sequential files is concerned, tapes have the advantage. Large capacity disk volumes (for example, those for IBM 3350 and IBM 3380 disk drives) are generally not removable from the drive unit. Where they can be removed (for example with the older IBM 3330 unit), the capacity is generally much lower and the volumes are bulky and expensive. Thus if sequential files must be kept for long periods, tape reels are commonly used because of the relatively low archival cost.

As far as information generation and report generation programs are concerned, there is no difference between tape and disk file processing, except that the program may run faster if we switch from tape to disk, or vice versa, depending on the model. However, with updating, the essential differences between sequential disk file and tape file processing appear.

Updating Sequential Files

In commerce, updating can be complex, involving many programs, files, and systems. We can distinguish four general types of updating:

a. **Insertion updating**. Additional records are inserted into the file.

b. **Deletion updating**. Records are physically removed from the file. An alternative to removing the records deleted is to change a deletion field, or tag, from a symbol denoting a valid record to a symbol denoting a deleted record. Thus a deleted record is still in the file, although marked as deleted, and will be retrieved when the file is read. A retrieval program must then be able to handle such deleted records. In this way deletion updating is actually transformed into change updating, defined next.

c. **Change updating**. One or more fields or a record are changed in value. Usually the primary key of a record is not change updated. If a primary key field needs to be changed, that is equivalent to deleting the record identified by the field and inserting a new record.

d. **General updating**. This involves any combination of insertion, deletion, and change updating

Updating on disk gives us a greater number of possibilities than updating on tape. The most radical difference arises when we deal with change updating or deletion updating using deletion tags. With tapes each record of a file being updated must be written out on a new reel of tape, whether or not it has been changed. With disks once a block of records has been read, that block continues to rotate under (or over) the read-write head, making it possible to alter the contents of the block before the next block is read. As a result, there is a COBOL command for use with sequential disk files that is not available for use with tape files. This is the REWRITE command introduced earlier (chapter 3), with COBOL syntax:

```
REWRITE buffer record FROM working-storage record.
```

The working-storage record must be the record most recently read with a COBOL READ command. In practice the REWRITE method with COBOL is quite simple to program. We read each master record in turn with a READ; if the record needs to be changed, we update it in working storage and then replace the original version in the buffer (and subsequently on disk) by means of a REWRITE command applied to the updated record in working storage. Later we shall see this used in a COBOL updating program excerpt. To put this REWRITE updating with disk files into perspective, we first look at the **classical method of updating**—typically used with tape files, but also used with sequential disk files.

Classical Updating Method

The **classical method of updating** originated with tape files.. Records of the master file to be updated are first sorted in ascending primary key order. The records of the transaction file are also sorted in primary key order (these records will be used to update the master).

Records of the two files are read sequentially. With both change and deletion updating, we scan through the master until we come to a record with a key that matches the latest transaction record key. As we scan we write out each master record encountered. When a match is reached we use the transaction record to update the master record before writing it out, if a change update is required; if a deletion update is needed, the matching master record is normally not written out.

With insertion updating, the scan takes us to just beyond the point of a theoretical match. Master records prior to this point are output to the new master; then the transaction record is used to construct a new record, which is also written out.

As a result of the different update activities, old unchanged master records, new inserted records, and changed records are all written out in the proper ascending key sequence. At the end we have the new updated master, the old master, and a transaction file. Some time later the new master itself will be updated from a further transaction file.

At this point we have three generations of the master file, commonly referred to as the **grandfather**, **father**, and **son** files. The grandfather and father files are generally archived, along with the three transaction files. Thus if the current (or son) master is lost, damaged, stolen, or just updated incorrectly, it will be possible to regenerate it from the previous archived generations.

Updating Methods with Disk Files

The classic updating method can be used with disk files, the only fundamental difference in principle being the awkward task of archiving the more expensive and bulky disk packs. Nevertheless we have some additional possibilities when the classic updating method is used with disk files. In its simplest form this method corresponds closely to tape processing.

We can take advantage of the huge data capacity of modern disks and keep the old master and the new master on the same disk pack. This saves the expenditure on an additional disk drive and requires archiving only one disk pack.

We can go further with this method and place the transaction file on the same disk pack as the master and old master. If the disk pack has sufficient capacity and the master is not likely to undergo net growth in size, we can go even further. We can keep grandfather, father, son, and the associated transaction files on a single disk, if necessary writing the output from the updating of the current master on top of the current grandfather. Thus we need only a single disk drive to hold all the files even during processing, which can be a significant saving for a small installation.

Remember that for classic updating with tapes we need three external storage devices, which is expensive. The disadvantage of having all the files on one disk is that processing is slowed down by the seeks, that result from reading and writing alternate files at different locations on the same disk.

REWRITE Updating

The final option when disks are available is to abandon the classical method altogether and use the REWRITE method, introduced earlier. Only one version of the master file is ever needed on disk; it is also possible to have the transactions on the same disk pack, thus reducing device costs.

Generally REWRITE updating is feasible only if the bulk of the updating is change updating and the remainder is deletion updating (carried out by the method of changing a deletion field value from valid to deleted). At regular intervals, but generally much less frequently than with classic updating, the file can be copied onto another disk location, but without the records marked as deleted. In a few cases it is also possible to have insertions, if the inserted records can be used to replace records deleted.

This method of updating is reasonably common with sequential files. It is even more common with indexed-sequential files (see chapter 6) since insertions are allowed in addition. However, this method can lead to a loss of data integrity (errors in the stored data) if precautions are not taken.

Once a field value has been updated, the original value is lost, so that if there is an error in updating, it may not be possible to correct it. The standard solution is to use a **log**, or **journal**, **file** on tape, where the **before-and-after** field values (or **images**) are recorded for each transaction. In addition, at regular intervals, the data in the master is **dumped** onto a **back-up tape file**, at which point a new log file is started. If anything happens to the master before the next dump, it can be regenerated from the previous dump and current log file.

Average Hit Rate Concept

At this point we need to introduce the **average hit rate** concept. It has a bearing on whether it makes sense to use REWRITE updating with sequential disk files, or to use classic updating. It even has a bearing on whether sequential file organization is the correct one at all, and whether an indexed-sequential file (permitting both direct as well as sequential processing) is more appropriate.

Suppose that T is the total number of transaction records used to update a master file containing M records. The hit rate in percent is then 100T/M. Thus we can loosely say that an average hit rate of 20 percent means that on average an update takes place at every fifth record of the master.

In the classic method of updating even records that are not in any way updated must be both read and written. In the REWRITE method all records must still be read, but only those updated are rewritten. Therefore no matter which method we use, a very low hit rate (0.01 percent) is very wasteful, although it is somewhat less wasteful in the case of the REWRITE method.

A high hit rate (greater than 5 percent) means efficient processing with sequential files, since many master records accessed will need updating. Note that with a very high hit rate the difference between the classic updating method and the method that relies on using REWRITE largely disappears, from a performance point of view. With the classic method all master records are read and written; with the REWRITE method all are read and most are also written.

There are two methods of dealing with the waste caused by updating with a very low hit rate. The simplest involves updating less frequently, so that there are considerably more transaction records when the updating does take place, resulting in a higher hit rate and less waste. This is not always an acceptable method since it generally results in a lower grade of service to users of the data in the master. The other alternative is to permit direct access to the file, so that only records needing updating are actually accessed, and the equivalent with insertions. We shall look at this method in the next chapter on indexed-sequential files. It is very important and commonly used.

SOME CONTRASTING COMMERCIAL UPDATING EXAMPLES

In this section we look at an example of classic updating strategy and an example of REWRITE updating strategy. The classic method is used with the updating of a customer master file; the REWRITE method is used with a file of investment data. In this section we merely discuss what is involved with updating the customer and investments files. In a subsequent section we present the COBOL programs.

Using Change, Insertion, and Deletion Updating with a Customer File

Our customer file contains records that describe customers of a firm. Because the file is used in many systems it is an important one (we saw that it was used in the invoice system in chapter 3). Because such information as customer credit rating changes with time, we often need to change update the file. Furthermore the appearance of new customers and the demise of former customers require that the file also be insertion and deletion updated. For these reasons we use the classic updating method.

The three types of updating can be carried out in separate updating programs or they can be combined into a general updating program. In this section we ultimately consider the combined updating method. This is unfortunately complicated by a problem involving mismatches and unmatched records. We therefore begin by looking at what is involved if change, insertion, and deletion updating are carried out separately.

Change Updating

In principle change updating is simple. However, in practice it is complicated by the occurrence of unmatched transaction records. Con-

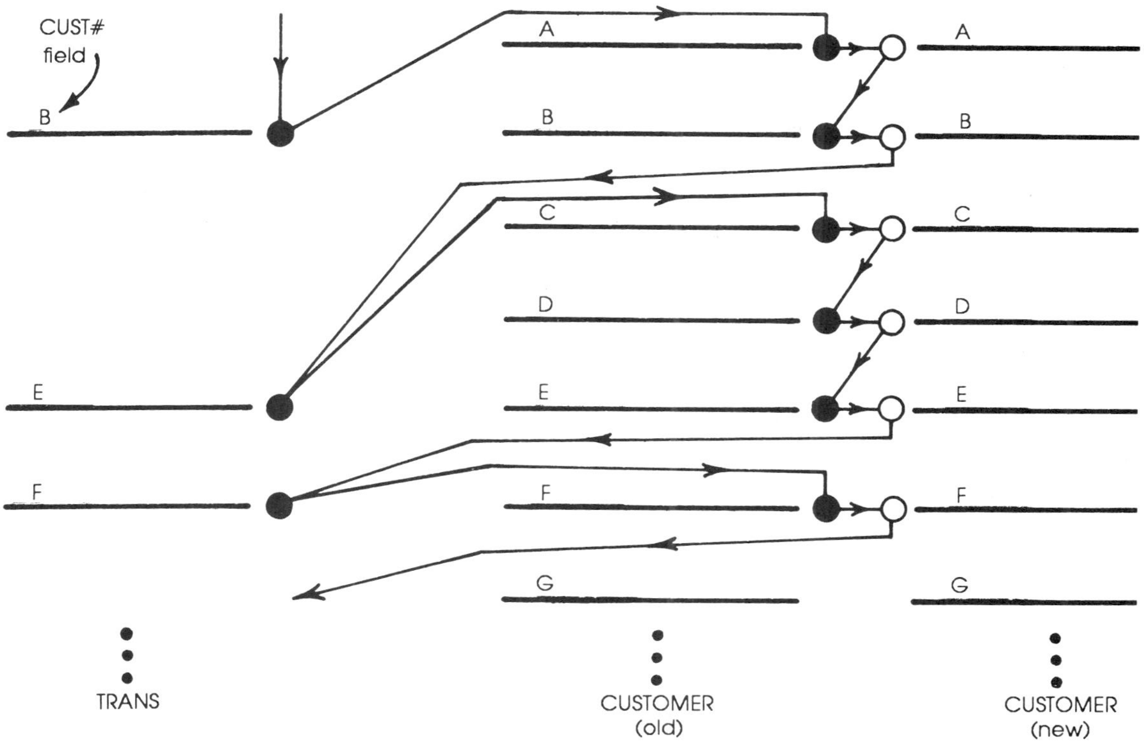

FIGURE 4.1 Simplest possible (classic) method for change updating a master file (CUSTOMER) from data in a transaction file (TRANS); both files are assumed sorted in ascending primary key order (CUST# filed). The method also assumes no possibility of an unmatched TRANS record. Where there is a matching TRANS record for the CUSTOMER record, that record is updated and written out; otherwise it is merely written out unchanged. The method can be modified to take care of multiple mismatches.

sider a master file, CUSTOMER, containing customer records, to be change updated from a transaction file, TRANS. A customer number field, CUST#, is used in both files as the primary key field.

The simplest conceivable processing involves reading the next (or first) TRANS record and then continuing with a scan of CUSTOMER(outputting records encountered) until a match is found. An updated CUSTOMER record is then output (see Figure 4.1). In practice we can have unmatched TRANS records; these unmatched records can appear in sequence and can occur at the end of the TRANS file.

Fortunately it is not difficult to modify this simple change updating method to handle a succession of unmatched TRANS records. The essentials of the modification are illustrated in Figures 4.2a and 4.2b. The logic that generates the file navigation pathway can be explained using the concept of **current records**. We denote the most recently read TRANS record as CUR(trans) and the most recently accessed old CUSTOMER record as CUR(oldcust). The necessary logic is:

```
A.  CUST# in CUR(oldcust) < CUST# in CUR(trans).
```

ACTION. Write out CUR(oldcust) as the lastest new CUSTOMER record (provided the CUR(oldcust) record is not a dummy beginning of file (BOF) record). Read in the next old CUSTOMER record.

```
B.  CUST# in CUR(oldcust) = CUST# in CUR(trans).
```

ACTION. Use CUR(trans) to update CUR(oldcust). Do not write it out (yet). Read next TRANS record.

```
C.  CUST# in CUR(oldcust) > CUST# in CUR(trans).
```

ACTION. Write message about unmatched CUR(trans) record.READ next TRANS record.

Notice that we do not immediately write out an updated, current old CUSTOMER record (see Case B, and Figure 4.2a but not Figure 4.1). If we did, the above logic would be ruined. Case B must be followed by Case A, the action for which will cause the updated record to be written out. If we include a WRITE in the action for Case B, we would write out an updated record twice. Readers should check that the above logic generates the pathway in Figure 4.2a. We assume a beginning of file (BOF) record for convenience; it will have a null (the smallest possible) CUST# value. This permits us to apply the above logic as soon as the first TRANS record has been read.

To manage the possibility of a succession of unmatched TRANS records, at the end of the TRANS file we use an end of file (EOF) old CUSTOMER record. The above logic can then be applied, no matter how many unmatched TRANS records there are. Readers should check that the above logic generates the pathway in Figure 4.2b.

Insertion updating

As an example of insertion updating let us again suppose a transaction file (TRANS) and a master file ([old] CUSTOMER) as in the previous case of change updating. This time the entire contents of a

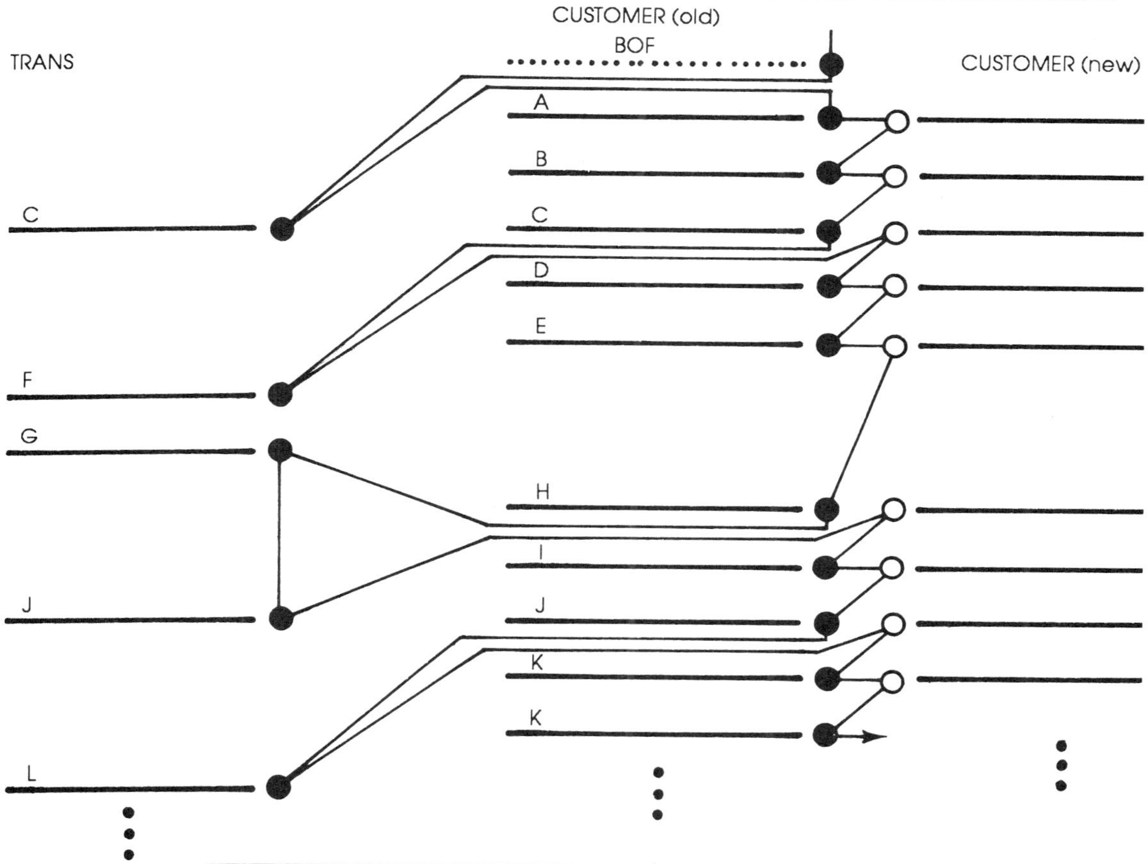

FIGURE 4.2a Extension of the classic method of change updating (from Figure 4.1) to cover the case of unmatched transaction (TRANS) records. Any number of consecutive unmatched TRANS records can be handled. The decision logic is discussed in the text. A beginning of file (BOF) record is introduced for the old CUSTOMER file in order to have a consistent processing method and to simplify programming logic.

TRANS record will be inserted into the new CUSTOMER file. We can assume that both TRANS and CUSTOMER are sorted in ascending CUST# order.

In principle the processing is quite straightforward. Essentially, if the current CUSTOMER record has a CUST# value less than the current TRANS CUST# value, we copy the current CUSTOMER record and

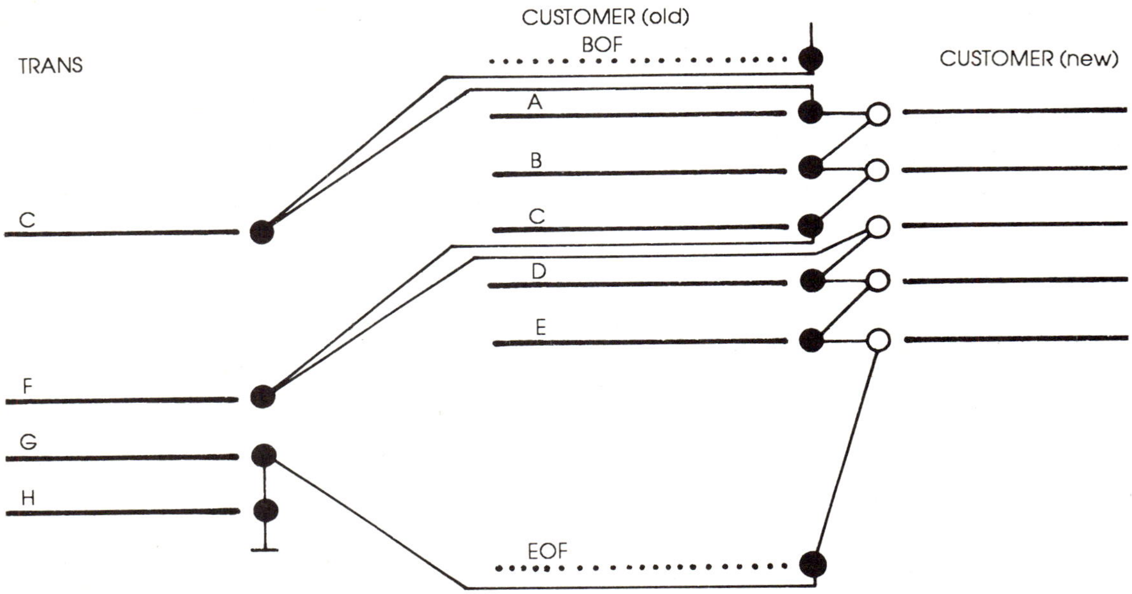

FIGURE 4.2b Classic method of change updating showing detail of the processing when unmatched transaction records occur at the end of the transaction (TRANS) file.

read the next CUSTOMER record; otherwise we copy the current TRANS record and read the next TRANS record.

Unfortunately in practice this basic method is too simple. Although unmatched records cannot be a problem here, since it is unmatched TRANS records that are to be inserted, matched TRANS records *are* a problem and must be rejected. The processing method must therefore be able to handle sequences of matched TRANS records, even if these occur at the end of the TRANS file.

We are therefore forced to modify the basic method. The following logic covers the case when a group of matched TRANS records is encountered. (Readers should draw file navigation diagrams for this case.)

```
A.   CUST# in CUR(oldcust) < CUST# in CUR(trans)
```

ACTION. Write out CUR(oldcust) as latest new CUSTOMER record (provided the record is not a dummy BOF record). Read next old CUSTOMER record.

```
B.   CUST# in CUR(oldcust) > CUST# in CUR(trans)
```

ACTION. Write out CUR(trans) as latest new CUSTOMER record. Read next TRANS record.

```
C.   CUST# in CUR(oldcust) = CUST# in CUR(trans).
```

ACTION. Print out CUR(trans) as erroneous matched record. Read next TRANS record.

Deletion Updating

The processing necessary for the general case of deletion updating is very similar to that for change updating. The only difference is that when there is a match between the TRANS and CUSTOMER records the CUSTOMER record is not output, instead of being updated and later output as in the change updating case. Thus only a minor modification of Figure 4.5 is required to cover deletion. Readers are invited to construct the necessary file navigation diagrams and develop the essential logic to generate the pathways.

General Updating

Once the individual cases of change, insertion, and deletion updating have been analyzed and the necessary logic understood, it is relatively simple to generate the logic for the general case where a transaction record can signal change, insertion, or deletion updating. We assume that the TRANS records now have an additional field, ACTION, indicating the purpose of the TRANS record. For example, an ACTION value "CH" could indicate that the TRANS record was to be used to change update a matching CUSTOMER record. The ACTION value "IN" would mean that a new CUSTOMER record was to be created from data in the TRANS record. An ACTION value of "DE" would mean that the matching CUSTOMER record was to be deleted.

Processing would involve comparing the CUST# values in the current CUSTOMER and TRANS records. Clearly if the current CUSTOMER CUST# value is less than the current TRANS CUST# value, the TRANS ACTION value is not relevant; we simply copy the current CUSTOMER record, writing it out as a new CUSTOMER record. When the current CUSTOMER CUST# value is either equal to or greater than the current TRANS CUST# value, the processing carried out depends on the ACTION value in the current TRANS record. For a given ACTION value, most of the logic given earlier for processing of change, insertion, and deletion updating can be used. The consolidated logic for the general updating case is:

`A. CUST# in CUR(oldcust) < CUST# in CUR(trans).`

PROCESSING: Write CUR(oldcust) out as next new CUSTOMER record (provided CUR(oldcust) is not a dummy record). Read next old CUSTOMER record.

`B. CUST# in CUR(oldcust) not < CUST# in CUR(trans).`

PROCESSING: Carry out Change-update, Insertion-update, or Deletion-update below, according to value in ACTION field in CUR(trans).

CHANGE-UPDATE:

`1. CUST# in CUR(oldcust) > CUST# in CUR(trans)`

ACTION: Print message, unmatched CUR(trans) record. Read next TRANS record.

`2. CUST# in CUR(oldcust) = CUST# in CUR(trans).`

ACTION: Update CUR(oldcust) from CUR(trans) data. Do not write it out (yet). Read next TRANS record.

INSERTION-UPDATE:

`1. CUST# in CUR(oldcust) > CUST# in CUR(trans)`

ACTION: Write out new CUSTOMER record from CUR(trans) data. Read next TRANS record.

`2. CUST# in CUR(oldcust) = CUST# in CUR(trans)`

ACTION: Print message, erroneous matched CUR(trans) record. Read next TRANS record.

DELETION-UPDATE:

`1. CUST# in CUR(oldcust) > CUST# in CUR(trans).`

ACTION: Print message, erroneous unmatched CUR(trans) record. Read next TRANS record.

```
2.  CUST# in CUR(oldcust) = CUST# in CUR(trans).
```

ACTION: Convert CUR(oldcust) to a dummy record, perhaps using null for the CUST# value, so that it will not be copied in (A) above. Read next TRANS record.

The above logic is admittedly fairly complex, taken as a whole. However, it must be remembered that it is for general updating, which involves complex processing. Clearly the best way to gain an understanding of general updating is to approach it first through change, insertion, and deletion updating, as we have done in earlier sections. The above logic is used later in this chapter with a COBOL program.

Note that the logic given above is not the only one for general updating, although it is typical of those normally used. Indeed there is still no general agreement on what is the best method of updating a master file.

Readers may be interested in developing the file navigation diagram for the above logic. Because of the many combinations of matched and unmatched TRANS records, and the three different types of TRANS record, a rather large piece of paper will be needed. This is the only reason why we have not included the diagram in this book. The diagram is nevertheless still useful for communicating the processing pathway through the files.

Updating a Common Stock (CS) Master File

Many organizations have very large sums of money that must be invested to provide for future income, often of a contractual nature. Examples are university, college, and hospital endowments, and foundation and pension funds. This money must be invested with the twin aims of (a) preservation of the principle in current dollars and (b) maximization of income commensurate with (a). Depending on the fund, a percentage will be invested in common stock.

To make informed decisions about common stock investment, a great deal of information about the health and prospects of corporations is required. Prices of common stock fluctuate a great deal under the influence of the hopes and fears of the mass of investors, the business cycle, interest rates, and so on.

Conservative fund managers and their research staff normally devote considerable time to uncovering stocks of companies that are undervalued in the market, but which are financially sound, have an excellent record, and have honest and competent management devoted to the growth of their firms. It goes without saying that this is very difficult to do; this is where a computer file can help, since a great deal of information must be recorded and kept available for analysis. We will use a common stock (CS) master file as our example.

To get some idea of what is involved, suppose that the fund decides to keep track of the fortunes of 1000 companies listed on major stock exchanges. Information about these companies is to be recorded quarterly—the quarterly information about an individual company constituting a record of the file. (Most of the financial information for any quarter is taken from a company's quarterly report.) It would not be unreasonable to record information about the past 25 years for each company. This would give 100 quarterly records per stock, or about 100,000 records for the file. Each record could contain a large number of fields. Sample fields would be the stock name, the price at the end of the quarter, and an identifier for the quarter in question. The current quarter could be identified by 0, the previous one by 1, and the last quarter in the file by 99. Other fields would contain financial data.

Clearly there is a need for a major update every quarter. Suppose that information is held for no more than 100 quarters. Therefore updating involves insertions (of the latest quarterly records) and deletions (of the records for the quarter 99). It also involves an update of every remaining record, for as a new quarter commences, old quarter 0 becomes new quarter 1; similarly old quarter n becomes new quarter n+1. Thus the classic method of updating can be applied. The old master can be on disk or tape, and a new master generated on a new disk or disk location, or on a new reel.

However, even though both insertions and deletions are involved, in this particular case it is possible to update the old master on disk using the REWRITE method. This is possible because insertions exactly match deletions (see Figure 4.3).

As illustrated in the figure, consider updating the records for the stock Multoil. First we read the old record for quarter 0 and replace it (using REWRITE) with the transaction record (the new quarter 0) record. Then we read the old record for quarter 1 and replace it with the old record for quarter 0, at the same time changing the 0 to 1. We continue in this way, shifting each record down in position and in-

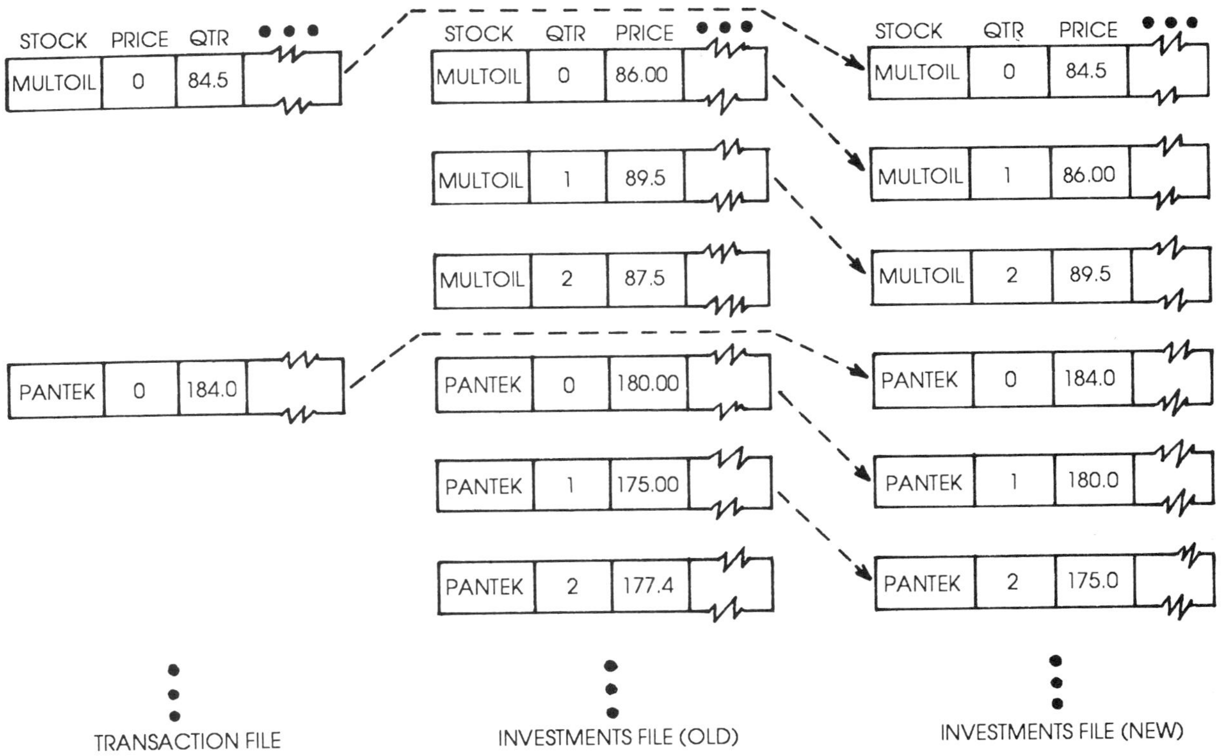

FIGURE 4.3 The basic method of updating the investments file. To make the diagram possible we are here assuming only 3 quarterly records for each stock. Following the updating the transaction record becomes the new record for quarter 0, the old record for quarter 0 becomes the new one for quarter 1, and so on. The old record for quarter 3 is deleted. It is possible to update the file on disk without writing out a new version.

crementing the quarter field. At the end there is no room for the old record for the last quarter, which is discarded (that is, not written out).

It should be understood that this tidy updating method is not in itself grounds for having the file on disk. However, it does mean that only one disk drive is required. In addition, since it is likely that the file will be used very frequently with information retrieval programs, it will be convenient to have it on disk. An investment manager normally makes decisions to maintain or alter a specific holding only after a great deal of research; such research involves a great deal of information retrieval from the investments file.

SOME COBOL FILE UPDATING PROGRAMS

In this section we present the basic cores of the COBOL procedures to update the customer and investment files described in the previous section. With the examples here and in many later sections, we shall not present detailed program specifications, hierarchy diagrams, and input/output diagrams, as we did in chapter 3. Instead we restrict our examples to the essential core of the COBOL processing and refer to relevant file navigation diagrams. This should enable any reader familiar with structured COBOL programming to construct a full, structured COBOL program, and associated documentation, for any of the examples. Essentially the methods outlined in chapter 3 should be used in any such endeavor.

Classic Update of a Sequential File

In carrying out the classic method of updating, we shall ultimately follow the method described in the previous section for an update involving changes, insertions, and deletions with allowance for arbitrary mismatches, unmatched records, and undesired matched records. The logic will be fairly complex, but has been discussed previously. The file navigation diagrams in Figures 4.1, 4.2a, and 4.2b should be referred to.

We shall update a customer file (OLDCUST) using a transaction file (TRANS), and generate a new customer file (NEWCUST). The primary key field for all three files will be the customer number field CUSTNUMB. The fields for these files are illustrated in Figure 4.4a, for readers' convenience. Note that the TRANS record has a field ACTION. The ACTION values "CH", "IN", and "DE" respectively indicate change, insertion, and deletion updating.

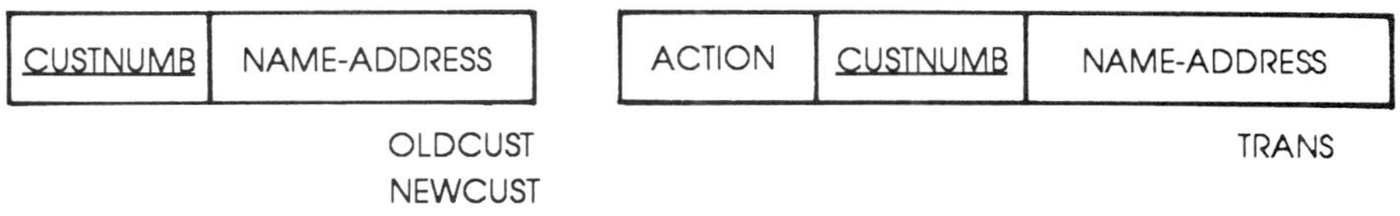

FIGURE 4.4a Fields for the files involved in the classic updating of OLDCUST from TRANS to form NEWCUST. The ACTION field in a TRANS record indicates whether the record will trigger a change, insertion, or deletion update.

We shall use a print file called EDIT-FILE in which we print information about mismatched TRANS records. Thus the system diagram in Figure 4.4b applies.

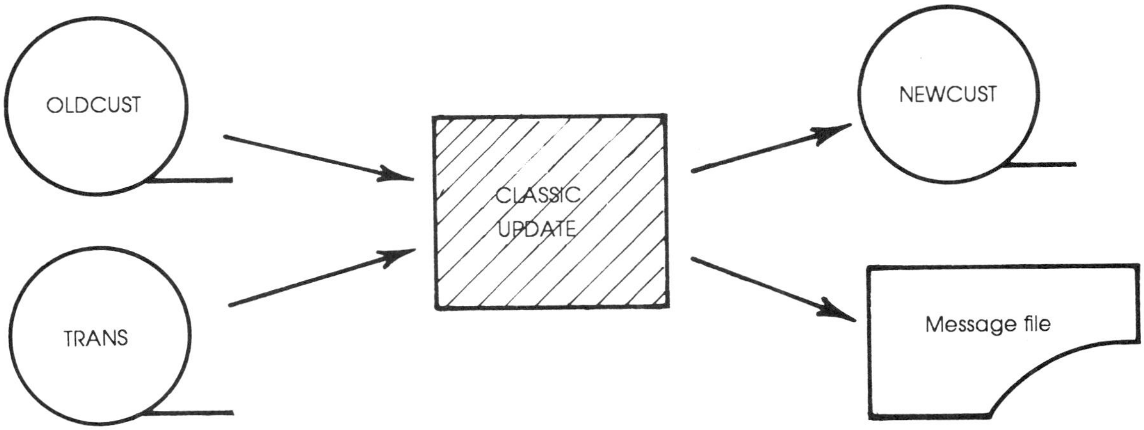

FIGURE 4.4b System diagram for the classic change updating of OLDCUST from TRANS to form NEWCUST.

COBOL File and Record Specifications

We omit the identification, environment, and data divisions of the program, to concentrate on the procedure. However, for reader convenience in Figure 4.5 we have listed the buffer and working-storage record names for each of the three data files.

Logical File Name	Buffer Record Name	Working-Storage Record Name
OLDCUST	OLDCUSTBUFREC	OLDCUSTREC
NEWCUST	NEWCUSTBUFREC	NEWCUSTREC
TRANS	TRANSBUFREC	TRANSREC

FIGURE 4.5 COBOL names associated with the files in Figure 4.4a,b.

COBOL Procedure for Change Updating Only

Because the procedure for the full classic update involving changes, insertions, and deletions is complex, we first give the following procedure, where only change updating is involved. (Arbitrary mismatches can be assumed, so that the file navigation diagrams in Figures 4.2a and 4.2b apply.)

```
PROCEDURE DIVISION.
MAIN-PARAGRAPH.
     OPEN INPUT TRANS,
          INPUT OLDCUST,
          OUTPUT NEWCUST,
          OUTPUT EDIT-FILE.
     MOVE ZEROS TO CUSTNUMB IN OLDCUSTREC.
     READ TRANS INTO TRANSREC,
         AT END PERFORM NO-RECORDS-PARAGRAPH.
     PERFORM TRANS-SCAN UNTIL CUSTNUMB IN TRANSREC = 99999.
     CLOSE TRANS, OLDCUST, NEWCUST, EDIT-FILE.
     STOP RUN.
TRANS-SCAN.
     PERFORM SCAN-OLDCUST UNTIL CUSTNUMB IN OLDCUSTREC
                  NOT < CUSTNUMB IN TRANSREC.
     IF CUSTNUMB IN OLDCUSTREC > CUSTNUMB IN TRANSREC
          THEN PERFORM UNMATCHED-ERROR MESSAGE
          ELSE MOVE NAME-ADDRESS IN TRANSREC
                  TO NAME-ADDRESS IN OLDCUSTREC.
     READ TRANS INTO TRANSREC,
```

```
          AT END MOVE 99999 TO CUSTNUMB IN TRANSREC.
SCAN-OLDCUST.
     IF CUSTNUMB IN OLDCUSTREC NOT = ZEROS
          THEN WRITE NEWCUSTBUFREC FROM OLDCUSTREC.
     READ OLDCUST INTO OLDCUSTREC,
          AT END MOVE 99999 TO CUSTNUMB IN OLDCUSTREC.
UN-MATCHED ERROR-MESSAGE.
.
.
.
(Current TRANS record printed).
```

Referring to Figures 4.2a and 4.2b, the BOF (beginning of file) OLDCUST record is assigned the CUSTNUMB value 00000, that is, the COBOL figurative constant ZEROS. Similarly for the CUSTNUMB value in both the EOF (end of file) TRANS and OLDCUST records, we use the value 99999.

We now give an extended version of the above procedure, where change, insertion, and deletion updating can occur according to the value in ACTION in the current TRANS record:

```
PROCEDURE DIVISION.
     OPEN INPUT TRANS,
          INPUT OLDCUST,
          OUTPUT NEWCUST,
          OUTPUT EDIT-FILE.
     MOVE ZEROS TO CUSTNUMB IN OLDCUSTREC.
     READ TRANS INTO TRANSREC, AT END
          PERFORM NO-RECORDS-PARAGRAPH.
     PERFORM TRANS-SCAN UNTIL CUSTNUMB IN
          TRANSREC = 99999.
     CLOSE TRANS, OLDCUST, NEWCUST, EDIT-FILE.
     STOP RUN.
TRANS-SCAN.
     PERFORM SCAN-OLDCUST UNTIL CUSTNUMB IN OLDCUST
          NOT < CUSTNUMB IN TRANSREC.
     IF ACTION = "CH"
          THEN PERFORM CHANGE-UPDATE.
          ELSE IF ACTION = "IN"
               THEN PERFORM INSERTION-UPDATE.
               ELSE IF ACTION = "DE"
                    THEN PERFORM DELETION-UPDATE
                    ELSE PERFORM BAD-TRANS-PARAGRAPH.
     READ TRANS INTO TRANSREC,
          AT END MOVE 99999 TO CUSTNUMB IN TRANSREC.
SCAN-OLDCUST.
     IF CUSTNUMB IN OLDCUSTREC > ZEROS
          THEN WRITE NEWCUSTBUFREC FROM OLDCUSTREC.
     READ OLDCUST INTO OLDCUSTREC,
          AT END MOVE 99999 TO CUSTNUMB IN OLDCUSTREC.
CHANGE-UPDATE.
     IF CUSTNUMB IN OLDCUSTREC > CUSTNUMB IN TRANSREC
```

```
                 THEN PERFORM UNMATCHED-CHANGE-UPDATE
                 ELSE MOVE NAME-ADDRESS IN TRANSREC TO
                      NAME-ADDRESS IN OLDCUSTREC.

******  Updated version will be written with next execution
******  of SCAN-OLDCUST.

INSERTION-UPDATE.
     IF CUSTNUMB IN OLDCUSTREC > CUSTNUMB IN TRANSREC
                 THEN MOVE TRANSREC TO NEWCUSTREC,
                 WRITE NEWCUSTBUFREC FROM NEWCUSTREC,
            ELSE PERFORM MATCHED-INSERTION-UPDATE.
DELETION-UPDATE.
     IF CUSTNUMB IN OLDCUSTREC > CUSTNUMB IN TRANSREC
            THEN PERFORM UNMATCHED-DELETION-UPDATE
            ELSE MOVE ZEROS TO CUSTNUMB IN OLDCUSTREC.
******  This means that OLDCUSTREC will not be copied to
******  NEWCUST next time we execute SCAN-OLDCUST.

UNMATCHED-CHANGE-UPDATE.
     Unmatched TRANS record written to EDIT-FILE.
MATCHED-INSERTION-UPDATE.
     Matched TRANS record written to EDIT-FILE.
UNMATCHED-DELETION-UPDATE.
     Unmatched TRANS record written to EDIT-FILE.
```

Arbitrary mismatches can occur anywhere in the program in any sequence without the program being impaired. Note that the program cannot handle correctly a sequence of duplicate primary key CUSTNUMB values in the TRANS records. This should not occur in practice, since in the editing and sorting of the TRANS records in preparation for update, duplicate key values would be detected.

Core COBOL Program for Updating the Investments File

We saw that the investments file can be updated without having to write out a new updated version of the file, provided the file is stored on disk. We shall base our core COBOL procedure on this method, which, as mentioned earlier, requires the use of the COBOL REWRITE command.

We need only be concerned with a few fields, such as the pair that identifies a record, namely, STOCK (name of stock) and QTR (number of quarter, with current quarter 0). The essential parts of the record formats are shown in Figure 4.6. The master file is called INVESTMENTS and the transaction file is TRANS.

The updating method involves replacing each record for quarter 0 by a transaction record, and each record for quarter n by the record

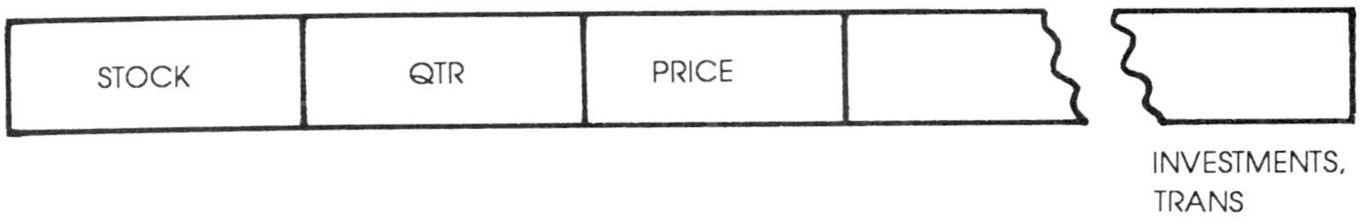

FIGURE 4.6 The essential part of the format for records of INVESTMENTS and TRANS.

for quarter n-1, at the same time increasing the QTR value by 1. In addition, each old master record for quarter 99 is deleted (see the file navigation diagram in Figure 4.7). The buffer and working-storage record names used in the program are shown in Figure 4.8a; the working-storage data items used are listed in Figure 4.8b. We must keep each record read so that it can be used to replace the next record. Thus we need an additional working-storage record structure, AUXIL-REC (see Figure 4.9).

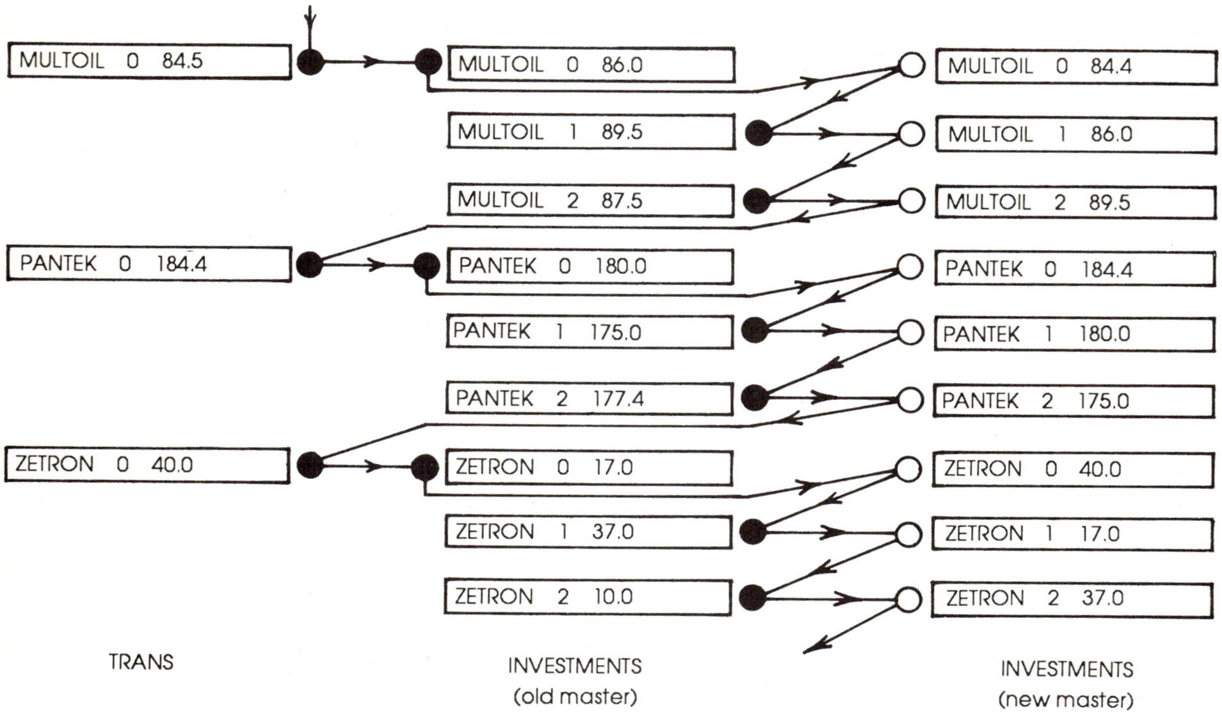

FIGURE 4.7 File navigation diagram for the update program in Figure 4.9. Every record of the old (INVESTMENTS) master is updated. The new master is not constructed as a physically distinct file. Each record of the new master is written out on top of a record of the old master. Note also that the number of insertions and the number of deletions individually equal the number of transaction records. It is this equality that makes it possible to update the transaction file without it being necessary to write out a new one. The diagram assumes that records for only 3 quarters are recorded for each stock. The program in 4.9 assumes 100 quarters.

Logical File Name	Buffer Record Name	Working-Storage Record Name
TRANS	TRANSBUFREC (not used)	INVESTREC
INVESTMENTS	INVESTBUFREC	INVESTREC AUXIL-REC

FIGURE 4.8a COBOL file and record names for the procedure in Figure 4.9.

Working-Storage Data Item Name	Type	Use
COUNTER	Numeric	For counting quarterly records for each stock
EOF-TRANS	Character	End of transaction file flag

FIGURE 4.8b COBOL working-storage names used in the program in Figure 4.9.

Note that at the beginning of the procedure, the file TRANS is opened for input (INPUT), whereas the file INVESTMENTS is opened for both input and output (I/O). Only a disk file can be opened for input/output, and it is only when a file has been opened in this way that a REWRITE command can be used. Note that the program is an essential core only. It does not take into account such an eventuality as a change of the name of the stock, for example, which would upset the sequential ordering in the file. Thus a commercial version of the program in Figure 4.9 would be much more complex.

```
PROCEDURE DIVISION.
     OPEN INPUT TRANS,
          I-O INVESTMENTS.
     MOVE "NO" TO EOF-TRANS.
     READ TRANS INTO INVESTREC,
          AT END PERFORM NO-TRANS-RECORDS.
     PERFORM PROCESS-TRANS-RECORDS UNTIL EOF-TRANS = "YES".
     CLOSE TRANS, CLOSE INVESTMENTS.
     STOP RUN.
PROCESS-TRANS-RECORDS.
     READ INVESTMENTS INTO AUXIL-REC,
          AT END PERFORM INVESTMENTS-ERROR.
     REWRITE INVESTBUFREC FROM INVESTREC.
     COMPUTE COUNTER = 1.
     PERFORM UPDATE-AND-SHIFT-DOWN UNTIL COUNTER = 100.
     READ TRANS INTO INVESTREC AT END MOVE "YES" TO EOF-TRANS.
UPDATE-AND-SHIFT-DOWN.
     MOVE AUXIL-REC TO INVESTREC.
     COMPUTE QTR IN INVESTREC = COUNTER.
     READ INVESTMENTS INTO AUXIL-REC,
          AT END PERFORM INVESTMENTS-ERROR.
     REWRITE INVESTBUFREC FROM INVESTREC.
     COMPUTE COUNTER = COUNTER + 1.
```

FIGURE 4.9 **Essential core of the program for updating the investments file on disk. The new master INVESTMENTS version is written out on top of the old master version.**

INFORMATION RETRIEVAL WITH SEQUENTIAL FILES

An important by-product of the processing of business files for generation of necessary business documents, such as invoices, is that the master files (and sometimes the transactions files) can be used for generating information of use to management. It is clear, for example, that an accounts receivable master can be very useful; many corporate funds are usually tied up in receivables, and management can make use of the file in deciding on courses of action to reduce the funds thus tied up.

It is important for readers to understand that information retrieval systems are really a by-product of otherwise essential file processing to generate required documents. Failure to grasp this has led in the to generate required documents. Failure to grasp this has led in the past to attempts to construct information retrieval systems based on files (and even on data bases) deliberately constructed for this purpose. Such attempts usually failed because they were too ambitious and expensive and not based on a readily available corporate resource, namely, the data in files used in the everyday business activities of the firm.

Some COBOL Information Retrieval with an Accounts Receivable (AR) Master File

We shall use an accounts receivable (AR) master file for our retrieval examples, since this is the kind of file from which management frequently wants to extract information. The AR master file is one of the most important files in a business organization, for its contents list the amount of money owed the firm on account of recent (and sometimes not so recent) sales, as well as who owes the money. In a well run business, management pays particular attention to the data in the accounts receivable file and tries to ensure that funds tied up in receivables are minimized. To minimize these funds, management must get customers to pay their bills promptly; one way to do that is to ensure that a clear statement of what is owing (the monthly statement) reaches each customer early at the beginning of the month.

Recall from chapter 3 that when goods are shipped to a customer, an invoice for those goods arrives a few days later. The customer may then pay part or all of that bill, or choose to defer payment. If the customer has received many different shipments and made only a few payments, at the month's end there will be a number of outstanding invoices with an amount still owing. The AR master file must be updated near the end of the month to reflect this, for it is from this master that a monthly statement for each customer is prepared. Typically that monthly statement will list all outstanding invoices for the customer and the amount owing.

To be useful for generating the monthly statements, the accounts receivable file must contain an up-to-date list of each invoice for which payment in full has not yet been made. A simplified version of an accounts receivable file, AR-MASTER, is illustrated in Figure 4.10. The primary key is the invoice number (INVOICE-NUMB); each record describes an invoice sent to a customer, so that we need a field for customer number (CUSTNUMB). Note that a customer can have many invoices not fully paid. The original amount of the invoice is in the field AMOUNT; the sum currently outstanding is in the field OWING.

CUSTNUMB	INVOICE-NUMB	INVOICE-DATE	AMOUNT	OWING
C15	IN67	3 March	15,400	9,200
C12	IN71	10 March	7,000	5,000
C14	IN79	4 April	12,000	12,000
C12	IN82	15 April	4,000	7,000
				AR-MASTER

FIGURE 4.10 Some records of the accounts receivable (AR) master file AR-MASTER. AMOUNT gives the amount originally billed, whereas OWING gives the sum currently owed by the customer.

Quite sophisticated updating procedures are needed to keep an accounts receivable file current (more about this in chapter 6). We now examine some retrievals with this accounts receivable file.

> Retrieval 1: Retrieve the invoice data for each invoice for which the amount owing is $10,000 or more.

We need only examine each AR record in turn. If the OWING field value is less than 10,000 we carry on to the next record in sequence; otherwise we print the record out. The core of the necessary COBOL procedure is:

```
PROCEDURE DIVISION.
     OPEN INPUT AR-MASTER,
     MOVE "NO" TO EOF.
     READ AR-MASTER INTO AR-REC,
          AT END PERFORM NO-RECORDS-PARAGRAPH.
     PERFORM SCAN-RECORDS UNTIL EOF = "YES".
     CLOSE AR-MASTER, STOP RUN.
SCAN-RECORDS.
     IF OWING IN AR-REC NOT < 10000
          THEN DISPLAY CUSTNUMB, INVOICE-NUMB, INVOICE-DATE,
          AMOUNT, OWING.
     READ AR-MASTER INTO AR-REC,
          AT END MOVE "YES" TO EOF.
```

Here AR-MASTER is the accounts receivable file (see Figure 4.10); EOF is the end of file flag. AR-REC is the working-storage record associated with the file.

> Retrieval 2: List the customer numbers for each customer whose total invoice debt is $10,000 or more.

This one is not quite so simple, but is typical of many requests. For each customer we must group all the invoices and sum the funds owing for each invoice. If the sum is 10,000 or more we print the customer number, otherwise we proceed to the next customer. Clearly a sort of AR-MASTER on the CUSTNUMB field will be necessary. Assuming that such a sorted version is available, the core of the necessary COBOL program would be:

```
PROCEDURE DIVISION.
     OPEN INPUT AR-MASTER.
     READ AR-MASTER INTO AR-REC,
          AT END PERFORM NO-RECORDS-PARAGRAPH.
     MOVE "NO" TO EOF.
     PERFORM SCAN-MASTER-FILE UNTIL EOF = "YES".
     CLOSE AR-MASTER, STOP RUN.
SCAN-MASTER-FILE.
     MOVE CUSTNUMB IN AR-REC TO CONTROL-CUSTNUMB.
     COMPUTE TOTAL = 0.
     PERFORM UNTIL CUSTNUMB IN AR-REC NOT = CONTROL-CUSTNUMB
          COMPUTE TOTAL = TOTAL + OWING IN AR-REC
          READ AR-MASTER INTO AR-REC,
               AT END MOVE "YES" TO EOF,
                    MOVE '99999' TO CUSTNUMB IN AR-REC.
     END-PERFORM.
     IF TOTAL NOT < 10000
          THEN DISPLAY CONTROL-CUSTNUMB.
```

The data item CONTROL-CUSTNUMB holds the customer number for a group of invoices, for each of which the sum owing (OWING field value) is extracted and added to a TOTAL data item. The TOTAL value is then used to determine whether the customer involved should be printed or displayed on a terminal. Assuming a terminal is being used, the COBOL verb imperative DISPLAY can be used to have the value of CONTROL-CUSTNUMB displayed. Note that the program uses a control break.

IBM DD-STATEMENT FOR THE INVESTMENTS FILE

With IBM systems, dataset definition statements (DD-statements) for sequential disk files are similar to those used for sequential tape files. The essential difference is the need for the SPACE parameter. As we saw in chapter 3, disks have a lot of storage capacity, so that many files can reside on a single disk pack. Furthermore, because of the direct access capability of disks, a sequential file anywhere on a disk is almost immediately available for processing, without the need for the equivalent of initial winding to the required start position, as would be the case with multiple files on a single tape reel.

Therefore it is possible for the creation of two distinct files on a disk to take place concurrently. Thus program A creating file FA can have its execution interleaved with that of program B creating file FB. In order to prevent competition for the same space on the disk, the operating system must be initially informed of the size of the file, so that an appropriate amount of disk space may be allocated.

The SPACE parameter specification can be quite complex, but the most common forms permit specification of one of the following:

a. The number of cylinders needed; for example, SPACE(CYL,50) means 50 cylinders.

b. The number of tracks needed; for example, SPACE(TRK,250) means 250 tracks.

c. The number and size of the blocks needed; for example, SPACE(2500,12000) means 12,000 data blocks, where the transmitted data block (or data subblock) is 2,500 bytes long. The system uses this information as well as information about the type of disk to compute how many cylinders and tracks are needed. We saw how to do this in the previous chapter.

As an example of a sequential disk file DD-statement, we examine the following for a program to create the file INVESTMENTS (used earlier in this chapter):

```
//INVESTMENTS DD DSN=INVEST1,UNIT=3350,VOL=SER=123,
//               DISP=(NEW,CATLG),
//               DCB=(LRECL=200,RECFM=FB,BLKSIZE=2400),
//               SPACE=(TRK,1500)
```

Here we assume that the record (see Figure 4.9) has length 200 characters and that there are 12 records per block. In addition we assume about 10,000 records. Consulting Figure 2.21 in chapter 2, this means 7 blocks per track, so that we need just under 1,500 tracks. Alternatively we could have specified SPACE(2400,100000). Note that the BLKSIZE specification is included only if the BLOCK CONTAINS clause in the COBOL program does not give the number of records per block.

SUMMARY

Sequential master files can be updated by either the classic method or the rewrite method. With the classic method the file being updated can be either on disk or tape; updates are taken from a transaction file and applied to the master file to generate a new master file. Three generations of master file (the son, father, and grandfather files) are always kept for security purposes.

With the rewrite method of updating, the file must be on disk; generally only change updating is possible, although you can have deletion updating if updated records are simply marked as deleted. With rewrite updating the records of the master needing updating are changed, so that the original version of the file is no longer available. With such updating a log, or journal, file is often used to record changes to the master for security purposes.

An updating operation can involve change updating, insertion updating, deletion updating, or any combination of these. With change and deletion updating the program must be able to handle mismatches, in any sequence and quantity, between transaction and master files; with insertion updating the program similarly must be able to handle unwanted matches.

Updating where change, insertion, and deletion updating are allowed is known as general updating; it can be quite involved because of the need to handle both unwanted mismatched and matched transaction records.

Retrieval of information from sequential files is a common activity for generating reports and other documents in business. Information retrieval programs read records sequentially and select those records that meet search criteria.

EXERCISES

1. With classic updating, give the method used for deletion updating when mismatches are involved.
2. Draw a file navigation diagram for deletion updating for the following cases: (a.) Mismatches occur at the end of the transaction file (b.) Mismatches occur at the beginning of the transaction file (c.) Mismatches occur randomly within the transaction file

3. Using a very large sheet of paper (computer printout paper, perhaps), draw a file navigation diagram for the general case of classic updating.
4. Create a PRODUCT file with fields product type number, product type description, and unit price. Also create a transaction file, TRANS, that contains new unit price information. Write a program for classic change updating PRODUCT from TRANS where mismatches can occur.
5. If TRANS (exercise 4) contains records for new product types, write a program for insertion updating of PRODUCT, given that unwanted matches may occur.
6. If TRANS (exercise 4) contains data about obsolete products, write a program for deletion update of PRODUCT, given that mismatches can occur.
7. Consider the master file INVESTMENTS in this chapter. Suppose that TRANS records describe changes in the name of stocks in INVESTMENTS. Write a program to use TRANS for updating assuming that mismatches can occur.
8. With the file INVESTMENTS, suppose that TRANS contains data about stocks that have been delisted from the stock exchange. Write a program to use TRANS for updating INVESTMENTS assuming that mismatches can occur.
9. Given the INVESTMENTS file, write a program to retrieve the names of stocks that have increased in price by more than 20 percent during the latest 2 quarters.
10. Given the INVESTMENTS file, write a program to retrieve the names and current prices of stocks whose price has increased by 10 percent or more in each of the previous 4 quarters.
11. Given the file INVESTMENTS, write a program to retrieve the moving average over the past 100 quarters for any stock entered at a terminal.
12. Given the file INVESTMENTS, write a program to retrieve the price history of any stock entered at a terminal for a period of recent quarters (also entered at a terminal).
13. Given the accounts receivable file AR-MASTER, write a program to retrieve the customer numbers for customers with at least one outstanding invoice on which more than 50 percent of the original amount is still owing.
14. Given the accounts receivable file AR-MASTER, write a program to retrieve the customer numbers for customers for whom every outstanding invoice has had less than 50 percent of the original amount repaid.

5 VARIABLE LENGTH RECORD FILE PROCESSING

In this brief chapter we look at files containing records that vary in length. It is a specialized topic, however, and may be skipped on the first reading of this text.

Readers should also be aware that files with variable length records are going out of style. The reasons are twofold. First, file processing programs that use variable length record files are more expensive to construct. Second, few query language systems can handle variable length record files; most query systems need the simpler fixed length record files. Nevertheless variable length record files are not uncommon; situations do occur where a variable length record file is the best solution, at least in the short run.

TYPES OF VARIABLE LENGTH RECORD FILES

There are three distinct types of variable length record files: **mixed category**, **repeating group**, and **variable field length**. We first examine these methods in general terms and then look at the COBOL facilities for handling them.

Mixed Category Files

Generally each record in a computer file describes an entity; all the entities described in the file belong to the same class. An **entity** can be taken as any thing in the physical world. For example, we could have the class of entity *person*. A file of records describing persons would have a single record for each person—that is, each entity—described. However, suppose that the file described persons associated with a business enterprise. We could divide such persons into different categories, such as *employees*, *stockholders*, *customers*, *suppliers*, and combinations of these. If a file of entities of a given class, such as *person*, contains different categories of that class, such as *employee* and *stockholder*, then the records of the file will in general be of varying length. For example, many of the fields of records describing employees and shareholders will differ substantially, since

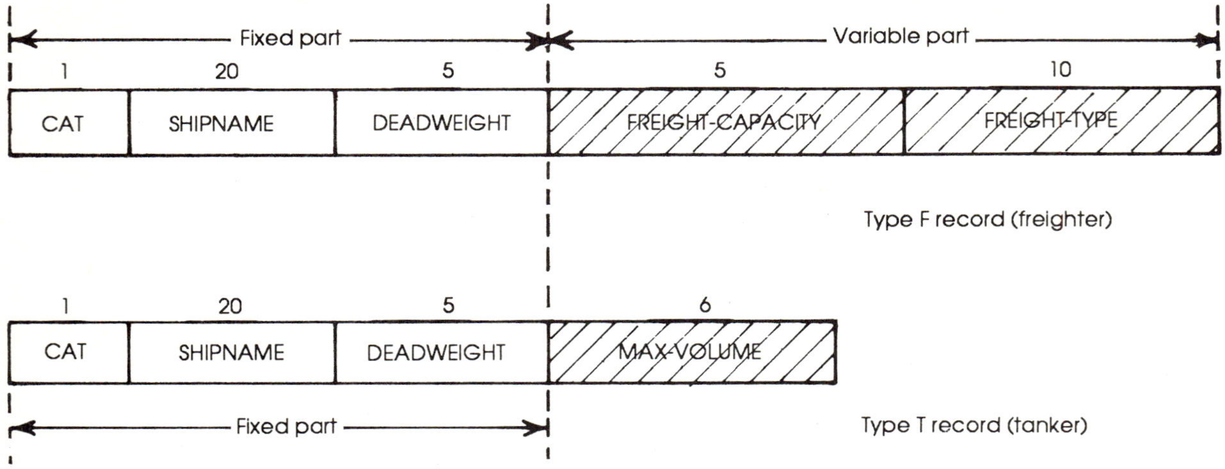

FIGURE 5.1 **Mixed category variable length records for the file SHIPPING. There are two types of records, each type describing an entity of a distinct category. Type *F* records describe freighters and type *T* records describe oil tankers. Both types of records have fields that are common (the fixed part of the record); the fields that are different make up the variable part of the record. The numbers above the fields give the field lengths in bytes and are used in examples involving COBOL processing. We can see that for the SHIPPING file the maximum record length (*F* type) is 41 characters and the minimum (*T* type) is 32 characters.**

an employee will have a salary, while a stockholder will have a number of shares and receive a dividend income. Such a file is a **mixed** category file.

To fix our ideas, let us take a simpler example of a file, SHIPPING, where only two categories are involved. Each record of the file describes a ship; the file can be considered the property of an insurance company dealing with shipping. Two categories of ship are included: Category *F* for freighter and category *T* for oil tanker. Simplified versions of the records are shown in Figure 5.1.

Both types of record have some field types in common, such as CAT (category), SHIPNAME, and DEADWEIGHT. These fields make up the fixed (format) part of the records. The other part depends on the type of record. A freighter can carry many different kinds of freight (and there is a field to describe this), whereas an oil tanker carries only oil. Thus each record has a variable (format) part as well. We shall make use of this example later when we examine how mixed category files can be handled.

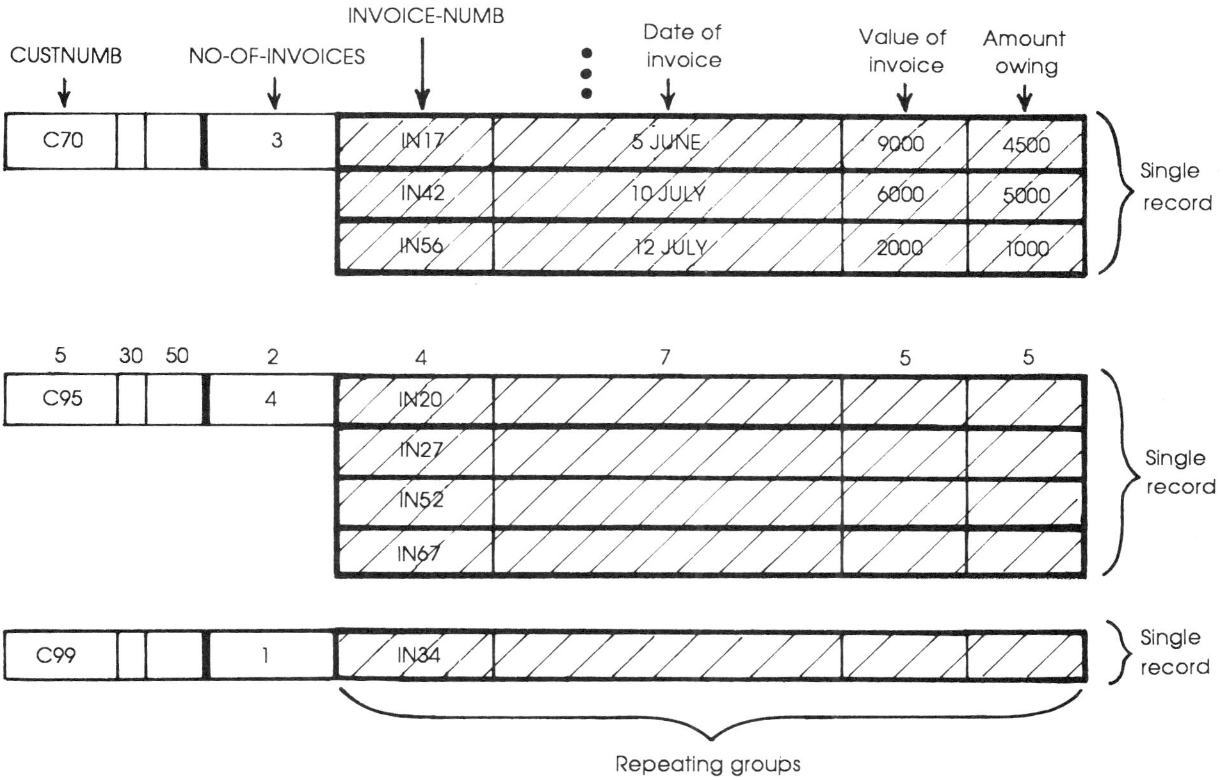

FIGURE 5.2 A file of records giving customer data followed by descriptions of a varying number of outstanding invoices. Each set of invoice data constitutes a repeating group of fields. The number of repeating groups in a record is contained in the NO-OF-INVOICES field. Field lengths are given above the second record.

Repeating Group Files

A **repeating group file** is the result of taking two files between which there is a parent-to-child relationship and constructing a new file in which a record combines a former parent record with its child records. We can illustrate this using the file CUSTOMER-MASTER and AR-MASTER. CUSTOMER-MASTER describes customers and has a key field, CUSTNUMB (or customer number). AR-MASTER (accounts receivable [AR] master file) lists each invoice for which there is an amount still owing. For each record in CUSTOMER-MASTER there will be 0 or more records in AR-MASTER with matching CUSTNUMB value. Thus there is a **parent-to-child relationship** between the two files. We have a parent-to-child relationship when for any one thing there are many related things, but not vice versa.

If we now take a CUSTOMER-MASTER record and attach to it the associated AR-MASTER records, we have a record with a number of fields that repeat, that is, a **repeating group of fields**, where each **repeating group** corresponds to an AR-MASTER record (see Figure 5.2). To rationalize things as much as possible we have removed the repeating CUSTNUMB fields from the repeating groups and added the field NO-OF-INVOICES. This new field is in the fixed part of the record, that is, the part not occupied by repeating groups; it contains the number of invoices outstanding for the customer and thus the number of repeating groups. This field is essential for reading the records, as we shall see.

Variable Field Length Files

Each record from a **variable field length file** has a fixed format part and a variable format part. The variable part normally contains only a single field, the length of which varies widely (see Figure 5.3). The classic example is a file describing books, perhaps maintained by a firm with a chain of outlets for the distribution of books. The fixed format fields contain the author name, publisher name, date of publication, and so on. The variable field is the title, which can vary from a few characters to many words depending on the book. To be able to read the records there must be information in the fixed part of each record giving the length of the variable length field. Thus we have the field FIELD-LENGTH in the fixed part of each record.

PROCESSING VARIABLE LENGTH RECORD FILES

Quite detailed techniques are needed to process variable length record files. It is also necessary to consider job control language (JCL) requirements with IBM systems.

The accompanying dataset definition statement (DD-statement) for a variable length record file does not depend on the type of variable length file. As was explained in Chapter 2, it is necessary only to specify the maximum possible record length (in the LRECL specification) and the maximum possible transmitted block size (in the

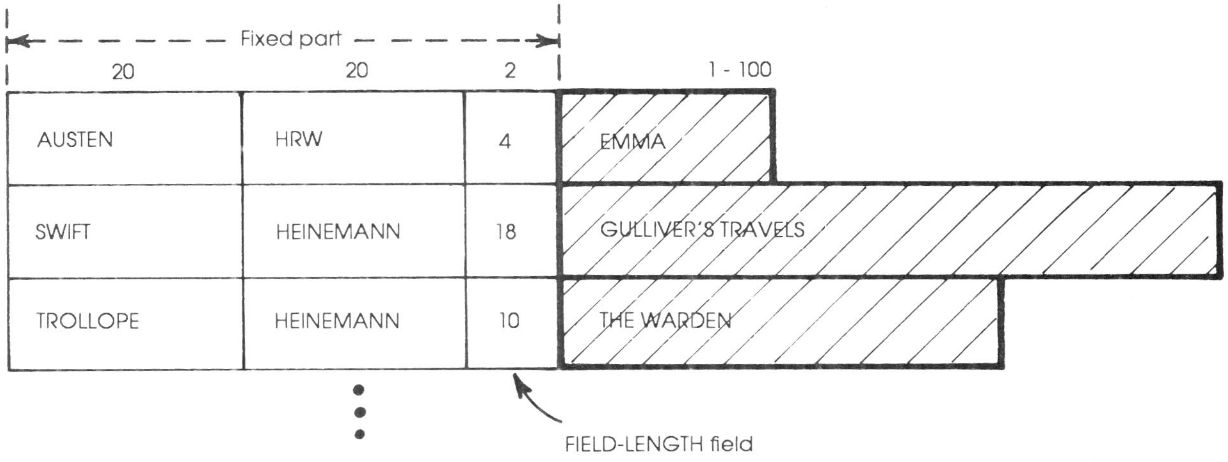

FIGURE 5.3 **A file about authors and book titles where the book title field can vary in length. The length of the varying field is given by FIELD-LENGTH in the initial nonvarying part of the record. Field lengths are shown above.**

BLKSIZE specification). We shall give an example of such a DD-statement presently.

Processing Mixed Category Files

Begin by considering how we can create a mixed category file. Suppose we need to create a file, SHIPPING, with records of the type shown in Figure 5.1. The first step is the definition of the two distinct types of buffer records and working-storage records for the file. COBOL lets us do this easily as follows:

```
DATA DIVISION.
FILE SECTION.
FD   SHIPPING.
     RECORD CONTAINS 32 TO 41 CHARACTERS
     BLOCK CONTAINS 0 RECORDS
     LABEL RECORDS ARE STANDARD
     DATA RECORDS ARE F-SHIPBUFREC, T-SHIPBUFREC.
01   F-SHIPBUFREC.
     02     CAT             PIC X.
     02     SHIPDATA        PIC X(40).
02   T-SHIPBUFREC.
     02     CAT             PIC X.
```

```
     02      SHIPDATA        PIC X(31).
WORKING-STORAGE SECTION.
01   F-SHIPREC.
     02      CAT             PIC X.
     02      SHIPNAME        PIC X(20).
     02      DEADWEIGHT      PIC 9(5).
     02      FREIGHT-CAP     PIC 9(5).
     02      FREIGHT-TYPE    PIC X(10).
01   T-SHIPREC.
     02      CAT             PIC X.
     02      SHIPNAME        PIC X(20).
     02      DEADWEIGHT      PIC 9(5).
     02      MAX-VOLUME      PIC 9(6).
```

In the file section we have specified a variable length record file called SHIPPING. The RECORD CONTAINS clause specifies the minimum record size in the file (32 characters) and the maximum size (41 characters). These are the sizes of the logical records and not the sizes of the physical records as stored on the disk or tape. This is important—failure to understand this is a frequent source of error when variable length record files are being set up. In the DATA RECORDS clause we have specified that two different types of buffer records will fit records of the file. The largest of these, F-SHIPBUFREC, clearly has 41 characters; this must equal the maximum record length specification in the RECORD CONTAINS clause. Note also that the largest of the buffer records must be specified first. (Technically the buffer records are redefined in terms of the first buffer record, which must therefore be the largest.)

The BLOCK CONTAINS clause is not to be interpreted literally. We use 0 RECORDS to indicate that the maximum block size is being specified in the accompanying DD-statement for the file if the file is being created, or is available from the system catalogue if the file was created during earlier processing.

In the WORKING-STORAGE section we specify two additional record structures corresponding to the two buffer structures. Many programmers do not specifiy such structures and do all processing using the buffer structures. Often such programmers are not aware that they are processing in the system buffer and that this is the cause of many of the peculiar errors that can result. We prefer to do all processing with working-storage structures, as was explained earlier.

If we use a ddname, SHIPPING, for the logical file, the DD-statement for creating the file on disk would be:

```
//SHIPPING  DD  DSN=SHIP0123,DISP=(NEW,CATLG),UNIT=DISK,
//              VOL=SER=123,SPACE=(CYL,100),
//              DCB=(LRECL=45,BLKSIZE=4504,RECFM=VB)
```

In this statement, we specify a new file whose specifications should be catalogued (DISPposition). We also specify that it is a disk file (UNIT) and that it will occupy up to 100 cylinders (SPACE). The data central block (DCB) specifications indicate that the records are blocked variable length (RECFM=VB), that the maximum physical record length is 41+4, as given by LRECL=45, and that the maximum transmitted block size is 4,504. The maximum transmitted block size can contain 100 of the largest records (100*(41+4) +4).

The essential Procedure Division COBOL statements for creating the file are WRITE statements using the two different buffer and working-storage structures. Thus the following excerpt writes out a long (F-type) record followed by a short (T-type) record:

```
WRITE F-SHIPBUFREC FROM F-SHIPREC.
.
.
.
WRITE T-SHIPBUFREC FROM T-SHIPREC.
```

In this way a random sequence of long and short records are written out onto the disk.

However, when we come to read the records back in again, the random sequence is something of a problem, for we do not know beforehand what type of record will be read next. Thus we cannot know the proper WORKING-STORAGE structure to be used.

The problem of reading variable length records is solved by using the two buffer structures (See Figure 5.4). This shows a sequence of records in the buffer (without the additional 4-byte length fields, which physically also are attached to the buffer records). As we saw earlier with fixed length records, as the file is read the buffer record structure physically moves along in the buffer (see Figure 3.1 in Chapter Three). However, this time we have two buffer structures that move through the buffer. They stick together and begin at exactly the same memory position. Thus we can say they partly overlap. Looking at Figure 5.4 again, it should be obvious that the fixed part of the two structures enjoy 100 percent overlap.

Now suppose that we issue the command READ SHIPPING. Both buffer structures move to the next record in the buffer. As yet we have no idea whether this next record is T-type or F-type. But we can examine the value in either CAT IN T-SHIPBUFREC or CAT IN F-SHIPBUFREC to find out. Once we know, we can move the record from the buffer to the appropriate WORKING-STORAGE record structure. The following COBOL excerpt illustrates this. We assume for purposes of illustration that the processing requires the total freight capacity (accummulated in TOTAL) for all the ships listed in the file.

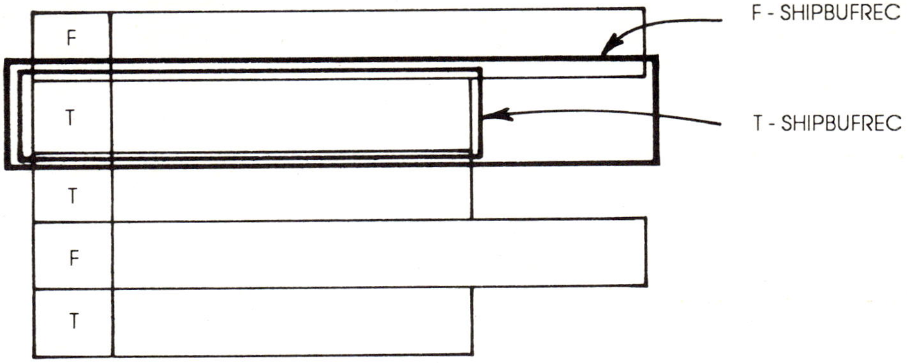

FIGURE 5.4 **Illustration of how mixed category variable length records are read. The buffer contains a random selection of *T* and *F* type records (see also Figure 5.1). As each READ command is executed, two coincident (or overlayed) buffer structures, F-SHIPBUFREC and T-SHIPBUFREC, move from the current record to the next record. By examining the CAT (category field) at the start of the record (and using either buffer structure to do this), the type of record can be determined by the program. The record is then moved to the correct working-storage structure.**

```
          MOVE "NO" TO EOF.
          COMPUTE TOTAL = 0.
          READ SHIPPING,
               AT END PERFORM NO-RECORDS-PARAGRAPH.
          PERFORM FILE-SCAN UNTIL EOF = "YES".
          DISPLAY TOTAL,
          CLOSE SHIPPING,
          STOP RUN.
     FILE-SCAN.
          IF CAT IN T-SHIPBUFREC = "F"
               THEN MOVE F-SHIPBUFREC TO F-SHIPREC,
                    COMPUTE TOTAL = TOTAL + FREIGHT-CAP.
          READ SHIPPING,
               AT END MOVE "YES" TO EOF.
```

EOF is an end of file flag. Notice that in the IF statement it makes no difference to replace CAT IN T-SHIPBUFREC by CAT IN F-SHIPBUFREC. Note also that while we process an F-type record in the WORKING-STORAGE record structure, we are forced to look initially at the CAT field in any buffer structure to determine what kind of record we are dealing with, and thus move it to the correct WORKING-STORAGE structure.

Processing Repeating Group Files

To illustrate the processing of records with repeating groups, we use the file in Figure 5.2 and give it the logical file name CUSTOMER-INVOICES. As in the previous case we must take care with the specification of the buffer and WORKING-STORAGE record structure. We assume that the maximum number of invoices a customer can have outstanding is 20, that the nonrepeating portion of a record occupies 87 bytes or characters, and that a repeated portion occupies 21 bytes as follows:

```
DATA DIVISION.
FILE SECTION.
FD      CUSTOMER-INVOICES
      RECORD CONTAINS 108 TO 507 CHARACTERS
      BLOCK CONTAINS 0 RECORDS
      LABEL RECORDS ARE STANDARD
      DATA RECORD IS CI-BUFREC.
01      CI-BUFREC.
      02      CUSTOMERDATA     PIC X(85).
      02      NO-OF-INVOICES   PIC S999 COMP-3.
      02      REPEATING-GROUP OCCURS 1 TO 20 TIMES
                          DEPENDING ON NO-OF-INVOICES.
              05      INVOICE-DATA     PIC X(21).
WORKING-STORAGE SECTION.
01      CI-REC.
      02      CUSTOMERDATA.
            05      CUSTNUMB           PIC X(5).
            05      CUST-NAME          PIC X(30).
            05      CUST-ADDRESS       PIC X(50).
      02      NO-OF-INVOICES             PIC S999 COMP-3.
      02      REPEATING-GROUP OCCURS 1 TO 20 TIMES
                            DEPENDING ON NO-OF-INVOICES.
              05      INVOICE-NUMB       PIC X(4).
              05      DATE               PIC X(7).
            05      AMOUNT             PIC 9(5).
            05      OWING              PIC 9(5).
```

In the RECORD CONTAINS clause we see that the minimum record size is 108 characters, made up of the nonrepeating, or fixed format, portion of the record (87 characters) and a single repeating group of fields (21 characters). The maximum record size will be 87 + 20*21, or 507 characters, since a repeating group repeats at most 20 times. In the BLOCK CONTAINS clause we specify that the block size will be specified in the accompanying DD-statement, as explained in the previous section. We specify that this time there is only one type of buffer record, CI-BUFREC, with CI-REC as the corresponding WORKING-STORAGE record.

In both CI-BUFREC and CI-REC we have the item REPEATING-GROUP, which repeats a number of times equal to the value in NO-OF INVOICES. Thus the lengths of CI-BUFREC and CI-REC are variable.

To create the file we carefully construct each record in CI-REC. We first place the data describing a customer in the fields under CUSTOMERDATA. This data will likely be obtained from a record of a file such as CUSTOMER-MASTER (see Figure 4.4a in Chapter Four), which can be accomplished by execution of the following, if we provide for the matching of the relevant field formats:

```
READ CUSTOMER-MASTER INTO CUSTOMERDATA, AT END ...
```

We must next determine how many repeating groups are needed. This can be done by retrieving and counting the number of records with matching customer number in a version of an AR master file that is sorted on customer number. The number of repeating groups is then moved to NO-OF-INVOICES in CI-REC. This determines the size of the record.

We can now fill in the items REPEATING-GROUP(1), REPEATING-GROUP(2), and so on. The completed record is then written out with:

```
WRITE CI-BUFREC FROM CI-REC.
```

When the buffer record CI-BUFREC receives the WORKING-STORAGE record, its length adjusts according to the value in NO-OF-INVOICES. Thus creating the file is quite straightforward.

The DD-statement for the file has the same parts as in the previous case. The figures for the LRECL and BLKSIZE differ of course. Using the data given in the COBOL file specification above, we specify LRECL=511 and BLKSIZE=3070 if we want a block to be able to hold at most six of the largest possible records. This means that the maximum block size must be (6*(507 + 4) + 4), or 3,070 characters.

What happens as records are read is partly illustrated in Figure 5.5. The buffer record structure (CI-BUFREC) is mobile in the buffer and changes its length to accommodate each record encountered. It can do this because of the value NO-OF-INVOICES field in each record encountered; it happens automatically without the programmer having to worry about it. To give a specific COBOL example of reading such a file, suppose that we need a printout of the total amount each customer owes. The essential COBOL follows:

```
OPEN INPUT CUSTOMER-INVOICES.
MOVE "NO" TO EOF.
READ CUSTOMER-INVOICES INTO CI-REC,
     AT END PERFORM NO-RECORDS-PARAGRAPH.
PERFORM SCAN-FILE UNTIL EOF = "YES".
```

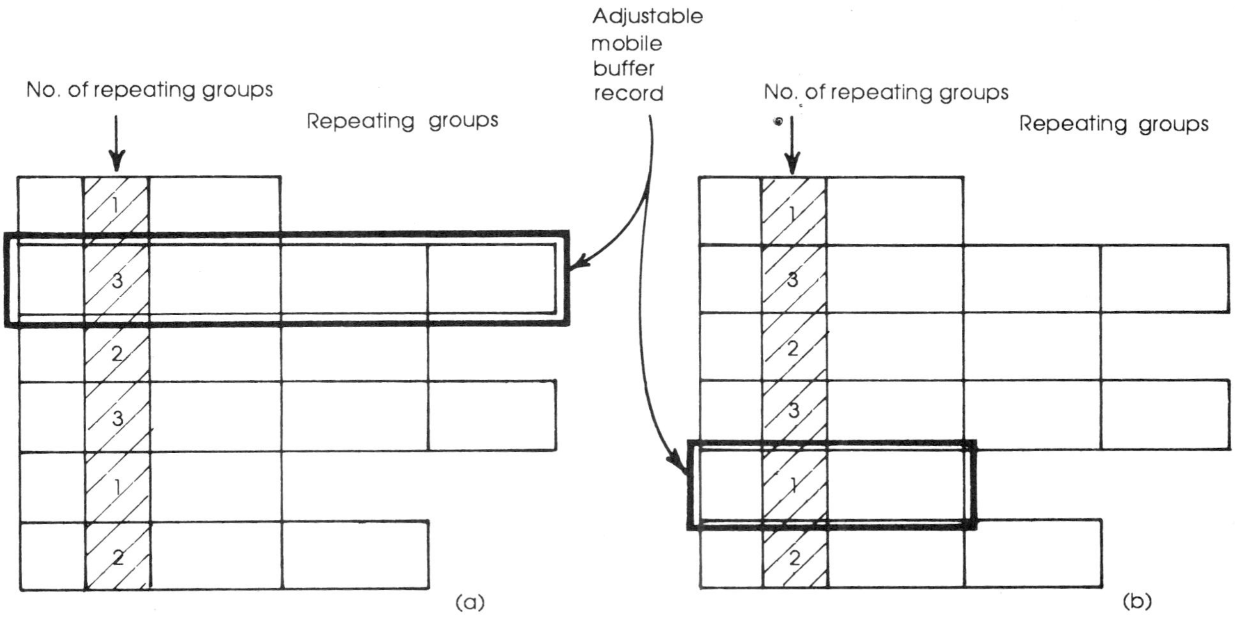

FIGURE 5.5 Illustration of how repeating group variable length records are read. Both buffers (a) and (b) show a buffer with a random collection of records with varying numbers of repeating groups (see also Figure 5.2). A single buffer record moves to the next record on execution of a READ command; the length of the buffer record adjusts to fit the length of the next record, the exact extent of the adjustment being determined by the field containing the number of repeating groups for that record.

```
        CLOSE CUSTOMER-INVOICES, STOP RUN.
SCAN-FILE.
        COMPUTE COUNT = 0,
        COMPUTE TOTAL-DEBT = 0.
        PERFORM COMPUTE-CUSTOMER-DEBT UNTIL
             COUNT = NO-OF-INVOICES IN CI-REC.
        DISPLAY CUSTNUMB IN CI-REC, TOTAL-DEBT.
        READ CUSTOMER-INVOICES INTO CI-REC,
             AT END MOVE "YES" TO EOF.
COMPUTE-CUSTOMER-DEBT.
        COMPUTE COUNT = COUNT + 1.
        COMPUTE TOTAL-DEBT = TOTAL-DEBT
                     + OWING IN REPEATING-GROUP(COUNT).
```

The READ statement causes the buffer record CI-BUFREC (not used above) to move to the next record in the buffer and to adjust to its length using the value in NO-OF-INVOICES. Then it causes the record to be transferred to the working-storage record CI-REC, which also adjusts its length using NO-OF-INVOICES. From then on it is merely a matter of summing the values in the OWING fields in the repeating groups using standard COBOL techniques for handling tables.

Some complications arise if updating a file like CUSTOMER-INVOICES involves either insertion or deletion of repeating groups. For example, if an invoice is paid up, the repeating group for that invoice needs to be deleted. Similarly if a new invoice is issued, a corresponding repeating group needs to be inserted. Unless insertions exactly match deletions, it will clearly not be possible to carry out such an updating without writing out a new version of the file. Two versions of CI-REC will then be needed working-storage. One of these is used to receive each record as it is read. If insertions or deletions are required, the new record is constructed in the second working-storage structure and written out (using WRITE, not REWRITE) as a record of the latest version of the file.

Processing Variable Field Lengths Files

Records of this type are processed in much the same way as records with repeating groups. Each character of the variable length field more or less corresponds to a repeating group; the number of characters in a particular record must appear in a field in the fixed part of the record. To see how this is done, suppose that we specify the COBOL file BOOK-FILE with the fields shown in Figure 5.3. We use the buffer and Working-storage records BOOK-BUFREC and BOOK-REC as follows:

```
DATA DIVISION.
FILE SECTION.
FD      BOOK-FILE
      RECORD CONTAINS 43 TO 142 CHARACTERS
      BLOCK CONTAINS 0 RECORDS
      LABEL RECORDS ARE STANDARD
      DATA RECORD IS BOOK-BUFREC.
01      BOOK-BUFREC.
      02  AUTHOR             PIC X(20).
      02  PUBLISHER          PIC X(20).
      02  FIELD-LENGTH       PIC S999 COMP-3.
      02  VARIABLE-AREA.
            05  BOOK-TITLE OCCURS 1 TO 100 TIMES
                       DEPENDING ON FIELD-LENGTH   PIC X(1).
WORKING-STORAGE SECTION.
01      BOOK-REC.
      02  ...
```

The buffer record BOOK-BUFREC and the Working-storage record BOOK-REC will have identical structures. Because of the OCCURS ... DEPENDING ON clause, the record structures adjust automatically to the length of the variable BOOK-TITLE field as contained in FIELD-LENGTH. Because of COBOL limitations, it is not possible to have two variable fields in a record. If AUTHOR also were variable, we would have to make a single field out of the fields AUTHOR and BOOK-TITLE, and use COBOL STRING and UNSTRING instructions to handle such a field (see a COBOL text).

SUMMARY

We have three types of variable length record files. They are mixed category, repeating group, and variable field length.

In mixed category files we have records that describe different categories of the same class of entity; for example, records that describe employees, stockholders, consultants, and auditors for the class of entity person. In such a file all records have a fixed part with a common format and a variable part with a variable format. When the file is being read, a field in the fixed part is used to indicate what category of record is being read by a READ command.

In repeating group files we have essentially a parent-to-child relationship between two types of entities, for example, customer and outstanding invoices. A record of the file describes the customer plus each of the outstanding invoices. A group of fields with the same format is used to describe each invoice; this group repeats for each invoice. The number of groups depends on the customer. In processing, a record is read by having a field (outside of the repeating group part of the record) that gives the number of repeating groups in the record.

In variable field length files we have a single field whose length can vary from one record to another. In processing, a record is read by having a field that gives the length of the variable length field.

Care must be taken with all variable length files when specifying the record and block sizes. With IBM systems a 4-byte record length field must be added to each record; further, a 4-byte block length field must be added to each block. Thus if r is the maximum record length and b is the blocking factor, then the maximum block size is $(b * (r + 4) + 4)$.

EXERCISES

1. In the logical records of a mixed category file, the fixed part is 50 bytes long and the maximum size of the variable part is 100 bytes. The minimum blocking factor is 10. What is (a) the maximum record length and (b) the maximum block size?
2. In the logical records of a repeating group file, the nonrepeating group portion is 100 bytes long and each repeating group is 20 bytes long. The minimum blocking factor is 5 and the maximum number of repeating groups is 10. What is (a) the maximum record length and (b) the maximum block size.
3. Write a program to create the file SHIPPING (used in this chapter). Data for the records is obtained from the files FREIGHTER and TANKER. Records of SHIPPING are written out in ascending SHIPNAME order.
4. Write a program to compute the volume of oil in oil tankers listed in the file SHIPPING (exercise 3).
5. Write a program to create the file CUSTOMER-INVOICES (described in this chapter). Data for the records is obtained from the files CUSTOMER and INVOICES.
6. Write a program to list the customers in CUSTOMER-INVOICES (exercise 5) who owe more than $10,000 on all their outstanding invoices taken together.
7. Write a program to create the file BOOK-FILE (described in this chapter). Data for the file should be taken from a fixed length record version of the file (called BOOK-FIXED), in which the BOOK-TITLE field is simply long enough to hold the longest title (say 200 bytes).
8. Write a program to process the file BOOK-FILE (exercise 7). The program simply prints the titles of all books by an author whose name is entered at the terminal.

6 INDEXED-SEQUENTIAL FILE PROCESSING

Sequential file processing is the most common type of file processing and normally is efficient, given the speed of disk and tape mechanisms. However, as pointed out in chapter 4, sequential file processing is not efficient for updating when the hit rate is very low. In other words if the updating involves only one record out of a thousand, we have to read (and probably also write) one thousand records on average for each one that needs to be processed.

It is clear that files permitting both conventional sequential access and direct access would be very useful. The sequential access feature could be used to permit sequential processing in the same manner as for conventional sequential files, whereas the direct access feature would permit the updating of only those records that needed updating when the hit rate was very low. In addition the direct access feature could be used to obtain information from just a few records without the need for reading the entire file.

For a record to be accessed directly, either the disk address of the record (in terms of cylinder number, track number, and block or sector number) must be available to the access method, or the access method must have a way of obtaining the disk address from some given value (such as a record key) that uniquely identifies the record. With what are known as *hash files* the correct disk address of a record must be presented to the access method. We look at this type of file in chapter 8. With **indexed-sequential files** we simply present a unique record key to the access method. This key is then used by the access method to uncover the disk address; to do this it uses an **index**. This explains the term *indexed-sequential file*.

There are two major types of indexed-sequential files in use. To be able to understand the difference, we must carefully examine the basic ideas behind them, and then look at IBM's ISAM and VSAM, which are the most common examples of the two types of indexed-sequential files. Then we shall look at the COBOL processing of indexed-sequential files and the broader implications of such processing.

BASIC IDEAS

Suppose that we have a rather large file called COMPANIES, each record of which describes a unique public corporation. The file could be for investment purposes or could be a file of customers for a widely used product. Each record is uniquely identified by the COMPNAME (company name) field; other fields are total assets, percentage of long-term debt, return on assets, profit margin, type of business, and so on, although for the purpose of the following discussion these nonkey fields need little concern us. The file is a sequential file, with the records ordered in ascending COMPNAME order.

Because of the large number of firms listed in the file, every day new information appears about the firms. There will be a daily list of bankruptcies; bankrupt companies will be deleted from the file; there will be a daily list of new public companies that will need to be added; there will be a list of firms for which changes will need to be made to nonkey fields. Nevertheless on any given day the total number of deletions, insertions, and changes to records will be a small fraction of the total number of records in the file, probably about 0.1 percent.

Such updating cannot be efficiently carried out using sequential processing. Despite the need to affect only about 0.1 percent of the file each day, sequential processing will require reading of all records and writing out all records (minus deletions but plus inserted records) into a new file. Nevertheless there will be many occasions when conventional sequential processing is both needed and efficient. At certain times of the year many corporate earnings reports will be issued; the necessary update to COMPANIES will involve a very high hit rate. There may be a frequent need for sequential searches through the file; for example, we may want to have a list of those firms, in ascending company name order, in a given line of business and with a profit margin exceeding 20 percent, since such companies might be targets for marketing a new product.

It is clear that the file COMPANIES is one where we have a need for both conventional sequential processing and direct access processing. Consider carefully what is involved in converting COMPANIES from a sequential file to one that can also be processed by direct access. Suppose that the blocking factor is 2. (A higher blocking factor makes no difference to the ideas we are pursuing, although it makes diagrams less convenient.) The beginning records for the files are shown in Figure 6.1 using this blocking factor. The file is on disk and starts at disk address cylinder 50, track 0, block 0. We show only the company names, using 3-character names for purposes of abbreviation only. We further assume that a track can have 4 blocks and that a cylinder contains 4 tracks.

It is clear that the file can be processed sequentially, since all sequential files are processed in ascending block number, track number, and cylinder order. In addition if we have an access method that retrieves the block at a given address, we then have some form of direct access. Thus in theory we can imagine the following COBOL command:

```
READ COMPANIES INTO COMPANY-RECORD DISK-ADDRESS (51,2,3)
```

The first time this is executed the first record of block 3 on track 2 of cylinder 51 is placed in the Working-Storage structure COMPANY-RECORD. Actually such a COBOL command is not available, but something close to it can be used with assembly language. Thus such a command can be carried out in system programs, such as the access method.

Unfortunately with a large file we are not likely to know beforehand which records are at a given address. For example, we may want to retrieve the record for the company called CAB. Thus if the direct access retrieval command available to the access method is like the READ command above, there must be a way for the access method to determine the disk address for CAB, for the proper READ command to be issued. A simple method is to keep a separate sequential file, each record of which lists a key value from the original file COMPANIES together with the address of that record. Such an auxiliary file is called a **dense index**. The term *dense* is used because there is an entry (or record) in the index (file) for every record in the original file. Thus our dense index can have the following entries:

```
KEY          ADDRESS
AAB          50  0  0
AAK          50  0  0
AAX          50  0  1
ABA          50  0  1
ABF          50  0  2
ABQ          50  0  2
ABW          50  0  3
ACB          50  0  3
ACE          50  1  0
ACK          50  1  0
ACM          50  1  1
 .              .
 .              .
 .              .
```

As shown, an address is composed of (left to right) cylinder number, track number, and block number. Now if we want to retrieve from the file COMPANIES a record with key value ACE, we use a program or subprogram to scan our dense index and recover the address for ACE,

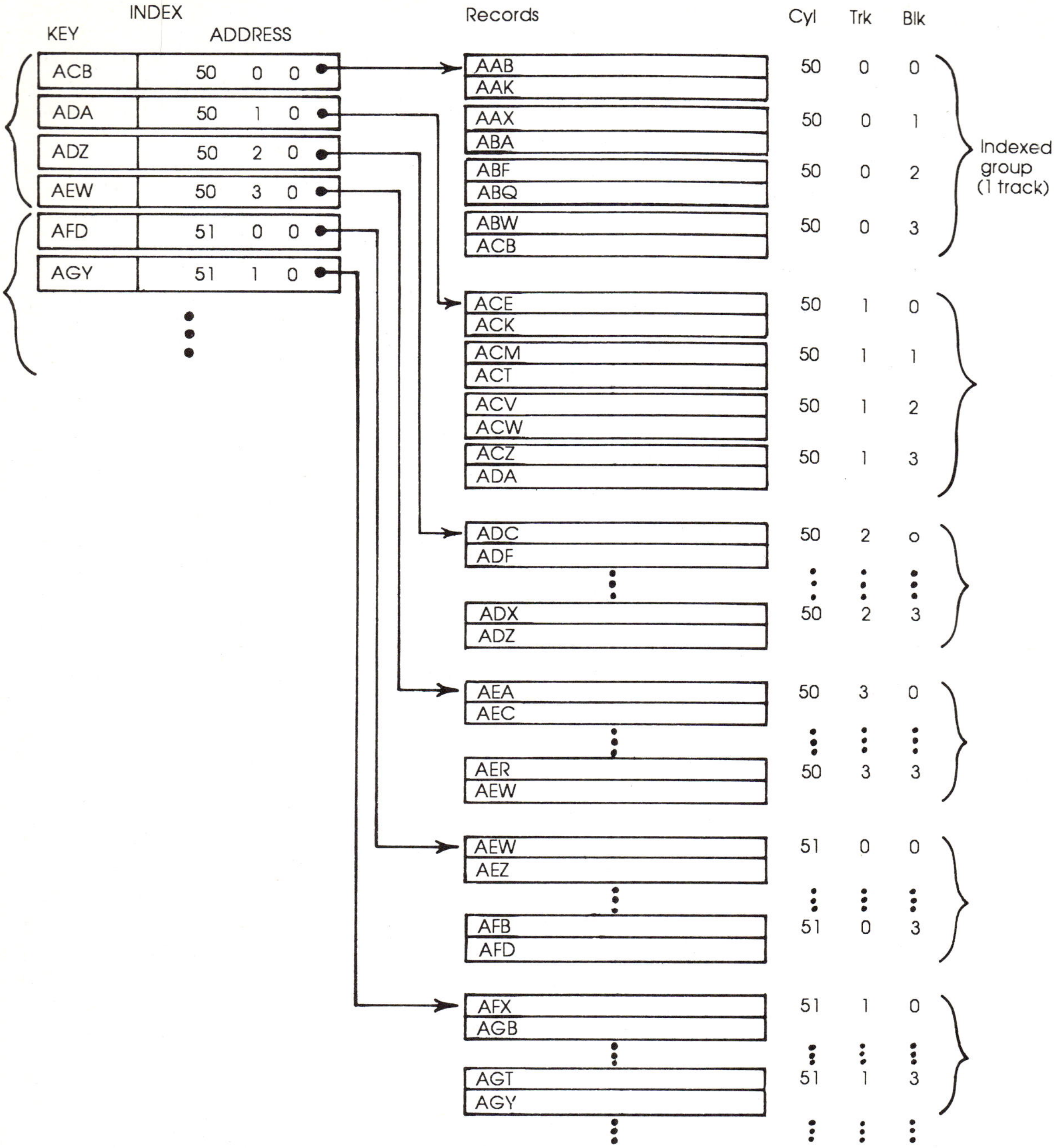

FIGURE 6.1 Showing the construction of a one-level sparse index for the file COMPANIES. There is an entry (record) in the index for every 4 blocks or 8 records of the file, that is, for the records on a track. Thus COMPANIES is divided into indexed groups of records. The index entry for a group contains the key of the last record of the group.

in this case 50 1 0. The program then issues a READ command, like the one discussed above, to retrieve the first record in block 0 of track 1 of cylinder 50. (If this record does not contain the required key value ACE, the READ command would be issued again and the second record in the same block retrieved.)

Thus a dense index enables us to access COMPANIES directly, given the key value of a required record. However, most readers will probably see that there is not a great advantage to the method we described; after all, there will be as many records in the index as in COMPANIES. And since we have to scan through the index records looking for a match with ACE, we might as well have scanned through the records of COMPANIES looking for a match. This criticism is valid—an improvement is to use a one-level **sparse index**, which is basic to indexed-sequential files and needs to be considered carefully.

One-Level Sparse Index

A **one-level sparse index** is shown in Figure 6.1 for the beginning portion of the file COMPANIES. The basic idea is that there should be an entry in the index (that is, a record in the index file) only for each group of records in COMPANIES. In Figure 6.1 we have arbitrarily chosen a group of 8 records. Generally a group of records is chosen that exactly fills a track, although this is not strictly necessary. The structure of an index entry is different from the trivial case of a dense index. For each group of records for which there is an index entry—that is, for each **indexed group of records**—we enter the key of the *last record* of the group and the disk address of the *first record* of the group. Following is a description of how an index is used.

Suppose we want to directly retrieve the record for the company called ACM. Our access program or subprogram scans through the index entries until it goes just too far—that is, until it comes to an entry with a key value immediately greater than that for the target record key ACM. In Figure 6.1 that is the entry for ADA. The address of the group of records containing the target record must therefore be 50 1 0. We can then read each block on track 1 of cylinder 50 in turn, until we come to the block (in this case block 1) with the required record.

In the diagram the blocking factor is only 2. In practice it will likely be a lot more than that. Nevertheless if count-key data blocks are used, it will help the scan of the track containing the target record. As each block of the track passes the read head, the controller can examine the key subblock. The first time a key value greater or equal to the target key is encountered in the key subblock, the controller reads the subsequent data subblock into the buffer.

Thus the basic method involves scanning the index until we find the address of the group of records, or track of records, containing the target record. Then the track is scanned, with the controller checking the key subblock of the blocks encountered, until a block containing the required record is found. This block will be the first encountered, with the last record having a key value greater or equal to the target key value.

Of course we would not be very interested in writing a program ourselves that involved instructing the disk controller to inspect the key subblocks of count-key data blocks. However, programs for doing this can be supplied by the manufacturer of the computer. In the case of IBM systems the access method passes commands to the operating system which causes execution of a channel program that directs the activities of the disk controller.

Thus we apparently have a feasible method for direct access based on presentation of a target record key. Unfortunately there is still a snag. Our sparse index will clearly be much smaller than the dense index discussed earlier. If we typically have about 25 records on a track, that would mean an index entry for every 25 records. Thus if we had 100,000 records in the COMPANIES file we would need 4,000 entries in the index; a big file of one million records would require 40,000 index entries. Thus the snag is time taken to search through the one-level sparse index to match the target key. The situation will be nowhere near as bad as with a dense index but it will still be serious with large files. The solution is the **multiple-level sparse index.**

Multiple-Level Sparse Indexes

A **multiple-level sparse index** can be two-level, three-level, and so on. We concentrate on a two-level index as this is sufficient to explain the principles involved. Essentially with a two-level index, in addition to the one-level sparse index to the file COMPANIES (as illustrated in Figure 6.1), we have another sparse index to the original one-level index.

To make it easier to search the first, or lower, level of the index, the index entries are grouped. Typically the entries of such a group are those that cover an entire cylinder of records from the original COMPANIES file. For each such group of first-level index entries there is a single entry in the second level of the index. This entry contains the key of the last entry of the group of entries and the disk address of the first entry of that same group of entries. Thus the second level

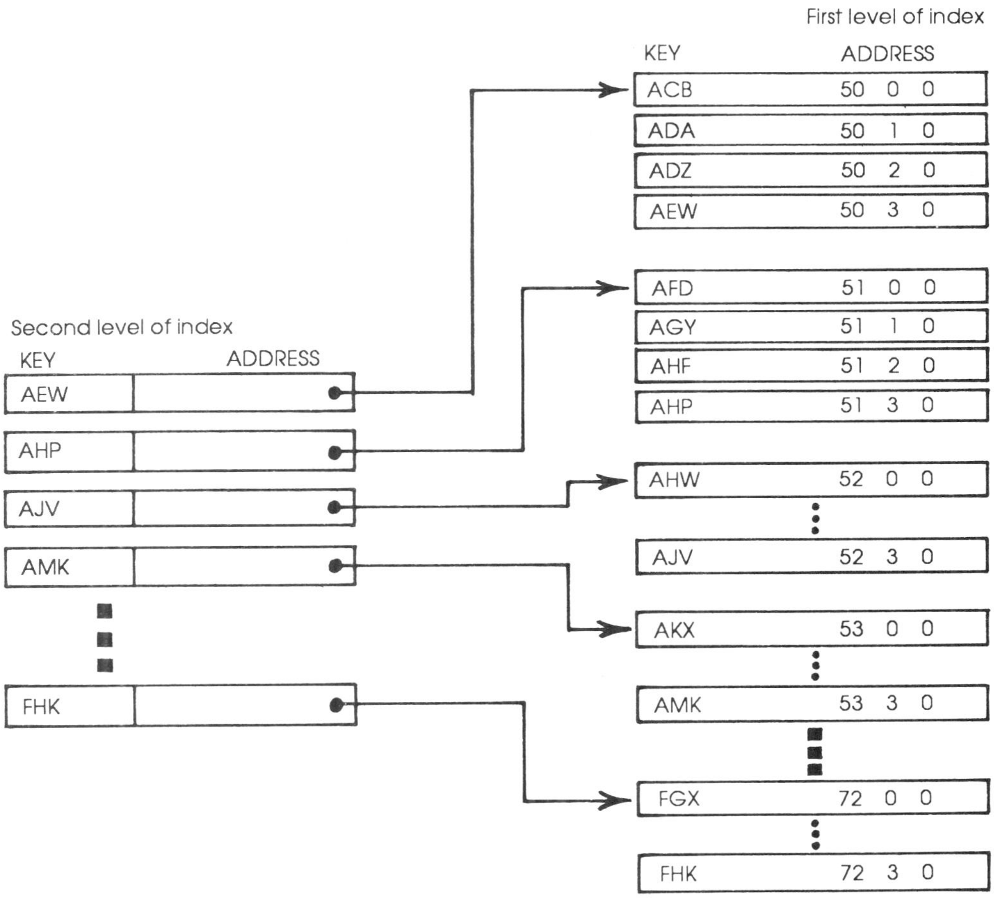

FIGURE 6.2 Structure of a 2-level index (or multiple-level index with two levels). At the first level of the index each entry is for a group (or indexed group) of records that takes up a single track. At the second level each entry is for a group of entries at the first level. Such a group of entries at the first level is normally for all the records on a single cylinder of the original file (as shown in Figure 6.1).

is a sparse index to the first level and the first level is a sparse index to the file of data. We have not shown the actual disk address values for the second level of the index and have used arrows to point to the lower-level entries addressed. It is for this reason that fields containing disk addresses are often called **pointers**.

To see how the index facilitates direct access on the basis of a record key, suppose that we need to retrieve the record in COMPANIES (see Figure 6.1) with key AGT. The following sequence must take place:

a. Search of second level of index.
   i. The second-level entries (Figure 6.2) are examined sequentially in ascending KEY order. The search ends when the first KEY value greater or equal to the target key value is found.
   ii. The second-level entry at the end of the search is re-trieved and the address value extracted. This is the entry with KEY value AHP.

b. Search of first level of the index.
   i. The entry for the first level of the index, whose address was retrieved above, is now retrieved. This is the entry for KEY value AFD. Beginning with this entry, the first level of the index is now searched, until we encounter a KEY value greater or equal to the target key value. This KEY value turns out to be AGY.
   ii. This first-level index entry with KEY value is re-trieved. It contains the ADDRESS value 51 1 0.

c. Search of file COMPANIES. The first block on track 1 of cylinder 51 is examined, and then the next block, until a block is encountered with a last record key value greater than the target key value. This turns out to be the last block on the track, which is then retrieved. The disk controller can examine the block keys without actually retrieving the block, since the key of the last record in any block is available for inspection in the key subblock of a count-key data block.

The search procedure is rather long, it is true, but the number of accesses to the index is much reduced compared to the case of a one-level index. With a search of a two-level index, we must begin with a sequential search of the second level, and on average we have to go through half of the entries. But the number of entries in the second level will only be a few percent of the number at the first level, so that the second level will require relatively few accesses. The search at the first level then involves only the entries for the tracks of a single cylinder, again a relatively small number. Thus a two-level index will require fewer accesses to the index than a one-level index.

In a similar fashion a three-level index will require fewer index accesses to search than a two-level index, and so on. Referring again to the two-level index in Figure 6.2, it is clear that a third level would be constructed as a sparse index to the second level, and so on. At each higher level the number of entries required for the level will be only a few percent of the number required for the lower level. Eventually if we have a high enough number of levels, the number of entries in the top level will be no more than a few.

It does not take many index levels for the top level to contain very few entries. Suppose that COMPANIES had 500,000 records with 100 records per track. The first level could easily have about 500,000/100 or 5,000 entries; the second level could have 5,000/20 or 250 entries; finally the third could have 250/25 or 10 entries. It is clear that the sequential search of this third or top level would be very fast indeed. In practice, because the top levels of an index contain very few entries, these are kept in main memory during processing of the file, so that disk accesses are not needed to access them. The larger lower levels of the index are normally on disk. However, entries for these levels are blocked, just like blocked records; therefore when a lower level is being searched following a search of a higher level, never more than one block of entries need be read. Thus it is possible to search an index in a few disk accesses for a file with hundreds of thousands of records.

Requirements for Creating an Indexed-Sequential File

Later in this chapter we shall examine in some detail the basic COBOL programming needed for creating an indexed-sequential file. For the moment, readers should understand that an index-sequential file processing program does not contain details either of the code necessary to create the index or to search and maintain the index. This is managed by the access method behind the scenes, so to speak. More technically we can say that index creation, searching, and maintenance are **transparent** to the program.

To create the file, the records are written out in sequence much as if a tape file were being created. The major difference is that the record keys must be unique and they must be written out in ascending order. (Duplicate or out-of-sequence keys will cause an errors.) As the records are written out with ordinary COBOL WRITE commands, the access method manages the creation of the index.

Thus it should be clearly understood that an indexed sequential file is a sequential file whose records are always maintained in ascending key order, and for which an index is available to permit direct access to any record on presentation of the record's key value. Once created, an indexed-sequential file can be read and updated sequentially, much as an ordinary sequential file on disk. But in addition, records can be read and updated by direct access using record key values. We shall see examples of how this is done later, using COBOL.

Record Insertions and the Two Major Types of Indexed-Sequential Files

Recall from our study of disk sequential files that record insertions are something of a nuisance. When updating a sequential disk file, it is possible to manage changes to field values (apart from changes to key values) without the need to create a new updated file elsewhere. Even with deletions it is possible to mark a record as deleted simply by changing a field value included in the record to serve as a valid/deleted record marker. However, an insertion normally makes the creation of a new file necessary, since there normally is no space in the old file to accommodate a new record.

Since an indexed-sequential file is primarily a sequential disk file, it is clear that it will cause a similar difficulty with record insertions. If we use the method of creating a new version of the file to accommodate insertion updating, we must create a new index as well. This may not sound so bad, but remember that indexed-sequential files can be updated by direct access. Are we to create a new file and accompanying index every time the file is opened for direct update and a few insertions take place? Clearly not—some other solution must be found.

Two solutions are common. One involves separate overflow areas and overflow chains or linked lists. The other involves splitting an indexed group of records whenever an insertion must be made into the group and there is no room. The overflow method is incorporated into IBM's ISAM (indexed-sequential access method) files; the indexed group splitting method is incorporated into IBM's VSAM (virtual sequential access method) indexed-sequential files. (VSAM has nothing to do with virtual storage as explained in chapter 2, except that the access method is very large and can be used only with virtual operating systems.)

FIGURE 6.3 (opposite) Organization of an ISAM indexed-sequential file, where the track index, prime data area, and overflow tracks occupy 12 cylinders. It is also possible to have a separate overflow area (not shown). Each track index entry has an additional component (not shown) that handles records overflowing from tracks.

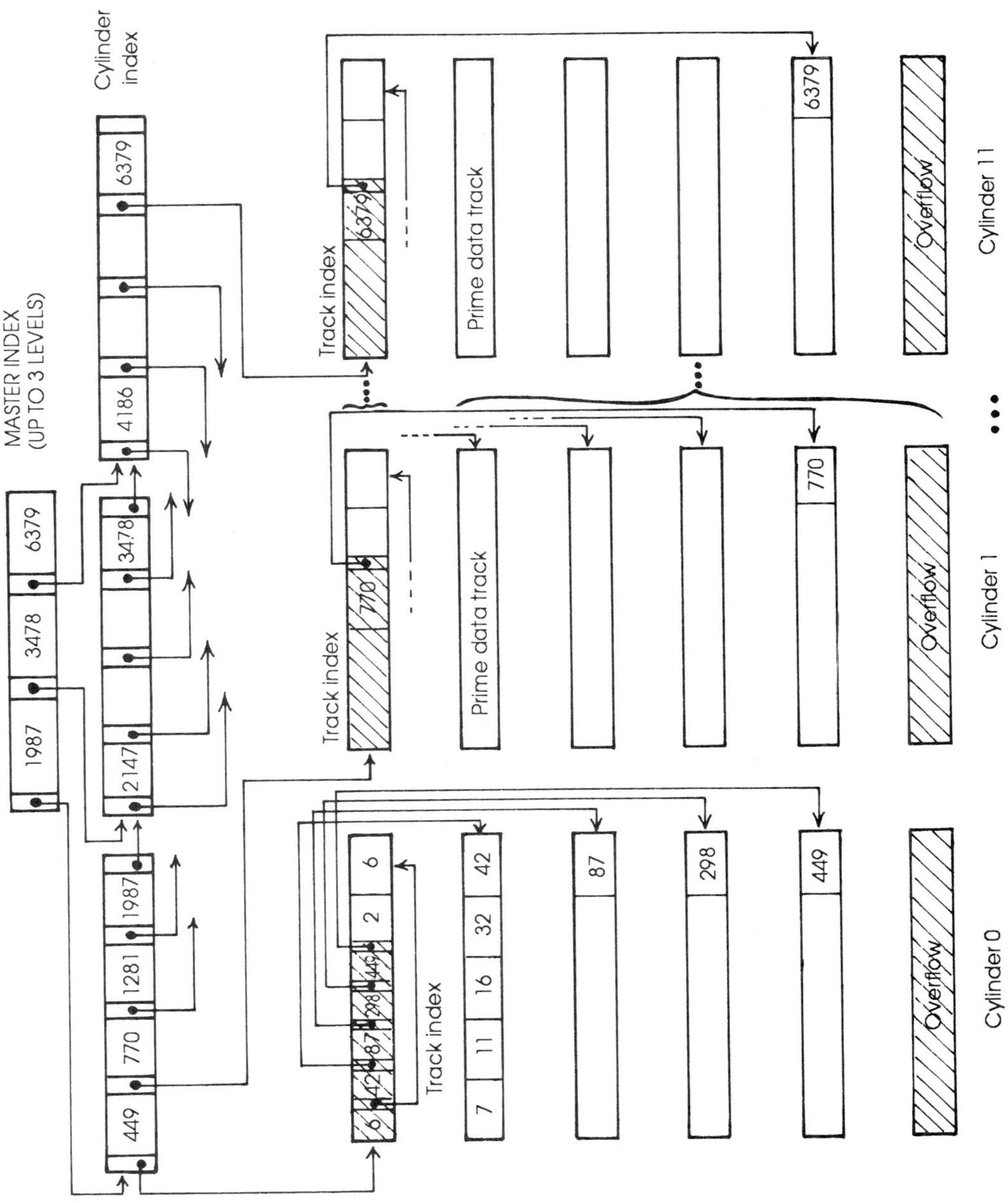
MASTER INDEX
(UP TO 3 LEVELS)
1987
3478
6379
Cylinder index
449
770
1281
1987
2147
3478
4186
6379
Track index
6
42
87
298
449
2
6
7
11
16
32
42
87
298
449
Overflow
Cylinder 0
Track index
770
Prime data track
770
Overflow
Cylinder 1
Track index
6379
Prime data track
6379
Overflow
Cylinder 11

ISAM and VSAM Indexed-Sequential Files

The two different methods for solving the problem of inserted records gave rise to the two major types of indexed- sequential files in common use. Rather than study these two methods in abstract terms, it is more instructive to study ISAM and VSAM. ISAM was the first to be introduced; VSAM came later and performs considerably better. Because VSAM is much more sophisticated than ISAM, and because it incorporates many other useful features (such as seondary key facilities, to be described in Chapter 7), VSAM costs more than ISAM. ISAM is rarely used in new applications anymore and has been largely replaced by VSAM. Nevertheless ISAM is still in wide use with older application programs; therefore it is still useful to study it.

ISAM FILES

In Figure 6.3 we have an overview of an ISAM file that takes up 12 cylinders. The records have keys with values 2, 6, 7, 11, . . . 6379 in ascending sequence. Each cylinder of the file contains a **track index** on track 0, a **prime data area** containing records from the file, and an **overflow area**, usually the last one or two tracks. In addition to these indexes, there are also a **cylinder** and **higher level indexes**.

An indexed group of records is a track; for a given cylinder the collection of entries for the tracks is the track index (track 0). If we refer to cylinder 0 in Figure 6.3, the last record on track 2 has key value 87. Thus there will be an entry in the track index containing key value 87 and the address (or pointer to) track 2. A small detail with ISAM files is that the track index on track 0 does not usually take up the complete track, so that there is room for some records on the remainder of the track. Thus the first track index entry on track 0 of cylinder 0 in Figure 6.3 is for the highest key value on track 0, which is 2. Note that the collection of track indexes for an ISAM file corresponds to the level 1 index.

Management of Record Insertions with ISAM

We mentioned that each cylinder of an ISAM file normally has one or more overflow tracks. However, the use of these tracks is not obvious

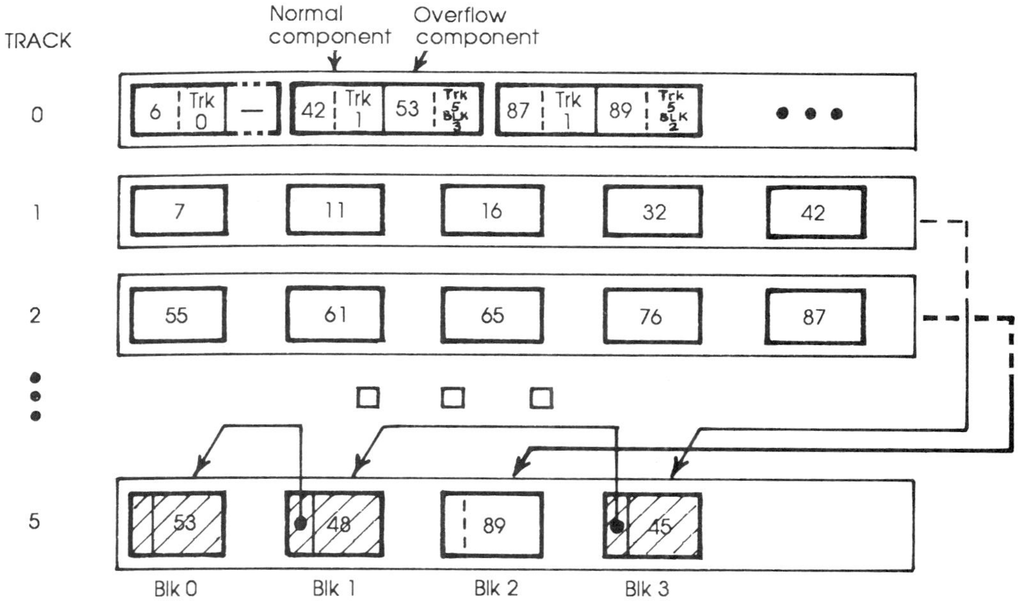

FIGURE 6.4 Detail from a typical ISAM cylinder. Each entry in the track index has two components; A normal component for the track indexed and an overflow component for records overflowing from the track indexed. In the entry for track 1, the normal component contains key 42, the highest key on track 1; however, the overflow component contains 53, the highest key of the overflow chain belonging to track 1. In addition the overflow component contains a pointer to the first record of the overflow chain, which is block 3 of track 5. Records in an overflow chain have blocking factor unity. Chains from different tracks are interwoven on the overflow tracks. If the overflow tracks for a cylinder become full, the chains can continue in a separate overflow area, which can take overflow records from all cylinders.

from the diagram in Figure 6.3. Essentially the overflow tracks of a cylinder are used to collect records overflowing from the prime data tracks of that cylinder. Overflow records arise because of record insertions.

To show the connection between record insertion and ISAM overflow records, we must look at a more detailed picture of a typical ISAM cylinder. We have therefore taken the cylinder 0 from Figure 6.3 and added a few details (see Figure 6.4). On the overflow track there are two chains of overflow records. One of these chains contains the records with keys 45, 48, and 53. The other has a single record with key 89. The long chain contains records that would be on track 1 if there were room for them; the record in the sort overflow chain belongs on track 2.

Notice that the overflow chains on track 5 in Figure 6.4 enable the records of the file to be read in ascending record key order. If we are reading the file sequentially we begin with track 0 and read records with keys 1 and 2 (Figure 6.3). Then we read the records on track 1 with keys 7, 11, 16, 36, 42; but then we continue with the overflow chain for track 1 and read the records with keys 45, 48, 53.. We then continue with the records on track 2, with keys 55, 61, 65, 76, 87, 89, and so on.

Note is made in each track index entry of any overflow records that belong to a track. Each track index entry is made up of a normal component and an overflow component. The normal component merely contains the key of the last record on a track together with the address of, or number of (pointer to), that track. The overflow component contains the key of the last record of the overflow chain for that track (53 in the case of track 1) together with the address of the first record of the overflow chain; in the case of track 1 this address must be block 3 on track 5. This means that the system takes overflow records into account when searching the index.

Suppose that the overflow record with key 48 is being sought. Following a search of the higher levels of the index, the search comes down to the track index for cylinder 0 (Figure 6.4). The track index entries are checked until a key with a value greater than or equal to the target key is encountered. Thus the overflow component of an index entry, namely, that with key 53 and address track 5 block 3, is retrieved. The system then follows the overflow chain that begins at block 3; eventually the target record is found. Each block on an overflow track contains a single record and the address of (or pointer to) the block containing the next overflow record of the overflow chain. Such a chain of records is also technically referred to as a **linked list**.

The Formation of ISAM Overflow Chains

Readers may have gained the impression that an inserted record that belongs on a given track automatically is placed in the overflow chain for that track. A moment's reflection will show that this cannot always be so, for ascending order of the record keys must always be maintained. If an inserted record belongs in the middle of a given track because of its key value, that is where it must be inserted. To make room for the new record, records already on the track with higher key values must be moved up; typically the last record on the track is *pushed off*

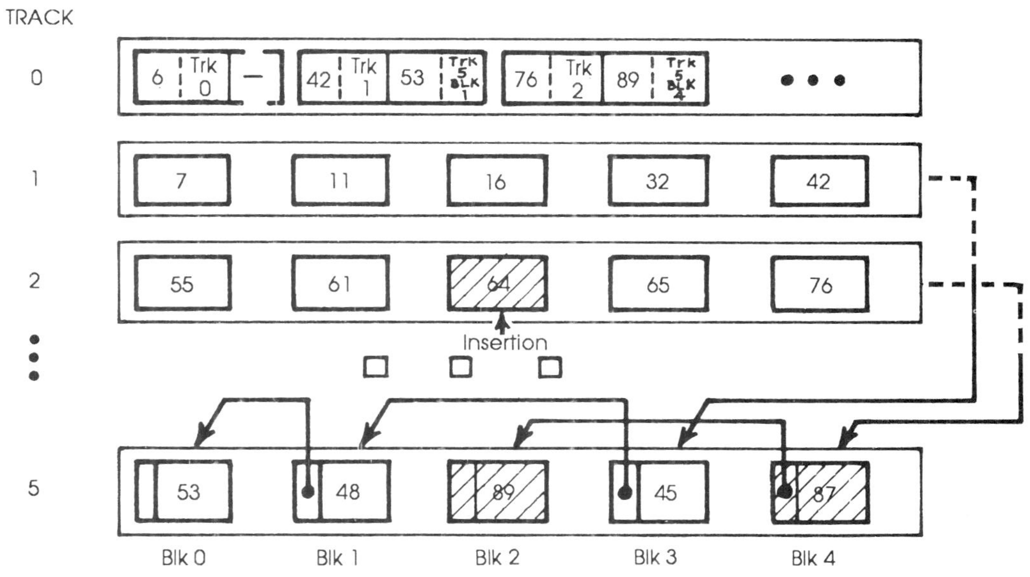

FIGURE 6.5 Showing the effect of inserting record 64 on track 2. The above diagram should be compared with Figure 6.4. To keep records in ascending key order, the insertion of record 64 pushes records up, or towards, the end of the track. This pushes the last record on the track into the overflow area for that track. Thus record 87 goes to the end of overflow track 5 but to the beginning of the overflow chain for track 2. Both the normal and overflow components of the track index entry for track 2 must be updated. The normal component is updated to reflect the new highest key on track 2, whereas the overflow component is updated to reflect the position of the start of the overflow chain.

and placed in the overflow area at the beginning of the overflow chain for that track.

The growth of overflow chains is illustrated in Figure 6.5. This shows what happens to the cylinder in Figure 6.4 after a record with key 64 is inserted. (Note that because insertion is always by means of direct access, the system first searches the index to find the track to which the record belongs.) The record belongs on track 2, and the records with keys 65, 76, and 87 are pushed up (pushed to the *right*) to make room. Therefore the record with key 87 will literally be pushed off the track and be placed at the end of the group of records on the overflow track. However, despite this physical placement at the end

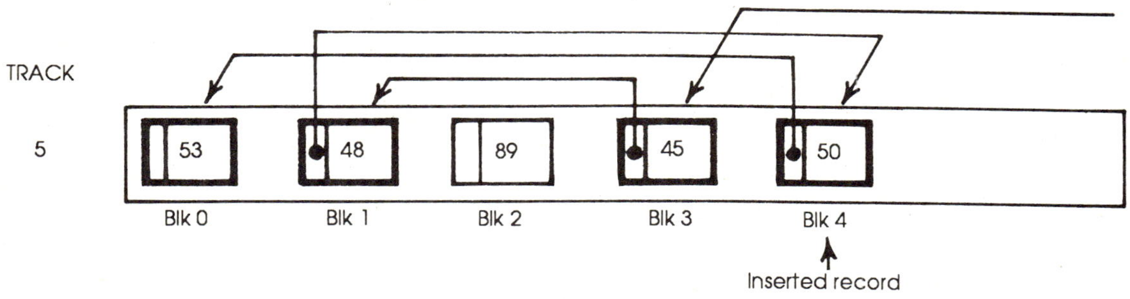

FIGURE 6.6. Illustration of the effect of inserting record 50 into the file shown in Figure 6.4. Record 50 must be inserted directly into the overflow chain in order that sequential order be maintained. However, the record is physically placed on the overflow track in the next available space, typically towards the end of the track. The pointer fields are simply adjusted as shown above to accommodate this. No change to the track index is required for this type of insertion.

of the overflow *track*, record 87 is also placed at the beginning of the overflow *chain* for track 2. In addition, the overflow component of the index must be changed to allow for the new address of the start of the chain. It is thus changed from track 5 block 2 to track 5 block 4.

Sometimes a record must be inserted into the middle of an overflow chain, without any moving up of records on the prime data track. For example, if record 50 (in Figure 6.4) is inserted, it would go straight into the overflow chain for track 1. Physically it would have to be placed at the end of the overflow track, although the pointer in the overflow chain would have to be adjusted to reflect the record's position in the overflow chain (see Figure 6.6).

When a record is deleted, the system places a deletion mark (the COBOL literal HIGH-VALUES, that is, the byte with bits '11111111') in the first character of the record. Thus the record will still be intact on the track following deletion, especially if the first byte of the record is a one-character field that is used only to indicate whether or not the record is deleted. Note that deleted records can be moved up along with valid records when a record is inserted into a track. Refer back to Figures 6.4 and 6.5 where we show what happens when record 64 is inserted; if record 76 were a deleted record, the moving up caused by record 64 insertion would still cause record 87 to move to the overflow area; deleted record 76 would move up to the end of the track. If record 68 were now inserted, only now would deleted record 76 be knocked off the end of the track; however, the deleted record is not moved to the overflow area, but is physically removed from the file.

Thus we see that with deleted records at the ends of tracks in the prime data area, record insertions on the tracks *will not give rise to an increase in the lengths of the overflow chains.* If the deleted records are distributed along the tracks, insertions will usually cause valid records to be knocked off the track ends into the overflow area. Only if an inserted record belongs exactly at the place where there is already a deleted record, will the insertion involve the occupation of the space taken up by the deleted record.

ISAM Performance

A useful measure of the performance of a direct access file is its average search length. This is defined as the average number of disk accesses required to retrieve a single record by direct access. Clearly the ideal average search length is unity, although this is rarely reached in practice. Immediately after creation of an ISAM file there are overflow records. Thus retrieval of a record by direct access requires a search of the index and access to the track containing the record. Sophisticated channel programs direct the disk controller during index searching to minimize seeks. In addition with a large file the master index is normally in main memory, so that it can be searched in negligible time compared with cylinder and track index searches. The result is that the average search length is about three disk accesses, two accesses being needed to search the index. This is about as good as one can expect with an indexed sequential file.

Unfortunately as time goes on and the file is subject to insertions, the overflow chains grow in length. Again ISAM brings sophisticated channel programs into action to direct the disk controller so that the number of disk accesses required to search an overflow chain is minimized. Thus it will normally require considerably less than seven disk accesses to search the full length of a 7-record chain. Nevertheless the increased number of accesses required to search the overflow chains causes the average search length to increase, so that file performance gradually deteriorates. The solution is periodic file reorganizations.

ISAM File Reorganization

Reorganizing an ISAM file is simple in principle. The aim is to eliminate all records from the overflow areas, so that average search length becomes once more the result only of accesses to search the index and the access to read prime data from a track. The file is opened for sequential output and the records read one by one in the order of ascending key value. As each record is read from the old low performance ISAM file, it is written out again as a record of a new ISAM file. Records written into the new ISAM file are placed only in the prime data area; deleted records on prime data tracks of the old file are not written out. Thus ISAM file reorganization is essentially a copying operation; a utility program is available for this purpose.

Delay of ISAM File Performance Deterioration

We mentioned earlier that if there is a deleted record at the end of a track, an insertion on that track causes the deleted record to be knocked off, but does not give rise to a new overflow record. It follows that when an ISAM file is first created, if we arrange for a number of dummy or deleted records at the end of each track, then it is possible to have many record insertions without corresponding additions to the overflow area. Creation of an ISAM file with end of track dummies will result in a best case average search length for quite a long time, if the number of dummies is sufficient to take care of the insertions; this method is recommended where speed of direct access is very important. Unfortunately the loading program for the file with dummies is specific for the type of disk used, since the number of blocks that can fit on a track varies from one disk to another. (A further complication is that track 0 for each cylinder contains a track index; only a portion of that track is available for records, whether valid or dummy.)

VSAM FILES

In Figure 6.7 we have an overview of a VSAM file. Although the file is made up of disk tracks and cylinders (as is an ISAM file), these units are not necessarily used to form natural groupings of records for purposes of indexing. Nevertheless it is convenient to imagine the file as having *logical cylinders and tracks*, which are merely groupings of

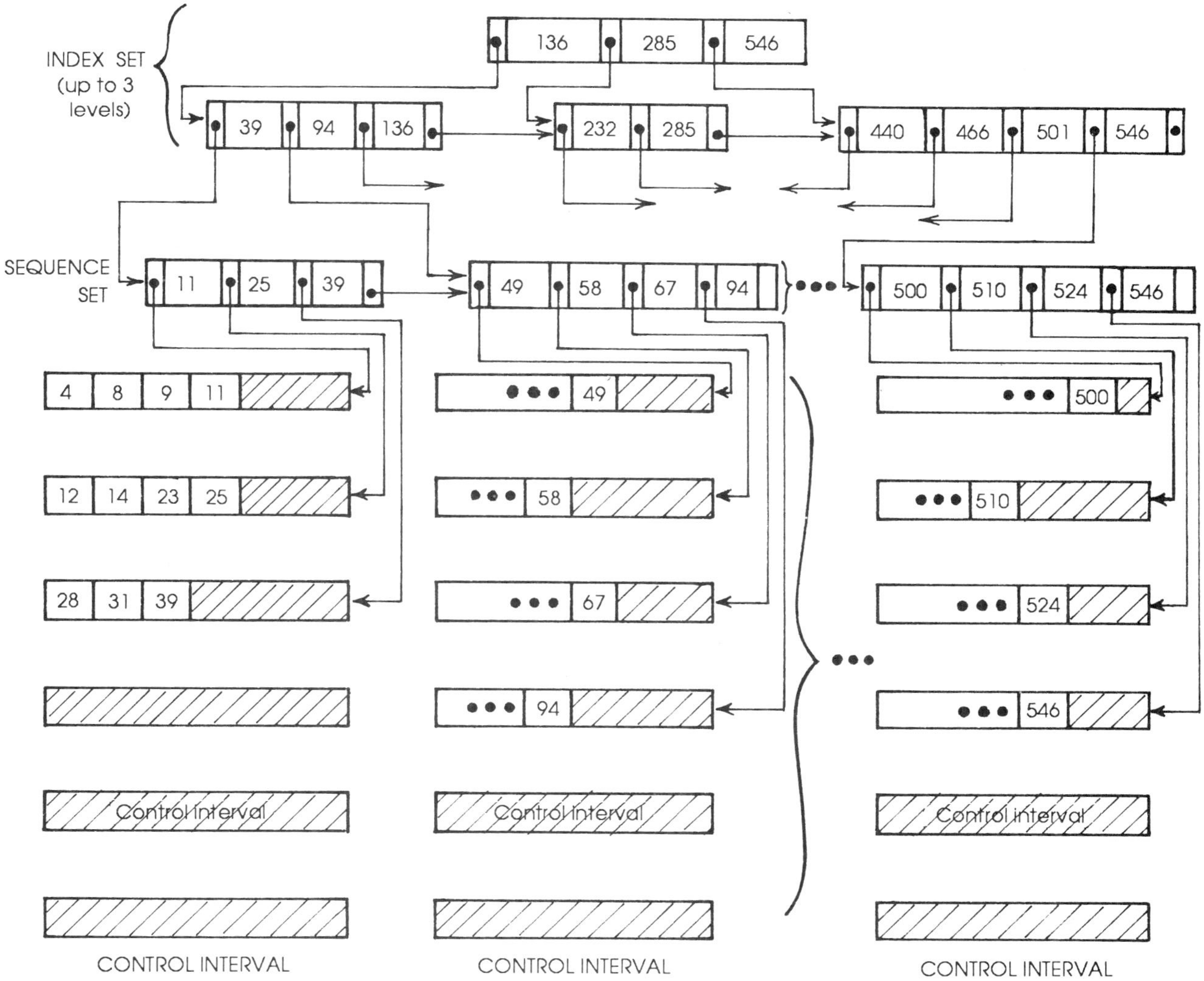

FIGURE 6.7. Structure of a VSAM indexed-sequential file. Records (numbered) are held in control intervals, which need not be full. Unused control interval space is shown shaded. A group of control intervals makes up a control area.

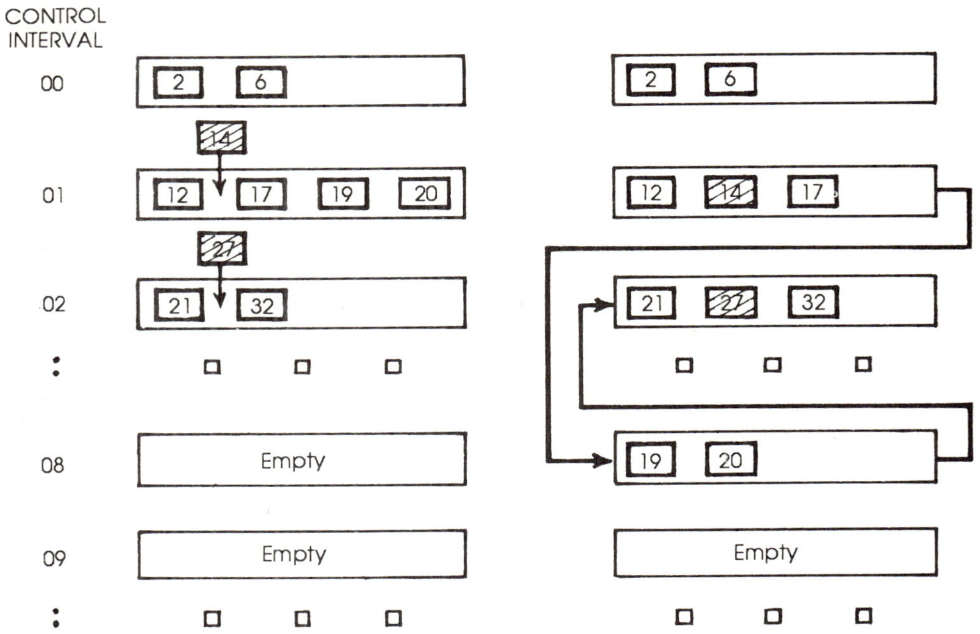

FIGURE 6.8. The diagram shows some control intervals of a VSAM indexed-sequentail file just before (on left) and just after (on right) insertion of the records with keys 14 and 27. Because there is space in control interval 02, record 27 can be inserted by moving records up. There is no space in control interval 01 for record 14, so that this control interval is split, using an empty control interval. A pointer chain maintains records in ascending key order following a split.

space for records that more or less correspond to the physical cylinders and tracks of an ISAM file. In VSAM jargon each **logical cylinder** is called a **control area**, and each **logical track** a **control interval**.

Each entry in the lowest level of the index contains the key of the last record in a control interval and the disk address of the first record in that control interval. Thus a control interval contains an indexed group of records, as does a track with ISAM. A difference is that a control interval is not necessarily a disk track, although it can be. The lowest level of the index is called a **sequence set**. We see in Figure 6.7 that the highest record key on control interval 1 of control area 0 is 22, for which there is an entry in the sequence set.

There can be up to three higher levels of the index. These are structured in the usual manner and are referred to as an **index set**.

However the entire VSAM index has built-in capability for growth, whereas an ISAM index does not. We shall return to this presently, when we have studied the method used in VSAM to handle insertions.

Management of Record Insertions with VSAM

Referring again to Figure 6.7, it can be seen that no control interval (logical track) is actually full. When a VSAM file is created, space for additional records is always left at the end of each control interval. As mentioned earlier this can also be done with ISAM, although the necessary code must be built into the file creation program. This is not necessary with VSAM. Instead a specification of how much empty space is needed must be made in the job control language (JCL) for the file creation program. As with ISAM, such empty space is used for insertions. When a record is inserted into a control interval, records with key values greater than that of the record being inserted are moved up, thus taking up some of the empty space at the end of the control interval in question. This is illustrated in Figure 6.8 with the insertion of the record with key value 27.

However, sooner or later a control interval becomes full, as with control interval 01 in Figure 6.8. If we now want to insert a record, such as the record with key 14, there is clearly no room for a new record. With ISAM such an insertion causes the last record of the track to be knocked off into the overflow area. With the VSAM logical track or control interval this does not happen. Instead the control interval is split.

Figure 6.8 illustrates how the splitting takes place. When the file is first created (along with an unused space at the end of each control interval), each control area contains a number of unused, or free, control intervals, such as control intervals 08 and 09 in the figure. When a control interval becomes full and an insertion into that full control interval is required, the control interval is first split. This means that the records in the last half are removed from the control interval and placed in an empty control interval, as shown for the splitting of control interval 01. The two control intervals resulting from the splitting and the next control interval in sequence (control interval 02) are connected by a pointer chain, so that ascending sequential key order for the records is preserved. When this has been done the new record (record 14) is inserted into the appropriate control interval, in which there must now be room.

However, this is not the end of the splitting process. Because there is now an extra control interval with records there must be an additional entry in the lowest level of the index (the sequence set); this entry must be in the correct sequential key order. To achieve this, insertion of the new index entry causes entries for higher key values (that is, for control intervals with higher key values) to be pushed up.

Occasionally there will be no empty control intervals in a control area to permit a split of a full control interval. When this happens the entire control area (logical cylinder) is split. Some empty control areas are normally included when the file is created. To split a control area, half the control intervals from the nonempty control area are copied into control intervals from an empty control area. Then the full control interval in turn splits using a newly provided empty control interval, following which the record is inserted.

When we have control area split we must also split the collection of lowest-level index entries for that control area, since instead of one control area there are now two. If this splitting process continues, it may even require adjustments to the higher level of the index.

It is clear that the technique of splitting control intervals and occasionally control areas is very powerful; it has little effect on the average number of disk accesses required to retrieve a record, since continued insertions do not give rise to overflow chains of records that must be searched, as with ISAM. Indeed the growth of a VSAM file through record insertions has been likened to the growth of a colony of microorganisms, each of which reproduces itself by splitting in two. And just as the growth of such a colony can continue indefinitely (given a supply of space and nutrients), the growth of a VSAM file can in theory continue indefinitely, given a ready supply of disk space and records.

COBOL Processing For Creation of a VSAM Indexed-Sequential File

Except for a few differences in the COBOL coding in the environment and data divisions, an indexed-sequential file is created as if it were a sequential file. Records must be written out in ascending key order, however. As they are written out using conventional COBOL WRITE commands, the access method constructs the index. This is true for both ISAM and VSAM files.

In general there are minor differences in the COBOL coding required for processing ISAM and VSAM. The differences are in no way fundamental, but in practice a COBOL program for processing an ISAM file would probably not run correctly with a VSAM version of the same file. The COBOL coding needed with VSAM files is much closer to ANS COBOL than is the case with ISAM files. We therefore assume

FIGURE 6.9 **Fields of the sequential (S-AR) and indexed-sequential (IS-AR) accounts receivable files. The key field is *INVOICE-NUMB*.**

VSAM files with our examples of COBOL processing. It should be understood that the same *programming methods* are used with both ISAM and VSAM files. The differences are at the COBOL coding level, are minor, even a nuisance. We note minor differences between VSAM and ISAM COBOL as we encounter them.

In this section we shall use an accounts receivable file as our main example. We use VSAM to create an indexed-sequential version of this file.

Creation of a VSAM Accounts Receivable File

Each record in a typical accounts receivable file describes an invoice for which some payment has yet to be made. In Figure 6.9 we list the fields of a sample accounts receivable file. They are the customer number, the invoice number (key field), the invoice date, the original value of the invoice, and the amount currently unpaid. The processing consists in reading in a (sequential) version of the file (called S-AR) from tape and writing out an indexed-sequential version (called IS-AR) on disk. This essential process is largely a copying operation, assuming that all necessary checking has previously been carried out when the sequential accounts receivable file was originally created. This is normally the case in practice. Even if a brand-new file is to be created as an indexed-sequential file, it is first created as a sequential file and all necessary checking of fields carried out, before being loaded as an indexed-sequential file. Very often a standard utility is used to load an indexed-sequential file from the sequential version. However, we shall examine the COBOL essentials necessary for such a loading program.

```
ENVIRONMENT DIVISION.
.
.
.
INPUT-OUTPUT SECTION.
FILE-CONTROL.
     SELECT S-AR
          ASSIGN TO UT-S-SAR.
     SELECT IS-AR
          ASSIGN TO ISAR              (ddname for DD-statement)
          ORGANIZATION IS INDEXED      (VSAM indexed-sequential
                                       file specified)
          ACCESS IS SEQUENTIAL        (RANDOM for direct access)
          RECORD KEY IS INVOICE-NUMB  (key field used in index)
```

Figure 6.10 Specification of the sequential file S-AR and the VSAM indexed file IS-AR. The ddnames for the DD-statements for the files are SAR and ISAR. We have specified that the indexed-sequential file is to be accessed sequentially (ACCESS IS SEQUENTIAL), since we intend to create the file. Later if direct access to the file is required, we would specify ACCESS IS RANDOM. A record key field (INVOICE-NUMB) must be specified; it must be a field in the buffer record for the file, specified in the data division (see Figure 6.11).

We first specify the logical files needed in the INPUT-OUTPUT section of the environment division (see Figure 6.10). The specification for the sequential file S-AR is similar to sequential file specifications in chapter 3. Note that in the ASSIGN clause SAR is the ddname, that is, the reference name to the dataset definition statement (DD-statement) containing the physical file specification (chapter 3).

The specification for the indexed file IS-AR is typical of that used for a VSAM file with IBM COBOL. The ddname for the accompanying DD-statement is ISAR. We must specify that the file organization is indexed-sequential with VSAM; this is the implication of ORGANIZATION IS INDEXED. (With ISAM instead of

```
ASSIGN TO ISAR
ORGANIZATION IS INDEXED
```

we specify:

```
ASSIGN TO DA-I-ISAR
```

where again ISAR is the ddname, DA denotes direct access, and I denotes indexed-sequential.)

```
DATA DIVISION.
FILE SECTION.
FD      S-AR
        LABEL RECORDS ARE STANDARD
        RECORD CONTAINS 26 CHARACTERS   (logical record length)
        BLOCK CONTAINS 0 RECORDS
        DATA RECORD IS S-ARBUFREC.
01      S-ARBUFREC      PIC X(26).

FD      IS-AR
        LABEL RECORDS ARE STANDARD
        RECORD CONTAINS 26 CHARACTERS
        DATA RECORD IS IS-ARBUFREC.
01      IS-ARBUFREC.
        02      CUSTNUMB        PIC 9(5).
        02      INVOICE-NUMB    PIC 9(4).  (key field:  must be
DISPLAY numeric or characters)
        02      INVOICE-DATE    PIC X(7).
        02      AMOUNT          PIC 9(5).
        02      OWING           PIC 9(5).
WORKING-STORAGE SECTION.
01      S-ARREC.
        02      CUSTNUMB        PIC 9(5).
.
.
.
```

Figure 6.11. Specification of the buffer and working-storage records for the sequential accounts receivable file S-AR; the indexed-sequential accounts receivable file is IS-AR. No BLOCK CONTAINS clause is needed in the specification for the indexed (VSAM) file, since blocks are no longer relevant because of the use of control intervals.

Continuing with the specification for the VSAM indexed file IS-AR, we next specify how the file is to be accessed. With VSAM the file will be either accessed sequentially or by direct access. Indexed-sequential files are created sequentially so we code ACCESS IS SEQUENTIAL. For processing with direct access we could code ACCESS IS RANDOM, as we shall illustrate in the next section.

Finally we must specify which field is to serve as the key field. This must be a field that uniquely identifies a record; in this case it is clear that INVOICE-NUMB is the required field. The access method must know what this field is, to be able to extract it from each record written and use it to build the index. For this reason also, the key field specified in the RECORD KEY clause must be a field of the buffer record.

```
PROCEDURE DIVISION
CREATE-PARAGRAPH.
     OPEN INPUT S-AR,
           OUTPUT IS-AR.
     MOVE "NO" TO EOF.
     READ S-AR INTO S-ARREC,
           AT END PERFORM NO-RECORDS-PARAGRAPH.
     PERFORM PROCESS-RECORDS UNTIL EOF = "YES".
     CLOSE S-AR, IS-AR.
     STOP RUN.
PROCESS-RECORDS.
     WRITE IS-AR-BUFREC FROM S-ARREC,
           INVALID KEY PERFORM ERROR-PARAGRAPH.
     READ S-AR INTO S-ARREC,
          AT END MOVE "YES" TO EOF.
ERROR-PARAGRAPH.
...
```

Figure 6.12. The essentials of a program to create the accounts receivable indexed-sequential file IS-AR from a sequential version of the file S-AR. It is assumed that the records of S-AR are sorted in ascending key (INVOICE-NUMB) order. Records must be written out in this order. If ascending order is violated—that is, if the latest record to be written does not have a key value greater than that of the previous record written—the INVALID KEY clause in the WRITE statement is executed. In the ERROR-PARAGRAPH, the nature of the invalid key would be investigated and a report issued. The access method constructs an index as the file is created, although this is not evident from (transparent to) the procedure.

The buffer and working-storage records for these files are specified in the data division in Figure 6.11. The buffer specifications for the sequential file are similar to those encountered earlier in chapter 3. With the indexed-sequential buffer specification we do not include a BLOCK CONTAINS clause since we are dealing with a VSAM file, which is made up of control intervals. The buffer record IS-ARBUFREC is specified as containing a field INVOICE-NUMB, which is the key field specified in the environment division.

In the working-storage section we specify the record S-ARREC, which can be used with both the sequential and indexed sequential versions of the accounts receivable file (illustrated in the essential core of the loading program in Figure 6.12).

It is clear that the loading is essentially a copying operation. Nevertheless it is necessary to check that records coming from the sequential file are in ascending key order. This can be done using the INVALID KEY clause of the WRITE statement, which is otherwise the same as a WRITE statement for a sequential file. If the next record to be written contains a key value equal to or less than the key value of the previous record written, then the INVALID KEY clause is executed. In the program in Figure 6.12, it would then be the task of ERROR-PARAGRAPH to determine whether a duplicate or out-of-sequence key was responsible and to output an appropriate message together with details of the record not written out. Records not written out can be manually checked at the end of the processing. Following any necessary alterations they can be input later as an insertion update operation.

Disk Space Allocation for a Newly Created Indexed-Sequential File

If the file created is an ISAM file, the space required is specified in the accompanying DD-statement. Actually it is rare for a single DD-statement to be enough, for in practice with a large ISAM file there will be three datasets, or physical files: One for the index, one for the records or prime data, and one for eventual overflow records. All of these DD-statements will be referenced by a single ddname. The DD-statements are quite complex and are beyond the scope of this book. Disk space is specified in each of them using the SPACE parameter.

The situation with VSAM indexed-sequential files is quite different. A great deal of specification effort is required for setting up VSAM files. However, much of it is performed by systems personnel and is valid for all VSAM files. When this specification effort has been completed only a simple DD-statment is needed for a specific VSAM file.

The VSAM specification effort is connected with setting up master catalogues of VSAM files and defining space that may be used only by VSAM files, called VSAM disk space. There is more about this at the end of this chapter. Briefly the specification effort involves three executions of a VSAM utility program called IDCAMS. (Note that IDCAMS is also called *access method services*.) The first execution sets up a master catalogue of all VSAM files; the second execution defines the entire VSAM disk space.

With the third execution of IDCAMS we define the space needed for the specific VSAM file being created. Here we also define the amount of free space to be left at the end of each control interval and the number of empty control intervals (see Figure 6.7). This free space affects the number of splits that will take place and so affects performance during insertion updating. There is a further discussion of this at the end of the chapter.

The details of these utility program executions and the parameters that control them are beyond the scope of this book. They also vary somewhat from one operating system to another.

When all these preparations have been completed, the program to load or process the VSAM file need only use a simple DD-statement such as:

```
//GO.ISAR   DD   DSN=IS001,DISP=SHR
```

Here ISAR is the ddname, IS001 is the dataset name, and SHR means that the file can be accessed by many users.

Cobol Processing for Updating the VSAM Accounts Receivable File

In this section we look at different kinds of updating for the indexed-sequential accounts receivable file IS-AR created in the previous section. We treat insertion, change, and deletion updating in turn.

In a business organization an updated version of an accounts receivable file must be available each month for generating the monthly billing statement to customers. Each record of the file gives the amount owing by a customer on a given invoice; for a given customer there can be many records, each for a different invoice.

During the course of each month new invoices are issued. These are first posted in an accounts receivable summary file. Near the end of the month the records from this file are inserted into the accounts receivable master (AR) file. Thus an insertion update is required.

During the course of a month cash payments are received from customers with funds owing on invoices, normally with instructions about which invoices the funds are to be applied to. These payments are recorded in a cash receipts file, in which a record describes a payment by a customer towards a particular invoice. Following insertion of the latest invoices into the accounts receivable master, there is a change update using the cash receipts file. In this update the sum paid on each invoice is deducted from the sum owing for the invoice. Thus a change update is required.

Following the change update some of the accounts receivable records will have a sum owing equal to (or very close to) 0. In a further processing step these records are deleted and a list of the deleted invoices printed. Thus a deletion update is required.

The monthly accounts receivable file updating can be carried out in three separate stages, as described above, or in a single (but more complex) processing step using sequential processing. The main reason for carrying out the update in a single step is the significant reduction in the number of times the accounts receivable records must be read. This is an important consideration when dealing with sequential updating. However, when the accounts receivable master is an indexed- sequential file, separate (and thus simpler) updating is attractive; it is not necessary to process the whole file, because of the direct access capability offered by the indexed-sequential organization. Thus we can deal with insertion, change, and deletion updates as separate processes.

Insertion Updating of the VSAM Accounts Receivable File by Direct Access

We cannot process an indexed-sequential file sequentially and carry out insertions. There is no COBOL facility that enables us to process the file with a specification of ACCESS IS SEQUENTIAL in the environment division, open the file with OPEN I-O IS-AR, and then use WRITE to insert new records. This is a basic restriction on the processing of indexed-sequential files and must be clearly understood. Instead we must process the file for direct access. Thus the ACCESS IS clause (see also Figure 6.10 for a specification of the indexed-sequential file IS-AR) must be:

```
ACCESS IS RANDOM
```

Only then can we open the file for updating with the procedure division instruction:

```
OPEN I-O IS-AR.
```

Suppose now that we have to update the indexed accounts receivable file from the accounts receivable summary file (AR-SUMMARY), and that the resulting insertions do not aways occur at the end of the accounts receivable file. Records of AR-SUMMARY will be read one by one and inserted into IS-AR. The order of the records in AR-SUMMARY does not matter since records are being inserted directly into IS-AR. As a precaution, before a record is inserted into IS-AR the access method checks that a record from IS-AR with the same key value as the record to be inserted is not already in the file, since duplicate keys are not allowed.

Before looking at the core of this updating procedure, it is instructive to examine just how we use the record key to directly access a record in an indexed file. Suppose that we want to read the record for invoice number 56. In the RECORD KEY clause in the environment division we must specify the name of the key field, in this case INVOICE-NUMB (see Figure 6.10 for an example). We make use of this as follows in the processing:

```
MOVE 56 TO INVOICE-NUMB IN IS-ARBUFREC.
READ IS-AR INTO IS-ARREC,
        INVALID KEY PERFORM ...
```

Using the MOVE statement we place the required key value in the *key field in the buffer record*, where it is available to the access method. The READ statement then causes the access method to search for the record with this key, using the index to come as quickly as possible to its disk location. If the record is found it is placed in the working-storage structure IS-ARREC; otherwise the PERFORM statement will be executed.

Similarly if we want to write a record by direct access, the index must be used to enable the access method to quickly come to the disk location where the record is to be inserted. To insert record 56 we code:

```
MOVE 56 TO INVOICE-NUMB IN IS-ARBUFREC.
WRITE IS-ARBUFREC FROM IS-ARREC,
        INVALID KEY PERFORM ...
```

If a record with that key is already in the file, the INVALID key phrase is executed.

Remembering therefore that ACCESS IS RANDOM and RECORD KEY IS INVOICE-NUMB must be specified for the indexed-sequential file IS-AR, the following excerpt is the core of the procedure to insert records from the accounts receivable summary file AR-SUMMARY:

```
        OPEN INPUT AR-SUMMARY,
             I-O IS-AR.
        MOVE "NO" TO SUMMARY-EOF.
        READ AR-SUMMARY INTO IS-ARREC, AT END PERFORM
             NO-RECORDS-PARAGRAPH.
        PERFORM INSERT-RECORDS UNTIL SUMMARY-EOF = "YES".
        CLOSE AR-SUMMARY, IS-AR.
        STOP RUN.
INSERT-RECORDS.
        MOVE INVOICE-NUMB IN IS-ARREC TO INVOICE-NUMB IN
             IS-ARBUFREC.
        WRITE IS-ARBUFREC FROM IS-ARREC,
             INVALID KEY PERFORM DUPLICATE-KEY-PARAGRAPH.
```

```
        READ AR-SUMMARY INTO IS-ARREC,
             AT END MOVE "YES" TO SUMMARY-EOF.
DUPLICATE-KEY-PARAGRAPH.
        . . .
```

In the above, SUMMARY-EOF is an end of file flag for the summary accounts receivable file; IS-ARBUFREC and IS-ARREC are respectively the buffer and working-storage records for the indexed file IS-AR.

Change Updating of the Indexed Accounts Receivable File

Change updating for an accounts receivable file is triggered by cash receipts against outstanding invoices. For a given invoice several payments may be made. Thus if a record for each payment is in a cash receipts file, then for one record in the accounts receivable file there can be many records in the cash receipts file with matching invoice number.

With sequential processing there is only one way to carry out such an update. The cash receipts records are first sorted in ascending invoice number sequence. Both accounts receivables and cash receipts files are then processed sequentially. When a match is encountered, all subsequent cash receipts records with the matching invoice number are then read and the total cash payment summed. This sum is then deducted from the OWING field in the matching accounts receivable record, which is then written out.

With an indexed-sequential version of the accounts receivable file we have three possible methods of carrying out this updating. The first method involves sequential processing and essentially is the same as the method used with a sequential disk version of the file where updated records are rewritten and other records are not. The indexed file would be specified with ACCESS IS SEQUENTIAL and opened with the COBOL statement OPEN I-O IS-AR. During the processing the COBOL READ and REWRITE statements are used in exactly the same way as with sequential disk files. The file navigation diagram is shown in Figure 6.13. The values in the PAYMENT fields for a given invoice number are summed and the total deducted from the OWING field of the matching IS-AR record. A matching IS-AR record must be searched for sequentially, so that every record of IS-AR is read, with only updated records being rewritten. This method is probably the most efficient if the hit rate is not low. Note that the method involves control break processing.

If the hit rate is very low, it probably pays to update the accounts receivable file by the second possible method, direct access (illustrated in Figure 6.14). Here only records that need updating are ever read. The indexed-sequential file must be specified with ACCESS IS RAN-

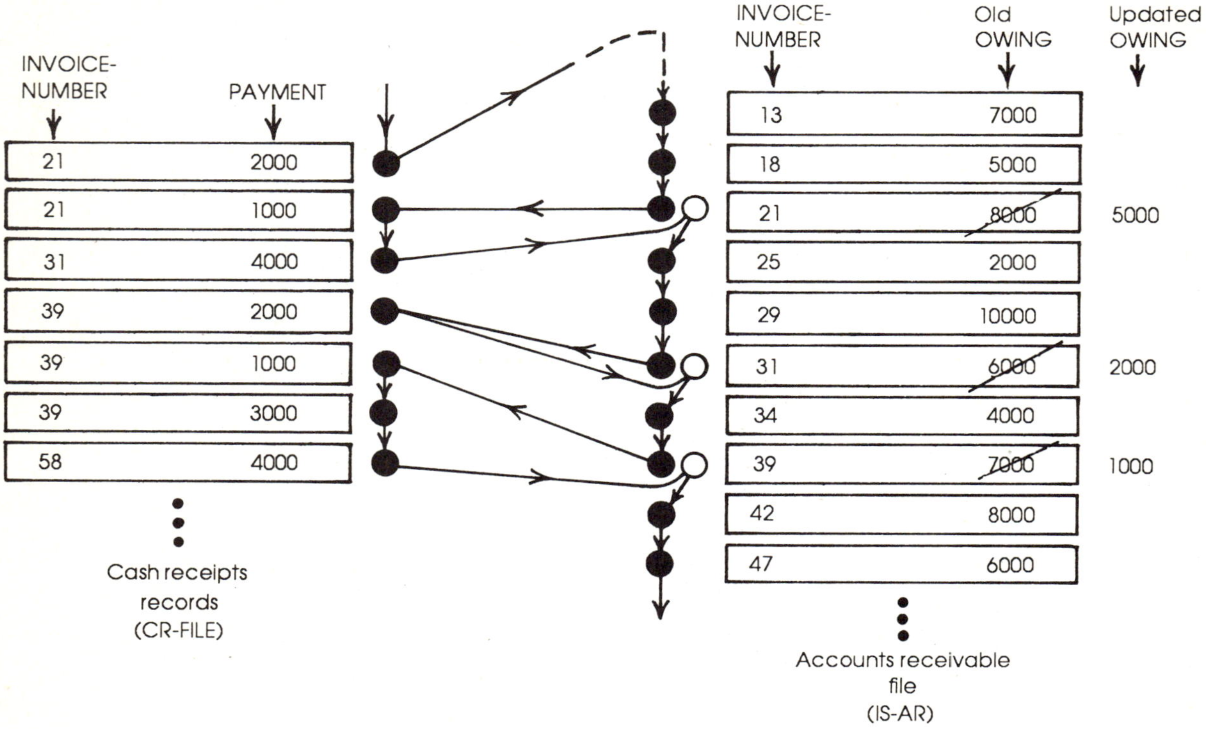

FIGURE 6.13. File navigation diagram for sequential updating of an indexed-sequential accounts receivable file from a cash receipts file. For a single invoice number there can be many cash receipts records, the PAYMENT fields of which must be summed before deduction from the OWING field of the accounts receivable record. Both files are sorted on invoice number. All accounts receivable records are read but only updated records are rewritten. The processing is typical of control break processing, and the invoice number is used for control.

DOM and the file opened with the COBOL statement OPEN I-O IS-AR. The cash receipts file is processed sequentially, however, and the PAYMENT field values for a given invoice number are summed before deduction from the OWING field of the matching IS-AR record. Thus an IS-AR record to be updated is first read and then rewritten. Since the access is direct a key must be used with the READ and REWRITE statements. This method also uses control break processing.

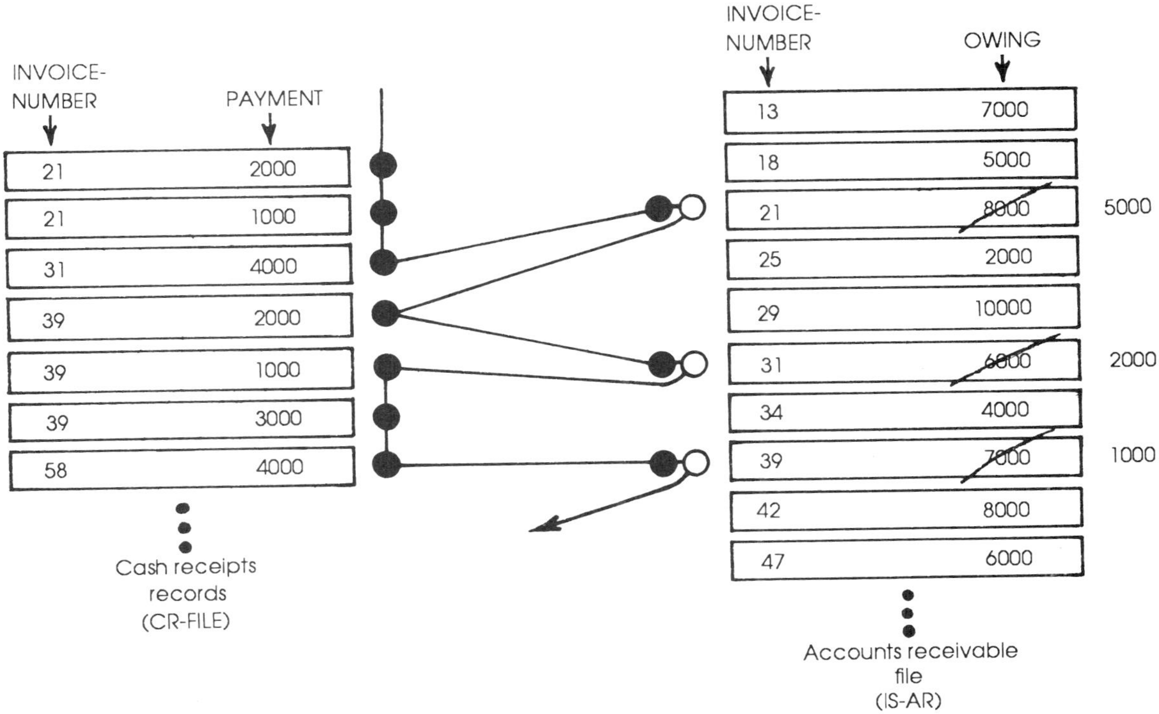

FIGURE 6.14. File navigation diagram for direct updating of an indexed-sequential accounts receivable file from a cash receipts file. Payments for a single invoice are summed before being deducted. Both files are sorted on INVOICE-NUMBER, which is also the key field for the indexed-sequential file. Only accounts receivable records to be updated are read. The method also uses control break processing with the invoice number used for control.

The third method is illustrated in Figure 6.15. Again the accounts receivable file is processed directly; the file is specified with ACCESS IS RANDOM and opened with OPEN I-O IS-AR as before. However, this time the cash receipts records are not necessarily in invoice number order. This means that the PAYMENT values are not summed before deduction from the OWING field of the matching accounts receivable record. Instead the PAYMENT value in each cash receipts record is deducted as it is read.

For invoice number 39 there are three cash receipts records and thus three payments and three deductions for the matching IS-AR record. The number of READ operations (and the number of REWRITE operations) applied to IS-AR exactly equals the number of matching records in the cash receipts file. As each cash receipts record is read, the PAYMENT value is immediately deducted from OWING field of the

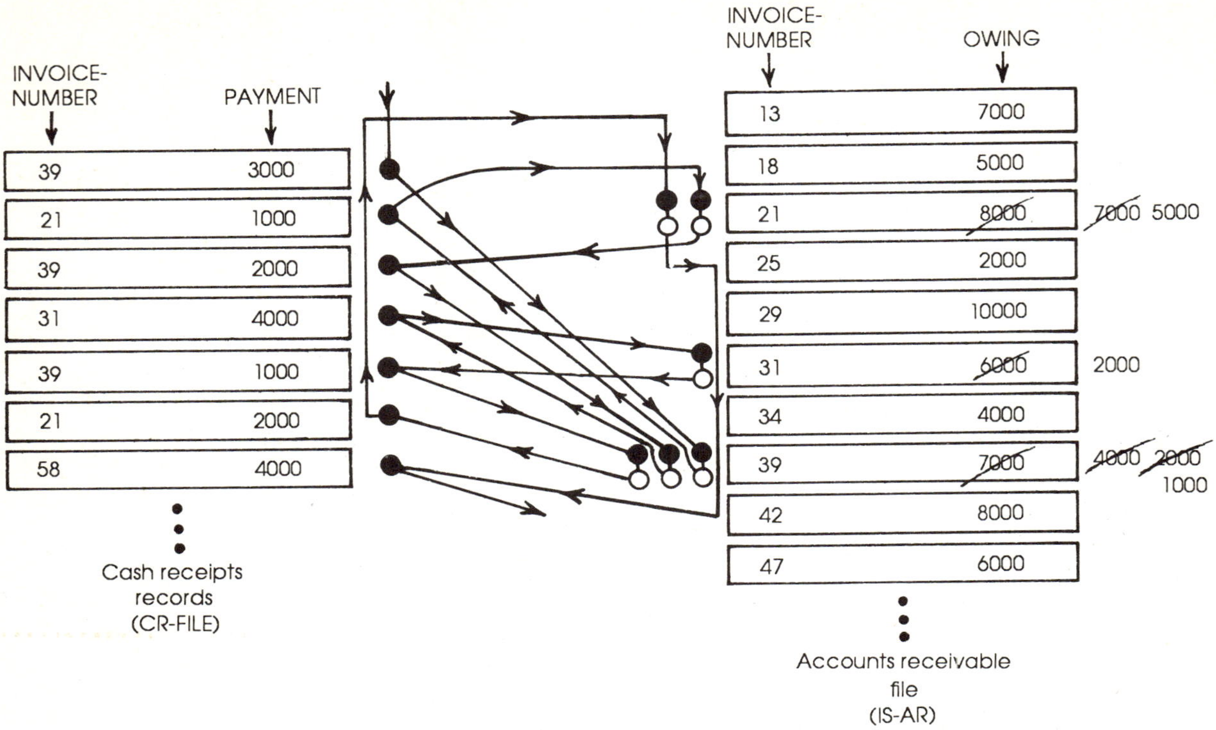

FIGURE 6.15. Another method of direct updating an indexed-sequential accounts receivable file from a cash receipts file. Payments for a given invoice are not summed before deduction. Cash receipts records are not necessarily in invoice number order, although the file is processed sequentially. The indexed-sequentail file is accessed directly. When a cash receipts record is read, the accounts receivable record with matching invoice number is accessed and the payment deducted from the sum owing. This means that the same accounts receivable record can be accessed many times, so that a sequence of deductions will take place. This is the method used for on-line updating.

matching accounts receivable record. The COBOL READ and REWRITE statements for the indexed file require that a key be specified, as with the previous method. The cash receipts file is processed sequentially. The following excerpt illustrates the core of the processing and how the key field (INVOICE-NUMB) in the buffer record (IS-ARBUFREC) is used with any direct access of the IS-AR file:

```
OPEN INPUT CR-FILE,
     I-O IS-AR.
MOVE "NO" TO CR-FILE-EOF.
READ CR-FILE INTO CR-REC, AT END PERFORM
       NO-RECORDS-PARAGRAPH.
PERFORM RECORD-PROCESSING UNTIL CR-FILE-EOF = "YES".
```

```
       CLOSE CR-FILE, IS-AR.
       STOP RUN.
RECORD-PROCESSING.
        MOVE INVOICE-NUMB IN CR-REC TO INVOICE-NUMB IN IS-AR-
BUFREC.
       READ IS-AR INTO IS-ARREC, INVALID KEY PERFORM
            ERROR-PARAGRAPH.
       COMPUTE OWING IN IS-ARREC = OWING IN IS-ARREC - PAYMENT
            IN CR-REC.
       REWRITE IS-ARBUFREC FROM IS-ARREC.
       READ CR-FILE INTO CR-REC,
            AT END MOVE "YES" TO CR-FILE-EOF.
ERROR-PARAGRAPH.
       ...
```

In the above excerpt CR-FILE is the sequential cash receipts file, CR-REC is the working-storage record for this file, and CR-FILE-EOF is a flag for the end of the file. Notice that when the READ IS-AR . . . and REWRITE commands are issued, the correct value of the record key is in INVOICE-NUMB in the buffer structure IS-ARBUFREC. The access method uses this key to search the index to locate the record to be either read or rewritten.

This third method would likely be used only if the hit rate were very low, so that the additional accesses to the indexed file would not be significant. The method is thus suitable for on-line processing, where small numbers of cash receipts are used to update the accounts receivable file at regular intervals. In such a case the cash receipts data is read from a terminal keyboard and will not be in ascending invoice number. Thus Figure 6.15 applies to the case of on-line updating, if we assume that the order of cash receipts records shown is the order in which they are input from an on-line terminal.

Deletion Updating of the VSAM Accounts Receivable File

With an indexed-sequential file, records can be deleted both during sequential processing and during direct processing. (Recall that records can be inserted only during direct processing.) As we would expect, with direct processing the key of the record to be deleted must be placed in the key field in the buffer record for the file. Thus if we want to delete invoice 56, we code:

```
MOVE 56 TO INVOICE-NUMB IN IS-ARBUFREC.
DELETE IS-AR,
INVALID KEY ...
```

If the record to be deleted is not in the file, the error paragraph specified following INVALID KEY will be executed.

A programming excerpt for sequential deletion is illustrative, since it demonstrates the COBOL commands involved and also serves as a reminder that sequential deletion is not possible with sequential files. The file must be indexed-sequential. Let us suppose that we need a program that scans sequentially through IS-AR, deleting each record for which the OWING field is less than one dollar, as might reasonably be done in practice. IS-AR must be specified with ACCESS IS SEQUENTIAL; the core of the deletion procedure is as follows (note that the DELETE statement deletes the record previously read):

```
        OPEN I-O IS-AR.
        MOVE "NO" TO IS-AR-EOF.
        READ IS-AR INTO IS-ARREC, AT END PERFORM
               NO-RECORDS-PARAGRAPH.
        PERFORM SCAN-RECORDS UNTIL IS-AR-EOF = "YES".
        CLOSE IS-AR,
        STOP RUN.
SCAN-RECORDS.
        IF OWING IN IS-ARREC < 1
             THEN DELETE IS-AR.
        READ IS-AR INTO IS-ARREC,
             AT END MOVE "YES" TO IS-AR-EOF.
```

As an example of deletion with direct access, suppose that we want to delete certain records for invoices that are many months overdue and not likely ever to be paid. Assume that a list of such delinquent invoices was compiled earlier in the file DELINQUENT. Thus we want to delete from IS-AR every record in DELINQUENT that had not already been deleted. IS-AR can be specified with ACCESS IS RANDOM as follows, whereas DELINQUENT is a sequential file (possibly on tape):

```
        OPEN INPUT DELINQUENT,
             I-O IS-AR.
        MOVE "NO" TO DELINQUENT-EOF.
        READ DELINQUENT INTO IS-AR, AT END
           PERFORM NO-RECORDS-PARAGRAPH.
        PERFORM PROCESS-RECORDS UNTIL DELINQUENT-EOF = "YES".
        CLOSE DELINQUENT, IS-AR.
        STOP RUN.
PROCESS-RECORDS.
        MOVE INVOICE-NUMB IN IS-AR TO INVOICE-NUMB IN
        IS-AR-BUFREC.
        DELETE IS-AR,
             INVALID KEY PERFORM NOT-FOUND-PARAGRAPH.
        READ DELINQUENT INTO IS-AR,
             AT END MOVE "YES" TO DELINQUENT-EOF.
NOT-FOUND-PARAGRAPH.
        ...
```

In the above we assume that a record of DELINQUENT has the type and number of fields as a record of IS-AR. Since access to IS-AR is direct, the order of the records in DELINQUENT does not matter. Note, however, that the key of the record to be deleted must be placed in the key field of the buffer record, before the DELETE command is issued.

INFORMATION RETRIEVAL FROM AN INDEX-SEQUENTIAL FILE

As mentioned earlier, an indexed sequential file must be looked upon primarily as a sequential file, where direct access is possible to any record for which the key is known. Thus a great deal of information retrieval and report generation involves sequential reading of the records, with records satisfying certain retrieval conditions being picked out for retrieval. In other words we can carry out the same kind of information retrieval as was possible with sequential files and with much the same programming methods.

Only if a retrieval condition involves a key field value will the direct access capability be any use to us. For example, the following request clearly requires a sequential scan of the indexed-sequential IS-AR file, with a record being picked for retrieval if its OWING field value exceeds 10,000:

```
"Retrieve the invoice numbers for all invoices for which
the sum owing exceeds $10,000."
```

On the other hand, the request that follows can be handled without a scan of the file being necessary:

```
"Retrieve the sum owing for invoice number 56."
```

It is merely necessary to use a COBOL READ statement with key value 56, as follows:

```
OPEN INPUT IS-AR.
MOVE 56 TO INVOICE-NUMB IN IS-AR-BUFREC.
READ IS-AR INTO IS-ARREC,
        INVALID KEY PERFORM NOT-FOUND-PARAGRAPH.
DISPLAY OWING IN IS-ARREC.
```

Here the DISPLAY command causes the retrieved OWING value to be displayed on the screen of a terminal.

There is a related type of information retrieval request for which an indexed-sequential file can save a lot of unnecessary accesses; for instance, when we want direct access to a certain position in the file from which we will continue processing by sequential access. Consider the retrieval request:

"Retrieve the sum owing for each invoice for which the invoice number exceeds 1234."

The COBOL procedure involves the use of the COBOL START command, illustrated by the following excerpt. The file is specified with ACCESS IS SEQUENTIAL.

```
        OPEN INPUT IS-AR.
        MOVE "NO" TO IS-AR-EOF.
        MOVE 1234 TO POSITION-INFO.
        START IS-AR KEY > POSITION-INFO.

*** The next (in this case also the first) READ statement
    executed
*** will deliver the first record with a key value exceeding the
*** value in POSITION-INFO.

        READ IS-AR INTO IS-ARREC
                AT END PERFORM NO-RECORDS-PARAGRAPH.
        PERFORM UNTIL IS-AR-EOF = "YES".
             DISPLAY OWING IN IS-AR.
             READ IS-AR INTO IS-ARREC,
             AT END MOVE "YES" TO IS-AR-EOF.
        END-PERFORM.
```

The START command can be given many times within a program. Thus if we want the OWING values for invoice numbers greater than 1234 but less than 2234 and greater than 4444 but less than 6666, we first issue:

```
START IS-AR KEY > 1234
```

Then we process sequentially until a record with key value greater or equal to 2234 is read. At this point we want to hop forward to a position just greater than 4444 and issue another START command:

```
START IS-AR KEY < 4444
```

Then we continue sequentially from that point. The access method employs the file index to locate the next record to be read after a START command execution.

With the START command the comparison operand *op* in the condition

KEY *op key-value*

can be =,> ,< or . When we employ KEY <> *key-value*, the key value does not actually have to be in the file, thus permitting the START command to be employed in generic retrievals.

To clearly understand how generic retrievals are accomplished in COBOL we must examine the key field more closely. Both VSAM and ISAM require that the field type be character, that is, either numeric (9(n)), alphanumeric (X(n)), or alphabetic (A(n)). The key field INVOICE-NUMB that we have been using was specified as being numeric with PIC 9(4). Thus we can imagine a generic search of the indexed-sequential file to obtain all those invoices where the first two digits of the invoice number is 55. To do this we can use the start command:

```
START IS-AR > KEY = 5500
```

This positions the system for reading the first required record, which can have the key value 5500.

On the other hand the key can be alphanumeric, perhaps with the first two characters alphabetic and the next two numeric, such as 'XY56'. In such a case INVOICE-NUMB would be specified with PIC X(4). Now suppose we want to retrieve all those invoices whose invoice numbers begin with 'PQ'. We can use either of the following START commands:

```
START IS-AR KEY > "PQ".

START IS-AR KEY > "PQbb".
```

The elementary collating sequence of character data is used here, so that PQ is less than PQOO, as is PQbb. Note that the INVALID key change can be used with the START command:

```
START IS-AR KEY = n,
      INVALID KEY PERFORM START-RECORD-NOT-FOUND-
      PARAGRAPH.
```

FURTHER VSAM FEATURES

There are some additional features of VSAM that must be understood by anyone planning to use the system. We cannot go into all the necessary details, but in this section we shall look at:

a. Management of free space in control intervals in order to minimize splitting,

b. How control intervals are formatted on disk, and
c. The management of VSAM datasets.

VSAM Performance Enhancement Using Free Space Management

As we saw earlier, with VSAM, inserted records are never stored in overflow chains that can cause performance degradation; thus there is no need for periodic reorganization, as is the case with ISAM. Some performance degradation is noticeable during extensive insertion updating, however, since a significantly increased number of disk accesses is needed to carry out the splitting and maintain the indexes. Nevertheless this is a fairly negligible price to pay overall; anyway the effect can be minimized by careful choice of the amount of free space to be left at the ends of the control intervals at file loading. If sufficient space is left, most record insertions can take place with very little splitting.

If we want the best possible performance out of a VSAM file, we should ensure that when the file is created we leave space at the end of each control interval for somewhat more records than the net number per control interval that we intend to insert. For example, if we have 10,000 control intervals and expect to insert 50,000 records and delete 20,000 over the life of the file, the net number inserted is 30,000 and the insertion level is 30,000/10,000, or 3 records per control interval. We get the best performance if we arrange space for 4 or 5 records at the end of each control interval when the file is first loaded.

Comparison of a VSAM Control Interval with an ISAM Disk Track

As we saw earlier the indexed group of records with an ISAM file is a track of records, with the index entry for the track consisting of the track address and the key of the last record on the track. The track itself consists of blocked records, using count key data format; records are typically fixed length blocked. (For track formats see Chapter 2.) These might be called the physical records.

We can also show some logical records and the underlying physical records on a disk track for an ISAM file. The logical records are the records seen by the program, while the physical records are those seen by the disk controller. In practice the program processing the file is not concerned with the details of the physical records on a disk track.

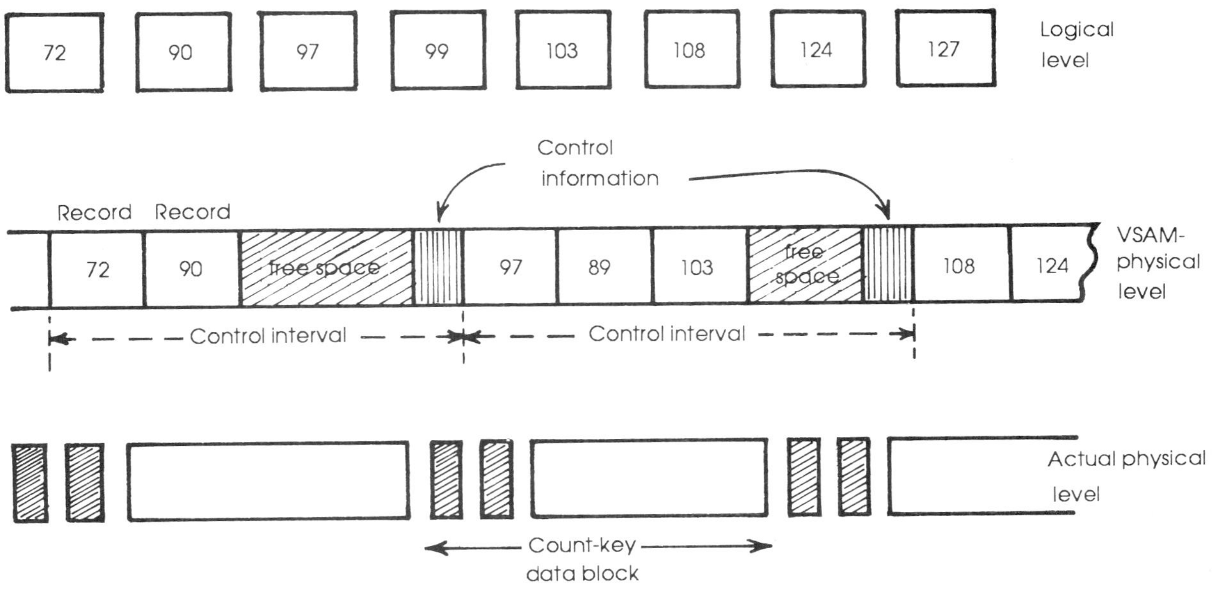

FIGURE 6.16. Logical and physical files when VSAM is used. The logical file is as with ISAM and other conventional files. However, there are two physical file levels; namely, the VSAM-physical level, at which the file consists of a sequence of control intervals, and the actual physical level made up of count-key date blocks.

It is useful to compare this with the case for VSAM. We have logical records, as with the ISAM file; with VSAM they too will be the records as seen by the program. But instead of only two levels of abstraction (logical and physical), with VSAM there are three levels; namely, the logical level, the VSAM-physical level (a name we have invented, for want of a better one), and the actual physical level (see Figures 6.16 and 6.17). In Figure 6.16 we show the logical records as the top level, followed by VSAM control intervals at the intermediate level, followed by the count- key data blocks at the bottom, or physical, level.

A control interval is best regarded as a group, or train, of data blocks, although in practice it is never necessary to be concerned with the lowest level. VSAM selects block sizes and looks after disk space automatically, so that we need never be concerned with the underlying data blocks. Thus with a VSAM file for all practical purposes the

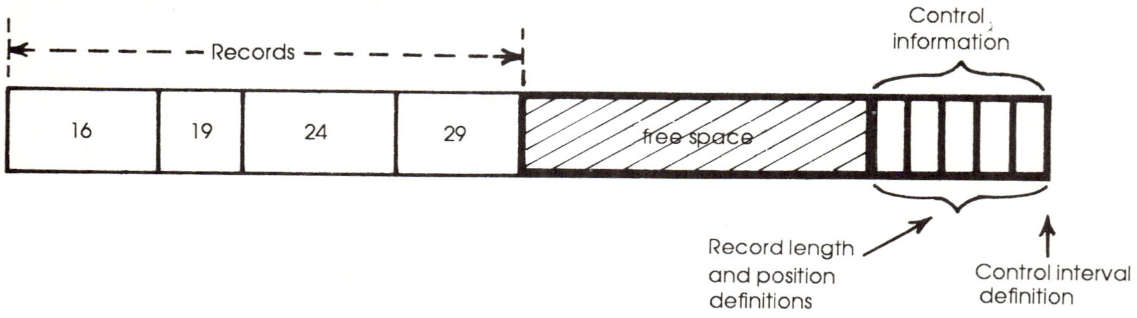

FIGURE 6.17. Details of the format of a VSAM control interval. Records may vary in length; there can be free space for insertions. Information about the start positions and length of records is kept at the end of the control interval.

control interval becomes the unit of data transmission between disk and input/output buffer in main memory.

The format of a control interval is shown in Figure 6.17. It consists of a sequence of records, possibly followed by free space for record insertions, followed by control information. The control information consists of lengths and positions of records within the control interval. Note that records in a control interval can be variable length. VSAM considers the control interval to be contiguous disk space, although in reality it is a train of conventional data blocks. VSAM also considers a file as made up of a continuous sequence of control intervals, that is, it considers the control intervals to be contiguous.

The advantage of all this is that a VSAM file becomes independent of the type of disk being used to store the file. VSAM chooses the length of the control interval (up to a maximum of 32,768 bytes) and the block size of the underlying data blocks. It then manages the layout of the control intervals on the tracks itself in such a manner that a track becomes irrelevant. If we wish we can imagine 2, 3, 4 or even 2 1/2 or 3 1/2 control intervals to a track, or 3 tracks per control interval—but it is a pointless exercise. Track lengths and how many records can fit on a track no longer matter. In the JCL for setting up the file, we simply ask for space for so many records of such and such a size; VSAM does the rest.

Other Disk Independent File Organizations

From our discussion in the previous section, it should be clear that there is more to a VSAM indexed-sequential file than simply a special indexed-group splitting technique to accommodate insertions. The use of control intervals (that is, the VSAM physical files as opposed to the actual physical file on a track made up of blocks of data), means that the file is independent of the nature of the disk used. Thus an ISAM file on an IBM 3350 disk is quite different from one on an IBM 3380 disk because the basic indexed group (a track) holds different records and different numbers of records. Therefore we have quite different indexes for the two disks. This is not the case with a corresponding VSAM file.

It is therefore natural to ask if we can have a sequential file (no direct access capability) that is independent of the disk used because records are stored in control intervals (logical tracks). There is no reason why not; as well as providing for indexed-sequential files, the original version of VSAM (released in 1973) also provided for sequential files using the control interval idea. In VSAM jargon the indexed-sequential file was called a **key-sequenced data set**; the sequential file an **entry-sequenced data set.** A VSAM entry-sequenced dataset is thus the functional equivalent of a conventional sequential file; with the exception of the JCL necessary to set it up, almost all the material in chapters 3 and 4 is applicable.

As with most successful software products, VSAM was extended. A later extension provided for constructing hash files that were disk independent, again using the control interval idea. In VSAM jargon such files are called **relative-record datasets**, and are the functional equivalent of the *relative* files discussed in chapters 8 and 9. Thus we can use VSAM to construct the three basic types of files, namely, sequential, indexed- sequential, and hash. A later extension to VSAM also allows for automatic construction of *inverted files* and *secondary keys*, covered in chapter 7.

VSAM and Central Control of Datasets

VSAM provides for central control of all VSAM datasets (whether key-sequenced, entry-sequenced, or relative-record) by means of a **master VSAM catalogue**, which contains information about all VSAM datasets and their sizes and locations. The VSAM datasets can be located on many different disk packs, each of which can contain non VSAM datasets. In the volume table of contents (VTOC) for a disk pack, there is a specification of the space that is available to VSAM files. All the VSAM space is under the control of VSAM and is registered in the VSAM master catalogue. An area of VSAM space on a disk pack is simply called a VSAM data space. Any part of a VSAM data space not being used is registered in the VSAM master catalogue and can be allocated to VSAM datasets as required.

SUMMARY

An indexed- sequential file is a sequential file, with records always available in ascending primary key order, where in addition there is a multiple-level sparse index that permits direct access on presentation of the primary key value of the record sought.

A problem with indexed-sequential files is insertions, which threaten ascending primary key order. Two methods are used to handle insertions and are illustrated in the two most commonly used types of indexed-sequential files, namely, IBM's ISAM and VSAM files.

With ISAM, inserted records are handled by linked lists and overflow tracks. With VSAM, inserted records are handled both by leaving space initially in the logical tracks (control intervals) for insertions and by splitting of logical tracks and cylinders in which there is no space left for insertions.

With ISAM files, insertions over the life of the file result in long overflow chains that cause perforamnce to deteriorate. This does not happen with VSAM files; ISAM files must be reorganized at intervals. VSAM files have largely replaced ISAM files in commerce as far as creation of new files is concerned. Older ISAM files remain in use since the COBOL code necessary for processing them is not quite the same as that for processing VSAM files.

EXERCISES

1. Referring to Figure 6.4:
   a. Give the contents of track 5, with pointer chains, if record 70 is placed in the file
   b. Give the contents of track 5, with pointer chains, if record 46 is placed in the file
   c. Give the contents of track 5, with pointer chains, if record 11 is deleted and record 36 is inserted

d. Give the contents of track 5, with pointer chains, if record 42 is deleted, and records 14 and 20 are inserted, in that order

2. Create the indexed- sequential file IS-AR, as described in the text. Use whatever access method is available on your computer.
3. Explain how the sequence set of a VSAM file is affected when a control interval splits.
4. Explain how VSAM files are independent of the disk on which they reside and why this is not true of ISAM files.
5. Explain why ACCESS IS RANDOM must be coded in a COBOL program that inserts records, even in ascending primary key order, into a VSAM file.
6. Complete the program in this chapter to insert records in IS-AR from the transaction file AR-SUMMARY.
7. Consider the file navigation diagram for sequential updating of IS-AR from a cash receipts transaction file (Figure 6.13). Write the program.
8. Consider the file navigation diagram for updating of IS-AR from a cash receipts file by direct access (Figure 6.14). Write the program.
9. Complete the update program for IS-AR according to the file navigation diagram in Figure 6.15.
10. Write a program that scans IS-AR, deletes each record where the amount owing is less than $5.00, and increases each amount owing over $5,000 by 10 percent.
11. Complete the updating program in this chapter for deleting records from IS-AR that are listed in the file DELINQUENT. Draw up a file naviagation diagram.
12. Rewrite the program for exercise 10, and insert code to allow for mismatches.
13. Write a program that sums the amount owing in each record of IS-AR where the invoice number is between 2000 and 3000.

REFERENCE

Trombetta, M., Finkelstein, S.C. *OS JCL and Utilities*, Addison Wesley, Reading, Mass., 1984

7 SECONDARY KEY ACCESS

Originally most file processing systems were built to satisfy the accounting needs of a business, since very great efficiencies can be achieved by the use of a computer for such accounting tasks as the generation of invoices, monthly statements, paychecks, and so on. In earlier chapters we saw how some of these systems depend on basic file processing principles.

However, in addition to the basic needs of accounting and finance, operating management also has a need for information. Some of this information is of an accounting or financial nature, but a great deal is not. For example in the case of a customer X, the accounting department may well be interested only in the credit limit of X, the amount owed by X for each of X's outstanding invoices, and X's address (so that X can be sent a monthly statement). That X is a manufacturer of aircraft landing gear need not concern accounting in the least. On the other hand, marketing may be very interested in the business of X, because of high hopes for the success of a novel light-weight high-strength material targeted at the aircraft industry.Thus there can be a basic conflict between the needs of operating management and the needs of accounting.

With most files, such as the ubiquitous CUSTOMER file, an obvious solution to the conflict of needs between accounting and management is an expanded version containing enough fields to satisfy both operating management and accounting. However, it frequently happens that operating management groups have their own version of files such as the CUSTOMER file, usually because the accounting system was set up before any other systems. (It would be expensive to redesign the accounting files since large numbers of accounting programs would also have to be redesigned.) Thus in the end there will be many files with data of interest to a wide segment of operating management.

Unfortunately it can be difficult for management to get needed information from many direct access files. Consider the version of CUSTOMER in Figure 7.1. The key field is customer number (CUSTNUMB). The other fields are the customer's business (BUSINESS), the state where the business is headquartered (STATE), the number of employees (EMPLOYEES), and the annual sales volume in millions of dollars (SALES). We can assume that the file is a direct access file (such as indexed-sequential) so that any record can be retrieved directly by presenting the primary key value.

CUSTMUMB	BUSINESS	STATE	EMPLOYEES	SALES
AB43	COMPUTERS	TEXAS	31,000	2600
DF33	AIRCRAFT	OREGON	17,000	1200
ED78	COMPUTERS	NEW YORK	8,000	650
GH12	TRUCKING	TEXAS	3,000	260
JK39	OIL	COLORADO	3,000	460
LK14	AIRCRAFT	NEW YORK	11,000	880
MH10	OIL	TEXAS	14,000	1600
PX25	AIRCRAFT	OREGON	2,500	290
TY66	OIL	TEXAS	1,200	155

CUSTOMER

FIGURE 7.1. Some data from a file of customer records that could be of interest to operating management. The customer number (CUSTNUMB) field is the key; we can assume the file to be direct access on this key. BUSINESS holds the primary field of business of the customer, STATE the state where the firm is headquartered, EMPLOYEES the number of employees, and SALES the latest annual sales for the customer in millions of dollars. Although direct access is possible on presentation of the key, direct access on any other field, such as BUSINESS, will not be possible. The primary key field is underlined.

With this file it is easily possible to carry out any retrieval of the following type:

> Retrieve customer data (any field or fields from a CUSTOMER record) for customer X.

Typically an interactive program is written for a manager; he or she simply enters the required value for X. The program executes efficiently since few direct accesses are required to fulfill a request.

Unfortunately operating management may well be rarely interested in data for just one customer. Consider a retrieval of the following type:

> Retrieve customer data for customers in the oil business in Texas.

With the CUSTOMER file this can be carried out only by a sequential inspection of each record, selecting each record for which the BUSINESS and STATE fields have the values OIL and TEXAS respectively. Thus the primary key and direct access facility do not help; and the processing can take a long time if the file is large.

In chapter 2 we saw that even with the fastest disks currently available it takes about 10 milliseconds to read a block of data, giving a maximum possible reading speed of about 100 blocks per second, if we are lucky. However, the speed is likely to be a lot less than that because of delays while the operating system takes care of competing jobs (assuming a multiprogramming operating system). For a file of 500,000 records the time required can easily be an hour or more.

The solution to the problem involves the use of *secondary keys* and associated *auxiliary file structures*. This solution is widely used both with conventional files and data bases, although it comes at considerable cost as well, as we shall see.

Two major types of **auxiliary file structures** are used with such secondary keys, namely, *inverted files* (or file inversions) and *multiple linked lists*. We look at each of them in detail. In addition to these two basic types of structures there are many variations of the theme, as we shall see. Note that auxiliary file structures for *secondary keys* are sometimes called secondary indexes.

SECONDARY KEYS AND INVERTED FILES

Our aim is to obtain direct access to a file, such as CUSTOMER, on the basis of a field other than the main, or primary, key, such as CUSTNUMB in CUSTOMER. By the primary key we mean a field or combination of fields that has a unique value for each record and that may be used to construct the index for an indexed- sequential file. If direct access is possible on a field other than the primary key, that field is called a **secondary key**.

Referring again to the file CUSTOMER in Figure 7.1, suppose that the field BUSINESS is were a secondary key. That means that we can directly retrieve all the records for which the BUSINESS value is *OIL*, for example. Note that we say "all the records", for clearly there are more than one. In other words a secondary key value does not have to be unique and can occur in many different records. Thus in general a retrieval on the basis of a secondary key value retrieves many records, whereas a retrieval on the basis of a primary key retrieves only one record.

This gives us a clue to a solution to the problem of secondary key access. To have primary key access we relate each primary key value to the address of a record, by means of an index in the case of indexed-sequential files. Clearly to have access on the basis of a secondary key we must relate each secondary key value with the group of records

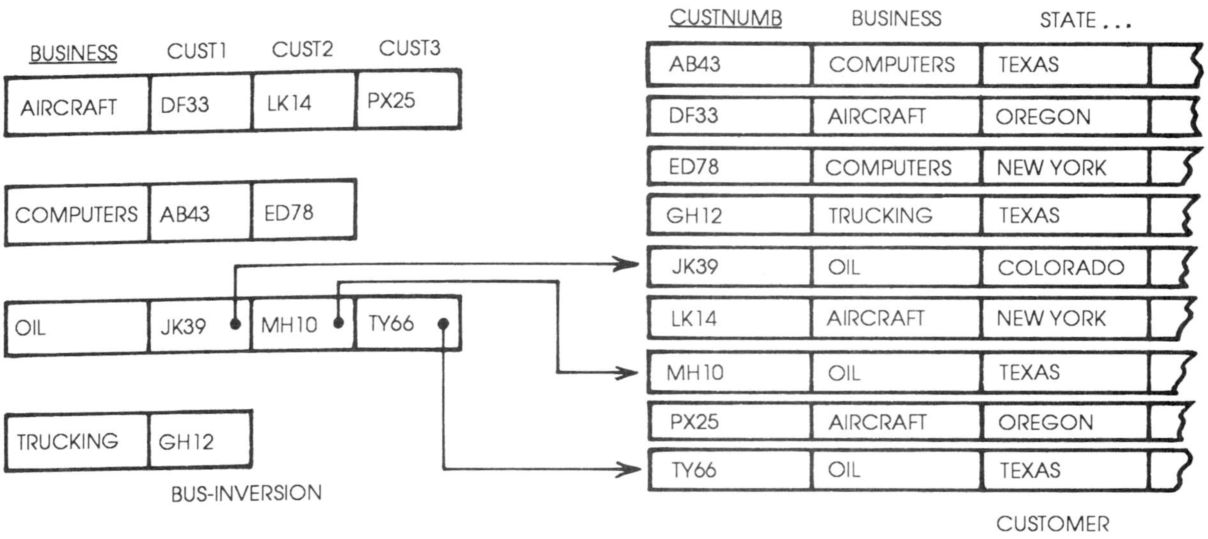

FIGURE 7.2. The auxiliary file BUS-INVERSION is an inversion on the field BUSINESS in CUSTOMER. In CUSTOMER the field BUSINESS is a secondary key, whereas in the inversion BUS-INVERSION it is the primary key. Both CUSTOMER and BUS-INVERSION are direct access files. Essentially a record in BUS-INVERSION contains a BUSINESS value from CUSTOMER followed by a list of pointers pointing to those records in CUSTOMER that contain the record's BUSINESS value. The pointers above are symbolic because they give the primary keys of the records to which they point, as opposed to their addresses. Primary key fields are underlined.

containing that secondary key. An inverted file is one way of doing that.

The Inverted File Concept

In Figure 7.2 we show the files CUSTOMER again, this time accompanied by the inverted file BUS-INVERSION, which is an inversion of the CUSTOMER file on the (secondary key) field BUSINESS. Now consider the value OIL that occurs in the BUSINESS fields in CUSTOMER.It occurs exactly 3 times in CUSTOMER, since oil is the business of customers JK39, MH10, and TY66. This information is stored in a record of the inversion on the field BUSINESS. We have a record in BUS-INVERSION with the BUSINESS field value OIL, followed by fields CUST1, CUST2, and CUST3 containing JK39, MH10, and TY66. In addition for each distinct BUSINESS value that occurs in CUSTOMER there is a single record in BUS-INVERSION with that value; following it we have a list of the CUSTNUMB values from CUSTOMER for which that BUSINESS value holds.

If we wish we can look at a BUS-INVERSION record as consisting of a BUSINESS value, followed by pointers to each CUSTOMER record containing that BUSINESS value. Unfortunately,BUS-INVERSION is a variable length record file, since a given BUSINESS value can be in any number of CUSTOMER records. BUS-INVERSION will be implemented as a direct access file with BUSINESS as the primary key field. Thus BUSINESS is a secondary key in CUSTOMER but a primary key in an inversion of CUSTOMER on BUSINESS.

Using an Inverted File

The principle behind the use of an inverted file is simple enough. Suppose we take the retrieval we had earlier, where we wanted the customers and their sales volume if the business was oil in Texas. We can carry out the following steps:

1. Retrieve the BUS-INVERSION record with primary key value OIL
2. Extract the CUST-NUMB values from this record (JK39, MH10, TY66)
3. Use each of these values in turn to directly access the CUSTOMER file
4. For each record so accessed extract the CUST-NUMB value and SALES value, provided the STATE value is TEXAS

The total file accesses is four, one to the inverted file and three to CUSTOMER. With a large file, if n is the number of customers in the oil business, we need 1+n file accesses, which is quite good (although it can be improved upon, as we shall see).

Note that a file access is not the same as the number of underlying disk accesses required to retrieve a record from a file. If each of the two files in Figure 7.2 were indexed-sequential files, it would likely take about 3 disk accesses to carry out a file access—that is, about 2 disk accesses to search the index of an indexed-sequential file and 1 to access the required record. That means that our 4 file acceses for the retrieval above would be 4*3 or 12 disk accesses. If we take direct disk access time (including a seek) as 25 milliseconds, then the time involved is 0.3 seconds. Not very fast by computer standards perhaps,

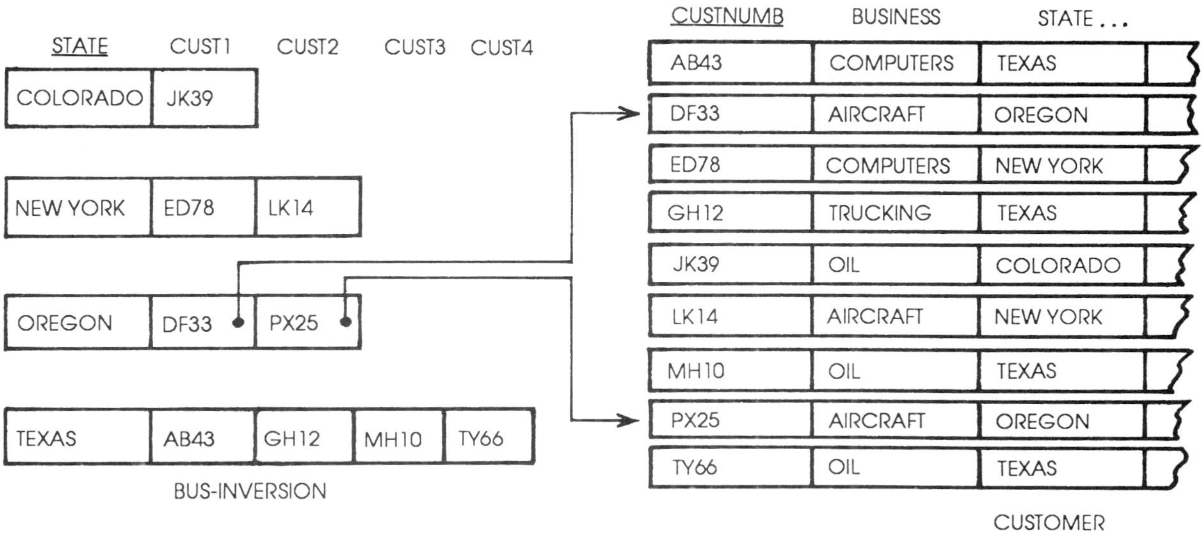

FIGURE 7.3. The auxiliary file STATE-INVERSION is an inversion of the file CUSTOMER on the field STATE. Primary key fields are underlined. Both files can be taken as direct access files. The pointers in STATE-INVERSION are symbolic.

but very much better than the time required to make a sequential search of CUSTOMER.

We can reduce the time required to carry out a retrieval if we have additional inversions at our disposal. Suppose that we have the inversion on STATE, which we call STATE-INVERSION (Figure 7.3). Let us now reconsider our request to retrieve the customer number and sales volume for each customer in the oil business in Texas. By accessing BUS-INVERSION using OIL as the primary key value, we retrieve the following customer number values:

JK39 MH10 TY66

If we then access the STATE-INVERSION file using TEXAS as the primary key we can retrieve the following customer number values:

AB43 GH12 MH10 TY66

The customer numbers that are common to both lists must be for those customers that are in both oil and Texas, namely, MH10 and TY66. We can then use these values to access the CUSTOMER file and retrieve the required SALES values. Thus use of the two inversions enables us to zero in on precisely those records in CUSTOMER that are of interest.

In the above example we needed 4 file accesses, one for each of the two inversions and two for the 2 CUSTOMER records, so we did not apparently save anything. However, suppose that CUSTOMER is large, with 100 records for customers in the oil industry and 60 customers in Texas with only 7 customers in both the oil industry and Texas. The method of using the two inversions requires (2 + 7) or 9 file accesses. If we use BUS-INVERSION alone we need 1 + 100 file accesses; or 1 + 60 file accesses if we use STATE-INVERSION alone.

This seems to be quite attractive, but as mentioned earlier there is a cost. Before we go into this aspect, however, we should be aware that we can use two distinct types of pointers in an inverted file, namely, **symbolic** and **physical** pointers, which we now examine.

Physical and Symbolic Pointers

The pointers used in the inversions in Figures 7.2 and 7.3 are **symbolic pointers**. A symbolic pointer contains a primary key value of the record pointed to.

Consider the typical symbolic pointer JK39 in the inversion record with key OIL in Figure 7.2. To obtain the record in CUSTOMER with key JK39, the access method uses the physical address of that record. If CUSTOMER is an indexed-sequential file then the access method obtains the record's (approximate) address by a search of the index. (If CUSTOMER is a hash file [Chapter 8] then the program first must obtain the address by hashing the key value JK39.)

An alternative uses **physical pointers** containing actual record addresses. Each record in CUSTOMER has a physical address, so that following a BUSINESS value in the inverted file we need only have a list of the addresses that contain records that contain that particular BUSINESS value. If CUSTOMER is an indexed-sequential file it is a difficult practical matter to load the inversion BUS-INVERSION with the disk addresses of the records pointed to. (However, if CUSTOMER is a hash file then the relative address of each record—whether home or overflow record—may be easily obtained for use in BUS-INVERSION.)

In general it is faster to use an inversion with physical pointers, but not always. Assume an indexed-sequential BUS-INVERSION with physical pointers. Assume also that CUSTOMER is an indexed-sequential file where we can get the disk addresses of the blocks. To carry out the retrieval of customer numbers and sales volumes for customers in the oil business in Texas, it will take 4 file accesses, as we saw earlier. The inverted file access will take about 3 disk accesses and the 3 CUSTOMER file accesses will take close to 3 disk accesses. This gives a total of 6 disk accesses, which is fewer than the corresponding case with symbolic pointers.

However, suppose that we simply wanted to retrieve the customer numbers for customers in the oil business in Texas. With symbolic pointers we need only access the inverted file BUS-INVERSION, for the pointers themselves in this file give the required customer numbers; thus we need 1 file access or about 3 disk accesses. In the case of physical pointers we must access the inverted file to obtain the pointers to the records in CUSTOMER (1 file access); then we must access the 3 records pointed to, to get the required customer numbers (3 more file accesses) for a total of 4 file accesses or 1*3 + 3*1 or 4 disk accesses, which is greater in every respect than for the case of symbolic pointers.

So which type of pointers should be used? In practice direct access files such as CUSTOMER are more often indexed-sequential files so that symbolic pointers are much easier to implement; on balance it is probably best to use them, even if they are somewhat slower than physical pointers. (When a file such as CUSTOMER is a hash file, either symbolic or physical pointers can be conveniently used.)

Symbolic pointers have an advantage over physical pointers that becomes apparent only when it is time to reorganize a file. Suppose that the file to be reorganized has a secondary key whose auxiliary structure uses physical pointers. When the records of this file are written out anew (in carrying out the reorganization), most of them will mostly have new disk addresses; therefore all the pointers in an inversion based on physical pointers would need to be changed, but not those in an inversion based on symbolic pointers.

For these reasons, and for the convenience of the reader, in the remainder of this chapter we confine our study to cases where *symbolic pointers* are used. Readers should simply remember that physical pointers are always a possibility, and that they usually give somewhat better results for the number of disk accesses required for any given processing task. Neverthless these results are not so different that radically different conclusions must be drawn.

Maintenance of an Inverted File

The snag with inverted files (and most other auxiliary structures for secondary keys) is that they are expensive to maintain in the face of updates, whether insertion, change, or deletion updates. Most of the difficulties can be seen from a consideration of insertion updates, which we look at first.

Insertion Update of CUSTOMER with a Record for a Customer in a Listed Business

Suppose that we insert into CUSTOMER the following new record:

QW99 TRUCKING NEW YORK 2,400 180

It takes 2 file accesses to place this record in CUSTOMER. One access is needed to attempt to read a record with key QW99 from the file to check if it is there already; another is needed to write the record into the file.

However, we must reflect this new record in the record in BUS-INVERSION (Figure 7.2) for the BUSINESS value TRUCKING, that is, the following record:

TRUCKING GH12

First we read this record (1 file access) and then we add the CUSTNUMB value QW99 to it and write it out, giving the following:

TRUCKING GH12 QW99

This is another file access, which is a total of 2 for the inverted file. (Notice also that the inverted file record grows, which is another problem we shall return to later.)

If we have an inversion on STATE, the inversion record with key NEW YORK also needs to be updated at cost of 2 file accesses. Thus the existence of an inversion doubles the number of file accesses required to insert a record of the type shown above. The existence of 2 inversions triples this number.

Insertion Update of CUSTOMER with a Record for a Customer Not in a Listed Business.

Suppose that we insert into CUSTOMER the following new record:

ZZ47 CHEMICALS OHIO 5,000 270

As before it takes 2 file accesses to place this record in CUSTOMER. To reflect this new record in the inversion for BUSINESS, we first attempt to read the inversion record for the BUSINESS value CHEMICALS. If we take the file as given in Figure 7.2, no record is found, although the exercise still costs a file access. We must then construct a new BUS-INVERSION record as follows:

CHEMICALS ZZ47

We must insert this into BUS-INVERSION, at the cost of another file access. Thus we need 2 file accesses to update the inverted file with this quite different type of insertion. We can conclude that no matter what kind of record is inserted, each inversion costs an additional 2 file accesses.

If we delete a record, each inversion also costs an additional 2 accesses. Suppose we delete the following record:

ED78 COMPUTERS NEW YORK 8,000 650

It takes two file accesses to read the record and then delete it. We must then read the inversion record with BUSINESS value COMPUTERS, that is, the following record:

COMPUTERS AB43 ED78

We must then remove the pointer ED78 and rewrite the record as follows:

COMPUTERS AB43

All this clearly takes an additional 2 accesses. We can thus conclude that deleting a record costs 2 additional file accesses for each inversion.

Change updating is the most expensive as far as file access is concerned. Suppose that customer ED78 decides that the future looks brighter in the aircraft industry, so that CUSTOMER record

ED78 COMPUTERS NEW YORK 8,000 650

is change updated to

ED78 AIRCRAFT NEW YORK 5,000 840

To reflect this in the inverted file, we first read the following record:

COMPUTERS AB43 ED78

We must then remove the pointer ED78 and rewrite the record as

COMPUTERS AB43

which costs 2 file accesses. But we are not finished. We must then read the record

AIRCRAFT DF33 LK14 PX25

and insert the new pointer ED78, so that we might then write out the following:

AIRCRAFT   DF33 ED78 LK14 PX25

This costs an additional 2 accesses. We thus conclude that change updating costs a total of 4 file accesses for each inversion.

In summary then, each inversion costs an additional 2 file accesses for an insertion, 2 file accesses for a deletion, and 4 file accesses for a change involving a field for which there is an inversion. Thus a file that is very volatile—that is, a file that is updated a great deal—is not suitable for secondary keys, since updating is severely slowed by the presence of one or more inversions.

It follows that great care must be taken when selecting a field for a secondary key. Ideally it should be a field that occurs very frequently in the conditions for retrieval of a record, is rarely if ever change updated, and is in a file that undergoes few deletions and insertions. Unfortunately such ideal circumstances are not often encountered in business, so that inversions tend to be kept to the absolute minimum that can be accepted.

This is a fundamental problem in file management and also in data base management. Although widely researched, no satisfactory solution is in sight. Other auxiliary structures for secondary keys, such as multiple linked lists, have similar difficulties with updates, as we shall see presently.

Since computer data bases generally are collections of direct access computer files linked by cross references, we have the same problem with secondary key access to a data base file. However, because of the large number of files in a data base, all of which are supposed to be available for information retrieval, the problem is compounded; data base systems are notorious for their poor performance as a result. Currently a great deal of research effort is directed towards finding a solution, although for the foreseeable future there is no alternative in commerce to secondary keys implemented by means of auxiliary files such as inverted files; we have to live with the performance problems.

Practical Considerations in the Construction of an Inverted File

It is clear from Figures 7.2 and 7.3 that a simple inverted file contains varying length records. An inverted file is also a direct access file and can in theory be either indexed-sequential or hash. A hash inversion file (with varying length records) is generally regarded as too difficult

BUSINESS	SEGMENT	MORE	CUST1	CUST2
AIRCRAFT	1	YES	DF33	LK14
AIRCRAFT	2	NO	PX25	—
COMPUTERS	1	NO	AB43	ED78
OIL	1	YES	JK39	MH10
OIL	2	NO	TY66	—
TRUCKING	1	NO	GH12	—

BUS-INVERSION

FIGURE 7.4. A version of the inverted file BUS-INVERSION from Figure 7.2 that does not involve variable length records. For each group of (in the above case two) pointers there is a record with a key made up of a BUSINESS value and a SEGMENT value. The pointers are thus segmented into groups numbered 1, 2, 3, and so on. To retrieve the pointers for the BUSINESS OIL we access the record with primary key OIL 1, then the key OIL 2, and so on. When there are no further segments to be retrieved the MORE field holds the value NO. The primary (and composite) key fields are underlined.

to construct, so that the indexed sequential technique is almost always used. We could use VSAM with IBM systems. However, the exercise would be pointless if VSAM were available, even though VSAM permits indexed-sequential files with variable length records. *VSAM has facilities for automatic construction of an inversion for a specified secondary key.* We shall look into this later. For now we want to look at how we can construct an inverted file if VSAM (or equivalent) is not available.

There is an immediate difficulty if we try to construct an inversion using ISAM, for most COBOL compilers do not support ISAM variable length record files. (Note that variable length files can be constructed with ISAM and PL/1.) If hash files are too difficult and ISAM cannot be used, there seems to be no alternative to installing VSAM. However, there is a reasonable alternative; it involves using an inverted file structure without variable length records.

This type of inverted file is illustrated in Figure 7.4. Each record in the inverted file can hold up to a fixed number of pointers. In the diagram we have an inversion of CUSTOMER on BUSINESS; the maximum number of pointers allowed is just two. In practice many more would be used. If a particular value of BUSINESS is associated with a number of records greater than the fixed number of pointers, an additional inversion record is used. If that is not enough we use a third record and so on. Thus the logical record of an inversion can be regarded as being broken up into a number of fixed length record segments. Each segment is numbered (SEGMENT value); the last segment for a given BUSINESS field value has a MORE value equal to NO, indicating no more segments.

To load the inversion of CUSTOMER on the BUSINESS field, the first step is to obtain the record key values for each value of BUSINESS. This can be done easily simply by sorting CUSTOMER on the field BUSINESS. The resulting file CUSTOMER-SA is shown in figure 7.5; we can assume that this is a tape file. We now load the inverted file from CUSTOMER-SA. During the loading we use sequential input for the tape file and sequential output for the inverted file.

CUSTNUMB	BUSINESS	STATE ...
DF33	AIRCRAFT	OREGON
LK14	AIRCRAFT	NEW YORK
PX25	AIRCRAFT	OREGON
AB43	COMPUTERS	TEXAS
ED78	COMPUTERS	NEW YORK
JK39	OIL	COLORADO
MH10	OIL	TEXAS
TY66	OIL	TEXAS
GH12	TRUCKING	TEXAS

CUSTOMER-SA

FIGURE 7.5. To load an inversion file the first step is a sort. Thus we sort the CUSTOMER file in Figure 7.1 on the field BUSINESS to load the inversion of CUSTOMER on BUSINESS shown in Figure 7.4. It is thus possible to use the sorted version of CUSTOMER (the file CUSTOMER-SA above) to sequentially write out BUS-Inversion records with the same BUSINESS value and increasing SEGMENT value (see Figure 7.4) The primary key is underlined.

The method used in the loading program is rather obvious now. We read a CUSTOMER-SA record; as long as the BUSINESS field value remains the same, we keep inserting the CUSTNUMB values into CUST(n) fields in BUS-INVERSION records with that BUSINESS value, remembering to increment the SEGMENT value as each BUS-INVER-

SION record is filled and written out. This ensures that each composite record key in BUS-INVERSION is greater than that of the previous record written out as well. (If we do not have ascending order, the INVALID KEY clause following a WRITE statement is executed.)

Practical Aspects of Updating an Inverted File

It is best to maintain the orderly arrangement in Figure 10.5. If we do not—that is, if we allow the development of dummy pointers anywhere within the arrays of pointers—we will complicate retrieval and updating programs. Since we can expect that retrieval programs will be very common, the simplest possible retrieval programs are desirable as well as an orderly arrangement of the pointers.

But this raises another question. Assume that we only allow dummy pointers at the end of the last record of a group for a given BUSINESS value (as illustrated in Figure 7.4). Suppose now that the following CUSTOMER record is inserted, so that new pointer KS20 is needed in the inversion:

```
KS20   OIL   TEXAS ...
```

The group of inversion records for the oil business are as follows:

```
OIL   1   YES   JK39   MH10
OIL   2   NO    TY66   -
```

The question now is whether the pointer KS20 should be inserted as follows:

```
OIL   1   YES   JK39   MH10
OIL   2   NO    TY66   KS20
```

That is, whether it should be inserted in the first available space at the end of the last record of the group for OIL, or whether it should be inserted so that the pointers are in ascending order, as follows:

```
OIL   1   YES   JK39   KS20
OIL   2   NO    MH10   TY66
```

This latter insertion is more complex, but it ensures that we can retrieve CUSTOMER records in ascending CUSTNUMB or primary key order given a BUSINESS value such as OIL. Readers will notice (see Figure 7.5) that the inversion records are loaded so that the pointers are in ascending order; this type of insertion merely maintains that order.

Clearly if the pointers are not maintained in ascending order, it is often necessary to use a sort with retrieval, since it is most likely that retrieved data from CUSTOMER will be required in ascending CUSTNUMB (symbolic pointer in an inversion of CUSTOMER) order. Unfortunately the cost of maintaining pointers in ascending order is high. With the example above of the insertion of pointer KS20, we must update both records of the group with BUSINESS value OIL, since pointers are *moved up* to make room for the new pointer in the correct position. If the group contains a large number of records, this is expensive, since on average half the records of the group need to be accessed.

Similar considerations apply to change updating of the BUSINESS field in CUSTOMER, since this results in a deletion of a pointer value in one inversion record and an insertion of a pointer value in another. Thus, unless updating is accompanied by moving up of pointers in the inversion records, the ascending order of the pointer values in the insertion following loading is rapidly destroyed.

We mentioned earlier that VSAM has facilities for automatic construction of an inversion for a given field. This system loads the inversion pointers in ascending order, but *fails to maintain this ascending order in the face of updates*, as we shall see later. (Many data base systems provide for inversions of fields in the files that make up the data base; in such cases it is normal that the system be able to maintain the pointers in the order in which they were initially loaded.)

In conclusion we can say that maintenance of the pointer order is to be preferred, but that this has a price. The decision about whether to pay the price must depend on the importance of the applications of the particular inverted file.

SECONDARY KEYS AND MULTIPLE LINKED LISTS

Another method of implementing a secondary key involves the use of **multiple linked lists**. Readers should be already familiar with the concept of a *linked list.* For example, ISAM used a linked list to link together all overflow records overflowing from a single prime data track (see chapter 6). With a secondary key implementation, the basic idea is to link all records with a common secondary key value, using a linked list.

The Multiple Linked List Concept

The basic concept of an implementation of a secondary key using multiple linked lists is illustrated in Figure 7.6. Here we implement a secondary key BUSINESS in the CUSTOMER file (Figure 7.1). As can be seen, each record in CUSTOMER is given a pointer field (PT-BUS); in the base of Figure 7.6 the pointer is a symbolic pointer holding the primary key of some other CUSTOMER record. For a given CUSTOMER value, such as OIL, all CUSTOMER records are chained together using the pointer field.

To begin a traversal of an individual linked list of records, we must have the primary key of the first record of the list. For this purpose there is an auxiliary structure, called a **linked-list index**. It is usually an indexed-sequential file, especially if the number of BUSINESS values is large. A record of this file (or linked-list index entry) consists of a BUSINESS value and the primary key of (pointer to) the first CUSTOMER record with that BUSINESS value. An obvious alternative is to use physical pointers in both CUSTOMER and the index. A BUSINESS value is a primary key in the linked-list index.

For a given file such as CUSTOMER, for each secondary key implemented, there is a pointer field in the file and a separate linked-list index. In Figure 7.6 we show a version of CUSTOMER with a (multiple) linked-list index (MLLI-BUS) for the secondary key BUSINESS and another index (MLLI-STATE) for the secondary key STATE. The pointer fields in CUSTOMER are respectively PT-BUS and PT-STATE.

Using Secondary Keys with Multiple Linked Lists

Let us first look at information retrieval using the single secondary key BUSINESS with the multiple linked list in Figure 7.6. Suppose that we have the following retrieval request:

> Retrieve the customer number and volume of sales for each customer in the oil business in Texas.

We carry out the following steps:

1. Access the linked-list index (MLLI-BUS) using the BUSINESS value OIL as the primary key, thus retrieving the PT-BUS value JK39.
2. Place the PT-BUS value in the data item CURRENT-POINTER.

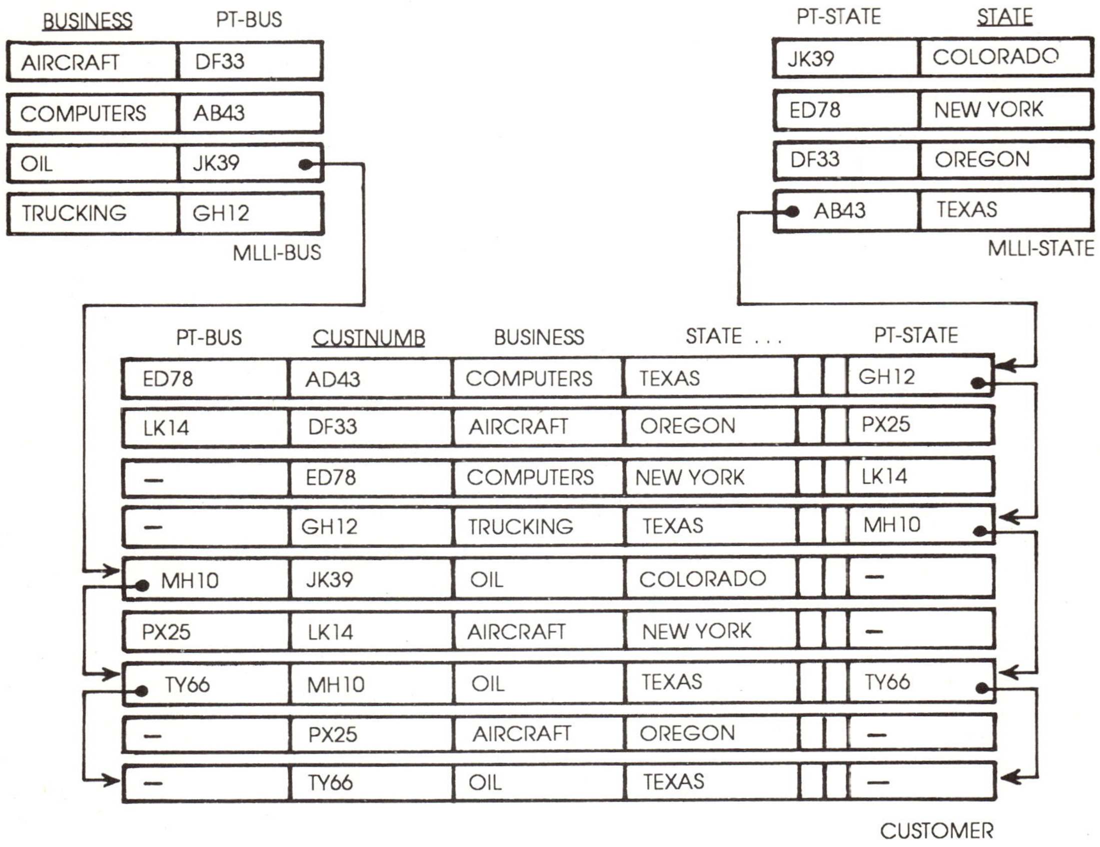

FIGURE 7.6. Use of one set of linked lists based on the pointer field PT-BUS and index MLLI-BUS to implement the secondary key BUSINESS in CUSTOMER, and another set of linked lists based on the pointer PT-STATE and index MLLI-STATE to implement the secondary key STATE. All pointers are symbolic. Primary key fields are underlined. The CUSTOMER file and the two index files are direct access files. The arrows trace the linked lists for OIL and TEXAS.

3. Retrieve the CUSTOMER record with primary key equal to the value in CURRENT-POINTER. Move the PT-BUS value in the record retrieved to CURRENT-POINTER.

4. If the STATE value in the record retrieved is TEXAS, print the CUSTNUMB and SALES values (see Figure 7.6.).
5. If the CURRENT-POINTER value is not null, then return to step 3, otherwise stop.

We see that in the case of the data in Figure 7.6, the retrieval involves 4 file accesses, one to the index, and three for the 3 records in CUSTOMER with BUSINESS value OIL. In general we need 1 + x accesses, where x is the number of records with the target secondary key value.

We saw earlier that the same number of file accesses were required with an inversion (if records of the inversion are allowed their natural varying length), but that a reduction in file accesses can be achieved by using two inversions. We cannot achieve any certain reduction by using two sets of multiple linked lists, however, because of the need to traverse a linked list to obtain the primary keys of those CUSTOMER records with a given secondary key value.

To see this, suppose we attempt the above retrieval using multiple linked-list implementations of the secondary keys BUSINESS and STATE (as illustrated in Figure 7.6). Earlier we saw that the ideal way to carry out the retrieval is by obtaining the CUSTNUMB values for BUSINESS value OIL, the CUSTNUMB values for STATE value TEXAS and selecting those CUSTNUMB values common to both. Only the CUSTOMER records for such common CUSTNUMB values need then be accessed, which often significantly reduces the number of file accesses (compared with accessing each CUSTOMER record with a given secondary key value and checkings its contents). However, we cannot obtain the set of CUSTNUMB values for OIL and TEXAS, in the case of multiple linked lists, without first traversing the lists. Since traversing a linked list involves a file access for each record of the list, no reduction in file accesses is possible. It must be concluded that for retrievals involving several secondary keys, inverted files are superior to multiple linked lists.

Note that the availability of a second set of linked lists gives us an alternative retrieval method, which may achieve a minor reduction in the number of file accesses; it may also give rise to an increase instead. Thus to retrieve the customer numbers and sales volumes for the oil business in Texas, we can alternatively use the following retrieval procedure:

1. Access the index MLLI-STATE using TEXAS as primary key. Take the PT-STATE value retrieved (AB43) and place it in the data item CURRENT-POINTER.

2. Retrieve the CUSTOMER record with primary key value equal to the value in CURRENT-POINTER. Move the PT-STATE value retrieved to CURRENT-POINTER.
3. If the BUSINESS value in the record retrieved is OIL, print the CUSTNUMB and SALES values.
4. If the CURRENT-POINTER value is not null, then return to step 2, otherwise stop.

With this version the number of file accesses is 1 + y, where 1 access is required to obtain the initial pointer from the index, and there are y records in CUSTOMER with the STATE value TEXAS. We saw that the number of accesses using the secondary key BUSINESS was 1 + x, where x was the number of CUSTOMER records with BUSINESS value OIL. If the CUSTOMER file has few business values then x is big on average, so that the use of the secondary key STATE is faster; furthermore, if the number of STATE values in CUSTOMER is small, then y is large, so that use of the secondary key BUSINESS is faster. The converse of this also holds.

We can conclude that since there is no benefit from using several secondary keys in a retrieval (if the secondary keys are implemented by multiple linked lists), the best secondary key to use is the one for which there the most distinct values and therefore the fewest records with any given secondary key value.

Maintenance of Secondary Keys with Multiple Linked Lists

Just as changes, insertions, and deletions affect the pointers in an inverted file, so too do these operations affect the pointer system in an implementation of a secondary key by means of a multiple linked list. In a nutshell, in addition to the normal file accesses to update a file such a CUSTOMER, additional file accesses are needed to update the pointer system. Furthermore the additional file accesses required usually exceed the number needed for the case of an inversion.

Consider the case of deletion updating. Referring initially to Figure 7.6, suppose that we want to delete the record for customer MH10. In addition to the file accesses for the deletion of this record (one to read it and another to delete it), we must repair the resulting gap in the linked list for the secondary key value OIL.

We have a similar problem if we change a secondary key value. If the BUSINESS value OIL in record MH10 is changed to something else, record MH10 must be dropped from the linked list for OIL, and the chain must be repaired just as with a deletion. In addition the record

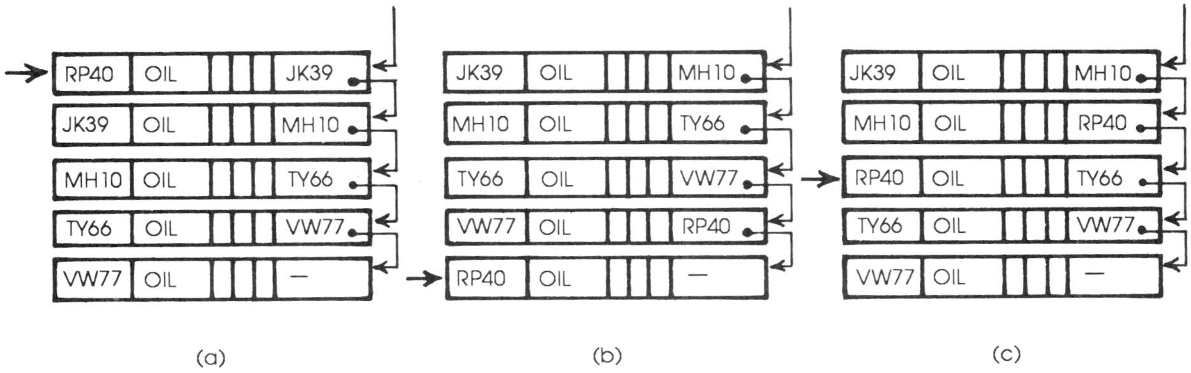

FIGURE 7.7. Three ways of maintaining the linked list for a given secondary key value in the face of insertions, as illustrated above by insertion of the record with primary key value RP40. In (a) the new record is placed at the beginning of the list, so that the records are maintained in LIFO order and form a stack. In (b) the new record is placed at the end of the list, so that the records are maintained in FIFO or chronological order. In (c) the new record is placed in the list so that the records appear in ascending primary key order; the records of the list are said to be maintained in sorted order.

MH10 must be placed in a new chain for the new value of BUSINESS; and this operation is equivalent to insertion of a new record, as far as chain repair is concerned.

Insertion of a new record brings us to a problem encountered earlier with inversions as well. Assuming that CUSTOMER is an indexed sequential file, any record inserted goes into the file in ascending primary key order. But suppose that we insert the following record:

RP40 OIL COLORADO ...

then the chain for OIL must be updated to allow for the new record. The question is where on the chain the record should go.

We have three convenient possibilities, as illustrated in Figure 7.7. The inserted record can go at the beginning of the chain, so that the last record inserted is the first retrieved by means of the secondary key (in this case OIL). Records of the list are thus maintained in LIFO order (last in, first out) and are said to form a **stack**, as in (a) in Figure 7.7.

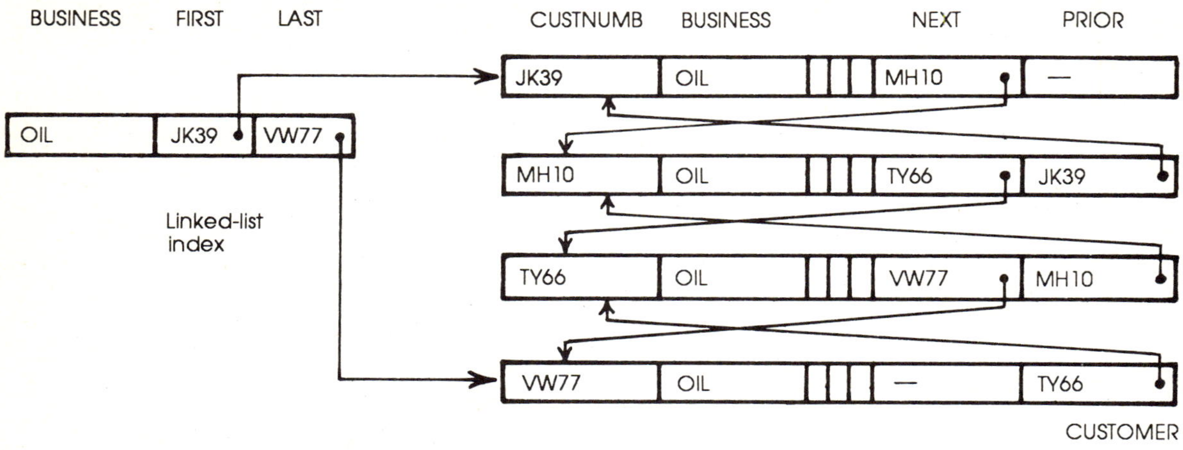

FIGURE 7.8. A single two-way linked list from a multiple two-way linked list version of the CUSTOMER file. For each linked list there is an index entry with a pointer to the first record of the list and a pointer to the last record of the list. The two-way list enables a list to be repaired following a removal of a record from the list without it being necessary to traverse the list from the beginning.

Another possibility is to place the inserted record at the end of the linked list, so that the first record in is the first out (FIFO technique). When this method is used the records with a given secondary key value are said to be retrievable in **chronological order**, as in (b) in Figure 7.7.

The final possibility is that a record can be placed in the chain so that records with a given secondary key value may be retrieved in ascending primary key order. That is, the records are said to be stored, or are available, in **sorted order**, as in (c) in Figure 7.7.

Sorted order is normally the most desirable of the three, since it is most likely that records with a given secondary key value will need to be displayed in ascending primary key order. Unfortunately the maintenance of sorted order, and also of chronological order, requires traversals of the relevant linked lists and thus increases the number of file accesses required for updating.

This need for chain traversals, both with information retrievals and with simple updates, is the primary disadvantage of secondary keys implemented by means of multiple linked lists, as compared with inverted files. The immediate advantage of multiple linked lists is that no variable length files are needed. However, we saw earlier that it is easily possible to implement an inverted file without the need for variable length records. It thus appears that inversions are superior in every way. This is not quite true, however, because with updates and multiple linked lists, some chain traversals can be avoided by using two-way linked lists or chains.

Two-Way Multiple Linked Lists

We illustrate implementation of the secondary key BUSINESS in the CUSTOMER file by means of a two-way linked list in Figure 7.8. For each record in the list there is a pointer to the prior record and the next record. In addition, in the index entry for a given BUSINESS value there is a pointer to the first record of the list and the last record.

It is possible to delete a record from the list without a chain traversal, since the record to be deleted contains the primary key of the prior and next records, and only these two records are needed to repair the chain. If the BUSINESS value in a record must be changed, then again that record is removed from an existing chain, although not from the file. This removal can also be accomplished without the need for a chain traversal. However, if a record must be inserted into the file and thus into a chain, or if a record simply must be reinserted into a chain following a prior removal, then a chain traversal is needed.

VSAM SECONDARY KEY FACILITIES

American National Standard (ANS) COBOL allows for the use of secondary keys in direct access files. However, as we have seen, to access a file directly by means of a secondary key, there must be an auxiliary inverted file or multiple linked-list system. If such a facility is to be available in COBOL merely by the specification of the desired secondary keys, then the underlying file access method must be equipped to create, maintain, and utilize the necessary auxiliary structures. In other words, before secondary key facilities can be incorporated in a COBOL compiler there must be a file access method capable of handling secondary keys automatically. *IBM's VSAM is such an access method.* In chapter 6 we decribed the indexed sequential file facilities of VSAM; we now look at how VSAM can be used with secondary keys.

When a VSAM indexed-sequential file is created using COBOL, it is possible to have VSAM create an inverted file (or **alternate index**, in VSAM jargon) for each secondary key specified in the indexed-sequential file loading program. An inversion is created automatically by the access method, without the user being aware of it, in much same way as an index is created for the primary key of the indexed-sequential file. As with the primary key index, the access method looks after all updating for the inverted files.

We now examine how secondary keys are specified using COBOL and how they are used. We assume that we are using IBM COBOL with VSAM as the underlying access method.

Creation of a COBOL Indexed-Sequential File with Secondary Keys

We shall use COBOL and VSAM to create a version of the file CUSTOMER (Figure 7.1) with primary key CUSTNUMB and secondary keys BUSINESS and STATE. All three keys must be specified in the environment division; they must also be specified in the data division as part of the buffer record for the indexed-sequential file. This is illustrated in the complete environment and data division specifications below for loading the file CUSTOMER and associated index and inversions. Assume that the records to be loaded are taken from a file SOURCE-CUSTOMER on tape (not specified below).

```
ENVIRONMENT DIVISION.
.
.
.
INPUT-OUTPUT SECTION.
FILE CONTROL.
        SELECT CUSTOMER ASSIGN TO CUST123
        ORGANIZATION IS INDEXED
        ACCESS IS SEQUENTIAL
        (Use DYNAMIC for direct access to all records with a
          secondary key value)
        RECORD KEY IS CUSTNUMB (primary key)
        ALTERNATE RECORD KEY IS BUSINESS
                WITH DUPLICATES
        ALTERNATE RECORD KEY IS STATE
                WITH DUPLICATES.
DATA DIVISION.
FILE SECTION.
FD CUSTOMER.
        LABEL RECORDS STANDARD
        RECORD CONTAINS 45 CHARACTERS
        DATA RECORD IS CUSTBUFREC.
01     CUSTBUFREC.
02     CUSTNUMB         PIC X(4).
```

```
        02      BUSINESS        PIC X(15).
        02       STATE           PIC X(15).
        02      EMPLOYEES       PIC 9(6).
        02      SALES           PIC 9(5).
WORKING-STORAGE SECTION.
01      CUSTREC (like CUSTBUFREC) ...
```

We see that the secondary keys are specified in the envirnoment division using the ALTERNATE KEY clause. These secondary key fields must also occur in the specification for the buffer record structure (CUSTBUFREC) for the file.

In the procedure division the COBOL code for loading the file is the same as for any straight VSAM indexed-sequential file; there are no references to the secondary keys. However, VSAM creates the necessary inversions as the file is written out, in much the same manner that it creates the index for the primary key.

Order of Records with the Same Secondary Key Value

In earlier sections we discussed the problem of the order in which records with the same secondary key value were to be available. In detail this is the problem of the order of records in a linked list or the order of the pointers in an inversion record. We saw that we could have chronological order (first in, first out), sorted (in ascending primary key) order, and even a stack (last in, first out).

With VSAM we can say that chronological order is used to maintain records with the same secondary key value. Note that because records of a VSAM indexed file are loaded in ascending primary key order, the records with the same secondary key value are also in ascending primary key order immediately after loading. Records inserted later with the same secondary key value are available only in chronological order.

Direct Access on the Basis of a VSAM Secondary (or Alternate) Key Value

When ACCESS IS RANDOM is coded in the file section of the environment division, we can directly access a record on the basis of the primary key, as we saw in chapter 6; however, we can directly access only *the first of a group* of records with the same secondary key value. To access all of the group of records we must specify ACCESS IS DYNAMIC. This permits **direct access** to the first record of the group and **sequential access** (in chronological order) to the remaining records of the group.

For example, suppose that we want to retrieve the first record in CUSTOMER with BUSINESS value OIL. Referring to Figure 7.2, we issue the following modified COBOL command:

```
MOVE "OIL" TO BUSINESS IN CUSTBUFREC,
READ CUSTOMER INTO CUSTREC,
        KEY IS BUSINESS IN CUSTBUFREC.
```

As a result the record with primary key value JK39 becomes available in CUSTREC, the working-storage structure. In addition, VSAM makes note of this record as the **record of reference**.

To retrieve the next record of the group, we now read the file sequentially in chronological secondary key order. We do this by issuing sequential READ statements:

```
READ CUSTOMER INTO CUSTREC, AT END ...
```

Each of the group of records is retrieved by a READ statement; each becomes the new record of reference when it is read. When the record of reference finally has a different secondary key value, the imperative following AT END is executed.

Retrieval Example Using a VSAM Secondary Key Value

Suppose now that we want to carry out the following retrieval request:

> Find the customer number and sales volume for each customer in the oil business in Texas.

Assuming that we have coded ACCESS IS DYNAMIC in the file section of the environment division, the essentials of the COBOL procedure are as follows:

```
MOVE "OIL" TO BUSINESS IN CUSTBUFREC.
COMPUTE TOTAL-RECORDS = 0.
MOVE "YES" TO MORE-RECORDS.
READ CUSTOMER INTO CUSTREC,
        KEY IS BUSINESS IN CUSTBUFREC,
        INVALID KEY MOVE "NO" TO MORE-RECORDS.
IF MORE-RECORDS = "YES" AND STATE IN CUSTREF = TEXAS
 THEN
        COMPUTE TOTAL-RECORDS = TOTAL-RECORDS + 1,
        PERFORM DISPLAY-DATA.
PERFORM SCAN-RECORD-SET UNTIL MORE-RECORDS = "NO".
IF TOTAL-RECORDS = 0 THEN
        DISPLAY "NO DATA SATISFIES CONDITIONS".
CLOSE CUSTOMER,
```

```
        STOP RUN.

SCAN-RECORD-SET.
** The file is now being accessed sequentially in secondary key
** order.
        READ CUSTOMER INTO CUSTREC,
                AT END MOVE "NO" TO MORE-RECORDS.
        IF MORE-RECORDS = "YES" AND
                STATE IN CUSTREC = "TEXAS" THEN
                    COMPUTE TOTAL-RECORDS = TOTAL-RECORDS + 1,
                    PERFORM DISPLAY-DATA.
DISPLAY-DATA.
        DISPLAY "CUSTOMER NUMBER    ", CUSTNUMB IN CUSTREC,
                "SALES VOLUME       ", SALES IN CUSTREC.
```

The retrieval involves both a direct access to the first record of the group and a sequential scan of the remaining records.

With VSAM there is no facilitiy for READ command to access a record satisfying more than one secondary key value, although such a command is possible in principle. For example, suppose that we specify alternate keys for both BUSINESS and STATE; we can imagine the following command sequence:

```
MOVE "OIL" TO BUSINESS IN CUSTBUFREC.
MOVE "TEXAS" TO STATE IN CUSTBUFREC.
READ CUSTOMER INTO CUSTREC,
        KEY IS BUSINESS IN CUSTBUFREC,
        KEY IS STATE IN CUSTBUFREC.
```

Clearly the READ command retrieves the first record describing a customer in the oil business in Texas. It is worth repeating that such a command is not currently available with VSAM. Commands of this type are in fact available only with the most sophisticated data base systems.

SUMMARY

To obtain direct access to a file on the basis of the primary key, an index is needed. But to obtain direct access on the basis of a nonprimary key field, either an inverted file structure or a multiple linked-list index is needed. A nonprimary key field on which direct access is possible is called a secondary key field.

An inverted file has a record for each secondary key value; such a record contains pointers to records of the original file that contain a particular secondary key value. A linked-list index has a record for each secondary key value; such a record contains a pointer to the first record in the original file with that secondary key value; the remaining records with that secondary key value are linked by a linked list.

Pointers can be either symbolic or physical. A symbolic pointer contains the primary key of a record, whereas a physical pointer contains the disk address of a record.

Updates to the original file mean updates to the auxiliary structure that supports a secondary key, so that secondary keys reduce performance. They should not be installed without careful consideration of consequences.

The VSAM access method has a facility for automatically creating an inverted file for a specified secondary key as an indexed-sequential file is created. Secondary keys are maintained in chronological order.

EXERCISES

1. Using the file CUSTOMER (Figure 7.2) and the inversion BUS.INVERSION, give a retrieval procedure and the number of file (but not disk) accesses required to execute it, for each of the following retrieval requests:
   a. What business areas are New York customers in?
   b. What Texas customers are in the oil business?
   c. What Oregon companies are not in the aircraft business?
   d. What customers are in either the computer or the oil business?
2. Using the file CUSTOMER (Figure 7.3) and the inversion STATE-INVERSION, give a retrieval procedure and the number of file (but not disk) accesses required to execute it, for each of the following retrieval requests:
   a. What business areas are Oregon customers involved in?
   b. What customers are either in Oregon or Colorado?
   c. What Oregon customers are in the aircraft business?
   d. What computer businesses are not located in Texas?
3. For the CUSTOMER file and inversions in Figures 7.2 and 7.3, give the updating procedures and number of required file accesses for the following:
   a. The number of employees at customer ED78 is increased to 9,000
   b. The number of employees for all customers in the oil business is increased by 10 percent
   c. Customer AB43 moves from Texas to New York

d. Customer LK14 switches from the aircraft business to the trucking business
e. A new Oregon customer in the oil business is entered
f. A new New York customer in the computer business is entered
g. Customer MH10 is deleted
h. Customer JK39 is deleted

4. Using the linked-list index and linked lists in Figure 7.6, repeat exercise 1.
5. Using the linked-list index MLLI-STATE in Figure 7.6, repeat exercise 2.
6. Using the linked-list indexes in Figure 7.6, repeat exercise 3.
7. Assume a two-way linked list index, like that in Figure 7.8, for the secondary key BUSINESS in Figure 7.6. Repeat exercise 3 using this assumption.
8. Using VSAM or some other access method that permits secondary keys, create an indexed-sequential version of CUSTOMER with BUSINESS and STATE as secondary keys.
9. Using CUSTOMER created in exercise 8, write programs to find:
   a. The customer number and volume of sales for each customer in Texas
   b. The total sales of all New York customers in the computer business
10. Using the CUSTOMER file from exercise 8, write an interactive program that retrieves all information about customers in state S in business B where S and B are entered at a terminal.

8 HASH FILES

In chapter 6 we mentioned that there were two fundamental types of direct access files, namely, indexed-sequential files and hash files. Sequential files are of course the most common, with indexed-sequential the next most common. After that come hash files, which have a narrower but nevertheless very important band of use. Indexed-sequential files allow both sequential access and direct access on the basis of a record key. Hash files in practice permit only direct access, although with some (inconvenient) auxiliary structures it is possible to process a hash file in ascending key order, just like a sequential file. It is this inconvenience of sequential processing that restricts the use of hash files.

Some readers may wonder why we need to bother with hash files at all. After all, with indexed-sequential files we can process both sequentially and by direct access. So why should we be concerned with a type of file that largely permits only direct access?

The answer lies in the speed of direct access. We saw that the access method needs the disk address of a required record before the channel program and disk controller can be directed to the record's disk location. We also saw that with indexed- sequential files, the information relating record keys to disk addresses is held in an index, which must be searched before direct access can commence. This index is largely located on disk, so that disk accesses are consumed in the initial search of the index. Thus the average number of disk accesses required to retrieve a record directly (the average search length) from an indexed-sequential file is about 3 disk accesses. Remembering that a disk access costs 30 milliseconds, this means that direct access is very slow with an indexed file.

With a well-designed hash file the average search length can be very close to one disk access per direct record retrieval. Thus hash files are useful in applications where sequential access is rarely needed and speed of direct access is vital. Common areas where they are used include military systems, on-line file systems, and the underlying files of data bases.

Well-designed hash files are the fastest available; the high speed is due to the use of a hashing routine to relate a record key with a disk address. A hashing routine involves a standard calculation procedure applied to the record key; the result of the calculation is a disk address called the record's **home address.**

Most hash file records are stored in their home addresses. This means that to find the record with key 56 we first apply the hashing routine to 56 to get the record's home address. The access method is then directed to retrieve the record in this home address. Thus the retrieval requires only one access, since we escape the disk accesses involved in searching an index.

However, there are difficulties that cause the average search length to be always somewhat greater than unity; if the file is poorly designed the average search length can be worse than is the case for an indexed-sequential version of the file. Accordingly we must look carefully at the basic principles behind hash files to understand how to design them properly. Because of the relative ease of constructing an indexed-sequential file using VSAM, it is quite true to state that it cannot pay to do a sloppy job with the design of a hash file. It either should be done well or not at all.

BASIC PRINCIPLES

A good example of an application where a hash file organization is likely to be appropriate involves information about producing oil wells for a large oil company. The oil wells are scattered all over the globe, and individuals and departments in the oil company have a constant need for information about specific wells. To meet this need, an oil-well file can be constructed, with 1 record for each of the company's wells, with the well number as the record key.

Typically there is a large flow of requests for oil-well information, so that the file must be fast. If only one read/write head is available for the physical file (or dataset), an average search length of 3 disk accesses per record permits up to 30 different record accesses per second. If the average search length is close to unity, then we can accomodate up to 90 record accesses per second. Thus a hash file is probably called for if there is little need for sequential processing in ascending key order. In general ascending key order is not possible in a hash file without auxiliary structures, because the hashing routine scatters records all over the file. We return to this presently.

Updates for such an oil-well file typically arrive in an irregular stream, so that it is probable that the file is updated by direct access. Thus matching of transaction records with oil- well records by means of sequential processing in ascending key order is rarely advantageous. Some sequential processing for information retrieval may be necessary, but it is unlikely that this sequential processing would require processing in ascending key order.

As an example, if each record contains a field (FLOW-RATE) giving the rate at which oil is pumped (or flows) from the well, we might want to find the total flow from all wells. To determine this, each record must be read and the value in FLOW-RATE added to a SUM variable. This clearly requires sequential processing, but the records do not have to be read in ascending key order. Such sequential processing is quite convenient with a hash file, as we shall see. It is sequential processing in ascending key order that is difficult and indeed impossible without additional structures.

It is clear that our file of oil-well data might best be structured as a hash file. As shown in Figure 8.1, we assume for convenience of exposition that our oil-well file (OIL-WELL) has four fields, as follows:

WELL-NUMB The key field contains a 4-character alpha-numeric identifier

FLOW-RATE Oil-flow rate in hundreds of barrels per day

STATE Country containing the well (or state or province in a federation)

TERRAIN Indicates the kind of terrain in which the well is drilled

WELL-NUMB	FLOW-RATE	STATE	TERRAIN
AA11	8	TEXAS	OPEN
AB14	50	ALASKA	OFF-SHORE
AB74	6	COLORADO	MOUNTAIN
CD83	20	TEXAS	OFF-SHORE
...			

FIGURE 8.1. Records describing oil wells that are used to construct a hash file called OIL-WELL. The wells are assumed to belong to an oil company. The file is also assumed to be very large and is normally only accessed directly. Because of the large number of users, speed of access is very important, and so a hash file is preferred.

The figure contains some examples of oil-well records shown in ascending key order as they might appear in a sequential tape file.

The Basic Hashing Process

A hash file resides on a magnetic disk. We saw that each block on disk has an address, namely, its cylinder number, track number, and block number. The space occupied by a hash file is simply a sequence of such directly addressible blocks. Instead of having to address these

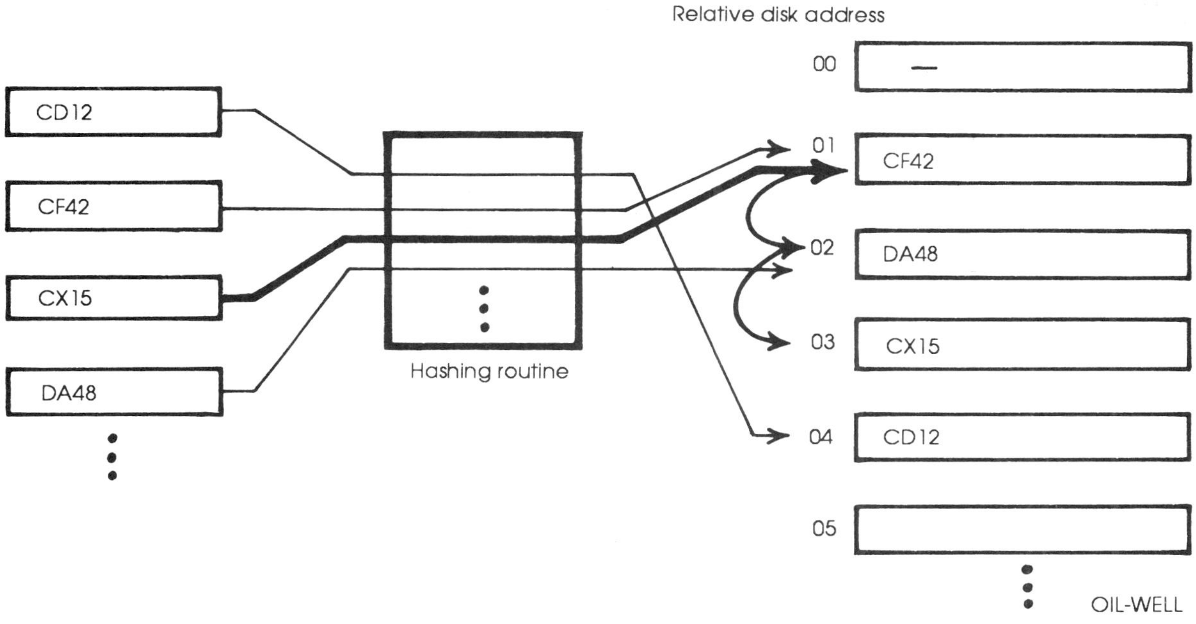

FIGURE 8.2. Basic idea behind the creation of the hash file OIL-WELL, each record of which contains information about an oil well. The hashing routine uses the primary key of a record (the WELL-NUMB) field) to calculate the disk address to which the record is to be assigned. This calculated disk address is called the home address of the record. Thus disk address 01 above is the home address of the record for well number CD12. The hashing routine applied to well number CD12 will always generate the address 01, so that it may be used to retrieve the record again. Not infrequently the hashing routine assigns two or more records to the same address. Thus above, the home address of record CX15 is also 01. When this happens the home address can overflow and the overflowing record (or records) must be placed in some other unused address.

blocks by their physical address (cylinder number, track number, and block number), we can use **relative addresses**. Thus the first block of the address space has address 0, the next address 1, and so on (illustrated at the right in Figure 8.2).

Figure 8.2 depicts the basics of the construction of the hash file OIL-WELL. The records could be available on tape. Using the WELL-NUMB value, the hashing routine calculates a disk address. For a given WELL-NUMB value the disk address calculated is always the same. Thus well number CD12 causes the hashing routine to generate the disk address 04, into which the record is placed using a COBOL

WRITE command and the address 04. This calculated disk address is called the *home address* of a record. If we need to retrieve the record for well number CD12 we use the hashing routine to calculate the record's home address, then use a COBOL READ command and this address to retrieve the record.

This sounds quite simple. Unfortunately there is a snag. Not infrequently the hashing routine calculates the same home address for two or more distinct record keys. As shown in Figure 8.2, this happens for keys CF42 and CX15. This phenomenon is sometimes called a **collision**; those records that hash to the same address are often called **synonyms**. If the address can hold only one record, as is often the case, then the additional records assigned to the address by the hashing routine are said to overflow from the address. These **overflow records** are normally placed elsewhere in the file in an unused address; thus **overflow records** are not in their home addresses.

Overflow records can have a serious effect on the average search length for a hash file. It is clear that to retrieve a home address record, it is necessary only to access the home address. To retrieve an overflow record, the home address must first be accessed (for otherwise we will not know beforehand that the record sought is an overflow record); then a search must be made of other nearby addresses to find the record. This search can take many accesses, so that if there are many overflow records in the file and it takes many accesses to find each one, the average search length can be high, even higher than with an indexed-sequential file.

It follows that the primary aim of hash file design is to keep the average search length low; this is done both by keeping low both the number of overflow records and the number of accesses required to retrieve those overflow records. This is the heart of the matter, which we shall return to again shortly.

COBOL READ and WRITE Commands for Hash Files

So far our discussion has been fairly abstract. To make things more concrete we must examine exactly how records are written into and read from a hash file using COBOL.

With ANS COBOL the file organization frequently used for hash files is called **relative file organization** and is specified in the input-output section with the clause ORGANIZATION IS RELATIVE. This file organization is also available with IBM COBOL. However, IBM COBOL allows for an additional file organization, called **direct file organization**, which can also be used for constructing hash files. Direct

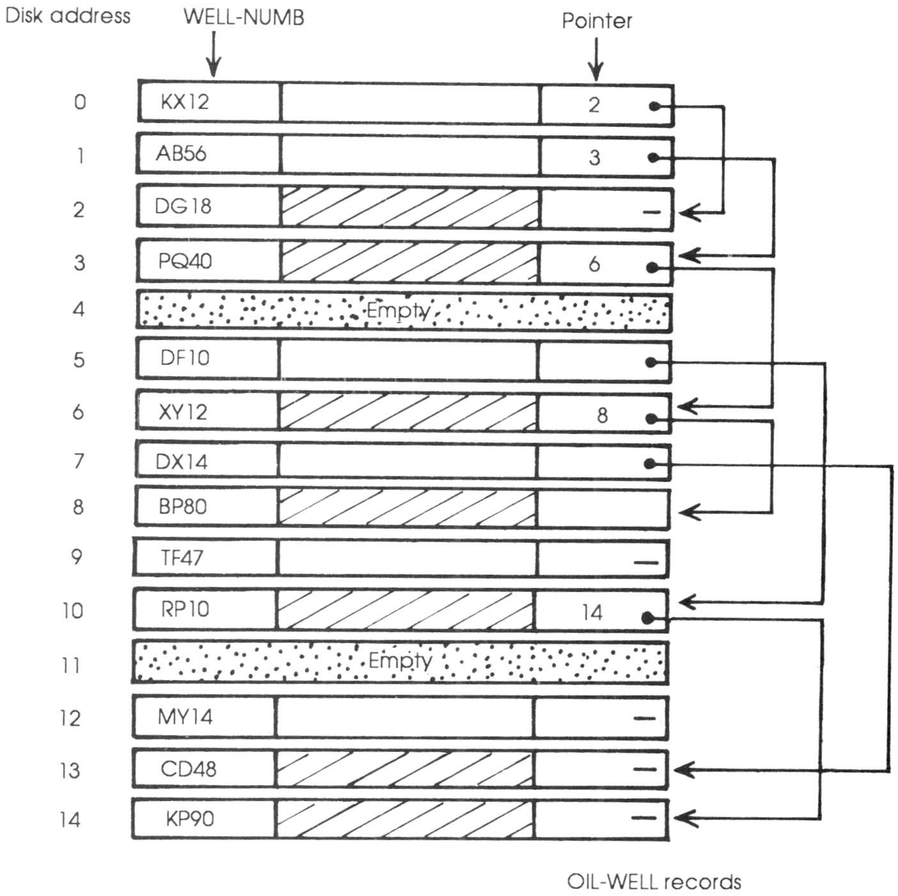

FIGURE 8.4. Illustration of the correspondence between relative disk address and physical disk address. In the above we assume 8 blocks per track and 6 tracks per cylinder. The access method keeps note of the physical address corresponding to relative address 0, and from this can calculate the physical address corresponding to any other relative disk address.

file organization is not part of ANS COBOL; it is specified with IBM COBOL compilers by placing ORGANIZATION IS DIRECT in the environment division.

The hash files constructed with direct file organization form a specialized subgroup of hash files that can be expensive in terms of disk space required. In this chapter we shall therefore illustrate hash file principles using relative file organization. Direct files are too specialized and not suitable for illustrating general principles. However, later when we have thoroughly examined hash file principles, we shall look at what direct file organization has to offer and at what cost.

Relative file organization takes its name from relative disk addresses. It provides for an address space on disk made up of a sequence of data blocks that can be addressed directly by specifying their relative position. We can refer to block 0 (address 0) for the first block of the file, block 1 (address 1) for the second, and so on. Thus the address of each block is relative to the first block, which is rarely physically the first block on the disk. Block 0 of a relative file could be block 2 of track 7 of cylinder 50.

When we use a READ command to read a record at relative address 7, the access method uses the physical address of block 0 to deduce the physical address corresponding to relative address 7. In this way we avoid having to refer to cylinders and tracks in a program. A sample correspondence between physical addresses and the first few relative addresses of a hash file is illustrated in Figure 8.3.

Suppose that we are creating the hash file OIL-WELL as a relative file. In the environment division with IBM COBOL we specify the following:

```
ENVIRONMENT DIVISION.
.
.
.
INPUT-OUTPUT SECTION.
FILE CONTROL.
        SELECT OIL-WELL
                ASSIGN TO DA-R-OWL
        ORGANIZATION IS RELATIVE
        ACCESS IS SEQUENTIAL
                NOMINAL KEY IS DISK-ADDRESS.
```

In the ASSIGN clause DA means direct access file, R means relative file, and OWL is the ddname for the dataset definition statement (DD-statement) for the file. Although this is a specification for creating the file, we specify that ACCESS IS SEQUENTIAL. The reason for this becomes clear when we examine loading methods. For now, a brief explanation is that the keys for the records are best hashed earlier so that the records can be loaded in ascending relative address order.

Finally in the above specification we specify NOMINAL KEY IS DISK-ADDRESS. DISK-ADDRESS is a COBOL variable or identifier to be specified in the working-storage section of the data division. It is this variable that will hold the relative disk address to be used by the access method for COBOL READ and WRITE commands. (Note that with ANS COBOL, as opposed to IBM COBOL, we specify RELATIVE ADDRESS IS DISK-ADDRESS.)

Now suppose that OW-REC is the working-storage structure for OIL-WELL records and OW-BUFREC is the buffer record structure. Suppose now that we have a record in OW-REC to be placed in the hash file in address 56. We code the following:

```
    COMPUTE DISK-ADDRESS = 56.
    WRITE OW-BUFREC FROM OW-REC.
```

The access method takes the record from OW-REC and places it in the buffer. It also extracts the record's disk address from DISK-ADDRESS and places the data block in the buffer (which will contain a single record) on disk at this relative block address.

It we want to read a record, we hash the record's key to obtain the disk address. Suppose the disk address is 27 and that the record involved is in its home address. We code the following:

```
    MOVE 27 TO DISK-ADDRESS.
    READ OIL-WELL INTO OW-REC.
```

The access method extracts the relative disk address from DISK-ADDRESS, converts it to the physical disk address, and causes the required block to be moved to the buffer, from which the record is extracted and placed in OW-REC.

If the required record is an overflow record, it will not be in its home address 27. Examination of the record retrieved from address 27 shows that it is not the record with the required oil- well number. Depending on how the overflow records are placed on the disk, we might then decide to look in address 28, then in address 29, and so on until we have checked perhaps the nearest 20 addresses. Suppose the required record is for oil-well number RT56. We code the following:

```
         COMPUTE DISK-ADDRESS = DISK-ADDRESS + 1.
         COMPUTE COUNT = 0, MOVE "NOT FOUND" TO SEARCH-MONITOR.
         PERFORM SEARCH-FOR-OVERFLOW UNTIL COUNT = 20.
         . . .
SEARCH-FOR-OVERFLOW.
         READ OIL-WELL INTO OW-REC.
        IF WELL-NUMB IN OW-REC = "RT56"
```

```
THEN COMPUTE COUNT = 20
     MOVE "FOUND" TO SEARCH-MONITOR
ELSE COMPUTE COUNT = COUNT + 1
     COMPUTE DISK-ADDRESS = DISK-ADDRESS + 1.
```

Where each overflow record is placed in an address ahead of or greater than its home address and has to be searched for in the manner of the above COBOL excerpt, the overflow management method is called **progressive overflow management**, or **open addressing**. We examine it next in some detail because it is commonly used.

Overflow Records and Progressive Overflow Management

To understand progressive overflow management more fully, imagine that we have only 15 relative addresses in our hash file for the oil-well records. The file has only 13 records, and they are assigned to the different addresses by the hashing routine. We can imagine an address to be a bucket and in this case a bucket that can hold only 1 record. It is convenient to imagine a record as a sphere that just fits a bucket. Where more than one record has been assigned to an address, we have overflow. We can imagine 7 overflow records. The remaining 6 are home address records.

After all home address records have been placed in their home addresses, the overflow records are loaded. Each overflow record is placed in the nearest empty address with an address value greater than the home address value. If there is no empty slot for an overflow record before the end of the file, then the search for an empty slot continues from the beginning of the file.

Chained Progressive Overflow

From the previous section it should be clear that the major problem with progressive overflow management is that the overflow records can increase the average search length far too much. The difficulty is that if a record is n addresses away from its home address, n+1 disk accesses must be made to get at it, since the record's home address must be accessed and all the intervening addresses as well.

A solution to this problem is a pointer field in the home address record; this pointer field should contain the address of the first record overflowing from that home address. The first overflow record in turn has a pointer field pointing to the next overflow record, (illustrated in Figure 8.4). By following a pointer chain in search of a record overflow-

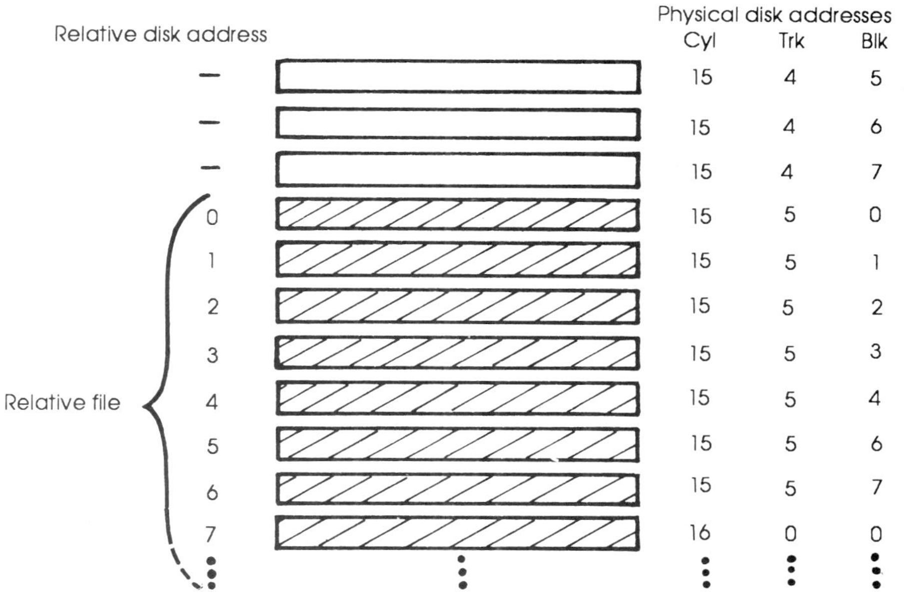

FIGURE 8.3. Part of a version of the OIL-WELL hash file that uses chained progressive overflow management. Each record has a space for a pointer or address field that contains the relative disk address of the next overflow record in any possible overflow chain.

ing from a home address, all intervening addresses are skipped. Such a pointer chain is called a **linked list**. We have already had examples of this type of pointer chain with the overflow records in ISAM files and secondary indexes.

In Figure 8.4 we have a number of pointer chains of varying lengths, all beginning at a home address (overflow records are shaded). This type of progressive overflow where the overflow records are tied together with pointers is called **chained progressive overflow**.

It is instructive to compare the average search length for the file in Figure 8.4 with the average search length if the overflow were plain progressive without the chains. We consider chained progressive overflow first.

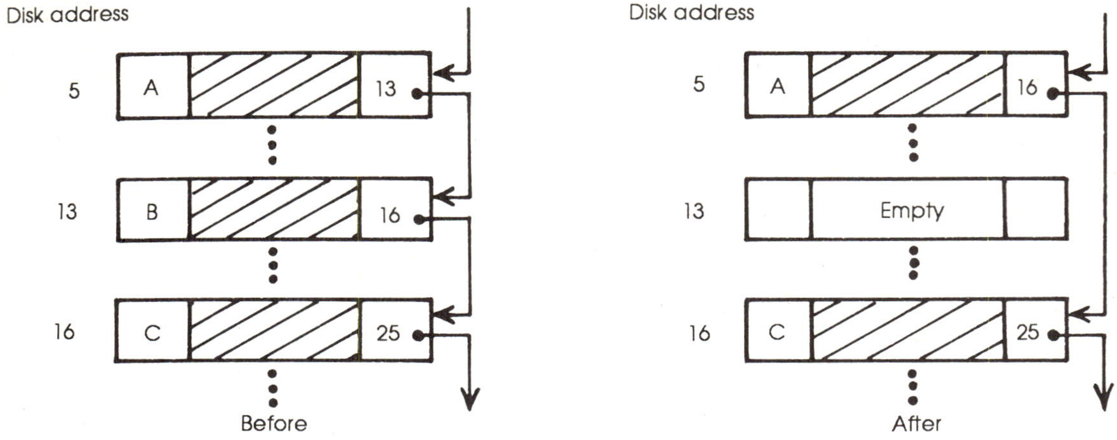

FIGURE 8.5. **Deletion of record B from an overflow pointer chain. All records (shaded) can be taken as overflow records.**

There are 6 chains in the file varying in length from 1 record to 4. The following table lists the different chains and the number of accesses required to retrieve records at random from these chains:

Number of chains	Records per chain	Total accesses	Records per chain
2	1	1	2
2	2	3	6
1	8		6
1	4	10	10
		Overall Total	24
		Average Search Length	24/13 = 1.84

To retrieve the record on a chain that is 1 record long takes 1 access. Since there are 2 such chains the total accesses required for them is 2*1 or 2. To retrieve in random order the 2 records on a chain that is 2 records long takes 1 + 2 or 3 accesses, so that the total for the 2 of these chains is 2*3 or 6 accesses. Continuing in this way we can complete the table above. The total accesses for all the records is 24. Since

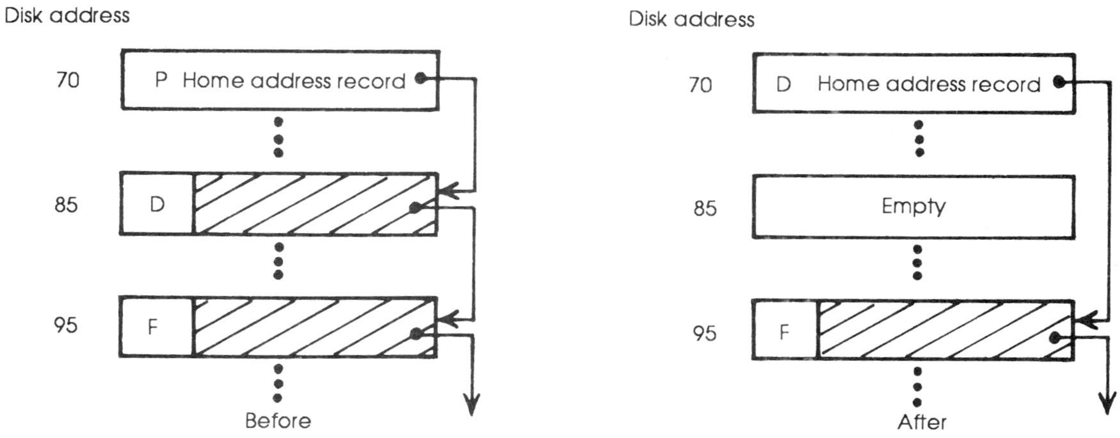

FIGURE 8.6. Deletion of a home address record P for which there is an overflow chain. The next record of the old chain (record D) is deleted and placed in the home address as the home address record for the chain. Overflow records are shaded.

the number of records involved is 13, the average number of accesses to retrieve a record (the average search length), must be 24/13 or 1.84.

In the previous section we saw how the average search length was computed for the case of progressive overflow. Applying this method to the records in Figure 8.4 and assuming no pointer chain, we get 48 for the total accesses required to retrieve all the records in random order. Thus the average search length is 3.69, which is much worse than with chained progressive overflow. It must be remembered that the example in Figure 8.4 is completely arbitrary; not too much should be read into the numerical values computed for the average search length.

Nevertheless, as we shall confirm later with more significant examples, chained progressive overflow gives a much lower average search length than does straight progressive overflow. Unfortunately the improved average search length comes at a price, the price of maintaining the pointer chains. Where we have at most 1 record per disk address (as is the case in Figure 8.4), the following management rules should be adhered to:

1. Each record must have a pointer field, capable of containing a relative disk address. The value is set to null if a pointer is not needed.

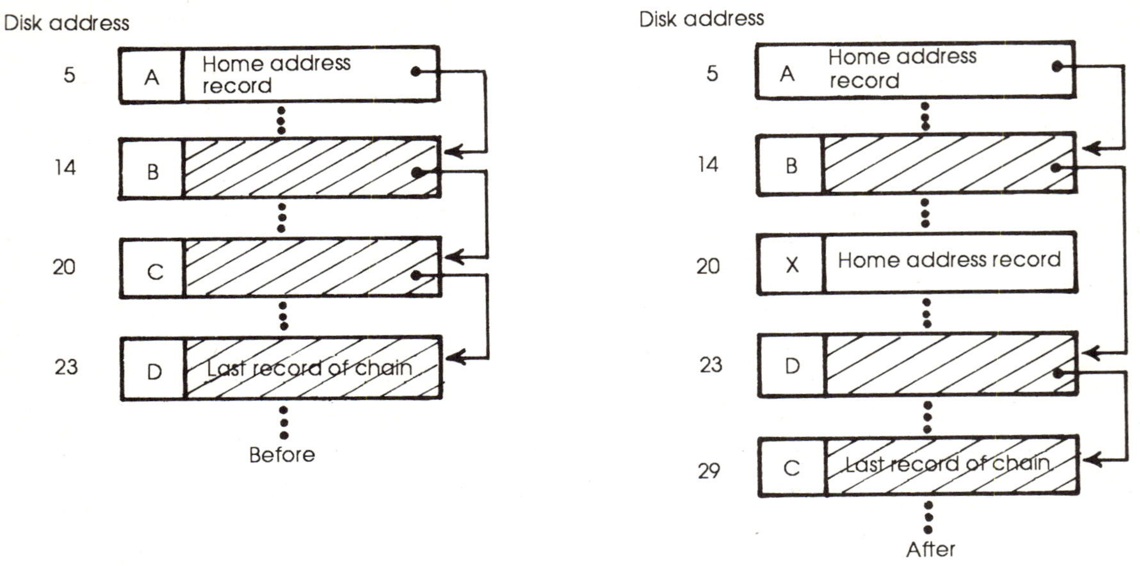

FIGURE 8.7. Illustration insertion of a record (X) that hashes to an address (20) already occupied by an overflow record (C) belonging to (or hashing to) another address (5). Record C must be deleted and placed elsewhere, usually at the end of the overflow to which it belongs. Record X can then be inserted at its home address. Overflow records are shaded.

2. When an overflow record is deleted, the overflow chain should be repaired (as illustrated in Figure 8.5). If A, B, and C are consecutive records of a chain and if B is deleted, the pointer field in record A must be adjusted to contain the address of record C.
3. If a record from a home address is deleted and there are overflow records for that home address, then a record from the overflow chain (usually the first) should be deleted and placed in the home address as the first record of the chain. The necessary pointer field adjustments are illustrated in Figure 8.6.
4. This rule applies to a quite subtle phenomenon (see Figure 8.7). Suppose that we have a chain of records A, B, C, D where record A is the home address record and record C is in address 20, for example. Suppose now that a new record (X) is to be inserted and hashes to address 20. Thus, if later further records hash

to address 20, X is the first record of a new chain beginning at address 20. Hence it is necessary that X actually be placed in address 20. Therefore record C must be deleted and placed at the end of the original chain and X is placed at address 20.

If a disk address is to be capable of holding more than 1 record (disk address capacity greater than 1), the pointer field must be a composite referring both to the relative block address (disk address) and to the number of the record within the block, or disk address. The management rules given above must be modified slightly for the case of address capacity greater than one. However, the basic aim is still the same—to keep the chains in good repair, and to make sure that an overflow record is always ultimately chained to its home (relative disk) address and that each home address record is actually in its home (relative disk) address. As we shall see later, an address capacity greater than unity contributes to a further reduction in average search length, because it reduces the number of overflow records likely to occur.

In the preceding section we examined the management of overflow records and the effect of management method on the all- important average search length. However, it is clear that if there are no overflow records at all, the average search length will be unity since only home address records will ever be retrieved. Thus an important method of reducing the average search length is to keep the number of overflow records as low as possible.

MINIMIZATION OF OVERFLOW RECORDS AND AVERAGE SEARCH LENGTH

The following are three main ways to reduce the number of overflow records in a hash file which we will examine in turn:

1. Ensure a distribution of the records as evenly as possible over the available disk address space
2. Use a low load factor, that is, have considerably more disk space available to the records than is actually needed
3. Use an address capacity greater than unity, that is, each disk address should be able to hold more than 1 record

FIGURE 8.8. In (a) we have ten records (circles) assigned to ten addresses (buckets) by a hashing routine. In (b) we illustrate how the distribution of the records in (a) can be depicted by a histogram. We see, for example that 4 addresses had no records assigned, and 3 addresses each had 1 record assigned.

Record Distributions

To reduce or even totally eliminate hashing collisions we need a routine that spreads the records over as many disk addresses as possible. Such is clearly not the case with the hashing routine that gave rise to the distribution of records in Figure 8.8(a). Here some addresses are assigned no records, while other addresses are assigned 2 or 3 records.

This method of illustrating a distribution of records is not very convenient for comparing the results of hashing routines. It is more convenient to use a histogram; and Figure 8.8(b) contains the histogram for the diagram in Figure 8.8(a). While a diagram becomes impossible when the number of addresses and records becomes large, a histogram is no more difficult to draw. From the histogram in Figure 8.8(b), we can see at a glance that 3 addresses are assigned 1 record, 2 addresses were assigned 2 records, and 1 address is assigned 3 records.

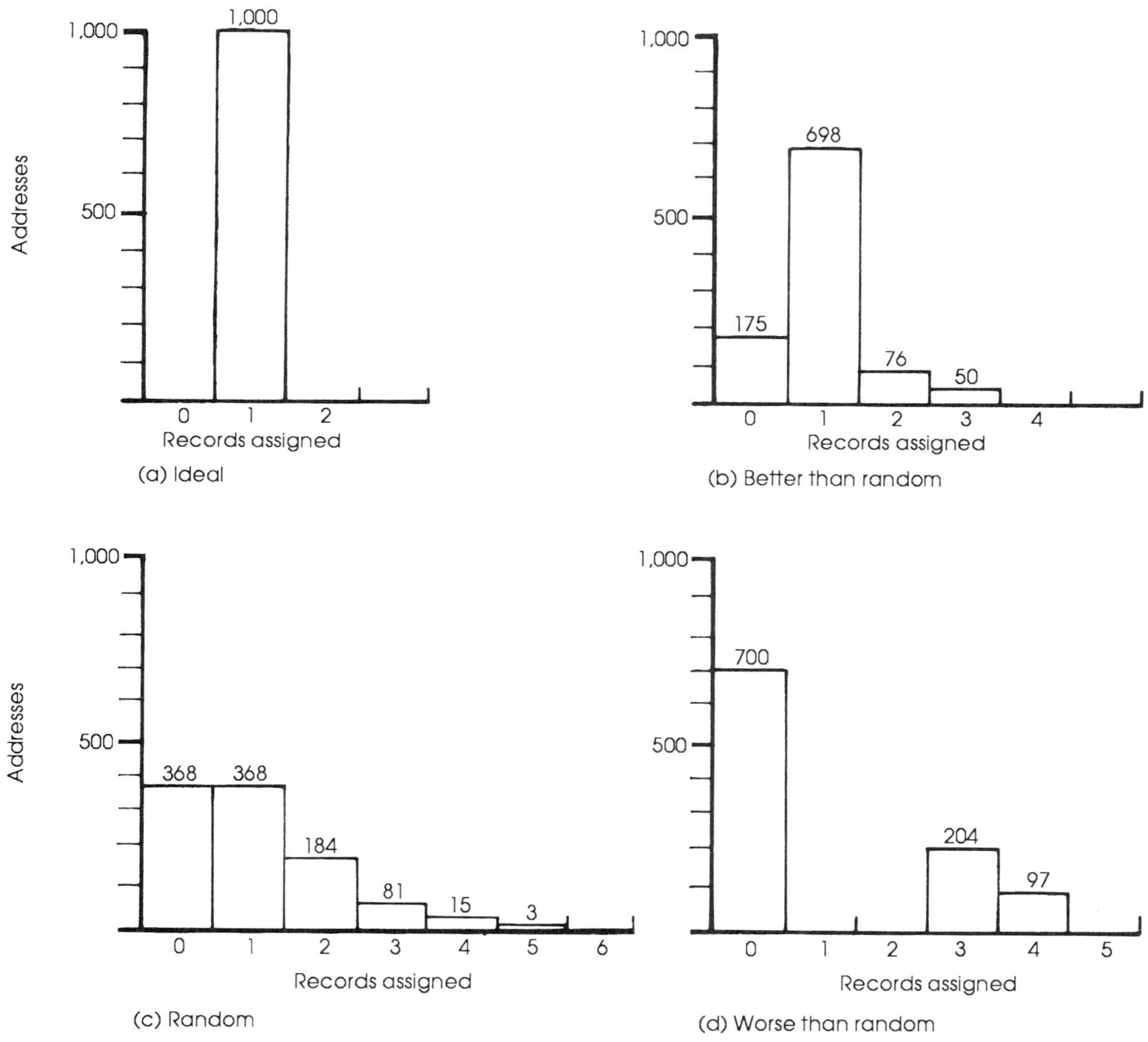

FIGURE 8.9. Examples of the possible distributions when 1,000 records are assigned by hashing to 1,000 addresses. You can assume any address capacity you like, but it is convenient to assume an address capacity of one record per address. The distributions in (a) and (b) are good, that in (c) is tolerable, whereas that in (d) is unacceptable.

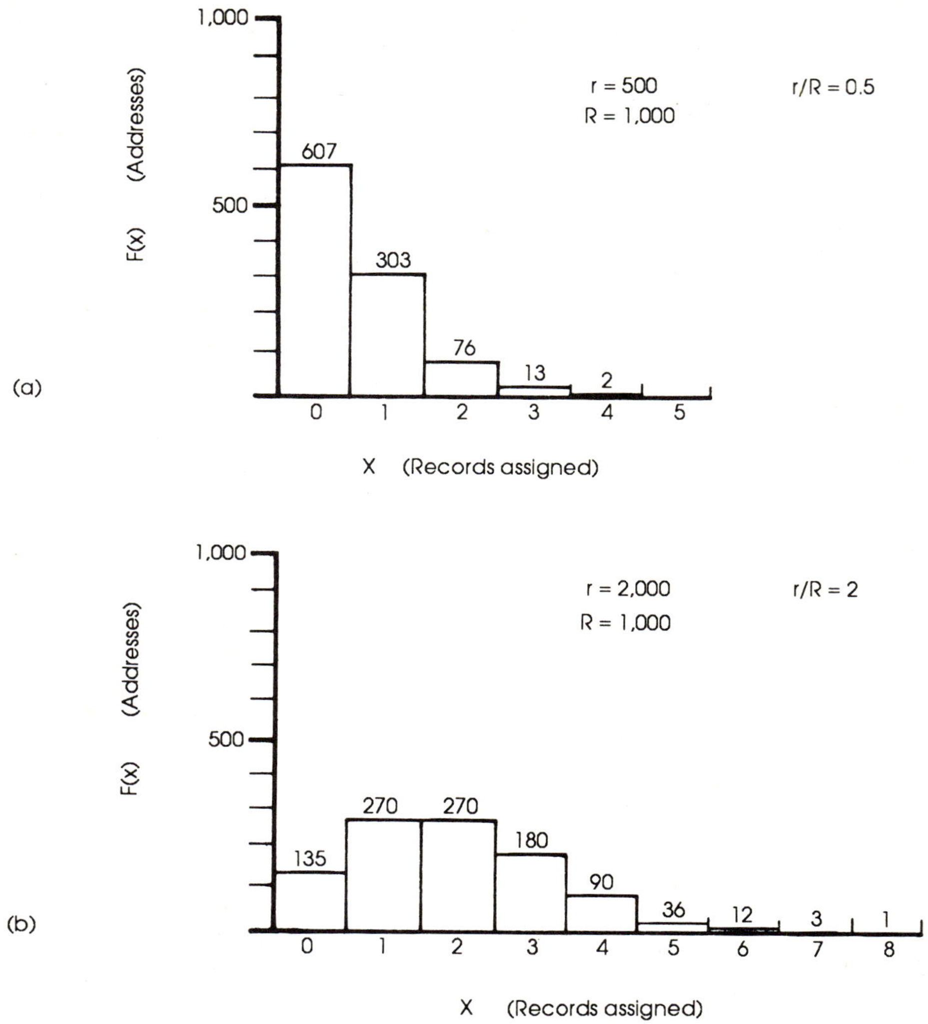

FIGURE 8.10. **Sample distributions resulting from the use of randomizing hashing routines. In (a) 500 records (r) are randomly assigned to 1,000 addresses (R), whereas in (b) 2,000 records as assigned to 1,000 addresses. It is r/R that controls the shape of the distribution, so that very many random distributions are possible.**

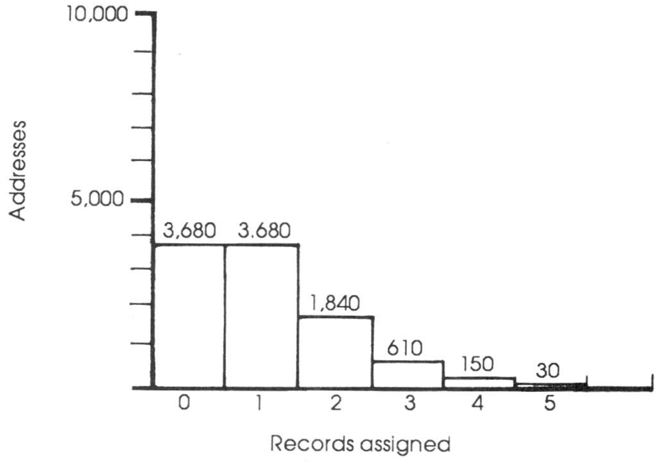

FIGURE 8.11. Illustration of how the number of addresses with a given number of assigned records depends proportionally on the total addresses (R) for a given value of the ratio r/R. Above we have the distribution for 10,000 records assigned randomly to 10,000 addresses. The ratio r/R is unity. The distribution is exactly the same as that in Figure 8.9(c) for 1,000 records assigned randomly to 1,000 addresses (with r/R also unity), except that above the address values are all 10 times greater.

A distribution of records over as many addresses as possible is called an *ideal*, or *uniform*, distribution and is an obvious design aim when constructing a hashing routine. Unfortunately such a routine is not normally available in practice, and we are forced to use hashing routines that give a distribution that is less than ideal. Thus we need to look carefully at the kinds of distributions that can occur; these range all the way from the ideal to the simply terrible.

In Figure 8.11, which illustrates the kinds of distribution, we consider the case of 1,000 records being assigned to 1,000 addresses by different hashing routines. For initial convenience the reader may assume that each disk address can hold at most 1 record, although this is not necessary, since a hashing routine does not take the address capacity into account, only the numerical range of the disk addressses, in this case from 0 to 99. We have isolated four important types of distribution in Figure 8.11 and we discuss them one by one.

Ideal distribution It is easy to see why the distribution in Figure 8.9(a) is ideal. Exactly one record has been assigned to each of the 1,000 addresses; no address has no records assigned, and no address has more than one record assigned. Thus there are no overflow records to worry about.

Random distribution A random distribution is shown in Figure 8.9(c). Here the hashing routine assigns a new record in a completely random (but reproducible) manner. By random manner we mean that when a new record is being assigned to a disk address, the hashing routine generates the disk address as if a 1,000- face die were being tossed in the air, so that every disk address is equally likely. (We can also consider the distribution in Figure 8.9(c) as being the distribution resulting from 1,000 hailstones falling randomly into 1,000 buckets; this analogy is actually useful in practice, as we shall see later.)

Note that the distribution in Figure 8.9(c) is but one example of a large number of random distributions. Thus if we assign 500 records to 1,000 addresses we get a different but still random distribution of the records over the addresses, as shown in Figure 8.10(a). Yet again, if we assign 2,000 records to 1,000 addresses we get the random but different distribution in Figure 8.10(b); clearly for this assignment to make any sense, each address must be able to hold more than 1 record.

Note that the shape of the distribution (histogram) is determined by the ratio of the number of records assigned (r) to the number of addresses (R) and not by the absolute values involved. Referring again to Figure 8.9(c), the histogram for 10,000 records assigned to 10,000 addresses would have the same shape, although the number of addresses with x records assigned would have increased by a factor of 10, as illustrated in Figure 8.11. In general, the random distribution histogram can be deduced from the Poisson distribution formula

$$F(x) = (r/R)^x (1/x!) \exp(-r/R)$$

where F(x) is the number of addresses assigned x records, R is the total addresses, and r is the total records. Thus if r = 1,000 and R = 1,000, the above formula reduces to

$$F(x) = (R/x!) \exp(-1) = (1000/x!) (1/2.7283) = 368/x!$$

so that F(0) = 368, F(1) = 368, F(2) = 184, F(3) = 61, . . . which is the distribution given in Figure 8.9(c). Figure 8.12 contains a table giving values of F(x)/R versus r/R.

It used to be thought that a random distribution of the records was most desirable in a hash file: the term *randomized file* is still used

POISSON DISTRIBUTION FUNCTION
Ratio of records to addresses (r/R)

	0.5	0.666	1	2	3	6	10
F(0)/R	.607	.770	.368	.135	.050	.002	
F(1)/R	.303	.513	.368	.271	.149	.015	
F(2)/R	.076	.171	.184	.271	.224	.045	.002
F(3)/R	.013	.038	.061	.180	.224	.089	.008
F(4)/R	.002	.006	.015	.090	.168	.134	.019
F(5)/R		.001	.003	.036	.101	.161	.038
F(6)/R			.001	.012	.050	.161	.063
F(7)/R				.003	.022	.138	.090
F(8)/R				.001	.008	.103	.113
F(9)/R					.003	.069	.125
F(10)/R					.001	.041	.125
F(11)/R						.023	.114
F(12)/R						.011	.095
F(13)/R						.005	.073
F(14)/R						.002	.052
F(15)/R						.001	.035
F(16)/R							.022
F(17)/R							.013
F(18)/R							.007
F(19)/R							.004
F(20)/R							.002
F(21)/R							.001

FIGURE 8.12. The Poisson distribution function displayed as a table. This table can be very useful in practice. Suppose that we assign 300,000 records to 100,000 addresses. This means that r/R is 3. From the table, the number of addresses that will be assigned 1 record is 0.149*100,000 or 14,900 addresses; the number of addresses assigned 2 records each is 0.224*100,000 or 22,400, and so on.

for a hash file. However, the random distributions in Figures 8.9(c), 8.10(a) and 8.10(b) show that many addresses are assigned more than one record, so that many overflow records are likely. The desired or ideal distribution is that shown in Figure 8.9(a).

Better than random distribution The ideal distribution in Figure 8.9(c) is not attainable in practice, so designers usually aim for a distribution that is better than random but less than ideal. Such a distribution is shown in Figure 8.9(b). It is clearly much closer to the ideal distribution than is the random distribution, for many more addresses have one record assigned.

Worse than random distribution In Figure 8.9(d) we have an example of a distribution that is worse than random. Very many addresses have no records assigned at all, and there are no addresses with exactly one record assigned. There is no excuse for using a distribution that is worse than random, for even if we cannot construct a hashing routine that gives a better than random distribution, there are well-known methods of at least constructing a hashing routine that gives a random distribution.

The clearest measure of whether a distribution is better or worse than random is a measure of the number of overflow records it gives rise to. Consider Figure 8.9 again; assume that the capacity of each address (b) is 1 record, that is, b = 1. In the case of the random distribution, there are 184 addresses with 2 records assigned. That means there are 184 addresses each with 1 record too many, which means that these 184 addresses give rise to 184 overflow records. There are 61 addresses each with 3 records assigned, that is, each with 2 records too many, so that these addresses give rise to 61*2 overflow records. Similarly the 15 addresses with 4 records assigned give rise to 15*3 overflow records. Thus the number of overflow records generated by the distribution in Figure 8.9(c) is as follows:

184*1 + 61*2 + 15*3 + 3*4 + 1*5 or 368 records

Thus about 37 percent of the records assigned become overflow records.

In the case of the better than random distribution in Figure 8.9(b), the number of overflow records is a follows:

76*1 +50*2 or 176 records

Thus only about 17 percent of the records assigned overflow in this case, which justifies our regarding this distribution as being superior to the random distribution.

In the case of the worse than random distribution in Figure 8.9(d), the number of overflow records is as follows:

204*2 + 97*3 or 699 records

Thus 70 percent overflow in this case, so that the distribution is undoubtedly worse than random.

It is worth noting that it is not the distribution itself (and thus the hashing routine) that solely determines how many overflow records there will be. This depends on both the distribution and the address capacity.

Consider once again the random assignment of 1,000 records to 1,000 addresses, so that the distribution in Figure 8.9(c) applies. Suppose that the address capacity is 2 instead of 1. It then follows that the 184 addresses that each have 2 records assigned so not give rise to any overflow records, since an address can hold 2 records. However, the 61 addresses that each have 3 records assigned each have only 1 record too many, so that only 61*1 overflow records are produced by these addresses. Similarly the 15 addresses each assigned 4 records generate 15*2 overflow records, and so on. Thus the total overflow records for this case is as follows:

61*1 + 15*2 +3*3 + 1*4 or 104 records

Therefore the overflow is just over 10 percent when the address capacity is 2, as opposed to 37 percent when the address capacity is 1. However, in the case of address capacity 2, we pay for our low overflow percentage by leaving half the file empty, for the 1,000 addresses can hold 2,000 records in all and only 1,000 have been assigned. Nevertheless, as we shall see shortly, this phenomenon can be used to reduce overflow.

Use of a Low Load Factor

The **load** (or **loading**) **factor** for a hash file is the percentage of the available space that is occupied by records. Thus if we assign 1,000 records to 1,000 addresses with address capacity equal to 1, the load factor is clearly 100 percent, since the file has only room for 1000 records. If we assign 1,000 records to 2,000 addresses with address capacity equal to 1, the load factor is clearly 50 percent.

Changing the address capacity also affects the load factor. Thus 1,000 records assigned to 1,000 addresses with address capacity 1 gives 100 percent load factor, but 1,000 records assigned to 1000 addresses with address capacity 2 gives 50 percent load factor.

The method of reducing overflow records by means of a low load factor assumes that that low load factor is achieved by means of additional addresses and not by means of increased address capacity. In other words we can reduce overflow by decreasing the load factor while holding the address capacity constant. Usually the address capacity is held at unity, since the relative file organization only allows for blocking factor of unity.

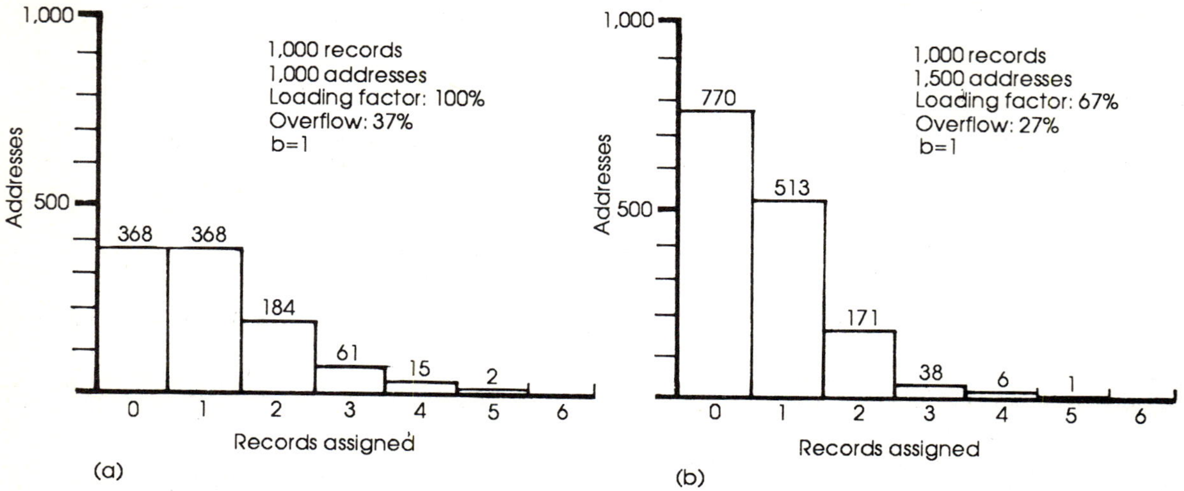

FIGURE 8.13. Illustration of the effect on overflow records of decreasing the loading factor, holding the address capacity constant. In (a) we randomly assign 1,000 records to 1,000 addresses. Assuming an address capacity of unity, the loading factor is 100 percent and the percentage of overflow records is 100 percent. In (b) we assign the same 1,000 records randomly to a larger address space (1,500 addresses), so that there is less likelihood of synonyms. Assuming address capacity of unity again, the loading factor falls to 67 percent and the overflow percentage to 27 percent.

We can easily see that decreasing the load factor reduces overflow. Consider once more the case of 1,000 records assigned to 1,000 addresses (address capacity 1), using a randomizing hashing routine, so that we get the distribution in Figure 8.9(c), and repeated in Figure 8.13(a). This gives 37 percent overflow. Now suppose that we increase the number of addresses to 1,500 but still assign 1,000 records randomly. Clearly the records now have more space so that synonyms are less likely. To be specific $r/R = 0.666$ and by using the Poisson table (or formula), we get the distribution shown in Figure 8.13(b).

If we now use the distribution in Figure 8.13(b) to derive the overflow percentage, it is clear that the number of overflow records is as follows:

171*1 + 38*1 + 6*3 + 1*4 or 269 overflow records.

Thus the overflow is reduced from about 37 percent to about 27 percent. To achieve this we decreased the load factor from 100 percent to 100*(1,000/1,500) or about 67 percent.

This result is found to be true in general. If we decrease the load factor and keep the address capacity constant, we significantly reduce the number of overflow records. The apparent wasted space is not a very high price to pay for this reduction, provided we do not have a load factor much less than about 70 percent. It is a good idea to leave some space in the file anyway, since we normally need space for insertions.

Another reason to leave some space in the file concerns the common overflow managment methods, namely, progressive overflow and chained progressive overflow. It requires fewer accesses to find an empty slot for an overflow record if the load factor is not high. In the extreme case of 100 percent load factor, if the last record loaded is an overflow record, then on average we must search halfway through the file, looking for that last empty slot in which to insert the record.

Use of Address Capacity Greater Than Unity

The most powerful method of reducing the overflow percentage, given the hashing routine, requires that we increase the address capacity while keeping the loading factor constant. Normally if we increase the address capacity, the loading factor falls. For instance, suppose we have 750 records assigned to 1,000 addresses with address capacity unity so that the loading factor is a reasonable 76 percent. If we then increase the address capacity to 4, there is space for 4,000 records; therefore the loading factor is reduced to 100(750/4,000) or an unacceptable 19 percent (which certainly reduces overflow, but at far too high a price).

We shall use two different methods to demonstrate that increasing the address capacity while keeping the load factor constant reduces overflow significantly, something that is not at all intuitively obvious. The first of these methods should appeal to the reader's intuition; the second is a technical argument, although we try to keep the technicalities to a minimum.

Let us go back to the simple case of 10 records assigned fairly randomly to 10 addresses as shown in Figure 8.14(a). Clearly we have 4

(a)

(b)

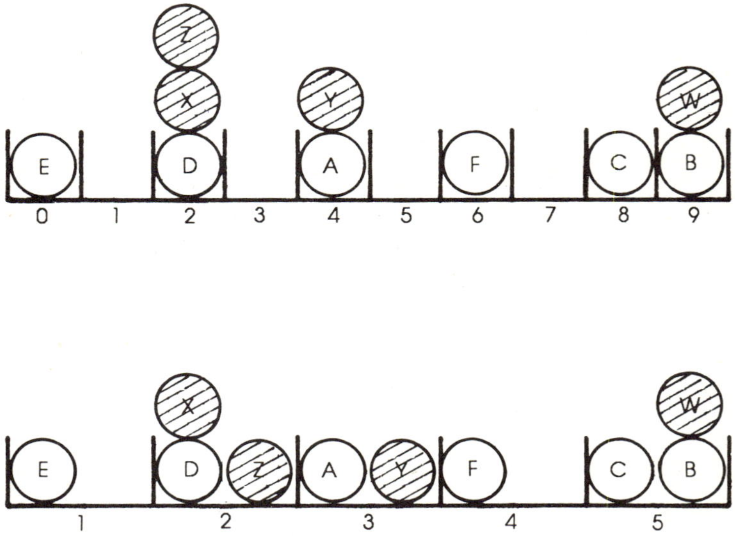

FIGURE 8.14. Simple demonstration (using the hailstone analogy) of how increasing the address capacity, while keeping the loading factor constant, reduces overflow. In (a) we see a typical (fairly random) assignment of 10 records (spheres) to 10 addresses where the buckets have been doubled in size, but the total space for records is still 10. The leading factor is thus still 100 percent, but the number of overflow records has been reduced because of an averaging effect.

overflow records, or 40 percent overflow. Now imagine that the records are analogous to hailstones falling ramdomly into 10 buckets, giving the distribution in Figure 8.14(a). Suppose now that we double the size of each bucket, but halve the number of buckets to 5, so that we still have room for 10 records, as in Figure 8.14(b). If the hailstones fall randomly as before into these buckets, the averaging effect will reduce the number of overflow records to 2. Note that in both (a) and (b) the load factor is the same, namely, 100 percent. Thus we have a simple intuitive demonstration of the most important single factor about hash files: *increasing the address capacity while holding load factor constant reduces overflow.*

We can also demonstrate this more technically. Suppose that we assign 1,000 records to 1,000 addresses with address capacity 1, using a randomizing hashing routine; we get the distribution in Figure

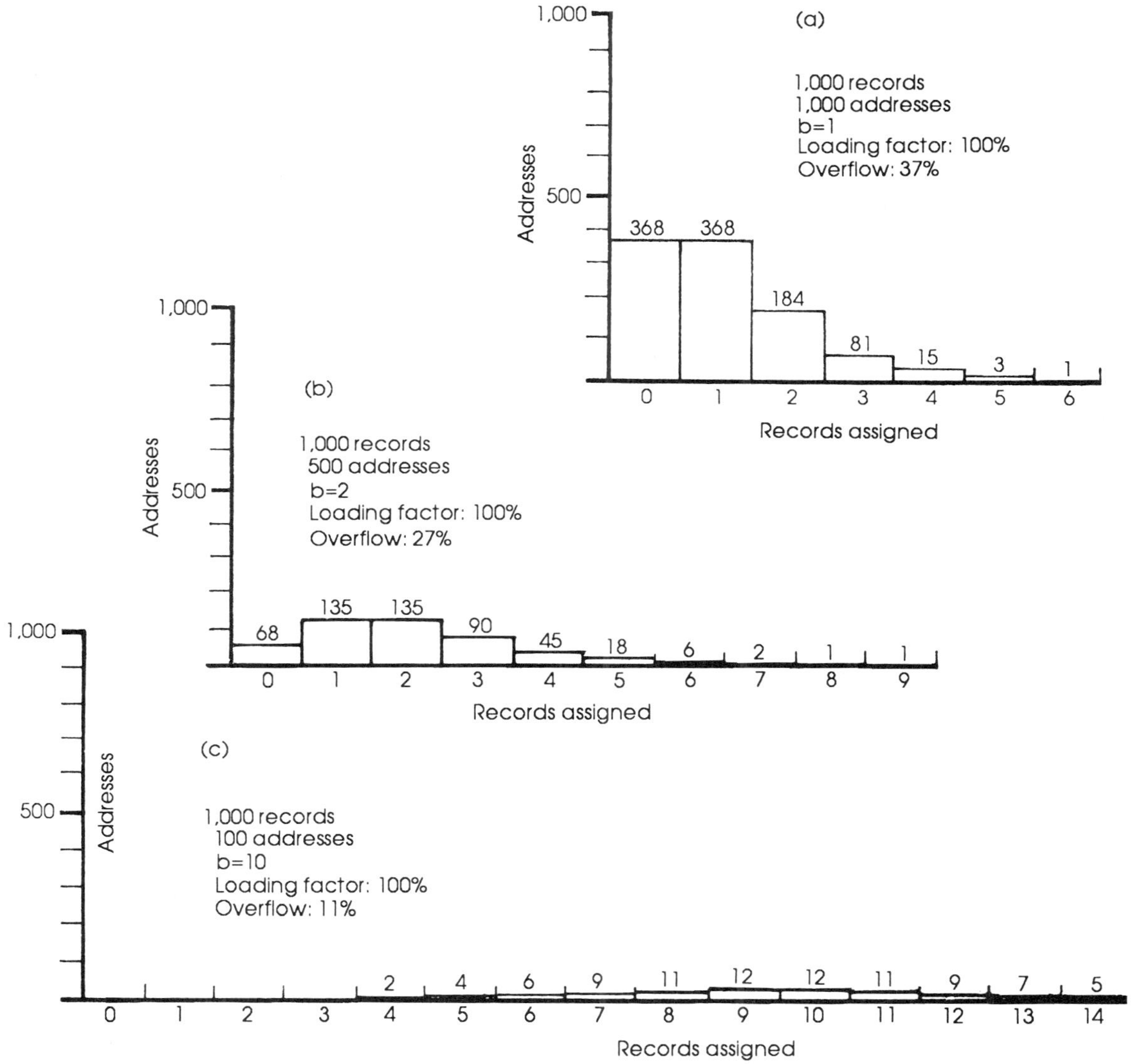

FIGURE 8.15. **Demonstration that the overflow percentage falls with increasing address capacity even if the loading factor remains constant. In (a), (b), and (c) above we have 1,000 records to assign, but as we increase the address capacity we decrease the number of addresses available so that the loading factor remains constant at 100 percent.**

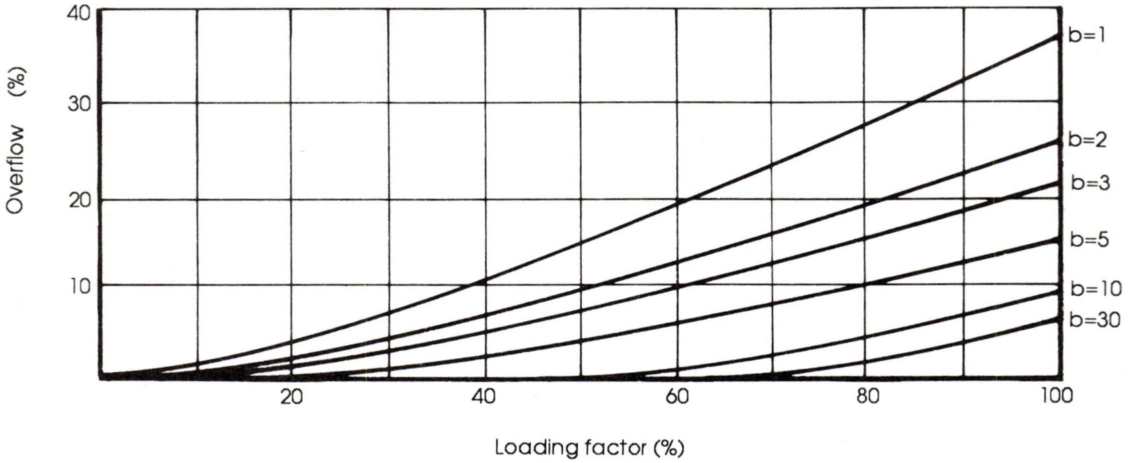

FIGURE 8.16. **With randomized hash file, the percentage of records overflowing versus the loading factor, for different address capacities (b).**

8.15(a) and 37 percent overflow. The loading factor is 100 percent. Let us now increase the address capacity to 2, keeping the loading factor constant. We can do this if we reduce the number of addresses to 500 with address capacity 2. The r/R = 1,000/500 or 2, and we get the distribution shown in Figure 8.15(b). The number of overflow records must be as follows:

90*1 + 45*2 + 18*3 +6*4 + 2*5 or 268 overflow records

This means 27 percent overflow, which is a significant reduction. Yet the loading factor is unchanged at 100 percent.

We can go further with this process. Suppose now that we increase the address capacity to 10, while at the same time decreasing the number of addresses to 100, so that the loading factor remains constant at 100 percent. The resulting distribution is shown in Figure 8.15(c). The number of overflow records is clearly as follows:

11+1 + 9*2 + 7*3 + 5*4 +3*5 + 2*6 + 1*7 + 1*8 or 112

This means 11 percent overflow, which is an even more significant reduction. Yet the loading factor remains unchanged at 100 percent.

We can go on increasing the address capacity in this way and getting less and less overflow, given the hashing routine. We can summarize the results of this and the previous section graphically, using the curves in Figure 8.16. The curves show the percentage overflow that we get versus the loading factor for different address capacity (b) values. If we take a constant loading factor of 80 percent, we see from the curves that when the address capacity is unity, the percentage overflow is a quite high 30 percent. However, if we increase the address capacity to 30, the overflow percentage drops markedly to only a few percent.

The curves also show that for a constant address capacity, the percentage overflow drops with decreasing load factor. With address capacity unity and load factor 100 percent, the overflow is 37 percent, (a result we computed in the previous section). From the same curve we see that if the loading factor is reduced to 67 percent, the percentage overflow falls to about 27 percent, (a result we also computed earlier). Note that the curves assume that the hashing routine is a randomizing one that generates random distributions to which the Poisson distribution function F(x) applies.

If we have a hashing routine that generates a distribution that is better than random, then the overflow percentages in Figure 8.16 are too pessimistic. Unfortunately in practice, the distribution is either random or only a bit better than random, so that the curves in the figure are of practical significance.

Average Search Length, Overflow Reduction, and Progressive Overflow Management

As we saw earlier the ultimate aim of hash file design is low average search length (with acceptable loading factor). Given the hashing routine, the address capacity, and the loading factor, the percentage of overflow records is determined (as can be seen from Figure 8.16). However, for a given percentage of overflow records, the average search length is determined by the overflow management method. We can now look at the interaction of progressive overflow, loading factor, and address capacity.

The curves in Figure 8.17 show the relationship between average search length, loading factor, and address capacity for progressive overflow, assuming random distributions of the records over the address space. If the distributions are better than random, the average

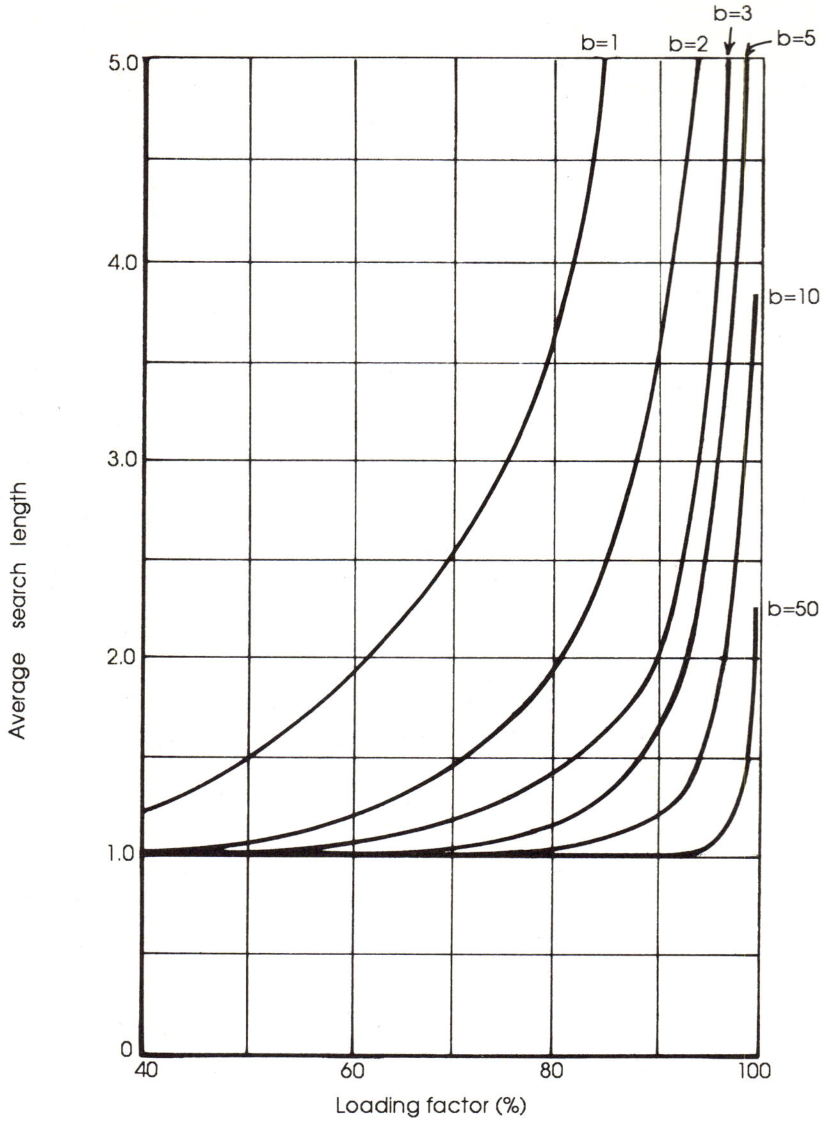

FIGURE 8.17. Average search length (in disk accesses) versus loading factor for different values of address capacity (b) in records per address. Curves assume a random distribution and are valid immediately after loading.

search lengths are lower. Curves such as these for progressive overflow can be derived from a mathematical analysis, but were first derived experimentally by Peterson at IBM (Ref. 2) in the 1950s. The more complete set of curves in Figure 8.17 were derived theoretically by the author (Ref. 1) and confirms Peterson's earlier results.

The curves are something of a disappointment for those wishing to construct a fast hash file using address capacity unity (the only address capacity explicitly supported by the COBOL relative file organization). We see that at loading factors between 65 percent and 80 percent, which would be reasonable in practice, the average search length lies between 2.0 and 4.0. Thus the file would probably not be any faster than a VSAM indexed- sequential file. To increase the speed we are forced to increase the address capacity. In practice, since each address in a relative file is a block, that means increasing the blocking factor.

The difficulty with increasing address capacity is that COBOL relative file organization does not explicitly support blocked records, so that a COBOL program for handling a relative file with address capacity greater than unity needs to incorporate code for blocking and deblocking records.

To demonstrate what must be done, suppose that the address capacity is 10. Then the buffer and working-storage structures can be designed to hold 10 records and can be declared using the OCCURS 10 TIMES clause. Such structures can then be read and written using READ and WRITE with relative files—that is, we always write 10 records into a relative address and read 10 records from a relative address. If we need to put only 7 records into an address, we still write 10 records, although 3 of them are marked as dummy records. In this way we incorporate our own blocking and deblocking and thus increase the address capacity at will. It is clear, however, that this makes writing COBOL programs for dealing with hash files more difficult and therefore more expensive. In the next chapter we shall study the COBOL necessary for creating the OIL-WELL hash file using progressive overflow.

We can undoubtedly get quite a low average search length with progressive overflow if we use quite a high address capacity. For example a loading factor of 80 percent and as address capacity of 10 places the average search length at about 1.05, which is near the theoretical minimum.

Unfortunately there is a minor snag. The curves in Figure 8.17 are for the average search lengths measured immediately after initial loading of the file. As time goes on there will be insertions and deletions. Even if the number of insertions matches the number of deletions, the average search length tends to increase. First consider the effect of deletions. The majority of records are in their home addresses. Thus deletions tend to remove home address records from the file, thus increasing the percentage of nonhome address records and thus increasing the average search length. Now consider insertions. Most insertions will hash either to an address occupied by a home address record or to an address occupied by an overflow record. If the address is occupied by a home address record, the inserted record becomes a new overflow record. If the address is occupied by an overflow record, as we saw earlier, then that overflow record moves further away to allow insertion of the new home address record. Either way average search length increases.

Experience shows that after between approximately 40 percent and 150 percent turnover of the records, the average search length stabilizes at a higher level. If we call the stable equilibrium average search length S and the initial search length I, then S and I are related as follows:

$$S = 1 + 3(I - 1)$$

Thus if we have an average search length of 1.05 after loading, it will likely rise to about 1.15 as the file ages. In contrast, if we have an average search length of 2.0 initially, it will likely rise to about 4.0.

In summary it is clear that we can design a very fast hash file using progressive overflow management only if we use a high address capacity, an acceptable load factor, and a hashing routine that gives a distribution not worse than random.

Average Search Length, Overflow Records and Chained Progressive Overflow.

Earlier in our studies of overflow management we saw that chained progressive overflow tends to give a significantly lower average search length than does straight progessive overflow. In Figure 8.18 the curves for chained progressive overflow show how the average search length depends on loading factor and address capacity. The curves were derived theoretically by the author and for technical reasons are worst case (except for the curve for b = 1 which is exact). Thus in practice we can get slightly lower average search lengths (by up to about 5 percent) than given in this figure.

It is clear that the average search length is generally lower than for the corresponding cases with progressive overflow (Figure 8.17). With address capacity of unity and an acceptable 80 percent loading factor, the average search length is 1.4, which is almost acceptable.

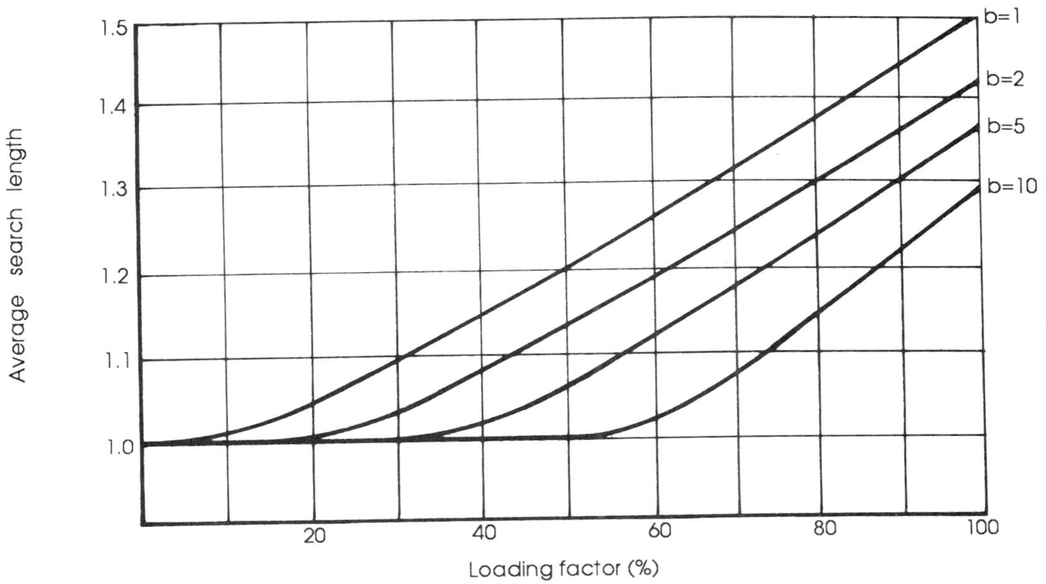

FIGURE 8.18. Average search length versus load factor with chained progressive overflow management; that is, records overflowing from a home address are placed in empty addresses and linked by a chain of pointers. The curves assume a random distribution of the records in the file. The curve for address capacity 1 is exact. The other curves are worse case; in practice average search lengths greater than 1.1 will be up to about 5 percent lower. The curves are reprinted from the author's File & Data Base Techniques, Holt, Rinehard and Winston, 1982.

Furthermore insertions and deletions do not significantly affect the average search length as the file ages, because of the existence of the chaining system. Note, however, that at high address capacities and loading factor between 65 percent and 85 percent, the average search length is comparable with the case where the overflow method is straight progressive.

We can conclude that at low address capacities and particularly when the address capacity is unity, the fastest hash files are those with chained overflow records. If very high address capacities can be used, it is probably less trouble to use straight progressive overflow, since the average search length is not significantly improved by switching to a chained system. Finally it should be emphasized that the curves in Figure 8.18 assume a randomizing hashing routine. If a routine can be constructed that gives a better than random distribution, average search lengths lower than those in the figure are obtained for a given loading factor and address capacity.

HASHING ROUTINES

When a hash file is being constructed for a large and important file, a great deal of effort must go into the construction of the hashing routine. A large hash file is an investment; like any other investment it generates a return for the capital invested. Part of this capital is for the construction of a hashing routine that minimizes overflow records. Thus we usually construct an array of routines and select the best one from those that give distributions better than random. We shall look at methods of testing hashing routines later. For now we concentrate on some commonly used methods for constructing them.

Methods of Constructing Hashing Routines

A hashing routine converts a record key to a relative address within the range of integers 0 to R-1, where R is the number of relative addresses. Keys frequently contain non-numeric characters, for example, AB56. The first step in generating an address is thus the conversion of the characters to numbers. A simple scheme is to convert A to 01, B to 02, and so on, so that AB56 is first of all converted to 010256. Many variations on this theme are possible, but the idea should be clear enough.

The next step is the generation of a relative address in the integer range 0 to R-1 from the numeric key resulting from the first step, if any. Remember that we seek a hashing routine that gives a distribution that is better than random. There is no method known that ensures such a result, but there are several methods and variations on these methods that have a good chance of generating the required distribution. However, should these methods fail and give distributions that are worse than random, there is a method, called *radix transformation*, that is practically certain to give a random distribution. We look first at methods that have a good chance of generating a better than random distribution.

The Division Method

If R is the number of addresses, **division** involves dividing the key by a divisor D and taking the remainder as the relative address. The value of D should be R or just greater than R. To take a simple example, suppose we have 20 addresses going from 0 to 19 and we have to assign records with 4-digit keys ranging from 0000 to 9999. If we divide the key by 20, the remainder lie between 0 and 19.

This is a very simple method and yet one of the best. A great deal of investigation and experience has shown that we are much more likely to get a distribution that is better than random if we use an odd number as the divisor and is best of all if we use a prime number. Thus, in the example above, instead of using 20 addresses, we might use either 19 or 23 and thus use 19 or 23 as the divisor.

The Truncation Method.

Truncation is simply a variation on the division method and really involves division by a power of 10. Suppose that we must assign 8-digit numeric keys to 4-digit addresses. A typical key can be 12345678. Truncation simply involves taking the right-most 4 digits as the address, (5678 in the case of the example).

The Extraction Method.

Extraction is a variation on the trunction method. It may be that some digits within a key vary more than others, so that it is natural to use the digits that vary most to form the disk address. Again suppose we have 8-digit keys being assigned to 4-digit addresses. A sample key is 12345678. We might want to extract the first, third, fourth, and eighth digits as the key, so that we would use 1348 as the address.

The Folding Method.

Folding involves folding the key on itself. Typically half the digits of the key are added to the other half. Suppose the numeric key is 12345678. We then take 1234 and add it to 5678 giving 6912. This value can be used as a 4-digit address. If the address must be less than 4 digits, we can apply the division, truncation, or extraction methods to this value.

A variation on this technique is called **boundary folding** and involves reversing the order of the digits in half of the key before addition. Thus if the key is 12345678 we take half of it (1234), reverse the order (giving 4321), and then add this to 5678 (giving 9999).

The Radix Transformation Method.

Radix transformation is best regarded as the method of last resort, to be used only when other methods fail to give a distribution that is better or even equal to random. It is practically certain to result in a random distribution. Suppose that our key is 12345678 and we seek a 4-digit address. This key is really the following expression since it is a decimal number (that is, a number based on the radix 10):

$$1*10^7 + 2*10^6 + 3*10^5 + 4*10^4 + 5*10^3 + 6*10^2 + 7*10^1 + 8*10^0$$

With a radix transformation we change the radix to a number, usually prime and greater than 10 (for example, 11). The above expression is thus transformed to the following, which on evaluation gives us the decimal number 23579476:

$$1+11^7 + 2*11^6 + 3*11^5 + 4*11^4 + 5*11^3 + 6*11^2 + 7*11^1 + 8*11^0$$

Normally truncation is applied to the decimal number to obtain the address. For a 4-digit address we would use 9476.

There are other methods of randomizing, but the radix transformation is probably the most effective. Note that when developing a hashing routine that is to be better than random, the more complex we make the conversion process and the more we involve powers, the less likely we are to achieve our goal and the more likely we are to develop another method of randomizing.

Testing a Hashing Routine

Testing a hashing routine involves generation of the distribution resulting from application of that hashing routine and then comparing that distribution with the corresponding random distribution. If the number of addresses involved is not too large (with System 370 COBOL compilers not larger than 65,000), it is not necessary to actually use a relative file for the test, as a COBOL table or array in main storage will do just as well and will be a lot faster. We will therefore illustrate the test method using a COBOL table and later point out the few minor variations required if a relative file must be used.

The records to be hashed must be available as a sequential file. Assume that we are dealing with the oil-well records discussed earlier and that these are available in the COBOL file TAPE-OIL-WELL. Suppose we need 50,000 addresses for the file. In the testing program we specify the following table:

```
01  TEST-TABLE
```

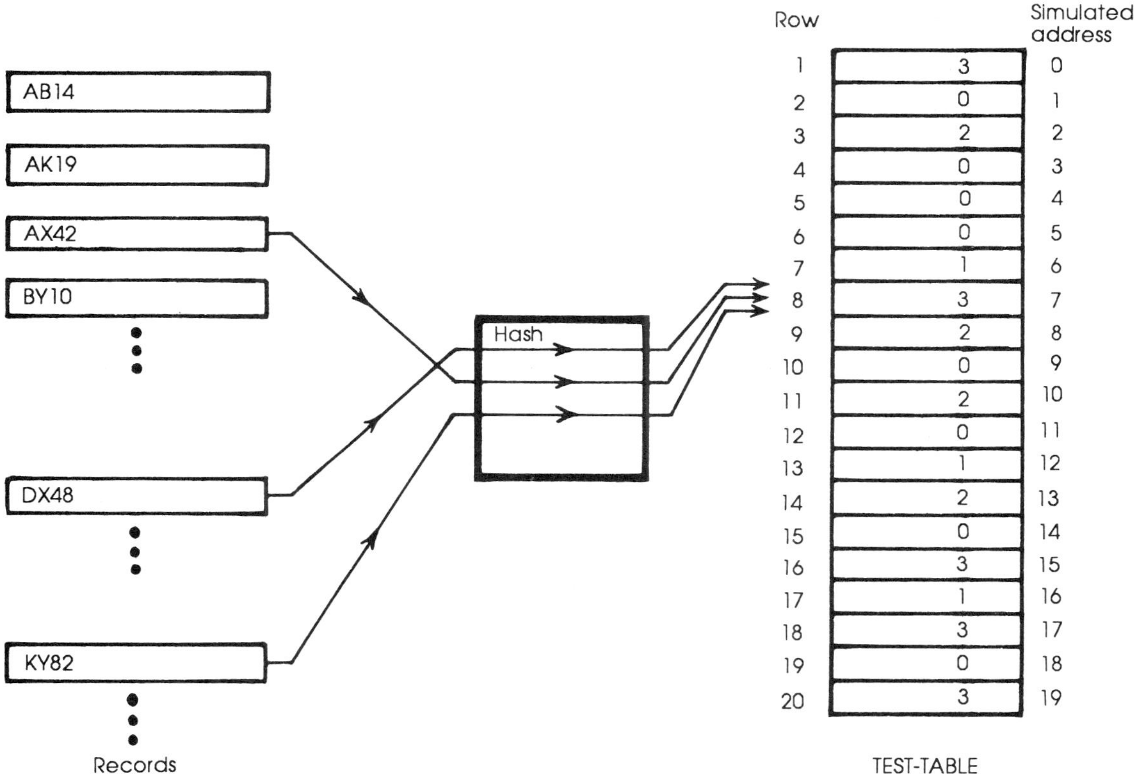

FIGURE 8.19. First step in testing a hashing routine, Instead of disk address space a table in main memory may be used, if the number of addresses intended to be used with the final disk file is not too large. Each element of the COBOL table TEST-TABLE above represents a space on disk with a relative disk address. Relative files start at address 0, but COBOL tables must start at element 1, so we are forced to regard table subscript 1 as simulated relative address 1, and so on. The records of the proposed hash file are read one by one and their keys hashed. If a key hashed to 7, then we increment the value at ROW (7 + 1). At the end of the processing we will have at ROW(8) the total number of records whose keys hashed to 7 and similarly for other ROW values.

```
01
   TEST-TABLE
   02   ROW   PIC S9999 COMP
              OCCURS 50000 TIMES.
```

This gives us 50,000 table elements going from ROW(1) to ROW(0) to ROW(49999). Unfortunately COBOL does not allow a table subscript

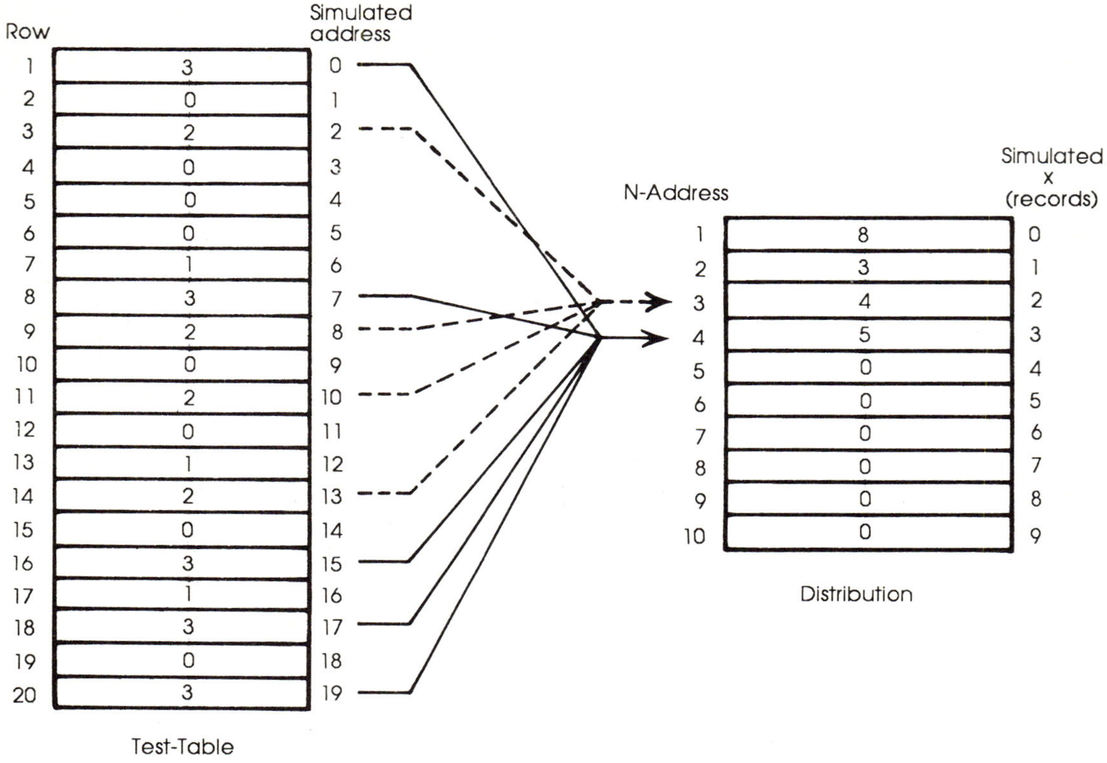

FIGURE 8.20. Second step in testing a hashing routine. Using the table generated in the first step (Figure 8.19), we can now generate the histogram for the distribution and place it in the table DISTRIBUTION, each element of which contains the number of addresses assigned x-1 records. Because COBOL does not allow the table element N-ADDRESS(x) as the number of addresses assigned x-1 records. During the processing, each element in TEST-TABLE is read. Suppose a value in TEST-TABLE is 2; then we increment N-ADDRESS(2+1). At the end of the processing, N-ADDRESS(2+1) contains the number of addresses assigned 2 records. Thus DISTRIBUTION contains the histogram of the distribution of the records over the address space.

of 0. This forces us to add 1 to every address generated by the hashing routine. Thus if we hash a key to 0, note is made of it in ROW(1), and so on.

A diagram of the first stage of the testing method is shown in Figure 8.19. To make the diagram possible we assume that the number of

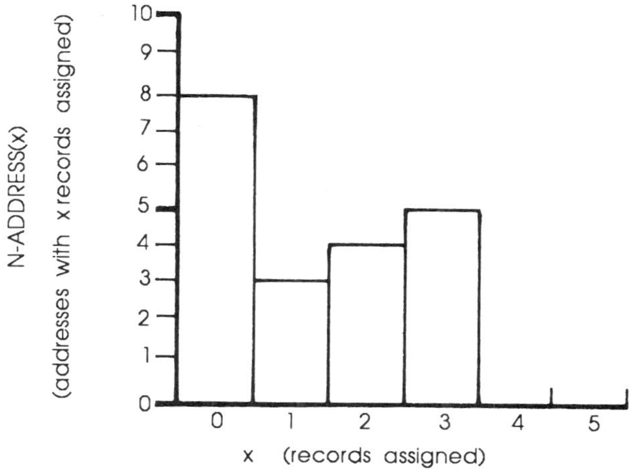

FIGURE 8.21. The actual histogram implicit in the table DISTRIBUTION in Figure 8.20.

addresses is only 20, instead of 50,000. Thus we have a table for disk addresses going from ROW(1) to ROW(20).

Records are read in one by one from the sequential file TAPE-OIL-WELL. The hashing routine is applied to each key in turn. When an address is generated, we simply increment the ROW value corresponding to the address (plus 1). Thus if a key hashes to address 09, we add 1 to the value in ROW(10). If ROW(10) is incremented 8 times in the course of the processing, that means that 8 records have been assigned to address 9. When all the TAPE-OIL-WELL keys have been hashed and corresponding table slots incremented, we are ready for the second stage of the processing (illustrated in Figure 8.20).

We need an additional table for the second stage. We can specify the following:

```
01   DISTRIBUTION.
     02  N-ADDRESS  PIC S999999   COMP
         OCCURS 10 TIMES.
```

Again we prefer elements ranging from N-ADDRESS(0) to N-ADDRESS(9). However, COBOL requires that we begin at N-ADDRESS(1).

The table will hold the histogram for the distribution, so that at the end of this stage of the processing, N-ADDRESS(1) holds the num-

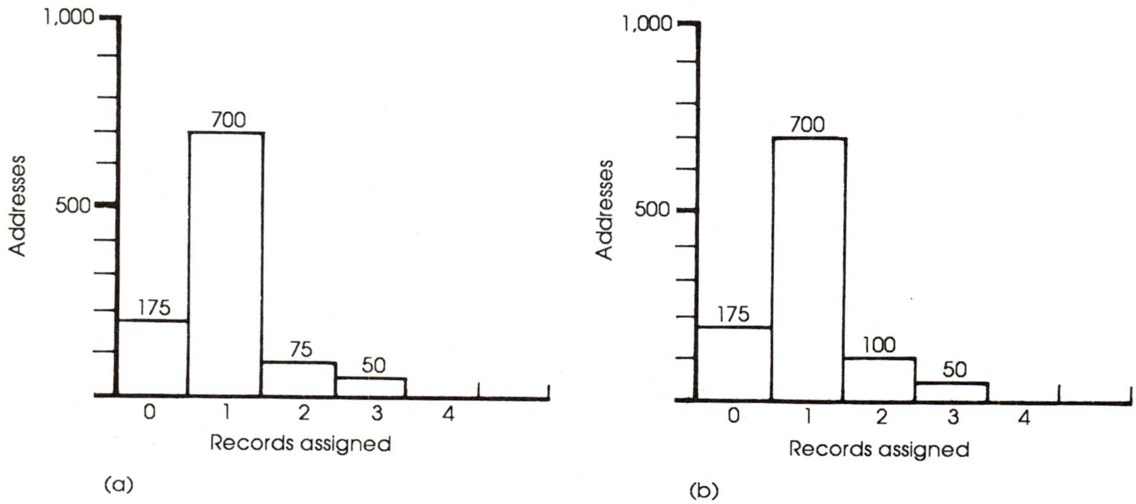

FIGURE 8.22. Illustration of how to check the validity of a histogram. Above we have two proposed histograms of 1,000 records assigned to 1,000 addresses. That in (a) is valid, whereas that in (b) is not. The total records and addresses given by the columns must each add up to 1,000. They do in the case of (a) but not in (b).

ber of addresses with 0 records assigned, N-ADDRESS(2) holds the number of addresses with 1 record assigned, N-ADDRESS(3) the number of addresses with 2 records assigned, and so on. At the end of the processing, the histogram for the distribution is in the table N-ADDRESS(n). For example, since there are 5 addresses (ROW(1), ROW(8), ROW(16), ROW(18), and ROW(20)) each containing 3 records, then the value of N-ADDRESS(3 + 1) at the end of the processing must be 5. This means that a total of 5 addresses were each assigned 3 records. The final step is a printout of the contents of the table DISTRIBUTION; the histogram that occurs as a result of the numbers used in Figures 8.19 and 8.20 is shown in Figure 8.21.

It is a good idea to check the validity of any distribution obtained. Two simple checks are sufficient. Suppose that we must assign 1,000 records to 1,000 addresses; following testing of the hashing routine we get the distribution shown in Figure 8.22(a). This histogram should be about 1,000 records and 1,000 addresses. The total addresses must be

```
175 + 700 + 75 + 50
```

that is, 1,000, which is correct. Similarly the total records must be

```
0*175 + 1*700 + 2*75 + 3*50
```

that is, 1,000, which is also correct. Had our testing program printed out the histogram in Figure 8.22(b), these checks would have revealed an error. The number of addresses adds up to 1,025 and the number of records 1,050, both of which are wrong, thus revealing an error in processing. It is a good idea to build such checks into a test program.

In Figure 8.19 we used the table TEST-TABLE to simulate our hash file addresses. If the number of addresses is very large then we can use a relative file, where each address can hold a single record containing a single numeric field such as COUNT. When we hash a key to an address, we retrieve the single field record at that address and increment the COUNT field. In this way, at the end of the first stage of the processing at any given address, the COUNT field will contain the number of records that hashed to that address.

This use of a relative file is not very efficient. First, each address contains a record with a single field. Relative files are in count-data format with blocking factor unity, so that the data subblock will be small compared with the count subblock and interblock and intersub-block gaps. Thus most of the disk space will be wasted. Second, each access to an address involves a seek. This costs many milliseconds compared with a few microseconds needed to access an element of a table in main storage. Since test programs are run many times in the search for a suitable hashing routine; and since a very large number of keys are hashed, the execution time for the testing program is an important consideration; the table should be used to simulate the hash file if possible. The basic limitation is the size of table allowed by the COBOL compiler used.

SUMMARY

A hash file has records scattered over a range of disk addresses, where the address for any record is computed from the record's primary key by means of a fixed routine called a hashing routine.

The capacity of each address in a hash file is fixed; records assigned to an address by the hashing routine in excess of the address's capacity are called overflow records. The address a record is assigned to is its home address. An overflow record does not reside in its home address but is normally placed in an empty address close to the home address.

The advantage of a hash file is speed. Most records are in their home addresses and so can be retrieved in a single disk access. For the few records that are not in their home addresses, many disk accesses are required. However, with careful design a hash file can be constructed so that the average number of disk accesses to retrieve a record (average search length) is greater than but close to 1.0

One common type of overflow management is progressive overflow, where the overflow record is placed in the nearest empty address greater than the home address. Another is chained progressive overflow, which is the same as progressive overflow except that the records overflowing from a single home address are chained to reduce the number of disk accesses required to retrieve an overflow record.

The average search length can be kept low by means of any of the following: A hashing routine that distributes the records evenly and so gives few overflow records; a low loading factor, so that the records are spread over many address reducing the chance of an overflow record; and a high address capacity, so that many records assigned to the same address produce few overflow records.

Hashing routines are commonly constructed using the division method and variations on it. Where these generate a distribution that gives more overflow records than a random distribution, the radix transformation method is employed; this invariably distributes the records randomly over the address space. A random distribution does give rise to significant overflow of records.

A hashing routine should be tested before being put to use. The test program should generate a histogram of the distribution of records over the address space.

EXERCISES

1. A hash file has 66,000 records in 100,000 addresses, each with an address capacity of unity. For a hashing routine that generates addresses randomly, do the exercises below:
   a. Compute the percentage of the records overflowing
   b. If progressive overflow is used, use curves to estimate the average search length just after loading
2. Repeat exercise 1 for the case where the address capacity is 2

3. If a hash file has 100,000 records that are assigned randomly to 50,000 addresses each with an address capacity of 2, do the exercises below:
   a. Compute the percentage of the records in home addresses
   b. If chained progressive overflow is used, estimate the average search length just after loading
4. If a hash file has 50,000 records that are assigned to 25,000 addresses, draw up a histogram to show the distribution of the records over the addresses. Why do we not concern ourselves with the address capacity in constructing such a histogram?
5. A hash file is constructed using progressive overflow. Just after loading, it is measured to have an average search length of 1.2. Give an estimate of the average search length after a great deal of insertions and deletions over the life of the file.
6. If a key of value 3456 is used with a hashing routine involving a radix transformation of 10 to 17, what is the address generated?
7. In Figure 8.12, compute a column for $r/R = 4$.
8. Using the histogram in Figure 8.11, show how you would confirm:
   a. That the number of records is 10,000
   b. That the number of addresses is 10,000
9. Take about 30 student ID numbers in your class and apply a simple hashing routine to them involving about 30 addresses. Write a program to generate a histogram showing the distribution of the records over the addresses. The histogram can be in the form of a table and does not have to be graphical.
10. Explain why increasing the address capacity is effective in reducing the number of overflow records even when the loading factor remains constant.

REFERENCES

1. Bradley, J., "Use of mean distance between overflow records to compute average search lengths in hash files with open addressing," *Computer Journal*, 29(2) (1986), pp. 167-170.

2. Peterson, W. W., "Addressing for random access storage," *IBM Journal of Research and Development*, 1(2) (1975), pp.130-146.

9 USING COBOL TO CREATE AND PROCESS HASH FILES

The major IBM operating systems (such as OS/MVS) and COBOL together provide us quite good facilities for creating and manipulating hash files. Two file organizations can be used, namely, the relative file organization and the direct file organization. The more basic hash files are constructed using relative organization, which was described briefly in the previous chapter. As we shall see, direct organization provides us with an easy method of constructing a hash file with high address capacity, although at a certain cost in terms of disk space.

We begin with a coverage of the creation of a hash file using relative file organization, address capacity of unity, and progressive overflow. Since this is a very basic type of hash file, we also show in detail how it can be updated and used for information retrieval. Then we outline how direct file organization may be used to construct a hash file with address capacity greater than unity. In the final section we show how relative file organization may be used to construct a hash file with address capacity greater than unity. This is not easy to do, because the blocking factor (that is, in practice the address capacity) is always unity for a relative file.

USE OF COBOL TO CREATE A HASH FILE WITH PROGRESSIVE OVERFLOW

In this section we illustrate the COBOL coding necessary to create a simple hash file using an address capacity of unity, progressive overflow, and a loading factor of about 67 percent. Referring to Figure 8.17, we see that this gives us an initial average search length of about 2.0 if we have a randomizing hashing routine, and less than 2.0 if we have a hashing routine that is better than random. To present the steps by means of diagrams we shall load only 10 records to 15 address—although, apart from the numbers involved, we would use the same methods to assign 100,000 records to 150,000 addresses.

Three major steps are involved. First we must prepare the records for loading; then we load the home address records; and finally we load the overflow records. It is important to load all the home address

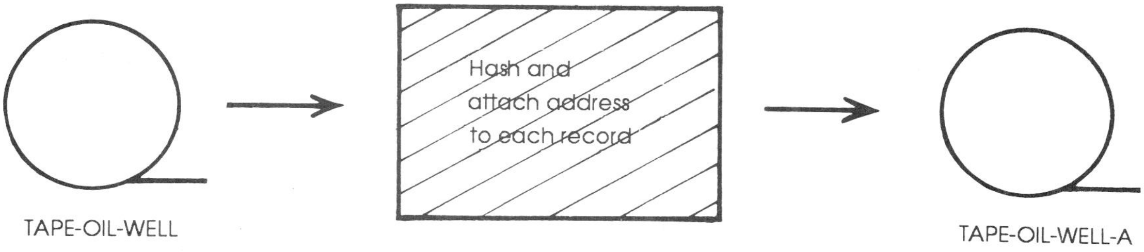

FIGURE 9.1a. The tape file TAPE-OIL-WELL is processed sequentially. The key of each record is hashed and the address generated attached to the record and output to the new version TAPE-OIL-WELL-A.

records before the overflow records. If we do not, it is likely that an overflow record will be assigned a slot that a later home address record should go into, thus forcing that home address record into some other address and thus increasing the average search length for the file. Since we must load the home address records first, part of the preparation of the records for loading involves separating records beforehand into home address records and overflow records.

We shall load records of the type illustrated in Figure 8.1 to form the hash file OIL-WELL. These records are assumed to be available on tape as the file TAPE-OIL-WELL. We also assume that when TAPE-OIL-WELL was created, all necessary checking was carried out on the data in the file, so that we need only be concerned with the mechanics of loading the records.

Preparation of the Records for Loading

First of all we must determine the addresses that the keys in TAPE-OIL-WELL hash to. At the same time we add an additional field ADDRESS to each record. This new field contains the address that the key of the record hashes to. This process is illustrated in Figure 9.1(a); the results of the processing are exemplified in Figure 9.1(b). We give the new file containing the additional ADDRESS field the name TAPE-OIL-WELL-A.

WELL-NUMB	FLOW-RATE	STATE	TERRAIN	ADDRESS
AA11	08	TEXAS	OPEN	04
AB14	50	ALASKA	OFF-SHORE	08
AB74	06	COLORADO	MOUNTAIN	12
CD83	20	TEXAS	OFF-SHORE	04
EF42	12	ALASKA	OPEN	08
EX99	36	TEXAS	OFF-SHORE	00
MU10	06	COLORADO	VALLEY	04
NP11	11	ALASKA	OFF-SHORE	12
QW47	17	ALASKA	MOUNTAIN	14
TX09	22	TEXAS	OPEN	12

TAPE-OIL-WELL-A

FIGURE 9.1b. Contents of TAPE-OIL-WELL-A generated by the process in Figure 9.1a.

The home address records are loaded in ascending relative address order, so that the next preparatory step involves a sort of TAPE-OIL-WELL-A on the ADDRESS field. We give the name TAPE-OIL-WELL-SA to the sorted file generated. In Figure 9.2 we show the records sorted primarily in ascending ADDRESS field order and secondarily in ascending key (WELL-NUMB) order. However, the secondary sorting does not matter.

We can see at a glance at how many records are assigned to a given address, since the sort has bunched all records together that have hashed to the same address. This is very convenient; it is now an easy matter to separate the home address and overflow records. We have an address capacity equal to unity, so that a given address can have at most one home address record. Thus we can take the first of each group of records in TAPE-OIL-WELL-SA and consider it to be a home address record; other records of the group will then be overflow records.

WELL-NUMB	FLOW-RATE	STATE	TERRAIN	ADDRESS
EX99	36	TEXAS	OFF-SHORE	00
AA11	08	TEXAS	OPEN	04
CD83	20	TEXAS	OFF-SHORE	04
MU10	06	COLORADO	VALLEY	04
14	50	ALASKA	OFF-SHORE	08
EF42	12	ALASKA	OPEN	08
AB74	06	COLORADO	MOUNTAIN	12
NP11	11	ALASKA	OFF-SHORE	12
TX09	22	TEXAS	OPEN	12
QW47	17	ALASKA	MOUNTAIN	14

TAPE-OIL-WELL-SA

FIGURE 9.2. The file generated by sorting TAPE-OIL-WELL-A (Figure 9.1b) on the ADDRESS field. The first record of each group with the same address value is a home address record.

We can see at a glance at how many records are assigned to a given e can thus generate two new tape files from a sequential scan of TAPE-OIL-WELL-SA (as illustrated in Figure 9.3). We have TAPE-HA containing the home address records, and TAPE-OF containing the overflow records. Both files are in ascending ADDRESS order. We are now in a position to load the home address records into the relative address disk space.

WELL-NUMB	FLOW-RATE	STATE	TERRAIN	ADDRESS
EX99	36	TEXAS	OFF-SHORE	00
AA11	08	TEXAS	OPEN	04
AB14	50	ALASKA	OFF-SHORE	08
AB74	06	COLORADO	MOUNTAIN	12
QW47	17	ALASKA	MOUNTAIN	14

TAPE-HA

WELL-NUMB	FLOW-RATE	STATE	TERRAIN	ADDRESS
CD83	20	TEXAS	OFF-SHORE	04
MU10	06	COLORADO	VALLEY	04
EF42	12	ALASKA	OPEN	08
NP11	11	ALASKA	OFF-SHORE	12
TX09	22	TEXAS	OPEN	12

TAPE-OF

FIGURE 9.3. The result of dividing the records of TAPE-OIL-WELL-SA (Figure 9.2) into two new files, TAPE-HA containing only home address records, and TAPE-OF containing only overflow records.

Loading the Home Address Records

With the home address records available in ascending address order in TAPE-HA, loading these records into the hash file OIL-WELL is quite straightforward. However, we need an additional field at the beginning of an OIL-WELL record that does not occur in the corresponding TAPE-HA record. This field takes up a single byte or character and is used for deleting records or for marking them as either valid or dummy. The first byte of any valid record in a relative file should contain the COBOL literal LOW-VALUES (binary code 00000000). To mark the record as deleted (or dummy, which is the same thing), the first byte is changed to the COBOL literal HIGH-VALUES (binary code 11111111). Thus we always leave space in a relative file record for this delete-byte or deletion tag. We shall call this field TAG, so that an OIL-WELL record has the format shown in Figure 9.4.

The deletion tag plays a role in sequential loading of the home address records. The hash file is opened for OUTPUT; as each record is

Relative disk Address	TAG	WELL-NUMB	FLOW-RATE	STATE	TERRAIN	ADDRESS
00	'b'	EX99	36	TEXAS	OFF-SHORE	00
01	'9'	—	—	—	—	—
02	'9'	—	—	—	—	—
03	'9'	—	—	—	—	—
04	'b'	AA11	08	TEXAS	OPEN	04
05	'9'	—	—	—	—	—
06	'9'	—	—	—	—	—
07	'9'	—	—	—	—	—
08	'b'	AB14	50	ALASKA	OFF-SHORE	08
09	'9'	—	—	—	—	—
10	'9'	—	—	—	—	—
11	'9'	—	—	—	—	—
12	'b'	AB74	06	COLORADO	MOUNTAIN	12
13	'9'	—	—	—	—	—
14	'b'	QW47	17	ALASKA	MOUNTAIN	14

OIL-WELL

FIGURE 9.4. The OIL-WELL hash file with only the home address records from TAPE-HA (Figure 9.3) loaded. The home address records are loaded sequentially in ascending address order; the loading program should place the COBOL literal LOW-VALUES (blank 'b') in the first byte (TAG field). The access method places dummy records into any addresses not used by the program; these dummy records have the COBOL literal HIGH-VALUES in the first byte (that is, the character '9'). When the file is later read these dummy records can be retrieved and inspected. During later loading of the overflow records (Figure 9.5), some of these dummy records will be replaced by overflow records. From a hash file point of view, the dummy records represent empty addresses.

read from TAPE-HA using a COBOL READ, it has a TAG field added containing LOW-VALUES (or ' ' value) and is output using a WRITE to the OIL-WELL relative address in the ADDRESS field. The OIL-WELL records are written out in ascending address order, as mentioned earlier. This means that not all addresses get an OIL-WELL record—that is, as the records are written, we leave empty addresses. Well, not quite, for the access method loads a record into every address. What happens is that every address skipped over by our COBOL WRITE command receives a dummy record from the access method; as we have seen, a dummy record has HIGH-VALUES (value '9') in the first byte. Also, when we have written the last record using a COBOL WRITE and have closed the file, the access method places dummy records in the remaining addresses up to the end of the address space. (Note that we can specify the number of addresses required in the dataset definition statement [DD-statement] for the hash file.)

When all home address records have been loaded, we have the situation shown in Figure 9.4. Some addresses have valid OIL-WELL records (these are the home address records), while the *unused* addresses contain dummy records, with TAG field value 9. Later if we attempt to read the record in an address containing a dummy, the record will be read normally. It is up to the program to check in the TAG field to see if it is a valid record.

Some COBOL code for this stage of the loading will be instructive. To focus attention on the hash file, we shall omit the specifications for the tape file. The tape file uses a working-storage structure called TAPE-HA-REC. We have already had the environment division specifications for OIL-WELL, but we repeat them below in the context of the program for loading the home address records:

```
ENVIRONMENT DIVISION.
.
.
.
INPUT-OUTPUT SECTION.
FILE-CONTROL.
        SELECT OIL-WELL
              ASSIGN TO DA-R-OWL   (OWL is an arbitrary ddname)
        ORGANIZATION IS RELATIVE
        ACCESS IS SEQUENTIAL
           NOMINAL KEY IS DISK-ADDRESS.
                (With ANS COBOL, replace NOMINAL with RELATIVE;
                NOMINAL is for IBM COBOL)
```

In the data division we specify the buffer and working-storage records in the usual way. Note that the address variable, or identifier (referred to in COBOL as the relative or nominal key), DISK-ADDRESS must be specified in the working-storage section:

```
DATA DIVISION.
FILE SECTION.
FD      OIL-WELL
        RECORD CONTAINS 36 CHARACTERS
        (BLOCK CONTAINS clause not needed, blocking factor is
```

```
        always unity)
        LABEL RECORDS STANDARD.
01      OW-BUFREC PIC X(36).
.
.
.
WORKING-STORAGE SECTION.
77      DISK-ADDRESS PIC 9(5).
01      OW-REC.
        02      TAG PIC X.
        02      OW-DATA.
                        03  WELL-NUMB    PIC X(4).
                        03  FLOW-RATE    PIC 99.
                        03  STAT         PIC X(12).
                        03  TERRAIN      PIC X(12).
                        03  ADDRESS      PIC 9(5).
```

The structure OW-REC gives the format of a valid record in the hash file OIL-WELL. Notice that the first character is for a deletion tag and that the home address of the record will be recorded in the field ADDRESS. Thus later it will easily be possible to determine if a record in the file is an overflow record; the address containing the record need only be compared with the address contained in the ADDRESS field of the record.

The loading procedure is now quite simple, since most of the processing has already been carried out in the preparation of the tape file TAPE-HA that contains the home address records (see Figure 9.3). The records of this file are now read in sequence and written out into the hash file OIL-WELL. Since not every relative address in sequence will get a valid OIL-WELL record, the DISK-ADDRESS identifier is used with WRITE as follows:

```
PROCEDURE DIVISION.
MAIN-PARAGRAPH.
      OPEN INPUT TAPE-HA,
OUTPUT OIL-WELL.
      MOVE "NO" TO TAPE-HA-EOF.
      READ TAPE-HA INTO TAPE-HA-REC,
AT END PERFORM NO-RECORDS-PARAGRAPH.
      PERFORM LOAD-HOME-ADDRESS-RECORDS
            UNTIL TAPE-HA-EOF = "YES".
      CLOSE TAPE-HA, OIL-WELL, STOP RUN.
LOAD-HOME-ADDRESS-RECORDS.
      MOVE LOW VALUES TO TAG IN OW-REC.
      MOVE TAPE-HA-REC TO OW-DATA IN OW-REC.
      MOVE ADDRESS IN OW-REC TO DISK-ADDRESS.
      WRITE OW-BUFREC FROM OW-REC.
      READ TAPE-HA INTO TAPE-HA-REC,
      AT END MOVE "YES" TO TAPE-HA-EOF.
```

When a WRITE command is executed the access method places the record involved in the address contained in DISK-ADDRESS; at the same time all intervening relative addresses since the previous WRITE command receive dummy records (Figure 9.4). The identifier TAPE-HA-EOF is merely an end of file flag for the tape file that contains the home address records (TAPE-HA).

Loading the Overflow Records

The overflow records are loaded from TAPE-OF, which contains the overflow records in ascending address order (see Figure 9.3). Thus TAPE-OF has groups of overflow records, each group being the records overflowing from the home address in the address field for that group.

To load a given group of overflow records, we must search through the addresses on the disk that are greater than the home address value. We conduct the search by reading the record in a relative address. If the record is a dummy, we can load an overflow record. If it is not, we carry on to the next address in sequence. If the search takes us past the end of the address space, we continue the search from address 0. This means that the file OIL-WELL must be open for direct access. Thus we code ACCESS IS RANDOM in the INPUT-OUTPUT section specification for OIL-WELL in the environment division. Otherwise OIL-WELL and associated record structures are specified as for loading the home address records.

Sometimes we search past the end of the address space; therefore the program must know how many addresses the file has. In the following excerpt we use 15, to enable the process to be diagrammed. As mentioned earlier this could be changed to 150,000 in the case where we are loading 100,000 records into 150,000 addresses.

The following is the essential core of the loading procedure; the file navigation diagram for the procedure is shown in Figure 9.5:

```
PROCEDURE DIVISION.
LOAD-OVERFLOW-RECORDS.
        OPEN I-O OIL-WELL,
             INPUT TAPE-OF.
        MOVE "NO" TO TAPE-OF-EOF.
        READ TAPE-OF INTO TAPE-OF-REC,
              AT END PERFORM NO-RECORDS-PARAGRAPH.
*TAPE-OF-REC is the WORKING-STORAGE structure for the
*overflow records of TAPE-OF.
        PERFORM LOAD-OVERFLOW-GROUP
              UNTIL TAPE-OF-EOF = "YES".
        CLOSE TAPE-OF, OIL-WELL.
        STOP-RUN.
LOAD-OVERFLOW-GROUP.
```

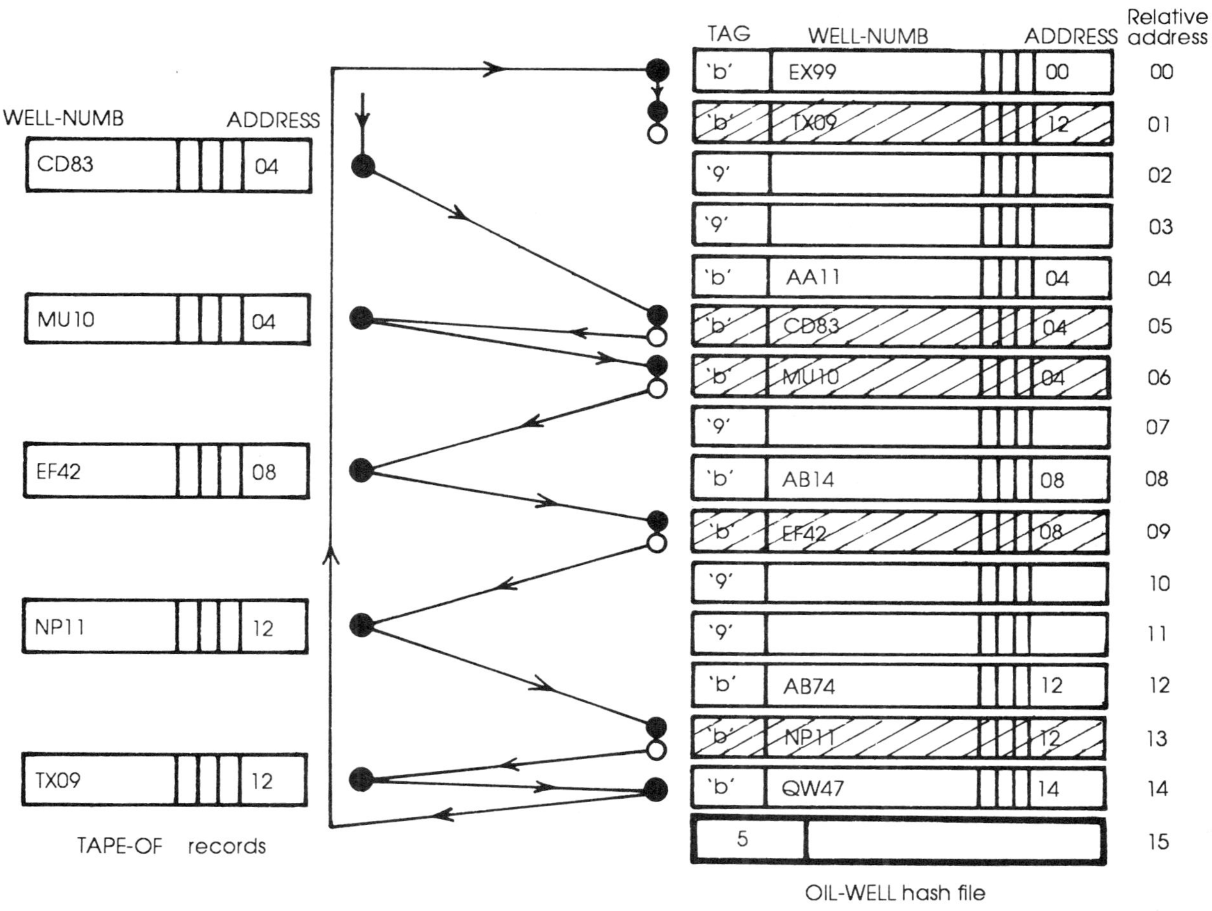

FIGURE 9.5. File navigation diagram for loading the overflow records from TAPE-OF (see also Figure 9.4) into the hash file OIL-WELL. Progressive overflow management is used for the overflow records. At the end of the field we show a special record in address 15. It is used for storing statistics about the file, particularly the maximum search length, which is 5 for the file above. Overflow records in OIL-WELL are shaded.

```
MOVE ADDRESS IN TAPE-OF-REC TO CONTROL-DISK-ADDRESS.
       MOVE ADDRESS IN TAPE-OF-REC TO DISK-ADDRESS.
       READ OIL-WELL INTO OW-REC.
       PERFORM SEARCH-AND-LOAD-RECORDS UNTIL
         ADDRESS IN TAPE-OF-REC NOT = CONTROL-DISK-ADDRESS.
```

```
SEARCH-AND-LOAD-RECORDS.
      PERFORM FORWARD-SEARCH UNTIL TAG IN OW-REC = HIGH-VALUES.
      MOVE LOW-VALUES TO TAG IN OW-REC.
       MOVE TAPE-OF-REC TO OW-DATA IN OW-REC.
       WRITE OW-BUFREC FROM OW-REC.
       READ TAPE-OF INTO TAPE-OF-REC,
           AT END MOVE "YES" TO TAPE-OF-EOF,
                  MOVE 99999 TO ADDRESS IN TAPE-OF-REC.
FORWARD-SEARCH.
        COMPUTE DISK-ADDRESS = DISK-ADDRESS + 1.
        IF DISK-ADDRESS = 15
             THEN COMPUTE DISK-ADDRESS = 0.
** Instead of 15 we would normally use the large number equal
** to the total addresses in the file.  Note that even in the
** present case the highest address is 14.  If the value in DISK
** ADDRESS exceeds 14 we recommence the search from address 0.
** READ OIL-WELL INTO OW-REC.
```

Calculation of Average Search Length and Maximum Search Length

Although not included in the above programs for loading the hash file OIL-WELL, it is good practice to get the loading program or programs to print out the average search length for the file loaded, and the maximum search length. This is not very difficult to arrange. Consider the average search length. By definition this is the total number of accesses to retrieve all the records at random divided by the total number of records. Getting the programs to increment a data item TOTREC following each WRITE to OIL-WELL is a simple matter. At the end of the loading, TOTREC contains the number of records. The total accesses required to retrieve all the records at random is the sum of the accesses required to retrieve the home address records plus those to retrieve the overflow records. Each home address record takes one access to retrieve it. Thus we can compute the accesses to retrieve the home address records in the program (or program step) to load the home address records, simply by summing them. The number of accesses required to retrieve a single overflow record is the value

```
DISK-ADDRESS - CONTROL-DISK-ADDRESS + 1
```

where DISK-ADDRESS contains the address at which the record is loaded and CONTROL-DISK-ADDRESS is the record's home address. These data items are used in the program to load the overflow records, so that the accesses required to retrieve all the overflow records may be summed in the data item TOTAL-ACCESSES, if we insert the following after each WRITE statement:

```
COMPUTE TOTAL-ACCESSES = TOTAL-ACCESSES + DISK-ADDRESS
                       - CONTROL-DISK-ADDRESS + 1
```

Thus if TOTHAREC is the total number of home address records, the average search length will be given by the following expression:

```
(TOTHAREC + TOTAL-ACCESSES) / TOTREC
```

Having this value printed out at the end of the loading program clearly signals whether the file has met its target for average search length and whether the design process has been a success. As such it is also a powerful tool for those trying to manage the hash file design process. Indeed it is the bottom line of hash file design.

The **maximum search length** is needed for use with programs that use the hash file. Maximum search length may be defined as the largest number of disk accesses required to retrieve a record—that is, it is the worst search length we can possibly encounter. This value must be available to any program searching for a record. Suppose that the maximum search length is 15 and that the home address of a record seeks hashes to 4567. The program looks in address 4567, then in 4568, then 4569, and so on. The program can determine that the record sought is not in the file when the search reaches 4567 + (15-1), that is, address 4581, without finding the record sought.

If the maximum search length is not available to the program, there is no way that the program can determine that a record is not in the file without searching the complete file. Thus the maximum search length is a fundamental operational parameter for a progressive overflow hash file. It is often stored in a separate record at the end of the address space, usually address R, where the file has R addresses. Before a file is processed for update or retrieval, the special record in address R is read, so that the maximum search length is available.

To compute the maximum search length during loading, the value of

```
DISK-ADDRESS - CONTROL-DISK-ADDRESS + 1
```

is compared with the value in a data item, MAX, following each WRITE command execution. Thus in the loading program for the overflow records we replace the WRITE command with:

```
WRITE-OW-BUFREC FROM OW-REC.
IF MAX < (DISK-ADDRESS - CONTROL-DISK-ADDRESS + 1)
   THEN COMPUTE MAX = DISK-ADDRESS
          - CONTROL-DISK-ADDRESS + 1.
```

At the end of the processing MAX contains the maximum search length, which can be printed out and also stored in a special record

At the end of the processing MAX contains the maximum search length, which can be printed out and also stored in a special record located at address R. The additional modifications of the program to achieve this are left to the reader.

USE OF COBOL TO UPDATE A PROGRESSIVE OVERFLOW HASH FILE

It would be next to impossible to update the file OIL-WELL in ascending key sequential order, at least as constructed in Figure 9.5. It can be done, however, if a more elaborate hash file is constructed, in which pointers are used to connect the records in ascending primary key order.

Updating a conventional hash file, such as the file OIL-WELL, is normally carried out by direct access. Often too, the file is part of some on-line system, so that all access is random. In this section we look at the necessary COBOL code for direct access updating of the OIL-WELL hash file in Figure 9.5. We consider change, insertion, and deletion updating.

Change Updating of the Hash File OIL-WELL

We may presume that flow rates for oil wells change from time to time, so that the FLOW-RATE field (given in hundreds of barrels per day) needs to be (change) updated from time to time. Suppose that the updating information is in the (transaction) file CTRANS, each record of which contains a well number and the latest flow-rate data for the well.

The records of CTRANS do not have to be in ascending key (WELL-NUMB) order, since OIL-WELL will be updated by direct access. We may assume that CTRANS is a tape file. (If interactive updating were being used, then CTRANS records could be accepted—using the COBOL ACCEPT verb—from a terminal by the updating program instead of being read from a tape.) We assume that the working-storage structure for CTRANS records is CTRANS-REC, with the following composition:

```
01      CTRANS-REC.
        02  WELL-NUMB  PIC X(4).
        02  FLOW-RATE  PIC 99.
```

To update a record it must first be found; if the record is an overflow record then a progressive search must be made for it. Thus the maximum search length must be available. We assume that it is available in a special record in address 15 that is used only for useful file statistics. The working-storage record structure used to retrieve this special record is as follows:

```
01      STATISTICSREC.
       02  MAX          PIC 999.
       02  STATINFO     PIC X(33).
```

It is the same length (36 characters) as the other records of the file. The essentials of the procedure to update OIL-WELL are as follows:

```
PROCEDURE DIVISION.
HEAD-PARAGRAPH.
     OPEN INPUT CTRANS,
          I-O OIL-WELL.
     MOVE 15 TO DISK-ADDRESS.
     READ OIL-WELL INTO STATISTICSREC.
     READ CTRANS INTO CTRANS-REC,
           AT END PERFORM NO-RECORDS-PARAGRAPH.
     MOVE "NO" TO CTRANS-EOF.
     PERFORM UPDATE-RECORD UNTIL CTRANS-EOF = "YES".
     CLOSE CTRANS, OIL-WELL.
     STOP RUN.
UPDATE-RECORD.
     PERFORM HASH-PARAGRAPH.
     MOVE HASH-RESULT TO DISK-ADDRESS.
     MOVE "NO" TO RECORD-FOUND.
     COMPUTE SEARCH-LENGTH = 0.
     PERFORM SEARCH-FOR-RECORD UNTIL
            RECORD-FOUND = "YES" OR
            SEARCH-LENGTH = MAX.
     IF RECORD-FOUND = "YES"
     THEN MOVE FLOW-RATE IN CTRANS-REC TO FLOW-RATE IN OW-REC
              REWRITE OW-BUFREC FROM OW-REC
```

```
          ELSE DISPLAY WELL-NUMB IN CTRANS-REC,
                 "NOT FOUND IN HASH FILE".
        READ CTRANS INTO CTRANS-REC,
                   AT END MOVE "YES" TO CTRANS-EOF.
SEARCH-FOR-RECORD.
        READ OIL-WELL INTO OW-REC.
        COMPUTE SEARCH-LENGTH = SEARCH-LENGTH + 1.
        IF WELL-NUMB IN CTRANS-REC = WELL-NUMB IN OW-REC
                  AND TAG IN OW-REC = LOW-VALUES
         THEN MOVE "YES" TO RECORD FOUND
         ELSE COMPUTE DISK-ADDRESS = DISK-ADDRESS + 1
                   IF DISK-ADDRESS = 15
                   THEN COMPUTE DISK-ADDRESS = 0.
HASH-PARAGRAPH.
**   In this paragraph, a WELL-NUMB IN CTRANS-REC value is
**   hashed giving a home address value that is placed in the
**   data item HASH-RESULT.
```

In the above procedure, CTRAN-EOF is the end of file flag for the transaction file CTRANS. RECORD-FOUND is another flag, used for searching for a record in OIL-WELL. Before beginning a search for a given OIL-WELL record, RECORD-FOUND is set to NO. It is set to YES if the record is found; and this is then used to determine whether or not to proceed with the update. During a search for a record (in the SEARCH-FOR-RECORD paragraph), we must keep incrementing the value in the address variable DISK-ADDRESS (which we recall is specified in the environment division as the data item from which the access method will extract the required disk address for a READ command execution). If the value of DISK-ADDRESS reaches R-1 (14 in the program), the next value of DISK-ADDRESS has to be 0, since the search will continue from the beginning of the file.

It is important that the number of accesses to obtain a record not exceed the maximum search length (MAX data item). Thus we use a data item SEARCH-LENGTH to count the disk accesses (number of READ OIL-WELL commands) carried out in a given search. However, apart from this rather tricky aspect of searching for a record in a hash file with progressive overflow, the updating is otherwise straightforward.

Insertion Updating of the Hash File OIL-WELL

The oil company that has developed the hash file OIL-WELL will no doubt continue to drill new holes, some of which will turn out to be producing wells. Thus we can expect insertion of new records from time to time. Some such records are assembled in the tape file ITRANS and have the same fields as OIL-WELL, except for the TAG field.

Note that we have an ADDRESS value in the ITRANS records. We may assume this has been added in an earlier processing step, by applying the WELL-NUMB values to the hashing routine and attaching the resulting relative addresses to the records. We have arranged the ITRANS fields in this way merely to keep the insertion update procedure as readable as possible. It is not strictly necessary, since the ITRANS key values can be hashed without difficulty as the records are read.

The OIL-WELL hash file is again processed by direct access. Before a record can be inserted at its home address (that is, the address the key hashed to), the contents of that home address in the file must be read to determine if the address is already occupied. If it is not, we can insert the record. If it is, the simplest strategy is to begin a progressive search for an empty address (that is, an address with a dummy record). This is the strategy coded in the procedure below.

We do not need the maximum search length to look for an empty address. Nevertheless the maximum search length may need updating as a result of an insertion for which the search length exceeds the maximum in the old version of the file. Thus the maximum search length is needed with insertion updating too.

The working-storage record for ITRANS is ITRANS-REC; we use OW-BUFREC and OW-REC as before for the buffer and working-storage records for the hash file OIL-WELL. The essential core of the procedure follows:

```
PROCEDURE DIVISION.
HEAD-PARAGRAPH.
     OPEN INPUT ITRANS,
          I-O OIL-WELL.
     MOVE 15 TO DISK-ADDRESS.
     READ OIL-WELL INTO STATISTICSREC.
     READ ITRANS INTO ITRANS-REC,
           AT END PERFORM NO-RECORDS-PARAGRAPH.
     MOVE "NO" TO ITRANS-EOF.
     PERFORM INSERT-RECORD UNTIL ITRANS-EOF = "YES".
     MOVE 15 TO DISK-ADDRESS.
     WRITE OW-BUFREC FROM STATISTICSREC.
     CLOSE OIL-WELL, ITRANS.
     STOP RUN.
INSERT-RECORD.
     MOVE ADDRESS IN ITRANS-REC TO DISK-ADDRESS.
     COMPUTE SEARCH-LENGTH = 0.
     MOVE "NO" TO SLOT-FOUND.
     PERFORM SEARCH-FOR-SLOT UNTIL SLOT-FOUND = "YES".
     MOVE LOW-VALUES TO TAG IN OW-REC.
     MOVE ITRANS-REC TO OW-DATA IN OW-REC.
```

```
          REWRITE OW-BUFREC FROM OW-REC.
          READ ITRANS INTO ITRANS-REC,
              AT END MOVE "YES" TO ITRANS-EOF.
     SEARCH-FOR-SLOT.
          READ OIL-WELL INTO OW-REC.
          COMPUTE SEARCH-LENGTH = SEARCH-LENGTH + 1.
          IF TAG IN OW-REC = HIGH-VALUES
            THEN MOVE "YES" TO SLOT-FOUND
            ELSE COMPUTE DISK-ADDRESS = DISK-ADDRESS + 1
               IF DISK-ADDRESS = 15
               THEN COMPUTE DISK-ADDRESS = 0.
          IF SLOT-FOUND = "YES" AND MAX < SEARCH-LENGTH
          THEN COMPUTE MAX = SEARCH-LENGTH.
```

In the above procedure, ITRANS-EOF is the usual flag for the end of the transaction file. The flag SLOT-FOUND is used for searching for an empty address greater to the home address of the record to be inserted. Before a search begins we set the flag to NO. When an empty slot has been found we set it to YES. During the search, with each OIL-WELL record read, we increment the data item SEARCH-LENGTH, so that when the search has ended (and SLOT-FOUND contains YES) SEARCH-LENGTH contains the number of accesses required to carry out the search for the empty slot. If this value exceeds MAX (the maximum search length hitherto) MAX is assigned this new value.

At the end of the processing (end of head-paragraph), the new value of MAX is stored once more in address 15 as a field of the record structure STATISTICSREC. Notice that if the search for a vacant address reaches the end of the address space, then as usual the search continues from address 0.

Deletion Updating of the Hash File OIL-WELL

Inevitably as an oil well ages, the flowrate diminishes until the day arrives where the flow rate is 0 or not economic. If we assume that our oil company only wants producing wells in the hash file OIL-WELL, records must be removed from the file on a continual basis. Suppose that the transaction file DTRANS contains records that each describe a well with a flow rate of 200 barrels per day or under and which are therefore to be deleted from OIL-WELL. As with the other updating procedures, ITRANS will be read sequentially and can be a tape file, whereas OIL-WELL will be updated by direct access. Before a record can be deleted it must be found, so that we encounter the usual search of the overflow records. Thus we must involve the maximum search length, to search for records to be deleted.

In theory, it is possible that we might also need to update the value of the maximum search length. For example, suppose that the maximum search length is 6 and that we delete a record whose search length is 6. If the record deleted is the only one with a search length of 6, then following the deletion the maximum search length will be less than 6. But how much less, and how does the program determine that the record deleted was the only one with a maximum search length of 6? It cannot be done if the only search length statistic maintained is the maximum search length. We need to maintain statistics about the number of records with the maximum search length, the number one less than the maximum search length, and so on. This is rarely done in practice, although the processing cost would be minimal.

Thus during the updating the maximum search length may decrease, but this will not be recorded in the file statistics. In other words the recorded maximum search length will be too high. However, no harm is done by this. It is a recorded maximum search length that is too low that could cause the system to deduce that records were not in the file when they actually were.

In the following procedure we assume that DTRANS records have the same fields as OIL-WELL, except for the TAG field. Thus we assume that in prior processing the ADDRESS value in each DTRANS record has been computed by hashing the WELL-NUMB value in the record. The working-storage record for DTRANS is DTRANS-REC. The essentials of the deletion updating procedure follows:

```
PROCEDURE DIVISION.
HEAD-PARAGRAPH.
     OPEN INPUT DTRANS,
          I-O OIL-WELL.
     MOVE 15 TO DISK-ADDRESS.
     READ OIL-WELL INTO STATISTICSREC.
     READ DTRANS INTO DTRANS-REC,
           AT END PERFORM NO-RECORDS-PARAGRAPH.
     MOVE "NO" TO DTRANS-EOF.
     PERFORM DELETE-RECORD UNTIL DTRANS-EOF = "YES".
     CLOSE DTRANS, OIL-WELL.
     STOP-RUN.
DELETE-RECORD.
     MOVE ADDRESS IN DTRANS-REC TO DISK-ADDRESS.
     COMPUTE SEARCH-LENGTH = 0.
     MOVE "NO" TO RECORD-FOUND.
     IF FLOW-RATE IN DTRANS-REC NOT > 2
       THEN PERFORM SEARCH-FOR-RECORD UNTIL
             RECORD-FOUND = "YES" OR
             SEARCH-LENGTH = MAX
       ELSE DISPLAY WELL-NUMB IN DTRANS-REC,
            "FLOW-RATE TOO HIGH FOR DELETION"
          MOVE " " TO WELL-NUMB IN DTRANS-REC.
```

```
          IF RECORD-FOUND = "YES"
            THEN MOVE HIGH-VALUES TO TAG IN OW-REC
               REWRITE OW-BUFREC FROM OW-REC
            ELSE IF WELL-NUMB IN DTRANS-REC NOT = " "
               THEN DISPLAY WELL-NUMB IN DTRANS-REC, "NOT IN FILE".
          READ DTRANS INTO DTRANS-REC,
               AT END MOVE "YES" TO DTRANS-EOF.
     SEARCH-FOR-RECORD.
          READ OIL-WELL INTO OW-REC.
          COMPUTE SEARCH-LENGTH = SEARCH-LENGTH +1.
          IF WELL-NUMB IN DTRANS = WELL-NUMB IN OW-REC
                                AND TAG = LOW-VALUES
            THEN MOVE "YES" TO RECORD-FOUND
            ELSE COMPUTE DISK-ADDRESS = DISK-ADDRESS + 1
              IF DISK-ADDRESS = 15
          THEN COMPUTE DISK-ADDRESS = 0.
```

Notice that to delete a record it is only necessary to alter the TAG field to HIGH-VALUES. Thus a REWRITE command is used instead of a DELETE, so that this deletion updating procedure is very similar to the change updating procedure given earlier. One difference is that careful checking is normally always carried out with an important file before a record is deleted. Thus in the procedure above we check that the flow rate actually is 200 barrels a day or less before a record for a well is deleted.

INFORMATION RETRIEVAL FROM A HASH FILE USING PROGRESSIVE OVERFLOW

Suppose that we want to know the total daily production of oil from wells in Texas, using the information in the hash file OIL-WELL in Figure 9.5. Clearly we have to examine each OIL-WELL record; if the STATE value is TEXAS, add the value in the field FLOW-RATE to a summation data item TOTAL, whose initial value is 0. A little thought shows that the order in which the records are accessed does not matter, as long as each record in the file is accessed. Thus we can process in ascending relative address order simply by checking in each relative address in turn, ignoring dummy records. This requires that ACCESS IS SEQUENTIAL be specified in the environment division; this is the method used in the procedure below. Note that processing in ascending key (WELL-NUMB) order is not possible with hash files in general and with the file OIL-WELL in particular.

```
PROCEDURE DIVISION.
```

```
MAIN-PARAGRAPH.
      OPEN INPUT OIL-WELL.
      MOVE "NO" TO OIL-WELL-EOF.
      COMPUTE TOTAL = 0.
      READ OIL-WELL INTO OW-REC.
      PERFORM CHECK-NEXT-RECORD UNTIL OIL-WELL-EOF = "YES".
      DISPLAY TOTAL.
      CLOSE OIL-WELL, STOP-RUN.
CHECK-NEXT-RECORD.
     IF TAG = LOW-VALUE
     THEN IF STATE = 'TEXAS'
          THEN COMPUTE TOTAL = TOTAL + FLOW-RATE.
      READ OIL-WELL INTO OW-REC,
          AT END MOVE "YES" TO OIL-WELL-EOF.
```

Note that dummy records are read during sequential reading of a hash file. Note also that the relative address data item DISK-ADDRESS is not used and *is not coded in the environment division this time*. In general we can say that sequential processing is used for information retrieval with a hash file when the retrieval does not depend on the record key field, in this case WELL-NUMB.

Information Retrieval by Means of Direct Access

Retrievals by means of direct access are straightforward, since they involve access to the file on the basis of a key. Suppose that we want to know what state well NP11 is in, as well as the location of some additional wells. We can imagine that the request is entered interactively at a terminal by the user, so that a COBOL ACCEPT command can read the target WELL-NUMB value into a data item TARGET-WELL-NUMB. We must specify ACCESS IS RANDOM in the data division, as well as the relative address specification NOMINAL KEY IS DISK-ADDRESS. Since the program is interactive it should prompt the user for the required or target record key.

In the following interactive retrival program, to make things more realistic we may assume that the user is likely to enter the required WELL-NUMB value incorrectly and will need a second chance. We also assume that the user is likely to need information about more than one well.

```
PROCEDURE DIVISION.
HEAD-PARAGRAPH.
     OPEN INPUT OIL-WELL.
     DISPLAY "OIL-WELL INFORMATION SYSTEM IN SESSION".
     MOVE 15 TO DISK-ADDRESS.
     READ OIL-WELL INTO STATISTICSREC.
```

```
          MOVE "YES" TO MORE-REQUESTS.
          PERFORM CARRY-OUT-REQUEST UNTIL MORE-REQUESTS = "NO".
          DISPLAY "SESSION TERMINATED, HAVE A GOOD DAY".
     CARRY-OUT-REQUEST.
          DISPLAY "GIVE WELL NUMBER".
          ACCEPT TARGET-WELL-NUMB.
          PERFORM HASH-PARAGRAPH.
          MOVE HASH-RESULT TO DISK-ADDRESS.
          COMPUTE SEARCH-LENGTH = 0.
          MOVE "NO" TO RECORD-FOUND.
          PERFORM SEARCH-FOR-RECORD UNTIL
                 RECORD-FOUND = "YES" OR SEARCH-LENGTH = MAX.
          IF RECORD-FOUND = "YES"
          THEN DISPLAY WELL-NUMB IN OW-REC, STATE IN OW-REC
          ELSE DISPLAY TARGET-WELL-NUMB, "NOT IN DATA FILE, SORRY".
          DISPLAY "FURTHER REQUESTS?"
          DISPLAY "ANSWER YES OR NO".
          ACCEPT RESPONSE.
          IF RESPONSE = "NO"
          THEN MOVE "NO" TO MORE-REQUESTS.
     SEARCH-FOR-RECORD.
          READ OIL-WELL INTO OW-REC.
          COMPUTE SEARCH-LENGTH = SEARCH-LENGTH + 1.
          IF TARGET-WELL-NUMB = WELL-NUMB IN OW-REC
                                   AND TAG = LOW-VALUES
          THEN MOVE "YES" TO RECORD-FOUND
          ELSE COMPUTE DISK-ADDRESS = DISK-ADDRESS + 1
               IF DISK-ADDRESS = 15
               THEN COMPUTE DISK-ADDRESS = 0.
     HASH-PARAGRAPH.
     **   Here TARGET-WELL-NUMB value is hashed giving result in
     **   HASH-RESULT.
```

Because we have to search for records, the maximum search length is needed, so that one of the first things the program must do is retrieve this information from the last address (address 15). The maximum search length is read into the data item MAX in the record STATISTICSREC. We need a flag MORE-REQUEST, which gets the value NO only when the user signals that no more requests for information are forthcoming. As such it functions in the program much like an end of file flag.

Each request is processed by CARRY-OUT-REQUEST. The program asks for the target well number, on receipt of which it is hashed and the resulting address moved to the relative (or nominal) address data item DISK-ADDRESS. In the search for the record (SEARCH-FOR-RECORD paragraph) as usual we count the number of accesses and call off the search if the maximum search length is reached without finding it. When a record has been found and the STATE value displayed, or not found and a message to that effect displayed, the user is asked to indicate (using YES or NO) whether or not there is a further request. The user's answer is collected in the data item RESPONSE; if it is YES the paragraph CARRY-OUT-REQUEST is repeated.

A sample session with the above procedure is given below. For the reader's convenience the users answers are in bold italics.

```
OIL-WELL INFORMATION SYSTEM IN SESSION
GIVE WELL NUMBER
```

NPI1

```
NPI1  NOT IN DATA FILE, SORRY
FURTHER REQUESTS?
ANSWER YES OR NO
```

YES

```
GIVE WELL NUMBER
```

NP11

```
NP11  ALASKA

FURTHER REQUESTS?
ANSWER YES OR NO
```

NO

```
SESSION TERMINATED, HAVE A GOOD DAY
```

Note that the rather long messages printed by the program are acceptable only if a video screen (cathode ray or liquid crystal) is being used. If a typewriter terminal is used, users tend to become irritated by long-winded messages that seem to take the typewriter forever to type. Thus brevity here may be desirable, at the expense of clarity and even politeness.

Increased Address Capacity with Relative Files

We have seen that relative file organization permits only a blocking factor of unity. This has two major disadvantages:

1. Since count-data format is usually used, the space taken up by a block on disk will be much larger than the space occupied by a single record.

2. The file will be relatively slow. A much lower average search length can be achieved if the address capacity is greater than unity.

Both these disadvantages can be eliminated by the use of a do-it-yourself blocking system with relative file organization—that is, a blocking system that is incorporated into the file processing application programs, as opposed to the access method. Unfortunately this method involves much more complex coding, and which is more expensive in terms of programming costs. Nevertheless it does result in highly efficient hash files, with little disk space wastage and low average search lengths. It is outlined in more detail later. The only other way to achieve a high address capacity is to use direct file organization, described next.

INCREASED HASH FILE ADDRESS CAPACITY USING DIRECT FILES

Direct files are not part of American National Standard COBOL but are available with the major IBM operating systems and are quite commonly used. From a programming point of view it is easier to maintain a file constructed using direct file organization than one with high address capacity using relative file organization. However, the ease of programming in the case of direct files usually comes at the cost of a very significant waste of disk space, as we shall see. In contrast, high address capacity hash files using relative file organization are very economical of disk space.

Basic Principles

With a direct file, the addressible unit of disk space is no longer a count-data block (as is the case with a relative file) but a complete track. Thus the address capacity is the number of records that can fit into a track. The records on a track are not blocked (which they are in count-key data format). It is this lack of blocking that can lead to significant waste of disk space (illustrated in Figure 9.6).

FIGURE 9.6. (opposite) General format and structure of a hash file constructed with direct file organization. Each relative address is a track starting at address 0. The address capacity is fixed at the number of records a track can hold (4 are shown above). Count-key data format is used and records are not blocked. Space not used is always filled with dummy records. A record is marked as dummy by the access method by means of HIGH-VALUES in the record key in the key subblock and not in the record. Overflow management is fixed at progressive overflow and is carried out automatically by the access method.

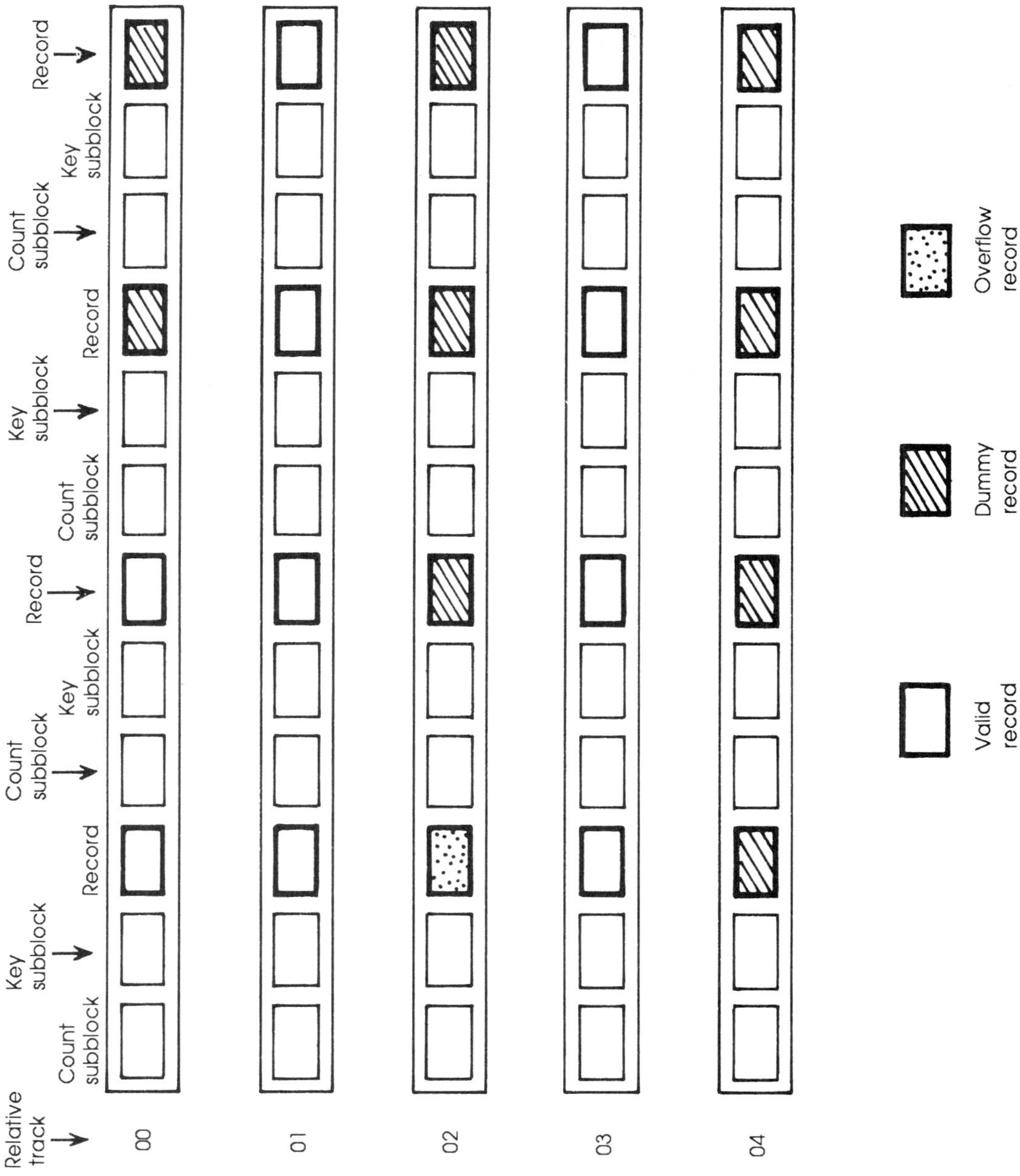
Relative track
Count subblock
Key subblock
Record
Count subblock
Key subblock
Record
Count subblock
Key subblock
Record
Count subblock
Key subblock
Record
00
01
02
03
04
Valid record
Dummy record
Overflow record

The file consists then of a number of addressible tracks; the addresses used are **relative track addresses**, not physical track addresses. Thus regardless of where a file begins on a disk, the first address is track 0. We note that if the addressible unit of disk space is always a track, then given the size of a record and the type of disk, the address capacity is always the same—that is, we have an unalterable but fairly high address capacity. This may place some limits on the flexibility of the hash file design, since address capacity is given right from the start.

A hash file constructed using direct organization is inflexible in another way too. It always uses progressive overflow. However, *progressive overflow management is built into the access method so that the program does not have to carry out searches for overflow records.* This is a significant advantage as far as reducing maintenance costs is concerned, since it simplifies hash file programs. This automatic progressive overflow management is described next.

Automatic Progressive Overflow Management with Direct File Organization

The basic principle of progressive overflow management with direct file organization is the same as that described earlier, except that the addressible unit is now a track. Record keys are hashed in the usual way; the result is a relative track address. If we present a new record to the access method with home address track 6, for example, and it is the case that track 6 is full, the access method automatically looks not only in track 6, but also in tracks 7, 8, 9, and so on, until it finds a track with space for the record.

The details of how records are handled are important. Consider retrieving a record with key XX13. Suppose that we hash XX13 and get track 6, the home address (or home track). Both the home track address (6) and the record key (XX13) must be presented to the access method. The access method first looks in track 6 (using the disk controller and an appropriate channel program, naturally) and checks to see if any of the records have key value XX13 in the key subblock. In the case of a relative file our retrieval program would have to do the equivalent of this. If the required record is not there, the next track is examined, and so on, until either the record is found or the maximum search length for the file is reached (see Figure 9.6). The access method knows the maximum search length, for it is coded in the DD-statement for the file.

Note that the tracks of a direct file are completely filled with records, either valid or dummy records. Valid records are normally at the beginning of the tracks and unused space at the ends is filled with dummy records.

Because of the automatic overflow management system, overflow management details do not have to be coded in a hash file processing program as is the case with a hash file based on relative file organization; this simplifies the COBOL coding required. A possible disadvantage of automatic progressive overflow management is that we cannot change it, perhaps to chained progressive overflow, which gives an even lower average search length. We can do this with a hash file based on relative file organization. Nevertheless this is hardly a serious drawback, since hash files with address capacity greater than unity using chained progressive overflow are not common (even if they give a very low average search length) because of the programming costs involved.

COBOL Specifications for Hash Files Based on Direct File Organization

Suppose that we are constructing another version of the hash file OIL-WELL with direct organization, so that the COBOL essentials can be compared with those given earlier for relative file organiztion. We begin with the environment division:

```
ENVIRONMENT DIVISION.
.
.
.
INPUT-OUTPUT SECTION.
FILE CONTROL.
         SELECT OIL-WELL ASSIGN TO DA-D-OWL (OWL is the ddname)
         ACCESS IS SEQUENTIAL (or RANDOM when direct access is
          used)
         ACTUAL KEY IS ADDRESS-KEY-COMBINATION
         TRACK LIMIT IS number of tracks in file
```

In the ACTUAL key clause we specify a group identifier, which we have arbitrarily called ADDRESS-KEY-COMBINATION, made up of an identifier to hold a relative track address and identifier to hold a record key. This group item is fully specified later in the working-storage section of the data division. It is this *actual key* ADDRESS-KEY-COMBINATION that is presented to the access method when we want to retrieve a record. The access method uses the relative track part to locate the home track; then it uses the record key part in its progressive search for the record.

The clause TRACK LIMIT is used only when the file is being created, usually by sequential access. Here we specify exactly how many tracks the file will contain. As with relative files the direct file is created by writing out records in ascending relative (track) address order. Tracks and portions of track not used are filled with dummy records. When the last record has been output, that part of the space remaining (up to the last track specified in the TRACK LIMIT clause) is also filled with dummies. Note that addresses start at track 0, so 1,000 tracks means addresses from 0 to 999.

To be able to correctly specify the number of tracks (number of addresses), we must know the number of records, the track or address capacity, and the required average search length. Suppose that we have 50,000 records, each 35 bytes long, as with OIL-WELL records, and suppose that the disk is an IBM 3350. The blocking factor is unity and count-key data is used. Thus a block takes up the following space on a track (we assume that the record key WELL-NUMB is 4 bytes long; see chapter 2 and Figure 2.22):

267 + (4 + 35), or 306 bytes

Thus the number of such blocks a track can hold is the integer below 19,254/306 or 62. Therefore the address capacity for the file is 62 records per address (or track).

We can now look up the curves for average search length versus loading factor for various address capacities and progressive overflow (see Figure 8.19). We do not have a curve for address capacity 62 but the one for 50 will do. Suppose we want an average search length less than 1.1 after loading. In that case we see that we are quite safe with a loading factor of 80 percent (assuming we do not intend to increase the number of records by more than about 15 percent during the life of the file).

A loading factor of 80 percent means that we must have space for more than our 50,000 records. We need space for 50,000/0.8 or about 62,000 records. Since the address capacity is 62, this means we need 1,000 tracks, which is what we would specify in the TRACK LIMIT clause.

In the data division we specify the usual buffer and working-storage records for the file. But we must also specify the *actual key* made up of track address and record key as follows:

```
DATA DIVISION.
FILE SECTION.
FD   OIL-WELL
      RECORD CONTAINS 35 CHARACTERS
```

```
      LABEL RECORDS ARE STANDARD
      DATA RECORD IS OW-BUFREC.
01    OW-BUFREC       PIC X(35).
.
.
.
WORKING-STORAGE SECTION.
01    ADDRESS-KEY-COMBINATION.
      02          TRACK-ADDRESS   PIC S9(8) COMP SYNC.
      02          RECORD-KEY.
                  03      DELETE-TAG      PIC X.
                  03      WELL-NUMB       PIC X(4).
01    OW-REC.
      02          WELL-NUMB       PIC X(4).
      02          FLOW-RATE       PIC 99.
      02          STATE           PIC X(12).
      02          TERRAIN         PIC X(12).
      02          ADDRESS         PIX 9(5).
```

The above specification illustrates several important points. First of all, the *actual key* ADDRESS-KEY-COMBINATION consists of the track address and a record key. The PIC specification for TRACK-ADDRESS should be as shown; before a record is read or written, the record's home track value should be moved to this data item, so that it is available to the access method. In addition RECORD-KEY must be initialized by the program before a record is written or read. LOW-VALUES (indicating a valid record) should be moved to DELETE-TAG and the key of the record (in this case the well number) moved to WELL-NUMB in RECORD-KEY. The combination of DELETE-TAG and WELL-NUMB is used in the search for the record once the home track has been found.

Notice that we do not have a deletion tag field in the working-storage record. A record (that is, a data subblock of a count-key data block) is not itself marked as deleted using the COBOL literal HIGH-VALUES in the first byte, as is the case with relative files. Instead the first byte in the key in the key subblock is marked as deleted using HIGH-VALUES. It is the value in RECORD-KEY in the group item ADDRESS-KEY-COMBINATION that is used in the key subblock; that is why we have a deletion tag in RECORD-KEY. If we do not include the field DELETE-TAG (and we are free to omit it), the access method uses the first byte of WELL-NUMB in RECORD-KEY to mark a record as deleted.

Loading the Hash File OIL-WELL Using Direct File Organization

As with relative file organization it is best to load the hash file in three stages. First we prepare two tape files TAPE-HA and TAPE-OF as before. We preprocess the records to be loaded and generate the track addresses using the hashing routine, followed by a sort on the track address value and a segregation of the records into home address records (to TAPE-HA) and overflow records (to TAPE-OF). This is much the same as the preprocessing used earlier to load the relative file version of OIL-WELL. This time, since we have an address capacity of 62, the first 62 records of a group with the same address value are taken as home address records.

The next step is to load the home address records. This is now little more than a copying operation, since the access method does all the work of arranging all records with the same address on the same track. We code ACCESS IS SEQUENTIAL for the file in the input-output section of the environment division. The procedure is:

```
PROCEDURE DIVISON.
      OPEN INPUT TAPE-HA,
           I-O OIL-WELL.
      COMPUTE COUNT-RECORDS = 0.
      MOVE "NO" TO TAPE-HA-EOF.
      READ TAPE-HA INTO OW-REC,
            AT END PERFORM NO-RECORDS-PARAGRAPH.
      PERFORM LOAD-RECORD UNTIL TAPE-HA-EOF = "YES".
      DISPLAY "TOTAL HOME ADDRESS RECORDS:", COUNT-RECORDS.
      CLOSE TAPE-HA, OIL-WELL.
      STOP RUN.
LOAD-RECORD.
      MOVE ADDRESS IN OW-REC TO TRACK-ADDRESS
                    IN ADDRESS-KEY-COMBINATION.
      MOVE LOW-VALUES TO DELETE-TAG IN ADDRESS-KEY-COMBINATION.
      WRITE OW-BUFREC FROM OW-REC.
      COMPUTE COUNT-RECORDS = COUNT-RECORDS + 1.
      READ TAPE-HA INTO OW-REC,
           AT END MOVE "YES" TO TAPE-HA-EOF.
```

Clearly this is quite a simple procedure. We intend to compute the average search length for the file, so we accumulate the number of records written out in the data item COUNT-RECORDS. TAPE-HA-EOF is the usual flag for the end of the source tape file TAPE-HA.

The final step is the loading of the overflow records from the source file TAPE-OF. This time the file is specified in the environment division with ACCESS IS RANDOM; the TRACK LIMIT clause is omitted, since the extent of the disk space for the file was fixed (for all time) when the home address records were loaded sequentially. Remember that the sequential loading of the home address records caused all the unused space to be filled with dummy records. The overflow records are loaded by direct access; the access method simply replaces dummy records with valid overflow records, complying at the same time with the basic idea of progressive overflow management. The loading program is again simple, since the access method does the work of searching for an empty slot within a track (that is, an address).

We must know on what track an overflow record is placed by the access method if we are to compute the average search length. For example, suppose that the home address of a record is track 20, and we place 20 in the TRACK-ADDRESS portion of the *actual key*. The access method might place the record somewhere on track 24. This means that the number of (track) accesses required to retrieve the record would be 24 - 20 + 1 or 5 tracks (access to track 20, 21, 22, 23, and 24). The problem is how we are to know that the access method placed the record on track 24. The answer is simple: Following a WRITE statement execution, the access method takes the address into which it has placed a record (not necessarily the home address) and places it in the TRACK-ADDRESS component of the *actual key*. Since the home address of the record will be in the ADDRESS field of OW-REC, the number of track accesses necessary to retrieve that record must be as follows:

```
TRACK-ADDRESS - ADDRESS + 1
```

In the program below we accumulate such values in the data item TOTAL-ACCESSES. Initially we add to TOTAL-ACCESS the number of records written out when the home addresses were loaded, since it takes exactly one track access to retrieve a home address record. Because we can compute the number of accesses required to retrieve each record loaded, we can also select the maximum value, which is the maximum search length.

```
PROCEDURE DIVISION.
      OPEN INPUT TAPE-OF,
           I-O OIL-WELL.
      ACCEPT TOTAL-RECORDS.
      COMPUTE TOTAL-ACCESSES = TOTAL-RECORDS.
      MOVE "NO" TO TAPE-OF-EOF.
      READ TAPE-OF INTO OW-REC,
          AT END PERFORM NO-RECORDS-PARAGRAPH.
      COMPUTE MAX-SEARCH-LENGTH = 0.
      PERFORM LOAD-RECORD UNTIL TAPE-OF-EOF = "YES".
      DISPLAY "AVERAGE SEARCH LENGTH:", AVE-SEARCH-LENGTH.
      DISPLAY "MAX. SEARCH LENGTH:", MAX-SEARCH-LENGTH.
      CLOSE TAPE-OF, OIL-WELL.
```

```
      STOP RUN.
LOAD-RECORD.
      MOVE ADDRESS IN OW-REC TO TRACK-ADDRESS.
      MOVE LOW-VALUES TO DELETE-TAG.
      MOVE WELL-NUMB IN OW-REC TO WELL-NUMB
          IN ADDRESS-KEY-COMBINATION.
      WRITE OW-BUFREC FROM OW-REC.
      COMPUTE TOTAL-RECORDS = TOTAL-RECORDS + 1.
      COMPUTE TOTAL-ACCESSES = TOTAL-ACCESSES + 1
              + TRACK-ADDRESS - ADDRESS.
      IF MAX-SEARCH-LENGTH < (TRACK-ADDRESS - ADDRESS + 1)
         THEN COMPUTE MAX-SEARCH-LENGTH = TRACK-ADDRESS
                - ADDRESS + 1.
      READ TAPE-OF INTO OW-REC,
           AT END MOVE "YES" TO TAPE-OF-EOF,
           PERFORM COMPUTE-AVE-SEARCH-LENGTH.
COMPUTE AVE-SEARCH-LENGTH.
      COMPUTE AVE-SEARCH-LENGTH = TOTAL-ACCESSES /
     TOTAL-RECORDS.
```

We use the COBOL ACCEPT verb at the beginning to read in the total home address records already loaded. This is equal to the total accesses required to access these records; therefore the value is placed in both TOTAL-ACCESSES (the total track accesses so far) and in TOTAL-RECORDS (the total records so far). At the end of the processing TOTAL-ACCESSES holds the total accesses required to retrieve all records randomly from OIL-WELL; TOTAL-RECORDS holds the sum of the home address and overflow records, thus permitting the average search length to be calculated.

Updating and Information Retrieval with Hash Files Based on Direct File Organization

We saw in loading the hash file OIL-WELL above that the coding is much simplified because the access method looks after the increased address capacity and progressive overflow management. The same is true for updating and information retrieval. No searches need ever be carried out by the program. The maximum search length obtained during loading is coded in the DD-statement for the file, so that the access method can always accurately determine whether or not a record is in the file. We look briefly at the essential COBOL coding for change, insertion, and deletion updating and for record retrieval. In all cases we assume direct access with ACCESS IS RANDOM coded in the environment division. We also continue with the hash file OIL-WELL as loaded above.

Change Updating

We use a READ statement (having presented the correct home address and record key combination) to read a record. We then change update the record and immediately use a WRITE (not a REWRITE) to replace that record. A WRITE replaces the record most recently read. Sup-ppose we want to update the record with key XX77 and home address 101 by changing the FLOW-RATE field value to 3,500 barrels per day, as follows:

```
MOVE 101 TO TRACK-ADDRESS.
MOVE LOW-VALUES TO DELETE-TAG.
MOVE "XX77" TO WELL-NUMB IN ADDRESS-KEY-COMBINATION.
READ OIL-WELL INTO OW-REC,
               INVALID KEY PERFORM RECORD-NOT-FOUND-PARAGRAPH.
COMPUTE FLOW-RATE IN OW-REC = 35.
**  Note that at this point the record's true track address is
**  in TRACK-ADDRESS and is not necessarily the home address.
WRITE OW-BUFREF FROM OW-REC.
```

Note the INVALID KEY clause. The access method searches for the record using the progressive overflow technique, if the record is not in its home address. When it reaches the maximum search length (coded in the DD-statement for the file) it gives up and the statements following INVALID KEY are executed. A previously deleted (but still physically present record) will not be retrieved.

Insertion Updating

We have already illustrated insertion updating in the third stage of loading the file. The file containing only the home address records was insertion updated using overflow records.

Deletion Updating

Suppose that we want to delete the record with key ZZ99 with home address 56. We must first read the record before we delete it:

```
MOVE 56 TO TRACK-ADDRESS.
MOVE LOW-VALUES TO DELETE-TAG.
MOVE 'ZZ99' TO WELL-NUMB IN ADDRESS-KEY-COMBINATION.
READ OIL-WELL INTO OW-REC,
      INVALID KEY PERFORM RECORD-NOT-FOUND-PARAGRAPH.
MOVE HIGH-VALUES TO DELETE-TAG.
WRITE OW-BUFREC FROM OW-REC.
```

We see that deletions involve setting the deletion tag in the *actual key* to the COBOL HIGH-VALUES literal and writing out the record again. Note that the WRITE must be issued after the record is read and before any other record is read. When the READ is issued, RECORD-ADDRESS holds the home address 56. Following the read, RECORD-ADDRESS holds the true track address, since the record in question may be an overflow record.

Record Retrieval

We have already had several examples of record retrieval, since a record must be read before it can be either change updated or deletion updated.

INCREASED HASH FILE ADDRESS CAPACITY WITH RELATIVE FILE ORGANIZATION

This section is highly specialized, and can be omitted on first reading. We have seen that relative file organization provides for only a blocking factor (and thus address capacity) of unity, and that one way to get a higher address capacity and thus lower average search length is to use direct file organization. Another method involves incorporating blocking and deblocking code in processing programs for hash files constructed with relative file organization. In this section we outline how such do-it-yourself blocking can be carried out. The advantage is very low average search lengths and minimization of wasted disk space.

Basic Principles

Consider the hash file OIL-WELL in Figure 9.5. We have 10 records assigned to 15 relative addresses with address capacity of unity, so that the loading factor is 66.6 percent. Suppose now that to reduce the average search length we increase address capacity to 2 and decrease the number of addresses to 8, so that the loading factor remains constant at about 66.6 percent. (We may ignore for the moment an additional address, address 8, for file statistics.) Our problem is how to achieve up to 2 records per address. COBOL and the relative file organization permits us to write only one record into an address.

The answer is simple, although it complicates the COBOL coding. We continue to write and read a single COBOL record with each address, but each of these COBOL records can contain up to 2 OIL-WELL records, so that a single OIL-WELL record becomes only a part of what is written and read using COBOL commands. In the case of address

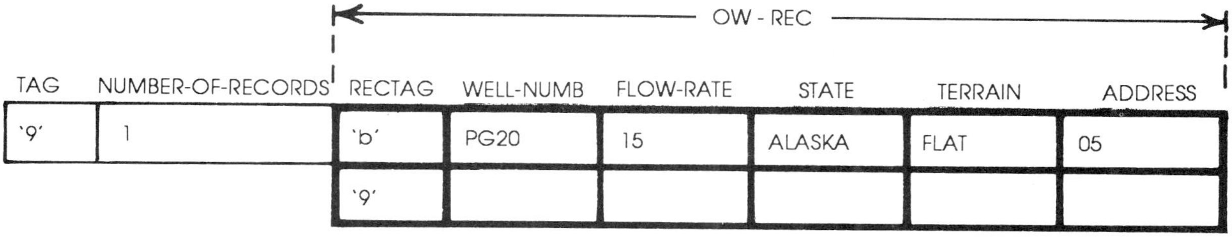

FIGURE 9.7. Structure of the group data item ARTIFICIAL-BLOCK. The entire group item is read or written with a relative file using the COBOL READ or WRITE commands. Thus the blocking factor is unity. However since ARTIFICIAL-BLOCK contains multiple occurrences of OIL-WELL records (only up to 2 in the case above), the effective address capacity has been increased. The initial TAG field indicates whether or not there are any valid records within the structure. NUMBER-OF-RECORDS gives how many valid records (above there is only one). In this example the first occurrence of the subgroup of data items OW-REC contains a record, whereas the second does not. RECTAG in OW-REC is used to indicate a valid or deleted record. ADDRESS in OW-REC holds the home address of the record.

capacity 2, we can structure the COBOL record (that is, the contents of a relative address) as follows:

```
01    ARTIFICIAL-BLOCK.
       02 TAG       PIC X.
       02 NUMBER-OF-RECORDS         PIC 99.
       02 OW-REC    OCCURS 2 TIMES.
                    03       RECTAG   PIC X.
                    03       OW-DATA.
                             04       WELL-NUMB PIC X(4).
                             04       FLOW-RATE PIC 99.
                             04       STATE     PIC X(12).
                             04       TERRAIN   PIC X(12).
                             04       ADDRESS   PIC 9(5).
```

These are the data items that occupy each address of the relative file (such a block is shown diagramatically in Figure 9.7). TAG is used to indicate whether there are any valid records in the address, LOW-VALUES indicating valid data and HIGH-VALUES indicating that the address is empty. NUMBER-OF-RECORDS indicates how many valid

OIL-WELL records are in the address (in this case the value is either 1 or 2). Then we have the two substructures OW-REC(1) and OW-REC(2); in each, RECTAG is used to indicate the presence or absence of a valid OIL-WELL record. As usual HIGH-VALUES indicates an empty slot and LOW-VALUES that the record is valid. The ADDRESS value in each substructure contains the home address of the record in the substructure.

To create the file we specify the environment division exactly as in the case of address capacity unity. We specify ACCESS IS SEQUENTIAL and the address data item DISK-ADDRESS with NOMINAL KEY IS DISK-ADDRESS. A COBOL record for the new version of OIL-WELL is now much longer; the above structure will be 2*(36 + 1) + 1 + 2 or 77 bytes long. Thus the data division specifications for OIL-WELL are as follows:

```
DATA DIVISION.
FILE SECTION.
FD OIL-WELL
         RECORD CONTAINS 77 CHARACTERS
         LABEL RECORDS STANDARD.
01      OW-BUFREC PIC X(77).
.
.
.
WORKING-STORAGE SECTION.
77 DISK-ADDRESS         PIC 9(5).
01 ARTIFICIAL-BLOCK.
    02   TAG             PIC X.
    02   NUMBER-OF-RECORDS        PIC 99.
    02   OW-REC  OCCURS 2 TIMES
                03      RECTAG ...
```

In the procedure division we may write in address 6, for example, using the following:

```
MOVE 6 TO DISK-ADDRESS.
WRITE OW-BUFREC FROM ARTIFICIAL-BLOCK.
```

We may read from address 6 using the following:

```
MOVE 6 TO DISK-ADDRESS.
READ OIL-WELL INTO ARTIFICIAL-BLOCK.
```

We may never write either of the following, as was possible when we had only a single record (OW-REC) in each address:

```
WRITE OW-BUFREC FROM OW-REC
READ OIL-WELL INTO OW-REC
```

WELL-NUMB	ADDRESS
EX99	00
AA11	02
CD83	02
MU10	02
AB14	04
AB74	06
NP11	06
TX09	06
EF42	07
QW47	07

TAPE-OIL-WELL-SA

FIGURE 9.8. Records intended for the OIL-WELL file are first fed to the hashing routine and the generated addresses are attached (ADDRESS field). They are then sorted on ADDRESS value giving this version of TAPE-OIL-WELL-SA. With the data above, the hash file is to have 10 records and 8 addresses, each capable of holding 2 records. The ascending ADDRESS order of the records permits them to be easily segregated into home address and overflow records.

Thus we always read and write 2 OIL-WELL records (or substructures), one or both of which can be dummies (indicating an unused slot).

Creating a Version of the Hash File OIL-WELL with Address Capacity Greater than Unity

The overall steps to create a hash file with address capacity greater than unity are no different from those used for address capacity unity. We must prepare two sequential files for the records to be loaded. Both should be in ascending relative address order, one containing home address records and the other the overflow records. Next we load the home address records and finally the overflow records.

We can follow the process for the records loaded earlier into the version of OIL-WELL for which the address capacity was unity (see Figures 9.3, 9.4, and 9.5 for comparison). This time we load the 10 records into 7 addresses, each with an address capacity equal to 2.

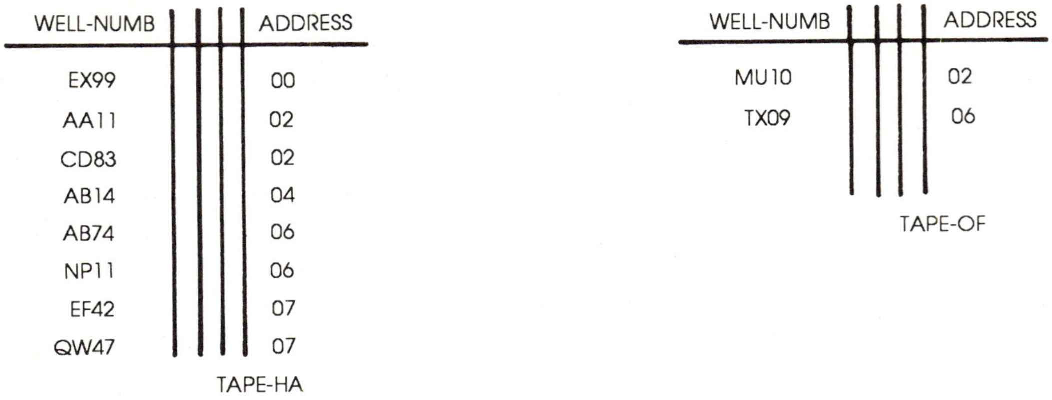

FIGURE 9.9. Result of segregating records in TAPE-OIL-WELL-SA (Figure 9.8) into home address records (file TAPE-HA) and overflow records (file TAPE-OF).

We first process these records sequentially; for each record the key is hashed and the resulting address (home address) attached in an ADDRESS field. Then we sort the file in ascending ADDRESS order; the result of this is the tape file TAPE-OIL-WELL-SA (Figure 9.8). We see that this tape file is made up of groups of records each with the same ADDRESS value. Since the address capacity in our projected hash file is now 2, the first 2 records of such a group (if there are 2 or more records) are home address records. If there is only 1 record in a group (such as that for well number AB14), that must also be a home address record. We can thus separate the records of TAPE-OIL-WELL-SA into the home address records in TAPE-HA and the overflow records in TAPE-OF (Figure 9.9).

In loading the home address records we use the COBOL record structure ARTIFICIAL-BLOCK, described in the previous section. The COBOL records are output in ascending relative address order; as before, the access method places HIGH-VALUES in the first byte of each relative address space that is not used. We take some care in filling the data items of ARTIFICIAL-BLOCK before it is output with a COBOL WRITE command. TAG is set to LOW-VALUES, and a value is assigned to NUMBER-OF-RECORDS; we also set the RECTAG byte in each of the OW-REC occurrences to LOW-VALUES when there is a record from TAPE-HA, otherwise to HIGH-VALUES, (see Figure 9.10).

Relative address	TAG	NUMBER-OF-RECORDS	RECTAG	WELL-NUMB	ADDRESS
00	'b'	1	'b'	EX99	00
			'9'	Empty	
01	'9'			Empty	
				Empty	
02	'b'	2	'b'	AA11	02
			'b'	CD83	02
03	'9'			Empty	
				Empty	
04	'b'	1	'b'	AB 14	04
			'9'	Empty	
05	'9'			Empty	
				Empty	
06	'b'	2	'b'	AB74	06
			'b'	NP11	06
07	'b'	2	'b'	EF42	07
			'b'	QW47	07

OIL-WELL

FIGURE 9.10. The state of the hash file OIL-WELL following loading of the home address records. Some addresses have 2 records, some 1 record, and some none. Total records (the sum of the NUMBER-OF-RECORDS values) is 8. Address 8, which holds file statistics such as maximum search length, is not shown.

in each of the OW-REC occurrences to LOW-VALUES when there is a record from TAPE-HA, otherwise to HIGH-VALUES, (see Figure 9.10).

Relative address	TAG	NUMBER-OF-RECORDS	RECTAG	WELL-NUMB	ADDRESS
00	'b'	1	'b'	EX99	00
			'b'	TX09	06
01	'9'			Empty	
				Empty	
02	'b'	2	'b'	AA11	02
			'b'	CD83	02
03	'b'	1	'b'	MU10	02
				Empty	
04	'b'	1	'b'	AB 14	04
			'9'	Empty	
05	'9'			Empty	
				Empty	
06	'b'	2	'b'	AB74	06
			'b'	NP11	06
07	'b'	2	'b'	EF42	07
			'b'	QW47	07

OIL-WELL

FIGURE 9.11. The state of the hash file OIL-WELL following loading of the overflow records from Figure 9.10. The NUMBER-OF-RECORDS field values now sum to 10.

In the loading of the overflow records, we begin the search for an empty slot at the address one greater than the home address. This time we do not reject out of hand an address for which the first byte (TAG field) contains LOW-VALUES, for it may be that the address contains space for an additional record. Thus we also examine the NUMBER-OF-RECORDS field, to see if the address is full. If it is we continue with the search; otherwise we check the OIL-WELL substructures within the address until we find an empty one. As usual, if our search for a nonfull address takes us to the end of the address space, we begin again at address 0. Most of these points are illustrated by the final hash file in Figure 9.11.

Updating and information retrieval procedures are similar to those given for address capacity unity earlier, except that in addition to progressive searches through the address space, we frequently also have to search the substructures within individual addresses (or COBOL records). This unfortunately adds an additional layer of complexity and thus increases the cost of maintaining such a file. Before constructing such a file, an analysis of the benefit (significantly reduced average search length if the address capacity is high) versus the cost should be carried out.

Space Utilization: Relative and Direct Files Compared

Earlier we considered the example of 50,000 OIL-WELL records in a hash file based on direct file organization. We saw that with a loading factor of 80 percent and a (given) address capacity of 62, exactly 1,000 tracks of an IBM 3350 disk are required.

At this point it is convenient to compare the number of tracks needed if we use an address capacity of 62 with a relative file. The blocking factor is always unity with such a hash file, although we can pack a single COBOL record with as many of the records as we wish using an OCCURS specification. The block size on a track of an IBM 3350 disk is then the following:

185 + 1 + 2 + 62*36 or 2420 bytes

The number of blocks per track is the integer below 19,254/2,420 or 7 blocks (see chapter 2). Thus a track can hold 7*62 or 434 records. We already know that we need space for 62,000 records to have a loading factor of about 80 percent, so that the number of tracks needed is 62,000/434 or 143.

In other words by using a relative file, do-it-yourself blocking, and the same address capacity and loading factor (and thus the same bottom line average search length), we need only 143 tracks as opposed to 1,000 tracks with a direct file. We can conclude that the price of the direct file method is a waste of 85.7 percent of the disk space. If larger records are involved, then the space wasted is a little less, but not much. This proves the assertion made earlier that the price of the convenience of programming hash files with direct organization is a very great waste of disk space.

SUMMARY OF HASH FILE DESIGN STEPS

In chapter 8 we covered the essential theory of hash files; in this chapter we cover the essentials of hash file practice using COBOL. This coverage should enable anyone requiring a hash file to construct one with a targeted average search length. Unfortunately the subject has many sides to it (as readers will no doubt have experienced), so a summary of the general steps to be taken in a design situation is probably useful. In addition, no two design problems are alike—the general steps given below may have to be modified in any given situation. Bearing this caveat in mind, we should proceed as follows:

1. Determine the required average search length for the application. If it is high—in the range 2.5 to 3 or above—use an indexed-sequential file. It is much cheaper.
2. Unless the average search length needed is extremely low, assume that progressive overflow management will be used. Chained progressive is expensive in terms of programming costs, but almost always gives a much lower average search length.
3. Determine an upper limit for the file's loading factor using anticipated net insertions. For example, if we initially have 80,000 records in the file and we expect a net insertion of 20,000 over the life of the file, we can say that 80 percent (or more conservatively, 75 percent) is the upper limit of the loading factor that can be used.
4. Obtain an approximation for the address capacity needed. Using our target average search length and our approximate idea of loading factor we can consult curves of average search length versus loading factor for different address capacities (see Figure 8.19 for progressive overflow and 8.20 for chained progressive overflow). The point on the curve selected gives the address capacity and initial loading factor.
5. Knowing the address capacity, loading factor, and the initial number of records to be loaded, we can determine the number of addresses required. For example, suppose we have an address capacity of 10, a loading factor of 80 percent and 200,000 records. That means we need space for 200,000*100/80 or 250,000 records. Since the address capacity is 10, we need 250,000/10 or 25,000 addresses (R).
6. Knowing the number of addresses, we can generate a hashing routine, the simplest being division of a numerical version of the key by R and taking the remainder as the address. A series of routines should be written and the resulting distributions ob-

tained. Select the best one and one that gives a better than random distribution. If none qualify, either try again or use a radix transformation. Remember that the curves used to determine required address capacity assume random distribution; therefore our hashing routine must give either a random or better than random distribution.

7a. Earlier if we decided to stay with progressive overflow, we now have a choice of relative file organization versus direct file organization. It is difficult to give firm rules here. If we derive an address capacity of unity then relative file organization gives a satisfactory bottom-line average search length—but we waste disk space because the records are not blocked, and progressive overflow management code must be incorporated into every program that uses the file.

If the derived address capacity is greater than unity we have a choice of a block-it-yourself relative file or a direct file. The relative file uses space efficiently but requires progressive overflow coding in all programs using the file. Programming is easy with the direct file but a great deal of space is wasted. Note that the derived address capacity is unlikely to equal the address capacity offered by the direct file, which is fixed by the record length at the capacity of a track. If the track capacity exceeds the derived address capacity, that is to the good since a somewhat lower target average search length will likely result; note that the number of addresses (R) derived in step 5 must be revised in the light of the fixed address capacity of the direct file. If the derived address capacity is greater than that offered by the direct file, use the relative file.

7b. Assuming that chained progressive overflow was decided upon earlier, we must use a relative file. If the derived address capacity is greater than unity, it is another case of do-it-yourself blocking.

8. Prepare the records for loading by attaching the home address of each record and sorting on ADDRESS value. Home address records can be placed in one sequential source file and overflow records in another.

9. Load home address records first, followed by overflow records. The loading program should generate the average search length for the file and the maximum search length. The average search length should be close to or lower than the original target average search length.

SUMMARY

A hash file can be created using either relative or direct file organization. With relative organization the address capacity is unity. To minimize overflow records, home address records are loaded first, followed by overflow records. The loading program should compute both the average and maximum search lengths. Code for the overflow management technique must be incorporated into the loading program.

With direct organization the address capacity is the capacity of a track and can be quite large. The records on a track are not blocked, so that a great deal of track space is wasted. The access method looks after overflow management.

It is possible to have an address capacity greater than unity with a relative file. To achieve this, the blocking and deblocking code must be incorporated in all programs that use the file.

EXERCISES

1. Create the hash file OIL-WELL using relative file organization, address capacity unity, and progressive overflow management. Print out the average and maximum search lengths.
2. Create the hash file OIL-WELL using relative file organization, address capacity unity, and chained progressive overflow management. Print out the average and maximum search lengths.
3. Suppose that some new records for OIL-WELL are available in a transaction file. Write a program to update OIL-WELL as created in exercise 1.
4. Suppose that some new records for OIL-WELL are available in a transaction file. Write a program to update OIL-WELL as created in exercise 2.
5. Suppose that a list of wells to be deleted from OIL-WELL are held in a transaction file. Write a program to update OIL-WELL as created in exercise 1.
6. Suppose that a list of wells to be deleted from OIL-WELL are held in a transaction file. Write a program to update OIL-WELL as created in exercise 2.
7. Suppose that a list of new flow rates for wells in OIL-WELL is held in a transaction file. Write a program to update OIL-WELL as created in exercise 1.

8. Suppose that a list of new flow rates for wells in OIL-WELL is held in a transaction file. Write a program to update OIL-WELL as created in exercise 2.
9. Write a program to create the hash file OIL-WELL using direct organization.
10. Suppose that some new records for OIL-well are available in a transaction file. Write a program to update OIL-WELL as created in exercise 9.
11. Suppose that a list of wells to be updated are held in a transaction file. Write a program to update OIL-WELL as created in exercise 9.
12. Supppose that a list of new flow rates for some wells in OIL-WELL are held in a transaction file. Write a program to update OIL-WELL as created in exercise 9.
13. A list of states is held in a transaction file. The transaction file contains less than 100 records. Write a program to obtain the total flow of oil in each state, using the file OIL-WELL as created in exercise 1.
14. Repeat exercise 13 using the version of OIL-WELL created in exercise 2.
15. Repeat exercise 13 using the version of OIL-WELL created in exercise 9.
16. Write a program to create OIL-WELL with relative address organization, progressive overflow, and address capacity of 10. The program must incorporate blocking techniques.
17. A list of wells to be deleted are held in a transaction file. Write a program to update OIL-WELL as created in exercise 16.
18. A list of records to be inserted in OIL-WELL are held in a transaction file. Write a program to update the version of OIL-WELL created in exercise 16.
19. Suppose that a list of new flow rates for some wells in OIL-WELL are held in a transaction file. Write a program to update OIL-WELL as created in exercise 16.
20. Repeat exercise 13 using the version of OIL-WELL created in exercise 16.

10 ON-LINE PROCESSING AND CICS

In chapter 1 we gave an overview of **batch** and **on-line processing** and showed in principle how a teleprocessing monitor is used with on-line processing. In later chapters we covered the essentials of file processing—but always with the tacit assumption that we were using either batch processing, or operating system batch processing facilities, or simply interactive processing using an interactive operating system (such as VM/CMS or UNIX). In this chapter we look in more detail at on-line processing, where a *teleprocessing monitor* is being used.

IBM's **Customer Information Control System** (CICS—sometimes pronounced *kicks*), is easily the most widely used teleprocessing monitor in commerce. It is also widely used on college campuses that have an IBM computer installation, but unfortunately is used almost exclusively for administration and rarely for education. The result is that few students are ever exposed to one of the most (if not *the* most) important and fundamental software systems used in business.

A problem with CICS from an educational point of view is that there is a great deal to know about it; entire books have been written about CICS. A COBOL application programmer at a CICS installation must know CICS to write a program, since the conventional READ and WRITE commands of COBOL (as well as other COBOL commands) must be replaced by CICS commands. In addition the inclusion of CICS commands in a COBOL program normally requires the coding of special procedures that are not necessary with conventional COBOL.

In addition to its effect on application programs, CICS requires that many tables holding detailed specifications (similar to job control language [JCL] specification) must be installed before on-line programs can be installed and executed. This task is normally carried out by systems programmers.

Even the business systems analyst must know CICS to design business systems. The analyst does not have to know all the etails, but he or she must be familiar with exactly what CICS can do and what jobs must be carried out for CICS to function.

We cannot go into all the various aspects of CICS in this book; space does not permit it for one thing, and for another, our mission is file processing. Instead our strategy is to give the reader a reasonable overall grasp of how CICS works and how it is used in general, coupled with fairly detailed coverage of how file processing is conducted with both CICS and COBOL. In this chapter we cover CICS concepts and the various components of CICS. In the next chapter we cover file processing with CICS and COBOL.

CICS CONCEPTS

A CICS facility is usually complex. It includes many types of remote terminals, complex communications hardware, and a wide variety of on-line application programs and associated files. In addition CICS is really an operating system within an operating system. Nevertheless, it is designed to handle the complexity, so that users can deal with it much more easily than you might think.

Overall we might say that CICS makes on-line programs independent of the hardware. Thus it is possible to make extensive changes to remote terminal types and communications hardware without a need to alter the on-line programs. Possibly equally important is that CICS provides very good response time to users at remote terminals.

It must be understood that with on-line systems most users are not computer experts. A user wants to do things such as enter the details of an order or inquire if any WK42 widgits are in stock. An on-line program must execute to accept the details of that order or to respond to the query about the widgits. And at any instant during a normal business day, hundreds and maybe thousands of users request such services at their remote terminals. The result is that many programs must execute in a very short time, to give each user a response in a short time (typically of the order of a few seconds at worst). CICS makes this possible; shortly we shall see how.

A further important aspect of CICS has to do with update interference prevention. Many on-line programs that are executing concurrently can be using the same file. The result is that the file update carried out by one of these program can be undone by the another program a fraction of a second later. This is *update interference*. We shall look at an example of this in the next chapter. With CICS it is possible to write programs that can concurrently use the same file without such update interference.

All these apsects of CICS are heavily intertwined. However, we can fix our ideas much better if we look at how a CICS on-line system fits into more conventional systems.

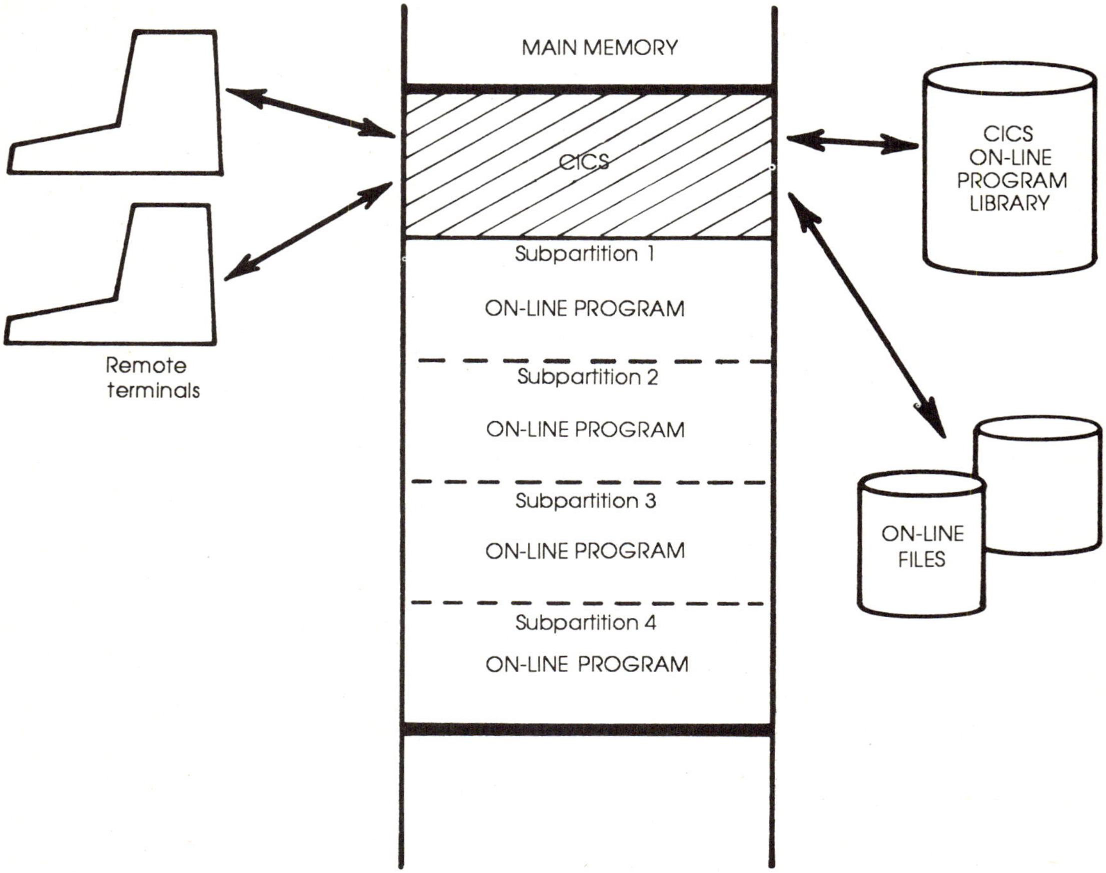

Figure 10.1 Some detail of the CICS on-line partition. The on-line partition is divided into subpartitions, each under the control of CICS. In response to a request for a service (corresponding to a CICS transaction code), CICS loads an on-line program from its library into a subpartition. When a program in a subpartition must wait for data from a file, CICS gives execution control to some other on-line program in another partition. The remote terminals deal with CICS directly and not with the application programs. It is also CICS (not the programs) that deals with the files.

CICS in a System Context

CICS normally runs in a partition of a batch operating system, such as OS/MVS. As far as the operating system is concerned, CICS is simply another job that occupies a partition or region. (The whole thing is paged in and out of course, but we just forget that.)

CICS is not a normal job, however. It has the highest priority of all jobs, so that other jobs in other partitions execute only when CICS is not busy. Typically CICS runs only during business hours, so that large batch jobs get priority to run and complete at night.

In the morning a systems programmer loads and executes CICS with normal IBM JCL commands. Part of the JCL for loading CICS with VSAM files might be:

```
//CICSRUN   JOB CLASS=W,REGION=4096K
//VERIFY    EXEC  PGM=IDCAMS
// ...
     ...
//CICS      EXEC PGM=DFHSIP,
     ...
/&
```

Altogether some 90 lines of detailed JCL are required to load CICS—we naturally spare the reader the details. In what is shown above, the program IDCAMS prepares VSAM disk space (see chapter 6). The program DFHSIP is CICS. When the above JCL has been carried out, the systems programmer has brought up CICS.

Earlier we stated that CICS is really an operating system within an operating system. An operating system looks after partitioning of memory (if we ignore paging, as usual) and input/output. The partition holding CICS can be quite large and is actually subpartitioned by CICS into subpartitions. These are controlled by CICS; each subpartition can hold an on-line application program (see Figure 10.1). The entire CICS partition is known as an **on-line partition**.

It is CICS (not the application programs) that is connected via the telecommunications hardware to the remote on-line terminals. A user at a terminal has a dialogue with CICS and not immediately with any on-line program.

Suppose that a user wants to know how many WK42 widgits are in stock. This is a specific type of CICS transaction, for which there is a transaction code that has been stored earlier by a systems programmer in a CICS table, called a **program control table (PCT)**. Suppose that the transaction code is INV1, and that in the CICS PCT entry this transaction is associated with an on-line program called INVWIDGE. The user then enters something like the following:

```
INV1 WK42
```

This is read by CICS. CICS looks up the transaction code INV1 in the appropriate table and determines that the program INVWIDGE is required. If this program is not already in one of the subpartitions, CICS takes it from its library of on-line programs (Figure 10.1) and loads it into a subpartition. Shortly afterwards CICS lets this program execute.

The data item WK42 is made available to the program by CICS. Actually, to get this data into the program's working storage, a CICS RECEIVE command must be executed, something like the following:

```
EXEC CICS
    RECEIVE INTO (WIDGIT-DATA) ...
END-EXEC.
```

This permits the program to have CICS place the value WK42 into a data name WIDGIT-NUMBER that is part of the COBOL group item WIDGIT-DATA. WIDGIT-DATA is specified in the working-storage section of the data division. Armed with the value WK42 the program then wants direct access to a file describing widgits. Suppose that this file, PRODUCT, is a VSAM indexed-sequential file with the field WIDGIT-NUMBER as the primary key.

The program cannot execute a COBOL READ to access the PRODUCT record for WK42. Only VSAM, under the direct control of CICS, can access the file. In the program a request to CICS to read a record must be coded to obtain the required record. A special CICS READ command is used for this. The necessary CICS command looks as follows:

```
EXEC CICS
     READ INTO (PRODUCT-RECORD) ...
               RIDFLD (WIDGIT-NUMBER) ...
END-EXEC.
```

This causes CICS to read the record with key WK42 into the COBOL structure PRODUCT-RECORD. CICS uses the WK42 value in the *record identifier field* (or RIDFLD) variable WIDGIT-NUMBER.

To actually do the reading CICS uses the VSAM access method, which uses the appropriate channel program. While CICS is waiting for the record, the on-line program INVWIDGE goes into a wait state (*inactive* status); CICS goes off either to deal with some other terminal or to give execution control to some other on-line program in one of its subpartitions. CICS is a busy bee.

Eventually the record for widgit WK42 becomes available—so CICS then gives the program INVWIDGE the status *active*, which means that the program is capable of running again when CICS gets around to letting it.

When our program INVWIDGE runs again, it will formulate a reply to the user. The essential data could be the quantity 150. Suppose that within the program this figure is held in the variable WIDGIT-QUANTITY. The program must request that CICS transmit this result to the user. The CICS SEND command is used for this as follows:

```
CICS-EXEC
    SEND FROM WIDGIT-QUANTITY ...
END-EXEC.
```

In the simplest case the user simply gets the value 150 displayed on his screen. But CICS has powerful capabilities here. The CICS programmer may have defined sophisticated **maps** for CICS to use; map defines the screen display for a specific terminal type. A map for our user might look as follows:

```
WIDGIT INVENTORY STATUS REPORT
QUANTITY ON HAND: .....
```

CICS looks up this map and displays on the user's screen the final message:

```
WIDGIT INVENTORY STATUS REPORT
QUANTITY ON HAND: 150
```

This relieves the programmer of the task of coding the details of the screen display in the application program INV. In addition the the screen formatting can be different for each of the many types of terminals in use in the system. CICS has a map for each type of terminal, so that the application program becomes independent of the terminal hardware. Constructing maps is a major task when designing on-line programs (more about this in the next chapter).

CICS COMPONENTS

In Figure 10.1 we show CICS in the context of a an on-line partition. This helps us to understand how CICS operates. We gain additional insight by looking at the major components of the system. These are the *data handling system*,the *data communications system*, *system*

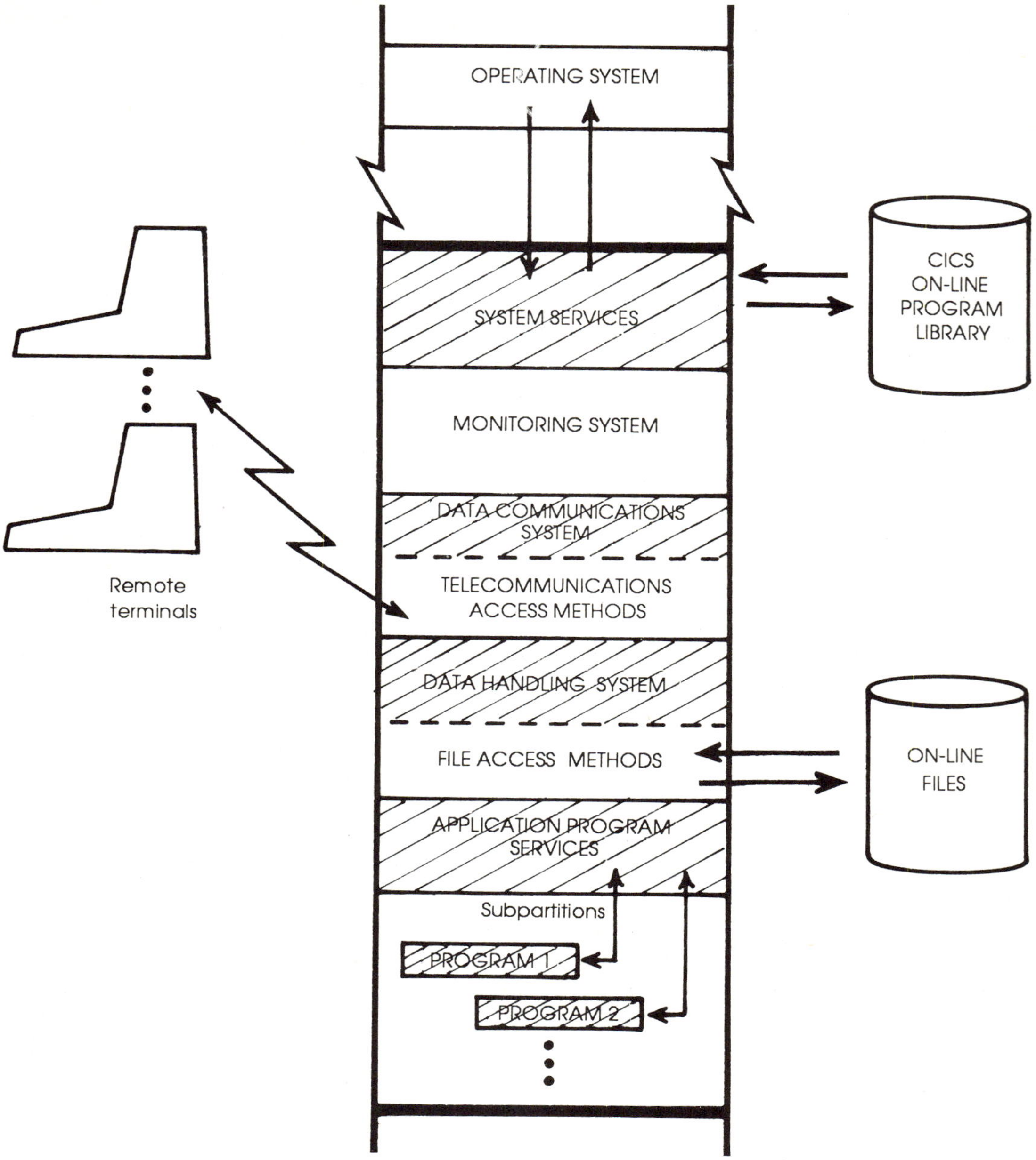

FIGURE 10.2. Detail of a CICS on-line partition showing the major components of CICS. Apart from the monitoring system, there is a component for dealing with the remote terminals, a component for the files, one for the operating system and one for dealing with the on-line programs.

services, the *monitoring system*, and *application program services* (see Figure 10.2). We now look at them in turn.

The Data Handling System

Earlier we mentioned that when an on-line program is running under the control of CICS, the program does not read and write records by directly calling up the services of the appropriate access method. Instead the program asks CICS to carry out the input/output. We saw that for a COBOL program there is a special CICS READ command. There is also a special CICS WRITE command. CICS carries out the input/output by calling up the access method directly (as illustrated in Figure 10.2).

At least as far as input/output is concerned, it may look as if CICS does nothing that cannot be done with ordinary COBOL READ and WRITE commands. This is not so. CICS carries out some fundamental data handling functions that are unique to the on-line environment. The most important of these functions have to do with maintaining the integrity of data in files. There are two types of situations that can cause a loss of data integrity, which the CICS **data handling system**is designed to prevent.

The first situation can occur because CICS permits a large number of on-line programs to compete concurrently. The problem is that two programs may attempt two different but concurrent updates of the same record in one file. As we shall see later, unless proper control is exercised, the updating from one of the programs can result in an unwarranted undoing of a legitimate update by the other program. The result is an inaccurate file, that is, a loss of **data integrity** for that file. This type of **updating interference** of one on-line program's activities by another is really due to the interleaving of the update activities of the two programs. The solution is the old-fashioned do-one-thing-at-a-time method. CICS simply permits one program to complete its updating before another program is allowed to start its updating.

In each program, CICS requires that code identifying complete transactions be included. A **transaction** is a unit of updating (or retrieval) that must be carried out without interruption by the activities of concurrent programs. CICS simply enforces the completion of transactions without interference. We shall look at this in detail later.

The other way in which CICS preserves data integrity has to do with the abrupt termination (for whatever reason) of an application program before it has completed a transaction. In other words, a program could have carried out, via CICS commands, some but not all of the updates necessary to complete a transaction at the point of an abnormal termination of the program. The data in the file is not consistent at this termination point; following further updates by other programs the inconsistency is compounded, so that the file continues to lose data integrity. CICS solves this problem simply by undoing the unfinished update. In other words it sets the file back to where it was before the aborted program began its update.

A final facility provided by the CICS data handling system has to do with restoring files when the entire system, or CICS itself, or the operating system, fails. When things are operating normally, each time a file is updated CICS notes the update in its *log (journal) file*, which is often simply a tape file. This journal file is used along with dumps of the on-line files. Periodically the on-line files are copied (dumped), and a new journal file is loaded. If some time later the system crashes, we have the dumps of the files plus all updates to those files since the dumps recorded in the journal. When the system is eventually started up again, CICS can restore the on-line files using the dumps and the journal file.

The Data Communications System

The **data communications system** carries out access to remote terminals via **telecommunications access methods** and the communications hardware. First of all we need to explain what a telecommunications access method is.

Readers should be familiar with the concept of an access method as used for reading and writing with files, which we covered in chapter 1. The access method looks after the details of blocking and unblocking records and getting channel programs to execute for block transmission. Essentially the access method looks after transmission of data to and from external devices (tape and disk drives in the case of file access methods).

A telecommunications access method essentially looks after transmission of data to and from remote devices, such as terminals. This sounds simple, but the details are anything but simple.

Usually the telecommunications access method is responsible for editing messages, for establishing and disestablishing a communications session with a remote device, and for the actual transmitting and receiving of complete messages. To do these things the access method normally interfaces to a hardware component called a **communications controller** (not shown in Figure 10.2), which is really a separate computer, analogous to the input/output (I/O) processor, or channel, in the case of a file access method. The communications controller may break a message down into smaller segments or packages, which are transmitted individually. The communications controller controls the transmission of these message packets via prearranged send/receive/acknowledge procedures. Such procedures are called **protocols** and are a study in themselves.

None of these details for the telecommunications access method and associated communications controller need concern the CICS programmer. The CICS data communications system looks after it all. There is one feature, concerning maps, that is a special concern, however. Earlier we saw that CICS maintains descriptions of the skeleton of the data that must be communicated to a given type of terminal. Such a description is a map. The important point is that the CICS data communications system looks after the details of contructing the messages to be sent to any specific type of terminal for a specific map. This means that the on-line program is independent of the type of terminal with which it communicates.

This independence is very important, since it means that we are free to change a terminal type (which happens all the time) without having to change the details in the on-line program. In addition the same display can be sent to many different types of terminals. Using the map, CICS data communications looks after the details.

CICS knows the details of every terminal's characteristics from information recorded in a **terminal control table (TCT)** when the system is set up. A new TCT entry is needed if a new type of terminal is added to the system. CICS can handle some fifty different kinds of terminals.

But there is a further consequence of interest to the application programmer. The concept of maps means that the on-line program is also independent of the format of the message displayed on the user's screen. To alter the format of a display, perhaps by using some upper-case characters where previously lower-case characters were displayed, only the corresponding map need be altered and not the on-line program.

System Services

We mentioned that CICS really functions like an operating system within an operating system. The CICS **system services** controls the overall functioning of the system, with all its subpartitions; system services loads an on-line program from the library in response to a given transaction code; system services is responsible for the management of the memory space within the CICS on-line partition—that is, system services essentially looks after creation and termination of the

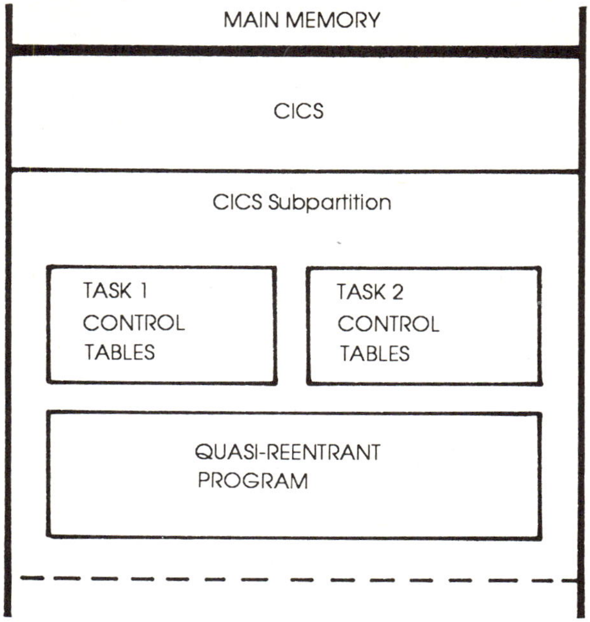

FIGURE 10.3. CICS allows different executions of the same program. These executions are concurrent; each is called a task. If two users at remote terminals want the same program, CICS loads only one version of the program into a subpartion, but creates an individual task for each user. The data in task control tables is used to keep the tasks distinct.

subpartitions of the on-line partition in which the on-line programs execute.

One feature of system services, the **task control facility,** is of fundamental importance to ensuring rapid response at the remote terminals. This facility permits a most ingenious feature of CICS, of which all users of the system should be aware. The feature has to do with multiple concurrent executions of the same on-line program in a subpartition (see Figure 10.3).

The diagram shows only one subpartition of the entire CICS online partition. (Other similar subpartitions are simply not shown). To understand exactly what goes on in the subpartition when the on-line program executes, it is necessary to return to the concept of how an executing program alters data in working storage, as explained at the beginning of chapter 1.

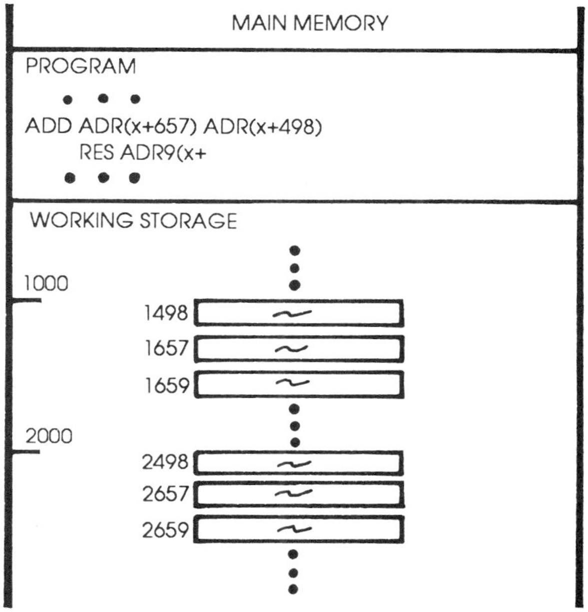

FIGURE 10.4. How the same program processes different sets of data in different concurrent executions. The addition instruction in the program processes the data in addresses (or memory cells) 1498, 1657, and 1659 when the value in X is 1,000, but will process the data in addresses 2498, 2657, and 2659, when the value in X is 2,000.

The instructions of a program are executed one by one; execution of a single instruction can cause an alteration to data stored in working-storage memory cells (perhaps by an addition, or a multiplication, or whatever). In such a situation the instructions are closely bound to the working-storage memory cells, both by the logic of the program and by the memory cell addresses that are an integral part of the program instructions. For example, a program instruction (in machine language) can be equivalent to the following:

```
ADD CONTENTS OF ADDRESS 657 TO ADDRESS 498
                  AND PLACE RESULT IN ADDRESS 659
```

Addresses 657, 498, and 659 are part of working storage for the program.

It is possible to break the close link between the program instructions and working storage to permit the instructions of the program to be used concurrently with more than one working-storage area. As an example (Figure 10.4), consider the instruction of a program that adds the numbers in two memory cells and places the result in a third. This program can use either the working storage beginning at address 1000 or at address 2000, depending on what value we give X. If X has the value 1,000, the instruction adds the number in address 1667 to the number in address 1498 and places the result in address 1659. On the other hand, if the value in X is 2,000, the addition refers to addresses 2657, 2498, and 2659.

A program with instructions of this type, where the working-storage memory cells referred to depend on some parameter X, is called a **reentrant program**. You can have concurrent executions of a reentrant program. Referring back to Figure 10.3, suppose that the on-line program in the subpartition is that shown in Figure 10.4. Now suppose that CICS has the value 1,000 for X stored in the TASK-1 control area and the value 2,000 for X in TASK-2 control area (and that addresses 1000-3000 lie within the subpartition). CICS can give control to the on-line program using the value 1,000 for X. This program then operates on the working- storage area beginning at address 1000. About halfway through execution of the program, CICS can stop execution, making note of the position of the next instruction, and place this in TASK-1 control area. It can then use the value 2,000 for X and start the program again. This time it manipulates the working-storage area beginning at address 2000. This time also CICS might let the program complete its execution. When the program is finished, CICS can restart it using the value of 1,000 for X, restarting it exactly at the position where it had previously stopped; the program, then continues manipulating the working-storage area beginning at address 1000.

Each such execution of a program in a subpartition is a CICS **task**. And as can be seen, CICS system services is capable of using any program in memory for multiple tasks. This speeds up processing (as the following example shows).

Suppose that a user at a terminal enters the transaction code XY, for which there is a corresponding on-line program in the CICS program library called XYPROG. CICS system services does not immediately load the program XYPROG from the library into a new subpartition. It first looks to see if XYPROG is already in a subpartition servicing another user. If it is, CICS simply creates a new task (as in Figure 10.3) for XYPROG—that is, provides it with an additional working-storage area and some tables to help control the task. The tables include a task control area (for holding the value of X and the position with XYPROG for a task that is not currently executing); there is also a need for a table to indicate exactly which terminal is using the task (for this there is a *terminal table*).

The net result of all this is that a single program in a subpartition may be concurrently servicing completely different requests from many different terminals. CICS, and especially CICS system services, is really smart.

Some readers may well wonder how we can get our on-line programs into reentrant form suitable for multiple concurrent tasks. The answer is that COBOL compilers generally generate object code that is not completely reentrant, but sufficiently reentrant to permit use of the object programs for CICS multitasking. Such COBOL compiler-generated object programs are said to be **quasi-reentrant.**

The Monitoring System

The **monitoring system** is used mainly by the system administrators. It collects and records information about the use of the various components of the entire on-line system. For example, how often a particular on-line program is used can be recorded, or how many messages are sent daily from a particular terminal, or how often a particular file is accessed. Such data can also be useful when a new on-line system is being designed.

Application Program Services

The application programmer comes into direct contact with **application program services**. When a CICS command is encountered in an on-line program being executed, it is the CICS application program services that is essentially called up by that CICS command. The services interprets the command and passes appropriate instructions to whatever other major components of CICS are appropriate. For example, if the CICS command in the program is for reading a file, then the data handling system comes into play at the request of application program services; if the CICS command in the program requests access to a terminal, then the data communications system comes into play, and so on.

An important subcomponent of application program services is the **CICS command translator**. Every CICS command embedded in a source program in COBOL (or any other language) must be sandwiched between an EXEC and an END-EXEC. Earlier we had the example of CICS READ command, written in COBOL as follows:

```
EXEC CICS
   READ INTO ...
END-EXEC.
```

If a COBOL program containing such CICS commands is submitted to a standard COBOL compiler, the program will not compile. The embedded CICS commands are not part of COBOL, so the compiler will not recognize them.

To compile a COBOL program with embedded CICS commands we proceed quite differently. Two translation components are needed—first the CICS command translator and then the ordinary COBOL compiler. The program is entered using an editor. You then use IBM JCL to have the CICS command translator process the source program. If you have made any mistakes in constructing your CICS commands in the program, the command translator gives you a listing of your errors. The command translator essentially replaces the CICS EXEC ...END-EXEC syntax with a very detailed COBOL syntax that calls up application program services when the program is executing.

The version of the COBOL program that results after processing by the command translator is now *all COBOL*, with no more EXEC ... END-EXEC syntax embedded in it. This version can now be translated into machine language by the COBOL compiler. Again if there are any errors in the COBOL, you get the usual compiler error messages.

At this point it is appropriate to discuss the final steps in getting a CICS COBOL program to execute. The object version generated by the COBOL compiler must now be processed by the linkage editor, which links the program to the CICS system. Remember that a CICS on-line program gets executed only when it is loaded from the CICS program library into a CICS subpartition (Figure 10.2), as a result of a request from a terminal that employs the proper transaction code. Thus the linkage editor must also place the program in the CICS on-line program library. The transaction code for this program must now be stored in the PCT; an entry is made in the PCT by a systems programmer, thus connecting this program with a specific transaction code.

You can now run the program by signing on to the CICS on-line system at a CICS terminal, just like any other remote user, and entering the transaction code for the program that you have just compiled and stored. It should then execute under the control of CICS.

Summary of CICS Tables

We have seen that CICS frequently refers to tables for the resources it has under its control. In setting up a CICS system it is the task of systems programmers to create these tables, called **system control tables**. The code used to define these tables is similar to JCL and is beyond the scope of this book. The main system control tables are discussed below:

Program Control Table (PCT)

Every on-line program under the control of CICS has a transaction code of up to 4 characters (such as INV1 earlier). This is the code entered by a remote user to gain access to the services offered by a specific program. In the PCT there must be an entry associating a specific transaction code with a specific on-line program. When a user at a remote terminal enters a specific transaction code CICS system services checks the PCT for the transaction code and uncovers the name of the associated on-line program. System services then initiates a new task for that program, if the program already is in a subpartition of the CICS on-line partition; if not, it loads the program from its on-line program library into a CICS subpartition.

Terminal Control Table (TCT)

Every terminal under the control of CICS must be known to the CICS data communications system. The characteristics of these terminals are listed in the TCT. The data communications system uses terminal specifications each time it deals with a message to or from a terminal. We saw that this facility in conjunction with maps permits a single on-line program to serve many kinds of terminals, without the need to incorporate terminal details in the program.

File Control Table (FCT)

Every file used by the on-line programs must be specified in the **file control table (FCT)**. Each file listed in the FCT must have a unique name with up to 8 characters. This name is used in CICS READ, WRITE, REWRITE, and DELETE commands within a COBOL program. (As we shall see in the next chapter, this file name is specified with the DATASET option in these CICS commands.)

Other information about a file is also specified in the FCT. For example, logical record length, primary key field length, location of the primary key within a record, and the access method required for the file are specified.

Sign-on Table (SNT)

The **sign-on table (SNT)** is of great practical importance to anyone wanting to use CICS. Every user must have a user identification name (**userid**) and a **password**, which are stored in the SNT, along with that user's priority and the kinds of resources that user is allowed to use. For example, if there is an on-line program in the system for raising salaries, the use of that resource will probably be denied most users.

The priority of a user is used by system services to determine which task will be allowed to execute next.

When you sign on to CICS at a CICS terminal, you must first enter a transaction code CSSN (even signing on a new user is a transaction for CICS, for which there is an on-line program). CICS then displays the following:

```
PLEASE SUPPLY PERSONAL DETAILS
NAME=
PASSWORD=
NEWPASWORD=
```

You fill in the first two blanks. If you wish to change your password you fill in the third blank with your new password. When sign-on is complete, you get the following display;

```
SIGN-ON IS COMPLETE
```

You are now free to enter a transaction code for any service that you are entitled to use.

SUMMARY

A teleprocessing monitor is used with a library of on-line programs and on-line terminals. A user at any terminal can ask CICS to load and execute any of the programs in the library; the programs can manipulate on-line files. In the coding of such programs, normal COBOL file manipulation commands cannot be used; instead special CICS commands must be used, CICS programming is a special skill.

CICS runs as a perpetual job in an on-line partition of memory in a batch operating system. CICS maintains a program control table (PCT) that links every program in its library to a transaction code. A user at a terminal can enter the transaction code, and CICS will execute the appropriate program.

CICS divides its partitions into subpartitions, each of which can hold a program currently in the process of execution. CICS controls which of these programs will actually execute. CICS prevents concurrently executing programs from interfering with each other when updating a file. By a process of generating multiple tasks from a single program, CICS can use a single program in a subpartition to satisfy two or more users at different terminals concurrently.

CICS makes application programs independent of the terminals. Details of screen displays are not coded in on-line programs. Instead they are stored in CICS maps. The program instructs CICS which computed or retrieved data is to be displayed; CICS embeds this data in a screen display based on an appropriate map.

When a CICS COBOL program is written it cannot be compiled by the COBOL compiler. It must first be processed by the CICS command translator, which converts CICS commands to COBOL calls. The resulting program can then be compiled normally.

EXERCISES

1. Explain the concept of a CICS transaction. How does it relate to a CICS transaction code?
2. Explain how multiple tasks can be generated from an on-line program in a CICS subpartition.
3. Explain how a CICS program is prepared for execution.
4. What are maps used for with CICS?
5. How does CICS permit programs to be independent of the terminal used?
6. How does a CICS program access a file?
7. Why is it more appropriate to talk about CICS tasks instead of CICS programs?
8. Explain what a program control table is used for.
9. Explain what the data communications component of CICS does.
10. Explain what a terminal control table is used for.

11 COBOL FILE PROCESSING WITH CICS

In this chapter we deal with CICS COBOL programming for indexed-sequential files; we will include the CICS methods for preventing interference between the file updating activities of concurrent programs. We begin the chapter by showing just how such update interference can take place. We then show how to use CICS to prevent update interference. We later show how deadlock between concurrent tasks can be prevented.

Because things can go wrong when CICS commands embedded in on-line COBOL programs are executed in the on-line environment, programs must be able to deal with many contingencies. Accordingly CICS provides the COBOL programmer with exception handling facilities, which we also look at briefly.

CICS COBOL PROCESSING WITH VSAM INDEXED-SEQUENTIAL FILES

Both indexed-sequential files and hash files are used in on-line processing. In chapter 8 we saw that unless care is taken in the design of a hash file, it may well turn out to be no faster than an indexed-sequential file—that is, the poorly designed hash file may have an average search length greater than the indexed file. Neverthless, even though a well-designed hash file is probably superior to an indexed file in an on-line environment, we shall concentrate on VSAM indexed files in this chapter for illustrating file processing with CICS. We do this only because hash file processing is more complex in general, even in a batch environment, and is thus less suitable for introducing the additional complexity of the CICS on-line environment.

A Product File for Use in an On-line Environment

In this chapter we assume a VSAM indexed-sequential file called PRODUCT. A record of this file describes a product that is available for sale by an electronic components wholesale firm. The full details of all the record fields need not concern us, but we can assume the following for the sake of the example:

PART#	Primary key, identification number for a part type
TYPE	Name of the type of part
QTY	Quantity on hand of a part type

Some examples of the records in PRODUCT are shown in Figure 11.1.

PART#	TYPE	QTY
P2	INDUCTOR	2300
P7	DIODE	1500
P11	RESISTOR	8600
P14	TRANSISTOR	2800
P22	DIODE	1700
P25	INDUCTOR	1200

PRODUCT

FIGURE 11.1. Some records of the file PRODUCT used in an on-line order-entry system.

File Update Interference in an On-line Environment

Assume that the on-line file PRODUCT is used as follows. Typically a salesperson at a remote terminal queries the file asking for the quantity on hand of a given part type. Assume that the sales person uses transaction code QYRQ for such a request, so that to find out how many P11 parts are on hand the salesperson enters:

```
QYRQ  P11
```

This causes the appropriate program to be loaded by CICS. This program might give the user the following response:

```
PART TYPE: P11
QUANTITY ON HAND: 8600
```

If the salesperson wants to sell a customer 5,000 P11 parts, it is clear that there are enough P11 parts on hand. After some time dealing with the customer, suppose that the saleperson informs the system that

5,000 P11 parts have been sold. Obviously the product file must now be change updated so that the QTY field for the P11 record shows 5,000 fewer parts, that is, 3600. Assume the the program that does this can be called up with the transaction code PTSL, so that the sales person enters:

```
PTSL P11 5000
```

The on-line program might then respond with either of the following messages:

```
ORDER FOR 5000 P11 PARTS ACCEPTED
3600 P11 PART REMAIN ON HAND

ORDER FOR 5000 P11 PARTS REJECTED
ONLY 2000 P11 PARTS ON HAND
INSUFFICIENT PARTS ON HAND
```

The second message can result even after the salesperson queries the data base and finds that there are sufficient parts. In an on-line system it can be assumed that there are many users; it takes only a second or so for some competing salesperson to sell a sufficient quantity of P11 parts to prevent a later order being fullfilled.

Let us give the CICS name PG1 to the program that updates the PRODUCT file in response to the user-entered transaction code PTSL, as illustrated above. Essentially PG1 first reads the values P11 and 5,000 from the terminal (via CICS) with the CICS RECEIVE command (as explained in the previous chapter). Then PG1 issues a CICS READ command to directly read the PRODUCT record for part type P11. The program then subtracts the 5,000 quantity from the quantity on hand in the working-storage record. If the result of the subtraction exceeds 0, the program issues the CICS REWRITE command to rewrite the P11 PRODUCT record with the updated P11 record in working storage; the program then issues a CICS SEND command to indicate acceptance of the order to the user. If the result of the earlier subtraction is negative, PG1 simply executes a CICS SEND command to inform the user of rejection of the order.

If we assume that the order is accepted, the file processing part of the updating procedure is as follows:

1. Execute CICS READ to retrieve PRODUCT record for part type P11 into working-storage structure PRODUCTREC
2. Subtract 5,000 from QTY IN PRODUCTREC
3. REWRITE PRODUCT for P11 using the data in PRODUCTREC

This looks simple enough, but it can go hopelessly wrong if there is a concurrent PG1 task updating the P11 record in PRODUCT.

Readers should recall that CICS is capable of multiple concurrent executions of a single on-line program; each independent execution is a task. In practice two multiple concurrent executions of the on-line program PG1 would occur if two different salespersons, Tom and Mary, want to record a sale of P11 parts at about the same time.

At Tom's CICS terminal, the entry is

```
PTSL P11 5000
```

whereas at Mary's CICS terminal the entry is

```
PTSL P11 3000
```

CICS typically responds by setting up two concurrent tasks based on the updating program PG1. Do not forget that CICS can switch execution control from one task to another very quickly, especially when a CICS file access command (READ, WRITE, or REWRITE) is executed. A program (or rather, a task) must wait for the results of such a command; CICS will almost certainly switch execution control to some other task while the task is waiting.

Now suppose that the following sequence of events takes place with the two tasks (based on program PG1) for Tom and Mary's update to the PRODUCT file. We call Mary's task *Mary-task* and Tom's task *Tom-task*.

Tom-task executes:

A. Execute CICS READ. PRODUCTREC gets the following values:

```
P11 RESISTOR 8600
```

Mary-task executes:

A. Execute CICS READ. PRODUCTREC gets the following values:

```
P11 RESISTOR 8600
```

Tom-task executes:

B. Subtract 5,000 from QTY IN PRODUCTREC. PRODUCT record for P11 is now as follows:

```
P11 RESISTOR 3600
```

C. Execute CICS REWRITE. Value in PRODUCTREC written onto disk. PRODUCT record for P11 is now as follows:

```
P11 RESISTOR 3600
```

Mary-task executes:

B. Subtract 3,000 from QTY IN PRODUCTREC giving the following record:

```
P11 RESISTOR 5600
```

C. EXECUTE CICS REWRITE. Value in PRODUCTREC written onto disk. PRODUCT record for P11 is now as follows:

```
P11 RESISTOR 5600
```

Clearly the interleaving of the two tasks has caused things to go wrong. We have update interference and a loss of data integrity. We began with 8,600 parts. Tom sold 5,000, leaving 3,600. Then Mary sold 3,000 leaving 600. But the file records a quantity on hand equal to 5,600 at the end of the processing.

This type of interference is prevented by defining complete *transactions* that may not be interupted by another task that uses the same record or records. These transaction definitions should not be confused with the transaction codes used at a terminal to permit CICS to identify which on-line program should be loaded.

Within a CICS COBOL program, the beginning and end of such a transaction is implicitly defined. The transaction begins when a CICS READ for UPDATE for a specific record (perhaps PRODUCT record P11) is executed. This command signals to CICS that the P11 record will be updated by the task (T1) that executed the command. CICS then gives the task T1 **exclusive** control over the P11 PRODUCT record. This means that even if execution control is subsequently switched away from the task T1, no other task can get control over the P11 PRODUCT record. For task T1 the transaction ends, that is, exclusive control over the P11 PRODUCT record is relinquished, whenever a CICS REWRITE command is executed by task T1.

Let us now look at what happens to the updating of the PRODUCT file with Tom and Mary's tasks based on the on-line program PG1, where the CICS READ command is a READ for UPDATE command:

Tom-task executes:

A. Execute CICS READ for UPDATE. PRODUCTREC gets the following data:

```
P11 RESISTORS 8600
```

Tom-task gets exclusive control over P11 record. Start of Tom-task transaction defined.

Mary-task executes:

A. Execute CICS READ for UPDATE for P11 PRODUCT record. Task denied control of P11 record. Task put in wait or inactive state.

Tom-Task executes:

B. Subtract 5,000 from QTY IN PRODUCTREC, giving the following record:

```
P11 RESISTORS 3600
```

C. Execute CICS REWRITE. Value in PRODUCTREC written onto disk. PRODUCT record for P11 is now as follows:

```
P11 RESISTORS 3600
```

Tom-task relinquishes exclusive control over P11 record. End of Tom-task transaction defined.

Mary-task executes:

A. Execution completed for CICS READ for UPDATE command. PRODUCTREC gets the following data:

```
P11 RESISTORS 3600
```

Mary-task gets exclusive control over P11 record. Start of Mary-task transaction defined.

Other task executes:

. . .

Mary-task executes:

B. Subtract 3,600 from QTY IN PRODUCTREC, giving the following record:

```
P11 RESISTORS 600
```

C. Execute CICS REWRITE. Value in PRODUCTREC written onto disk. PRODUCT record for P11 is now as follows:

```
P11 RESISTORS 600
```

Mary-task relinquishes exclusive control over P11 record. End of Mary-task transaction defined.

Thus this time the updating is carried out without any error caused by interference between the two concurrent tasks.

CICS COMMANDS

A large number of CICS commands may be embedded in a COBOL program. Full coverage of all of these commands is beyond the scope of this book. However, we can give a detailed account of the commands used for file processing. Our coverage of the other commands should be sufficient to permit the reader to write reasonably sophisticated online COBOL programs.

CICS File Processing Commands

In this section we summarize the CICS commands used for processing a VSAM indexed-sequential file. As far as possible we compare with conventional COBOL commands. In illustrating the commands, we use the logical file name PRODUCT (Figure 11.1), for which there is a working-storage structure PRODUCTREC, as follows:

```
01    PRODUCTREC.
    02   PART#    PIC X(4).
    02   TYPE     PIC X(15).
    02   QTY      PIC 9(6).
```

We also assume a working-storage variable RECKEY as follows, which can hold the value of the key of a record being sought:

```
77   RECKEY       PIC X(4).
```

which can hold the value of the key of a record being sought.

The OPEN Command

Unlike the case with conventional COBOL, there is no CICS command for opening a file. An on-line file is held permanently open by CICS.

The CICS READ Command.

To read a record from the file PRODUCT with primary key value P11, you code as follows:

```
MOVE "P11" TO RECKEY.
EXEC CICS
READ INTO(PRODUCTREC) DATASET("PRODUCT") RIDFLD(RECKEY)
END-EXEC.
```

The P11 record from the file PRODUCT will appear in the working structure aggregate variable PRODUCTREC. Note that the file name PRODUCT must be listed in the CICS file control (FCT) table and does not have to be specified with the COBOL program, as would be the case with a conventional VSAM indexed-sequential file.

If the command does not work, perhaps because no record with the specified key was found, an exceptional (error) condition, or simply **exception**, occurs. If no action is coded, a default message is displayed on the user's screen by CICS and the task terminated. This message is likely to be incomprehensible by the typical nonspecialist user. It is thus necessary for the programmer to code for things going wrong, that is, for exceptions.

Each exception that can occur with a CICS command has a name. The name for **no record found** with a READ command is NOTFND. The name for some general error is simply ERROR. Suppose that we want a COBOL paragraph called NOT-FOUND to handle the case of the NOTFND exception and a different COBOL paragraph called GENERAL-ERROR to handle an exception due to any other cause. In the COBOL procedure division we include a CICS HANDLE CONDITION command, as illustrated below:

```
PROCEDURE DIVISION.
    ...
    EXEC CICS
        HANDLE CONDITION
            NOTFND(NOTFOUND)
            ERROR(GENERAL-ERROR)
    END-EXEC.
    MOVE "P11" TO RECKEY.
    EXEC CICS
      READ INTO(PRODUCTREC) DATASET("PRODUCT") RIDFLD(RECKEY)
    END-EXEC.
    ...
NOT-FOUND.
    Code for no record matching target key.
GENERAL-ERROR.
    Code for any other error.
```

In the CICS HANDLE CONDITION command, the exception conditions to be dealt with are listed, with the exception handling paragraph named in parenthesis following the exception name.

The CICS READ for UPDATE Command

We have already explained why it is necessary for CICS to have a special on-line READ command, called READ for UPDATE, for CICS to be alerted to the need to give the task involved exclusive control over the record being read. Until the task eventually updates the record with a REWRITE, it retains exclusive control. This means that another task can update the record only after the the first task has relinguished exclusive control, thus preventing update interference.

To read a record from PRODUCT with primary key value P11, we code the following:

```
    MOVE "P11" TO RECKEY.
    EXEC CICS
        READ INTO(PRODUCTREC) DATASET("PRODUCT")
            RIDFLD(RECKEY) UPDATE
END-EXEC.
```

The requested P11 record appears in PRODUCTREC and the task is granted exclusive control over that record in the disk file. Exceptions can arise, which would be handled by the CICS HANDLE CONDITION command, and the exception handling paragraphs, as explained in the section on the CICS READ command.

The CICS REWRITE Command

The CICS REWRITE command simply uses the working-storage record in PRODUCTREC to update the corresponding record on disk in the file PRODUCT. CICS knows the key of the record involved since it has given the task exclusive control over that record. Once the REWRITE is executed, that exclusive control is lost by the task.

Suppose that we want to reduce the quantity on hand for part P11 by 5,000. We code the following:

```
MOVE "P11" TO RECKEY.
EXEC CICS
    READ INTO(PRODUCTREC) DATASET("PRODUCT")
RIDFLD(RECKEY) UPDATE
    END-EXEC.
**Record now in PRODUCTREC.
    COMPUTE QTY IN PRODUCTREC =
        QTY IN PRODUCTREC - 5000.
**Rewrite the updated P11 record.
    EXEC CICS
      REWRITE FROM(PRODUCTREC) DATASET("PRODUCT")
    END-EXEC.
```

Note that the REWRITE command merely specifies the working-storage record and the file involved, without any key specification.

The CICS DELETE Command

There are two versions of the CICS DELETE command. One is used after a CICS READ for UPDATE command. The READ grants the task control over a specific record. On execution of the DELETE command, this control is relinquished.

As an example of this first version of the command, suppose that we wish to delete record P11, provided the product type is a resistor. We can code the following:

```
MOVE "P11" TO RECKEY.
EXEC CICS
    READ INTO(PRODUCTREC) DATASET("PRODUCT")
        RIDFLD(RECKEY) UPDATE
END-EXEC.
IF TYPE IN PRODUCTREC = "RESISTOR"
THEN EXEC CICS
    DELETE DATASET("PRODUCT")
```

```
END-EXEC.
```

The READ gives the task exclusive control over the P11 record; execution of the DELETE causes that control to be relinquished. What happens if the DELETE is not executed because the IF-condition is false? In that case exclusive control remains with the task and must be relinquished by execution of a special CICS command called UNLOCK. We shall come to this presently.

The other CICS DELETE command simply deletes a record whose key is specified. For example, suppose that we want to delete the record for key P11. We can code the following:

```
MOVE "P11" TO RECKEY.
EXEC CICS
    DELETE DATASET("PRODUCT") RIDFLD(RECKEY)
END-EXEC.
```

The CICS UNLOCK Command

We have seen that a READ for UPDATE gives the task involved exclusive control over the record requested and that this exclusive control can be relinquished by execution of either a REWRITE or a DELETE command. It may happen, however, that neither a REWRITE nor a DELETE is ever executed for an exclusively controlled record. To keep the on-line system functioning effectively, at any given time as few records as possible should be under exclusive control of tasks. Thus it is important for a task to relinquish control of any record for which control is no longer required. This can be done easily using the CICS UNLOCK command.

As an example, suppose that we take a variation on the processing above, where we delete a P11 record provided its TYPE is RESISTOR. If the TYPE is not RESISTOR, we do not delete it; but since the record is under exclusive control because of an earlier unavoidable READ for UPDATE, an UNLOCK command is needed to relinquish control, as follows:

```
MOVE "P11" TO RECKEY.
EXEC CICS
  READ INTO(PRODUCTREC) DATASET("PRODUCT")
    RIDFLD(RECKEY) UPDATE
END-EXEC.
IF TYPE IN PRODUCTREC = "RESISTOR"
THEN EXEC CICS
    DELETE DATASET(PRODUCTREC)
  END-EXEC
ELSE EXEC CICS
    UNLOCK DATASET("PRODUCT")
  END-EXEC.
```

The CICS WRITE Command

The CICS WRITE command is used for adding new records to a file. It may not be used for relinguishing exclusive control over a record previously READ with a READ for UPDATE command. Suppose that we want to add the following record to the file PRODUCT:

```
P42 MICROCIRCUIT 2000
```

We can code the following:

```
MOVE "P42" TO PART# IN PRODUCTREC.
MOVE "MICROCIRCUIT" TO TYPE IN PRODUCTREC.
MOVE 2000 TO QTY IN PRODUCTREC.
MOVE PART# IN PRODUCTREC TO KEYREC.
EXEC CICS
    WRITE FROM(PRODUCTREC) DATASET("PRODUCT")
    RIDFLD(KEYREC)
END-EXEC.
```

The record in PRODUCTREC is placed in the PRODUCT file in ascending primary key order, with CICS and ultimately VSAM using the primary key in KEYREC to properly position the record in the file—and if necessary adjust the VSAM index for the file (see chapter 6 for VSAM details).

CICS Commands for Dealing with Remote Terminals

The two main commands that permit a CICS on-line program to communicate with a remote terminal are RECEIVE and SEND. We have already met these commands, but now look at them in more detail.

The CICS RECEIVE Command

The CICS receive command is used for reading a message from a terminal. As we have seen, a user at a CICS terminal typically inputs a CICS transaction code followed by some information that will be used by the appropriate application program.

Suppose that there is an application program called FYND that retrieves the quantity of a given part type on hand from the file PRODUCT (Figure 11.1). Suppose also that the transaction code for getting CICS to initiate a task involving FYND is FQTY. To find the quantity of part type P11, for example, the user can enter the following:

```
FQTY P11
```

The program FYND must be in a position to read the entire message, even though only CICS is interested in the transaction code FQTY. (Remember that CICS uses its program control table (PCT) to determine that the program FYND will process a transaction with code FQTY.)

In the program, for receiving the above message we can use the following data structure, specified in working storage:

```
01 IN-MESSAGE.
   02 TRAN-CODE          PIC X(4).
   02 FILLER             PIC X(1).
   02 INFO               PIC X(4).
```

This means that the maximum length of the input message is 4 + 1 + 4 or 9 characters. Notice that we need the FILLER variable to allow for the blank character between the FQTY and P11 entered by the user. CICS transmits the entire string containing a message, blanks and all. CICS also transmits the length of the message. For example, if the user enters:

```
FQTY P4
```

CICS transmits length 7. A message of length 7 does no harm. But if the user enters:

```
FQTY P4321
```

CICS transmits a message of length 10, which is larger than the length of the reception variable IN-MESSAGE. This causes an exception condition; without an appropriate exception processing paragraph, the user gets an unintelligible default message. We shall now see how to handle this situation.

First we need a variable to receive the length of the message; we can specify it in the working storage as follows:

```
77 MES-LEN  PIC S9(4) COMP.
```

(The S9(4) COMP is necessary.) If the message is too long the exception raised has the CICS standard name LENGERR. We shall use the CICS HANDLE CONDITION command to have the paragraph FAR-TOO-LONG executed if the value of MES-LEN exceeds the length of IN-MESSAGE.

The actual RECEIVE command is as follows:

```
EXEC CICS
    RECEIVE INTO(IN-MESSAGE) LENGTH(MES-LEN)
END-EXEC.
```

This puts the message into IN-MESSAGE and the length of the message into MES-LEN. If MES-LEN gets value larger than the length of IN-MESSAGE, the exception condition LENGERR is raised.

Let us now put this all together in a COBOL program excerpt as follows:

```
WORKING-STORAGE SECTION.
     77 MES-LEN     PIC S9(4) COMP.
     01  IN-MESSAGE.
         02 TRAN-CODE   PIC X(4).
         02 FILLER      PIC X.
         02 INFO        PIC X(4).
...
PROCEDURE DIVISION.
     EXEC CICS
         HANDLE CONDITION LENGERR(FAR-TOO-LONG)
     END-EXEC.
     MOVE "         " TO IN-MESSAGE.
     EXEC CICS
         RECEIVE INTO(IN-MESSAGE) LENGTH(MES-LEN)
     END-EXEC.
```

(Program now uses the primary key value in INFO to carry out a READ command to retrieve the PRODUCT record. It then executes a SEND command to forward the QTY value back to the user.)

```
...

FAR-TOO-LONG.
```

(This contains the code for the case where the message submitted by the user is too long for IN-MESSAGE. An appropriate message should be sent to the user, probably asking for a correctly formatted message next time.)

Notice that we put blanks in IN-MESSAGE before having the RECEIVE command executed. This is not really necessary in this case, but it is a good habit idea to develop because CICS always transmits a complete string of characters. This can cause problems when code like that above is part of a loop, if you do not blank the IN-MESSAGE variable before executing the RECEIVE command.

As an example of how it can all go wrong without the blanking, suppose that the RECEIVE command is in a loop and undergoes repeated executions. Suppose that the first execution is to receive the following user-entered message:

```
FQTY P768
```

This is a valid message; its value goes to IN-MESSAGE, with the value P768 in particular going to INFO. Suppose that the user next enters:

```
FQTY P4
```

This too is a valid message; it also goes into IN-MESSAGE, but *only into the first 7 spaces of IN-MESSAGE*. The last 2 spaces are left unchanged, so that IN-MESSAGE actually gets the following, which is wrong:

```
FQTY P468
```

Always blank the message variable before executing a CICS RECEIVE command.

CICS SEND Command

The CICS send command sends a message of a defined length from working storage. Suppose that we have the working storage variable OUT-MESSAGE as follows:

```
01 OUT-MESSAGE.
     02 TRAN-CODE     PIC X(4).
     02 FILLER        PIC X(1).
     02 OUT-TEXT      PIC X(15).
```

Suppose also that this is used to hold a message to be transmitted back to the user. We assume that the transaction code involved is FTYP, with a corresponding program FYNDTYPE. The program FYNDTYPE returns the user the type of part involved when it receives the part type number (the primary key). Thus the user might enter

```
FTYP P11
```

with the response

```
RESISTOR
```

The value RESISTOR would be in OUT-TEXT.

We also need a message length variable; we shall use MES-LEN, as defined earlier in working storage. The CICS SEND command is now the following:

```
EXEC CICS
     SEND FROM(OUT-MESSAGE) LENGTH(MES-LEN)
          ERASE
END-EXEC.
```

To illustrate how the MES-LEN variable is used, suppose that we place the value 13 in MES-LENGTH before execution of SEND. In that case, when SEND is executed, the first 13 characters (left to right) in OUT-MESSAGE are transmitted to the remote terminal and the data in OUT-TEXT is displayed on the user's screen.

You must be careful that the value you place in MES-LEN does not exceed the length of OUT-MESSAGE (which in this case is defined as 4 + 1 + 15 or 20 characters). Suppose that we use a MES-LEN value of 25. In this case the 25 characters in main memory (working storage), beginning where OUT-MESSAGE is located, are transmitted. In other words the 20 characters in OUT-MESSAGE are transmitted plus 5 additional unpredictable characters. The message might then be the following, or some such nonsense:

```
RESISTOR        %GTY&
```

That can certainly confuse the user. But what is worse is that it sometimes the nonsense characters cause something meaningful to happen with the terminal, such as beeps or flashes.

The word ERASE in the SEND command is optional. When included it causes the screen of the terminal to be cleared before the message is displayed.

The CICS RETURN Command

Only one additional command is needed for most elementary CICS COBOL programs: The CICS RETURN command. In a COBOL program the code for the command is simply the following:

```
EXEC CICS
      RETURN
END-EXEC.
```

Essentially RETURN is used where STOP RUN is used in a conventional COBOL program. An on-line COBOL program running under CICS is really a subprogram of CICS, so that when the program (or task based on the program) ceases to execute, execution control returns to CICS.

The RETURN command thus forces control to return to CICS. If there is only one task based on the COBOL program, the CICS subpartition or subregion holding the program is cleared, to make room for some other on-line program.

A More Comprehensive Example

We now show how to combine some of the above commands in a more comprehensive programming example. We assume a user who wants to execute the on-line program FYND using the CICS transaction code FQTY. FYND determines the quantity of parts on hand (in the file PRODUCT) given the part type number (the primary key). Thus the user can enter

```
FQTY P11
```

and get the response

```
8600
```

where we ignore any additional display that results from more comprehensive predefined screen formatting maps. If the part type is not in the file, FYND transmits the following text and then stops:

```
PART TYPE NOT FOUND
```

If the user enters a message that is too long, FYND transmits the following text and then stops:

```
USER ENTRY TOO LONG
```

The logic of the program is as follows:

1. RECEIVE message. If message is too long, execute paragraph that informs user and then RETURN to CICS.
2. READ the record from the file. If the record is not found, execute the paragraph that informs the user and then RETURN to CICS.
3. SEND message to user informing of quantity on hand and then RETURN to CICS.

We can see that the processing is fairly simple. Nevertheless it does illustrate the essence of CICS on-line programming. Most CICS programs are fairly short and carry out some single elementary task, like retrieving or updating a record and transmitting appropriate error messages when things go wrong.

No files need to be defined, as in conventional COBOL procesing; the PRODUCT file is predefined in the FTC for use by a large number of on-line programs. The program is as follows:

```
IDENTIFICATION DIVISION.
PROGRAM-ID. CICS-EXAMPLE.
ENVIRONMENTAL DIVISION.
```

```
DATA DIVISION.
WORKING-STORAGE SECTION.
77  RECKEY    PIC X(4).
77  MES-LEN   PIC S9(4) COMP.
01  PRODUCTREC.
     02 PART#  PIC X(4).
     02 TYPE   PIC X(15).
     02 QTY    PIC 9(6).
01 IN-MESSAGE.
     02 TRAN-CODE    PIC X(4).
     02 FILLER       PIC X.
     02 INFO         X(4).
01 OUT-MESSAGE.
     02 TRAN-CODE    PIC X(4).
     02 FILLER       PIC X.
     02 QTY          PIC 9(6).
01 ERROR-MESSAGE.
     02 TRAN-CODE    PIC X(4).
     02 FILLER       PIC X.
     02 ERROR-TEXT   PIC X(20).
PROCEDURE DIVISION.
     EXEC CICS
        HANDLE CONDITION NOTFND(NOT-FOUND)
                         LENGERR(FAR-TOO-LONG)
     END-EXEC.
     MOVE "          " TO IN-MESSAGE.
     EXEC CICS
        RECEIVE INTO(IN-MESSAGE) LENGTH(MES-LEN)
     END-EXEC.
     MOVE INFO IN IN-MESSAGE TO RECKEY.
     EXEC CICS
        READ INTO(PRODUCTREC) DATASET("PRODUCT")
             RIDFLD(RECKEY)
     END-EXEC.
     MOVE 11 TO MES-LEN.
     MOVE QTY IN PRODUCTREC TO QTY IN OUT-MESSAGE.
     MOVE " " TO FILLER IN OUT-MESSAGE.
     MOVE "FQTY" TO TRAN-CODE IN OUT-MESSAGE.
     EXEC CICS
         SEND FROM(OUT-MESSAGE) LENGTH(MES-LEN)
     END-EXEC.
     EXEC CICS
         RETURN
     END-EXEC.
NOT-FOUND.
     MOVE "FQTY" TO TRAN-CODE IN ERROR-MESSAGE.
     MOVE " " TO FILLER IN ERROR-MESSAGE.
     MOVE "RECORD NOT FOUND" TO
                 ERROR-TEXT IN ERROR-MESSAGE.
     MOVE 25 TO MES-LEN.
     EXEC CICS
        SEND FROM(ERROR-MESSAGE) LENGTH(MES-LEN)
     END-EXEC.
```

```
          EXEC CICS
             RETURN
          END-EXEC.
     FAR-TOO-LONG.
          MOVE "FQTY" TO TRAN-CODE IN ERROR-MESSAGE.
          MOVE " " TO FILLER IN ERROR-MESSAGE.
          MOVE "MESSAGE TOO LONG" TO
                         ERROR-TEXT IN ERROR-MESSAGE.
          MOVE 25 TO MES-LEN.
          EXEC CICS
             SEND FROM(ERROR-MESSAGE) LENGTH(MES-LEN)
          END-EXEC.
          EXEC CICS
               RETURN
          END-EXEC.
```

Terminal Control with CICS Basic Mapping Support (BMS)

We have seen how to use the CICS SEND and RECEIVE commands only for the simplest case of communicating single-line messages. However, if you want to communicate messages that occupy the entire screen, you must learn how to use SEND and RECEIVE for dealing with essential data embedded in an entire screen (or **panel**) of information. As mentioned earlier, the details of a standard panel are not part of the COBOL program, but the variables that hold such data are included in the program by the CICS command translator when the program is precompiled. The command translator gets the details from *maps* and **mapsets** that must be predefined by the programmer using a CICS facility called **basic mapping support (BMS)**. The result of this is that when users run the same application program from quite different terminal types, they all get the same message, but each sees a different message format.

Designing panels for use with CICS is a very large part of CICS application programming activities and is a special skill. Details are largely beyond the scope of this book, which concentrates on file processing. Nevertheless, for the sake of completeness, we briefly cover some of the ideas involved.

Each particular type of terminal in the system must have two kinds of *maps* available for each panel, or whole-screen message. There must be a **physical map**—unique for each terminal—that describes the format of a panel for the terminal. There must also be a **symbolic map**—identical for all terminals—that shows where each information quantity (transmitted by RECEIVE or SEND) is located within the panel or message.

Both physical and symbolic maps are constructed using BMS. Once constructed, these BMS maps are placed in a CICS library where they can be referenced when an on-line program is executed.

The format of a panel involves such low level detail as the size and type of display characters used, what kind of highlighting (color, underlining, blinking, and so on) is used, how data fields are located with respect to each other, the number of characters allowed per line, and the number of lines allowed per screen. Readers will appreciate that terminals differ in what kind of formatting they permit, which depends on **format control codes** that are embedded in the data to be displayed. The control codes are not displayed. A control code can dictate underlining of text, or boldface text, for example.

Suppose that we want to display the following panel on a number of different terminal types:

```
PRODUCT STATUS REPORT

Part Type Code:  P111
Part Type:       RESISTOR
```

The data that CICS actually transmits for a specific terminal looks something like that below. For a different terminal the control codes are different.

```
{control codes (CC)} PRODUCT STATUS REPORT {CC} PART TYPE CODE:
{CC} P111 {CC} PART TYPE CODE {CC} RESISTOR {CC}
```

For a specific terminal you can put the above string in a CICS SEND command. The message would appear properly, but the program would no longer be independent of the terminal; the message displayed on other terminals would be weird, if anything at all was displayed.

The string of data communicated to and from a terminal that includes the control codes is called a **native data stream**. Notice that the variable quantities P11 and RESISTOR are a part of the native data stream transmitted. It is the physical map that defines a native data stream for a terminal, with allowance being made for variable names that will include the variable data. The specification of the variable names is in the symbolic map. (Remember, this symbolic map is the same for all terminals for a given panel.) The names used in the symbolic map can be used in the program.

As an example, suppose that to transmit the panel above to four different types of terminals we need four distinct physical maps, W1, X1, Y1, and Z1. W1 thus specifies a specific native data stream, with reference to variables for the variable data. Suppose that the symbolic map for these four physical maps has the variables PARTNUMB and

PARTTYPE. To display the panel on the terminal that needs physical map W1, we can code the following in the CICS COBOL program:

```
MOVE "P11" TO PARTNUMB.
MOVE "RESISTOR" TO PARTTYPE.
CICS EXEC
    SEND MAP("W1") MAPSET("WXYZ")
END-EXEC
```

Here WXYZA refers to a mapset that contains the map W1. We shall return to mapsets presently.

It is likely that within a program more than one distinct panel must dealt with. Suppose that there are three. Then for each terminal there can be three types of panels, so that we can have the following physical maps:

Physical maps are defined by means of BMS macro instructions, which have to be translated by the IBM OS Assembler, link edited, and

	TerminalA	TerminalB	TerminalC	TerminalD
Panel1	W1	X1	Y1	Z1
Panel2	W2	X2	Y2	Z2
Panel3	W3	X3	Y3	Z3
MAPSET	WXYZA	WXYZB	WXYZC	WXYZD

placed in a CICS load library ready for use by an on-line program. All the physical maps for a given terminal used by a given on-line program (such as W1, W2, and W3 for TerminalA) are normally link edited to form a named physical *mapset*. Thus in the CICS SEND command above we assume that the physical map W1 is part of the physical mapset WXYZA.

(There are naming conventions for physical mapsets. Thus WXYZ can be the generic name for all the physical mapsets for this program, with WXYZA being the mapset for TerminalA, WXYZB the mapset for TerminalB, and so on; the suffix identifies the terminal, but must not be used in the SEND command. The details of defining physical mapsets are beyond the scope of this book.)

The symbolic maps are also defined by means of BMS macro instructions and translated by means of IBM OS Assembler. Details are also beyond the scope of this book.

As we have seen, there is a symbolic map for each panel communicated by a program, regardless of terminal type. For a given program all the symbolic maps may be link-edited together to give a symbolic mapset. The symbolic mapset is contained in an operating system (OS) library and contains COBOL statements.

To use a symbolic mapset in a COBOL on-line program, a COPY statement must be placed in the working-storage section. Together with appropriate job control language (JCL), this causes the necessary COBOL statements to be incorporated into the COBOL program at compile time. The net result is that it is possible for the program to refer to variables that can be used for putting variable data into a native data stream, defined for a terminal type by a physical map, and specified in a SEND command. Conversely, these variables can be used for receiving data out of a variable data stream with a RECEIVE command.

DEADLOCK

In this concluding section we look at how the phenomenon of **deadlock** is handled with CICS. Deadlock can be a problem with on-line processing. It occurs when two tasks cannot proceed because each is waiting for a resource held by the other. An example should clarify this.

Suppose that customer Tom at terminal A needs to update record P14 in file P and record Q20 in file Q. It also happens that customer Mary needs a different type of update (involving a different updating program) but also for record P14 in file P and record Q20 in file Q. Both customers cause the necessary updating programs to execute at about the same time, with Tom getting the task Tom-task and Mary the task Mary-task. These tasks are based on different programs, but could interleave as follows:

Tom-task executes:	READ file P key P14. Exclusive control of P14 to Tom-task.
Mary-task executes:	READ file Q key Q20. Exclusive control of Q14 to Mary-task.
Tom-task executes:	READ file Q key Q20. Exclusive control denied. Tom-task put in wait (inactive) state.
Mary-task executes:	READ file P key P14. Exclusive control denied. Mary-task put in wait (inactive) state.

Mary-task waits for Tom-task, and Tom-task waits for Mary-task. Thus we have a deadlock situation.

Now suppose that the order of asking for the records was different for Tom-task, as follows:

Tom-task executes:	READ file P key P14. Exclusive control of P14 to Tom-task.
Mary-task executes:	READ file P key P14. Exclusive control denied. Mary-task put in wait state.
Tom-task executes:	READ file Q key Q20. Exclusive control of Q20 to Tom-task.
Nora-task executes:	...
Tom-task executes:	Files P and Q updated. Tom-task relinquishes control of P14 and Q20.
Mary-task executes:	 Exclusive control of P14 to Mary-task.
Frank-task executes:	...
Mary-task executes:	READ file Q key Q20. Exclusive control of Q20 to Mary-task.
Jane-task executes:	...
Mary-task executes:	Files P and Q updated. Mary-task relinquishes control of P14 and Q20.

This time we clearly do not get deadlock. It should be clear that as long as two tasks do not attempt to get exclusive control of two records A and B, such that one task asks for A and then B, and the other for B and then A, we cannot have deadlock. Accordingly, it is an established convention that *all programs must request files for update in alphabetical order*. If it is a case of two records from the same file that are requested, then the order of requesting them is ascending key order.

SUMMARY

CICS prevents file update interference by providing for definition of a transaction, which gives exclusive control over a record of a file and prevents any other program from updating the records until the transaction is completed. A CICS READ for UPDATE command defines the beginning of a transaction; other common commands such as CICS

REWRITE and DELETE can define the end of a transaction. A CICS UNLOCK command is used to abort a transaction.

A HANDLE CONDITION command is used to define error processing paragraphs for use when error conditions arise. The CICS READ, REWRITE, DELETE, and WRITE commands are used for file processing. They have different syntax and semantics from the corresponding COBOL commands.

Maps are used for definitions of panels to be displayed on screens. These maps are stored in tables for use when data must be displayed on a terminal screen. They are not defined in a COBOL program. For any panel a physical and a symbolic map must be defined. The physical map contains the data that is always displayed. The symbolic map defines variables that will hold the variable data that is displayed in the panel. Since the variables from the symbolic map must be assigned data within a program, they must be known to the program. This is accomplished by a COPY command that inserts definitions of these variables from the symbolic map. A group of maps for a set of panels for a single terminal is called a mapset.

Deadlock occurs when two concurrent programs are each waiting for exclusive control of the same record. It is likely to happen to a program that needs control of two records before it can proceed. Deadlock is avoided if all programs ask for records in a standard sequence, namely, records from different files in ascending file name order, and records from the same file in ascending primary key order.

EXERCISES

1. Write a brief CICS COBOL program to accept a request for the quantity on hand of any product from the PRODUCT file.
2. Write a brief CICS COBOL program to accept a terminal request to reduce the quantity on hand of a product in the PRODUCT file by any amount.
3. Write a brief CICS COBOL program to delete any record listed in PRODUCT when its key is submitted by a user at a terminal.
4. Write a brief COBOL program to insert into PRODUCT a record specified at a terminal.
5. Write a brief COBOL program to compare, percentagewise, the quantities on hand of two distinct products specified at a terminal.

12 FILE PROCESSING WITH SQL

Since about the mid 1980s, commercial **relational data base systems** have become quite common. This has meant that a great deal of file processing that was formerly carried out by the conventional methods described in earlier chapters can nowadays be very conveniently carried out using **structured query language (SQL)**, the language of relational data base systems. The best known relational data base systems are IBM's DATABASE2, for use with mainframe operating systems, and the ORACLE system, which will run on a wide variety of computers. There is even an inexpensive version of ORACLE available for IBM personal computers and compatibles. A version of DATABASE2 for personal computers is expected. We shall be more specific about what a relational data base system is as we develop this subject.

DATABASE2 and ORACLE are very similar. Both use the language SQL. However, SQL is not only a query language. It is a comprehensive data base manipulation language; it can also be used for updating a data base and even for defining one.

Loosely speaking, a **data base** is a collection of computer files that cross-reference or relate to each other. A **data base system** is a software system used for manipulating a data base. But although the data base systems DATABASE2 and ORACLE are widely used for manipulating data bases, they can also be used for manipulating single files. Single-file manipulation is very easy using SQL with these systems and can save a great deal of conventional programming effort.

What makes SQL so convenient is that unlike COBOL and similar languages, SQL is a **nonprocedural language**. With COBOL you must specify the method, or procedure, required to process a file, which makes COBOL a **procedural language**. In contrast, with SQL you specify what is required and the data base system does the job of converting your requirement specification into a procedure. In a way, it can be said that with SQL you specify what you want, in terms of the desired result, and the system generates the program for getting that result.

SQL can be used in two ways. Because it is so powerful, in many cases it is necessary only to enter a few SQL commands at a terminal to get a job done that formerly would have required an extensive COBOL program. Thus one way to use SQL is directly at a terminal.

The other way is to embed SQL expressions in COBOL programs that are used in routine production. The SQL expressions substitute for a great deal of the COBOL code that would normally have been used for file processing. Thus COBOL-embedded SQL can be used to considerably shorten the task of writing a COBOL file processing program.

In this chapter we look at how SQL can be used to process a file directly at a terminal. In chapter 13 we look at how SQL for file processing can be embedded in COBOL programs.

First we look at how a file is specified with a relational data base system; then we look at how information can be retrieved from such a file using SQL; after that we look at file updating with SQL. Finally we look at the subject of views and security.

RELATIONAL FILE DEFINITION

In chapter 1 we pointed out that in addition to the logical file and the physical file of conventional file processing (that is, the storage file), we can also have a *conceptual file* and an *external file*. For the time being we shall ignore the external file idea. The conceptual file is what is important for getting a grasp of file processing with SQL. The concept of a conceptual file is closely tied to the concept of a **relation.** This leads to the concept of a *relational file*. It is a relational file that must be specified when we want to use a relational data base system and SQL for file processing.

Conceptual Files

We have seen that a physical (storage) file is the file that is physically stored on a storage medium (such as a disk) complete with system data, such as IBM count or key subblocks. The physical file plainly physically exists. The logical (storage) file is the collection of records as read into working storage. The logical file plainly does not physically exist, unless we have it printed out and get a hard copy.

As should be apparent from earlier chapters (particularly chapter 7 on secondary keys and chapters 8 and 9 on hash files) the logical file records may well contain pointer fields and other fields whose only purpose is to make it easier to access records. If we can imagine the logical file records with such extra fields, if any, removed, we then have a conceptual file.

A **conceptual file** simply contains the essential data of interest to a business. It will be the same as the logical file only if the logical file does not contains any pointers, deletion tag fields, and the like. For example, in the case of a logical file implemented as a VSAM indexed-sequential file, the logical file and the conceptual file are the same. In

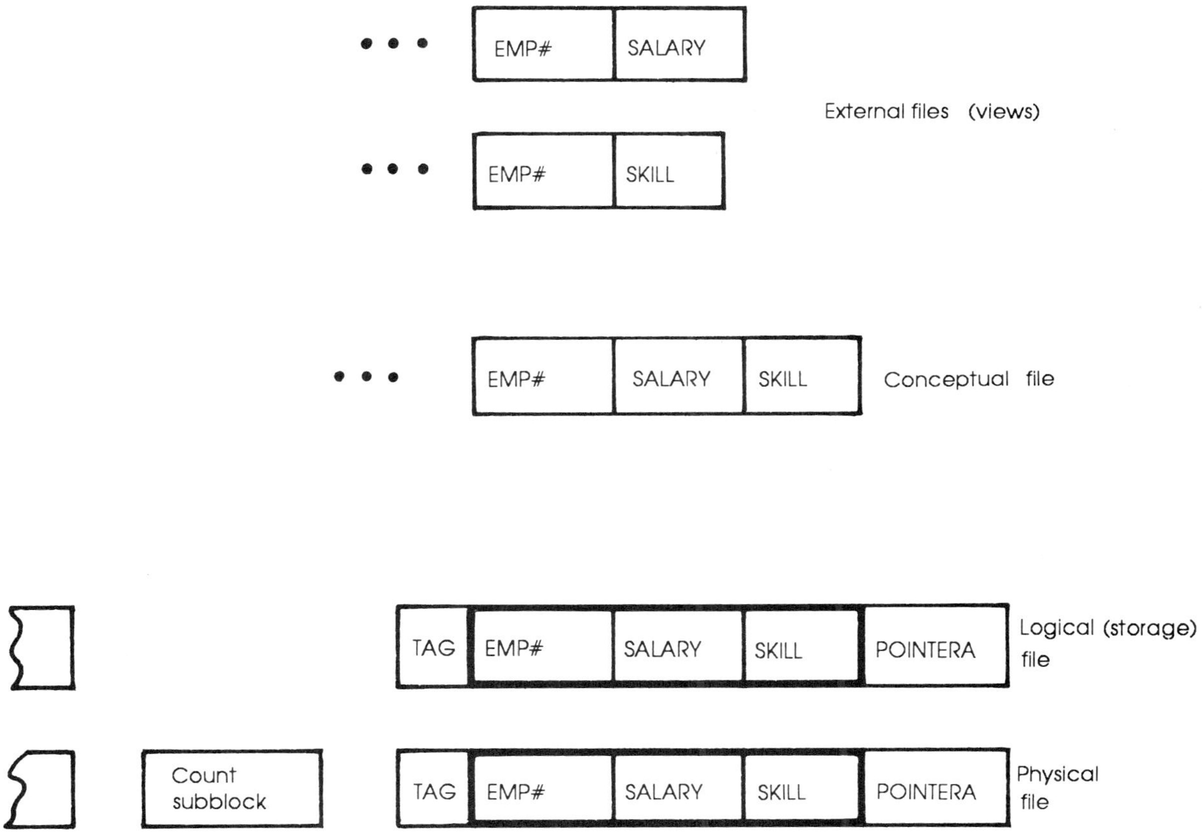

FIGURE 12.1 **Showing how the logical file, the conceptual file, and external files are all abstracted from the underlying physical storage file that physically exists, usually stored on disk.**

the case of a logical file that is a hash file with chained progressive overflow, the conceptual file is not the same as the logical file. In Figure 12.1 we illustrate the concepts of logical, physical, and conceptual files.

Relations and Relational Files

You can have conceptual files whose records vary in length, you can have conceptual files whose records vary in format (number and type of fields), and you can have conceptual files that contain duplicate records. A conceptual file for which none of these things are true is called a **relation**.

The concept of a relation is very important and really very simple. If the file is conceptual, that is, no pointers, and so on, and if it has the following, then it is a relation:

1. No varying length records
2. No records whose format varies
3. No duplicate records

A relation is the simplest possible conceptual file. Readers should thus not be overly concerned about understanding the concept of a relation. A relation is very simple and on paper looks like a regular table. The file EMPLOYEE in Figure 12.2 is thus a relation and very simple. The file PRODUCT in Figure 11.1 can also be considered a relation!

EMP#	DEPT#	SALARY	SKILL	YEAR
E2	D4	30000	ENGINEER	1988
E3	D6	18000	TYPIST	1987
E5	D4	25000	PROGRAMMER	1987
E6	D6	21000	SECRETARY	1986
E7	D5	25000	MANAGER	1987
E9	D4	22000	TECHNICIAN	1988

EMPLOYEE

FIGURE 12.2. Some records of the conceptual file EMPLOYEE. The file is also a relation (or relational file, or base table) since it has fixed length, fixed format unique records. The field EMP# is the primary key. Each record of EMPLOYEE describes an employee of a firm. EMP# gives the employee number, DEPT# the employee's department number, SALARY the salary, SKILL the main skill, and YEAR the year hired.

Remember that a relation is a conceptual file and thus exists only in our imaginations. In reality the relation will be implemented as a direct access physical storage file on disk, possibly with embedded pointer fields and possibly with associated indexes and even count and key data subblocks. When dealing with a relational data base system,

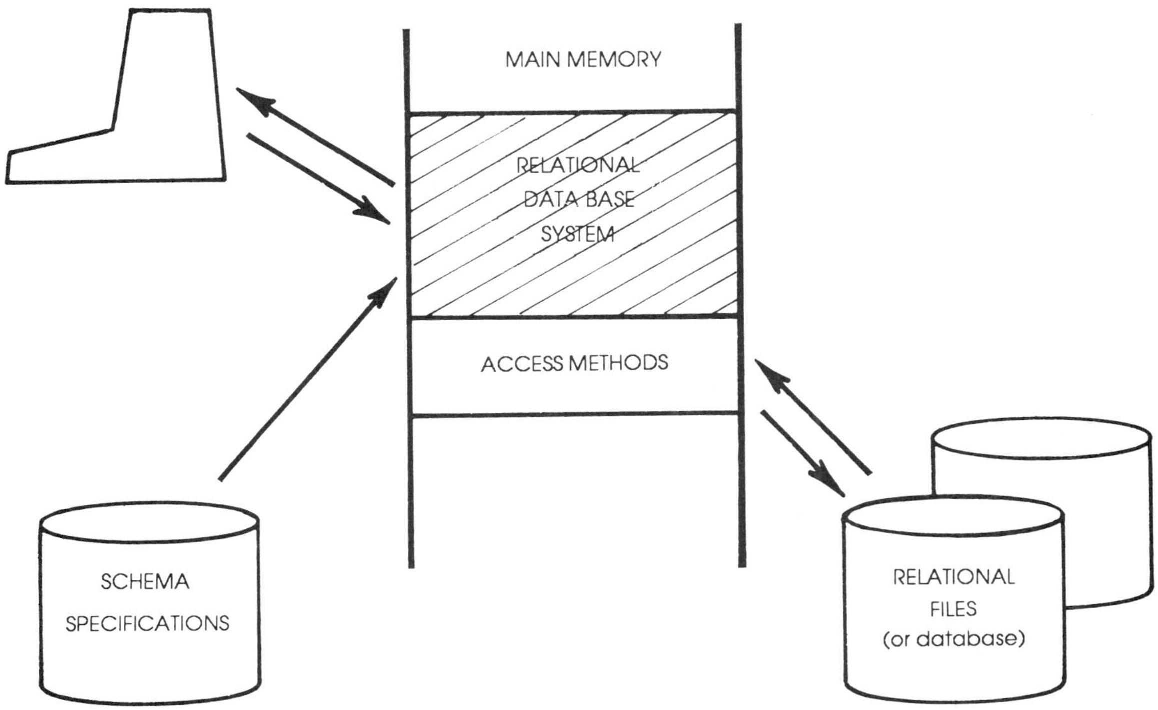

FIGURE 12.3. Overview of a relational data base system used at a terminal for entering SQL commands. The system can manage either individual (unrelated) conceptual files that are relations (base tables), or a collection of related base tables (a data base). The system requires specifications (schemas) for each base table it manipulates.

however, the user need only be concerned with the records of the relation and not with their underlying implementation on disk. This is very convenient, since it removes any need for the programmer or other user to be concerned about system data connected with the implementation of the relation.

A relation is sometimes referred to as a **relational file**. When a relational data base system is used for processing individual files, these files must be relations. Thus the term relational file seems appropriate for an individual file processed using a relational data base system. Nevertheless the term often used with IBM's DATABASE2 for a relation is **base table**, since a relation looks like a regular table with rows (records) and columns (fields). We shall also use the term *base table*. Readers should be clear that a base table is a conceptual file that is also a relation.

Specifying a Relational File (Base Table)

When a user enters an SQL expression at a terminal for execution, he or she expects some file processing to be carried out, either in terms of information retrieval or file updating. Essentially the relational data base system is an intermediate system and carries out the processing using a procedure that it has generated from the SQL expression. This process is illustrated in Figure 12.3. The diagram glosses over a great deal of the system detail, but does convey the essential idea.

The data base system is capable of processing any relational file (base table) according to SQL commands entered at the terminal. However, before it can do this it must have a prior definition or specification of the base table, together with a specification of how the base table should be implemented.

In other words, the system needs a specification of the conceptual file and the underlying storage file. The conceptual file specification is called a **conceptual schema**; the underlying storage file specification is called the **storage schema**. These schemas are entered at a terminal prior to SQL processing.

Conceptual Schema Specification

With IBM's DATABASE2 and similar systems, for each relational file specification we issue a CREATE TABLE command at a terminal. In this command we simply list the fields of the record together with data types. To define the relation EMPLOYEE in Figure 12.2, we specify the following:

```
CREATE TABLE EMPLOYEE (EMP#      CHAR(5) NOT NULL,
                       DEPT#     CHAR(4),
                       SALARY    INTEGER,
                       SKILL     CHAR(15),
                       YEAR     SMALLINTEGER);
```

A note about the data types may be needed for some readers. CHAR(n) corresponds essentially to PIC X(n) in COBOL. INTEGER means a binary number occupying 32 bits (or PIC S9(9) COMP in COBOL). SMALLINTEGER is a binary number occupying 16 bits (or

PIC S9(4) COMP in COBOL). (You can also specify DECIMAL(w,d) for decimal numbers; thus numbers up to 9999.99 could be specified as DECIMAL(6,2). You can also specify FLOAT for 8-byte (double precision) floating point numbers.) These data types have their origin in PL/1, the language in which DATABASE2 was originally implemented.

Notice that we have not specified a field as primary key. We do that with the storage schema specification with DATABASE2. We shall use EMP# (employee number) as the primary key, however; for this reason we have specified that the field may not contain a null value (NOT NULL). A null value is not the same as simply blanks. It means that there is a value, but it is not currently known. If we do not specify NOT NULL with a field, a null value for that field is allowed in a record.

Storage Schema Specification

Indexes are the major features that can be specified for the implementation of a base table with DATABASE2. A hash file implementation is not allowed. The underlying file organization used for all base tables with DATABASE2 is very close to VSAM organization. Readers will therefore not be surprized to learn that you can specify a primary index for the primary key and secondary key indexes (inverted files) for any of the other fields.

The primary index will have a structure close to that described for VSAM in chapter 6. A secondary key index will have a structure close to the inverted file structure used with VSAM (see chapter 7).

We want to specify a primary key index for EMP#, since this field will contain unique values and can be considered a primary key. The specification will be as follows:

```
CREATE UNIQUE INDEX
          EMP-INDEX ON EMPLOYEE(EMP#);
```

The name of the index is EMP-INDEX, which we are not likely ever to use. The word UNIQUE makes the index a primary key index.

We might want secondary key indexes for some of the remaining fields of EMPLOYEE. Generally, because of the expense of maintaining inverted files in the face of updates (chapter 7), we try to restrict secondary key indexes in the interest of performance. The best fields to index are those that are frequently used in retrievals but are rarely involved in updates (as we saw in chapter 7).

If we decide to have a secondary index for the field SKILL we specify the following, where SKILL-INDEX is the name of the index:

```
CREATE INDEX
```

```
SKILL-INDEX ON EMPLOYEE(SKILL);
```

Note that the nonexistence of an index will not deter SQL from delivering results. It may just take longer. For example, if we enter an SQL expression to retrieve the salaries of engineers and if there is no secondary index for the field SKILL, the system simply sequentially scans the EMPLOYEE file, selecting all records with SKILL value ENGINEER. On the other hand, if there is an index on SKILL, the system will be able to go directly to the ENGINEER records, without the need for a time-consuming sequential scan. The downside, of course, is that if the SKILL field is updated a lot, then the existence of an index slows down each update, since both the index and the EMPLOYEE file must be updated.

Putting Records into a Base Table

Once you have defined the base table EMPLOYEE, the system has a permanent recording of it, and, in fact, there exists a relational file EMPLOYEE. However, it will have no records in it. There are two ways to put records into it. If you have only a few records you can enter them one by one at the terminal with an SQL INSERT command. As an example, to enter the EMPLOYEE record

```
E2  D4  20000 ENGINEER  1988
```

we can code the following:

```
INSERT
INTO EMPLOYEE (EMP#, DEPT#, SALARY, POSITION, YEAR)
VALUES ('E2', 'D2', 20000, 'ENGINEER', 1988);
```

Quotes are needed for character field values.

The other way to get records into a base table involves transferring them from an existing conventional file. This method is normally used when a large number of records is involved. A COBOL program is written to accomplish this. A record is read from the conventional file using a COBOL READ statement. This record is then output to the base table using an SQL INSERT command embedded in the COBOL program. This process is repeated until the last record in the conventional file is transferred to the base table. Validity checks on the data are probably carried out during loading of the original conventional file. The use of SQL commands embedded in COBOL programs is covered in the next chapter.

In the next section we shall look at information retrieval. We shall use the base table EMPLOYEE and assume that it has been populated with the records shown in Figure 12.2.

INFORMATION RETRIEVAL WITH SQL

In this section we shall see how SQL may be applied to information retrieval using a single relational file (base table). We do not cover how SQL may be used with a group of base tables that are related, that is, with data bases. Readers interested in that subject should consult a data base text.

We begin with the structure of the SQL SELECT command. Then we look at general information retrieval. Finally we look at retrievals that involve computations.

The SQL SELECT Expression

To retrieve information from a base table we use an SQL SELECT expression. The simplest SELECT expression has the following structure:

```
SELECT fieldname, fieldname, ...
FROM  relation name
WHERE logical expression;
```

For example (referring to Figure 12.2), we might have the following, where we want to select the values in fields EMP# and SALARY, from (each record of) EMPLOYEE, where (or for which) the DEPT# field value is D4:

```
SELECT EMP#, SALARY
FROM EMPLOYEE
WHERE DEPT# = 'D4';
```

A logical expression follows WHERE in a SELECT expression. We can imagine that each record of the base table is checked, and for those records that satisfy the logical expression, the field values specified are retrieved. Note that in actual practice not all the records of EMPLOYEE may be individually checked. For example, if there is a secondary index for the DEPT# field, the system can select the required records directly, without having to scan through the entire relation.

The above SQL expression is a nonprocedural expression. We specify what we want; how the system goes about getting it does not concern us much (unless you are a system administrator concerned with performance). Nevertheless it is convenient to imagine that the system scans through all the records of the relation, selecting those that meet the specified logical condition.

Some SQL Retrievals

The following retrievals all refer to the relational file (base table) EMPLOYEE. We assume that EMPLOYEE contains the records shown in Figure 12.2.

Retrieval-1: Retrieve the department numbers for the departments in the firm.

```
SELECT DEPT#
FROM EMPLOYEE;
```

The result displayed is as follows:

```
DEPT#
D4
D6
D4
D6
D5
D4
```

What SQL retrieves (if computations are not involved) is another table. The table may contain duplicate rows. If we do not want them we specify the following:

```
SELECT DISTINCT DEPT#
FROM EMPLOYEE
```

The resulting display is as follows:

```
DEPT#
D4
D6
D5
```

In each of the above SQL expressions there is no WHERE clause. That simply means that all records from the file are to be selected and the DEPT# value extracted.

Retrieval-2 Retrieve all records for which the department number is D6.

We have two choices. We can use the following expression:

```
SELECT EMP#, DEPT#, SALARY, SKILL, YEAR
FROM EMPLOYEE
WHERE DEPT# = 'D6';
```

The resulting display is as follows:

```
    EMP#    DEPT#    SALARY    SKILL      YEAR
```

```
E3      D6      18000     TYPIST      1987
E6      D6      21000     SECRETARY   1986
```

Or we can use the following:

```
SELECT *
FROM EMPLOYEE
WHERE DEPT# = 'D6';
```

The asterisk (*) specifies that all field values from selected records should be retrieved. This is convenient when the number of fields in the relation is large, with difficult names that are easily misspelled.

Retrieval-3 Find the salaries and employee numbers for employees hired in 1987.

```
SELECT EMP#, SALARY
FROM EMPLOYEE
WHERE YEAR = 1987;
```

The result is as follows:

```
EMP#    SALARY
E3      18000
E5      25000
E7      25000
```

Retrieval-4 Find the employee numbers for employees who work in either department D6 or D5.

```
SELECT EMP#
FROM EMPLOYEE
WHERE DEPT# = 'D6' OR DEPT# = 'D5';
```

The result is as follows:

```
EMP#
E3
E6
E7
```

Simple logical expressions, such as DEPT# = 'D6', can be combined with other simple logical expressions using either the logical connective OR or AND.

Retrieval-5 Find the skills and salaries of employees in department D4 who were hired after 1987.

This should be interpreted as follows:

Find the skill and salary for each employee who (a) works in Department D4 and (b) was hired after 1987.

The SQL expression is as follows:

```
SELECT SKILL, SALARY
FROM EMPLOYEE
WHERE DEPT# = 'D4' AND YEAR > 1987;
```

The result is as follows:

```
SKILL       SALARY
ENGINEER    30000
TECHNICIAN  22000
```

Retrieval-6 Find the employee numbers and their salaries for employees hired before 1988 and display the data in ascending salary order.

```
SELECT EMP#, SALARY
FROM EMPLOYEE
WHERE YEAR < 1988
ORDER BY SALARY ASC;
```

The result is as follows:

```
EMP#   SALARY
E3     18000
E6     21000
E5     25000
E7     25000
```

If we want the data in descending SALARY order we must specify ORDER BY SALARY DESC. If we want data primarily in ascending order by field X and secondarily in descending order by field Y, we specify ORDER BY X ASC, Y DESC. SQL can thus be used for formatting reports.

Retrieval-7 Retrieve the department numbers for departments with an employee whose salary exceeds 48,000 D-marks. Assume US$1.00 = 2.00 D-marks. (Arithmetic expressions are permitted.)

```
SELECT DISTINCT DEPT#
FROM EMPLOYEE
WHERE SALARY*2  48000;
```

The result is as follows:

```
DEPT#
D4
D5
```

Retrieval-8 Retrieve the skills whose first three letters are PRO.

```
SELECT SKILL
FROM EMPLOYEE
```

```
WHERE SKILL LIKE 'PRO%';
```

The result is as follows:

```
SKILL
PROGRAMMER
```

Following LIKE, the string can include a percent sign anywhere to denote any missing set of characters; for example, with TYP%, %PIST, or %YP%, the character string TYPIST satisfies. If we want to deal with only one missing character, we use an underscore; thus T_PI_T can be satisfied by TYPIST. We can also combine these, so that _ANA% is satisfied by MANAGER.

Retrieval-9 Find the employees and their skills in department D6 and give an explanation of what is retrieved.

```
SELECT 'Employee number is:', EMP#, 'Employee skill:', SKILL
FROM EMPLOYEE
WHERE DEPTY# = 'D6';
```

The result is below. You can have any string displayed before field value as shown.

```
                    EMPNUMB                     SKILL
Employee number is: E3      Employee skill:     TYPIST
Employee number is: E6      Employee skill:     SECRETARY
```

Retrieval-10 What employees are engineers, programmers, or technicians?

```
SELECT EMP#
FROM EMPLOYEE
WHERE SKILL IN ('ENGINEER', 'PROGRAMMER', 'TECHNICIAN');
```

The result is as follows:

```
EMP#
E2
E5
E9
```

The IN in the above expression should be interpreted as meaning *is among*. In other words, we want the employee records where the SKILL value is among those listed, that is, those in the set of values in parenthesis.

Retrieval-11 What employees are in the same department as employee E5

We can approach this using two SQL expressions. First we find out what department E5 is in as follows:

```
SELECT DEPT#
FROM EMPLOYEE
WHERE EMP# = 'E5';
```

The result is department D4. Then we find out what employees are in department D4 as follows:

```
SELECT EMP#
FROM EMPLOYEE
WHERE DEPT# = 'D4';
```

The result is as follows:

```
    EMP#
    E2
    E5
    E9
```

But we can combine these two expressions into a more sophisticated SQL expression, with the following:

```
SELECT EMP#
FROM EMPLOYEE
WHERE DEPT# IN (SELECT DEPT#
                 FROM EMPLOYEE
                WHERE DEPT# = 'D4');
```

This expression contains an inner or **nested block** (the SELECT-FROM-WHERE block). The inner block evaluates to D4. Thus the expression resolves into the following:

```
SELECT EMP#
FROM EMPLOYEE
WHERE DEPT# IN ('D4');
```

This will clearly give the required result. SQL expressions can be nested to any number of levels, although three levels is usually more than enough in most cases.

Retrieval-12 What departments have hired nobody in 1988?

We can do this one using two expressions as well. First let us find the departments that have hired somebody in 1988, as follows:

```
SELECT DEPT#
FROM EMPLOYEE
WHERE YEAR = 1988;
```

The result is the set of department numbers {D4}. We therefore want the records whose DEPT# values are not in this set, as follows:

```
SELECT DISTINCT DEPT#
FROM EMPLOYEE
WHERE DEPT# NOT IN ('D4');
```

NOT is used in SQL to denote negation. The results are departments D5 and D6.

The above two expressions can be combined as follows:

```
SELECT DISTINCT DEPT#
FROM EMPLOYEE
WHERE DEPT# NOT IN (SELECT DEPT#
                     FROM EMPLOYEE
                    WHERE YEAR = 1988);
```

Note that to carry out this retrieval with conventional COBOL programming, you first need a version of EMPLOYEE sorted on DEPT#. Using sequential processing you then check each group of records with the same DEPT# value to make sure that none of the records have a YEAR field value equal to 1988.

Retrieval-13 What departments have nobody making $25,000?

```
SELECT DISTINCT DEPT#
FROM EMPLOYEE
WHERE DEPT# NOT IN (SELECT DEPT#
                     FROM EMPLOYEE
                     WHERE SALARY NOT = 25000);
```

The result is D6. Notice that the following expression, which the novice might be tempted to construct, is dead wrong:

```
SELECT DISTINCT DEPT#
FROM EMPLOYEE
WHERE SALARY NOT = 25000;
```

This retrieves D4 and D6, which is clearly wrong. To carry out the above retrieval using conventional COBOL file processing you first need a version of EMPLOYEE sorted on DEPT#. Using sequential processing you then check that each group of records with the same DEPT# value has no SALARY fields with value 25,000.

Retrieval-14 In what departments does everyone make more than $20,000?

```
SELECT DISTINCT DEPT#
FROM EMPLOYEE
WHERE DEPT# NOT IN (SELECT DEPT#
  FROM EMPLOYEE
  WHERE SALARY  < = 20000);
```

The result is D4 and D5. The logic of this should be considered carefully. The above English-language retrieval expression can be rewritten as below:

> Find the departments where there is no salary less than or equal to $20,000.

It is this structure that is mirrored by the SQL expression. Of course, the information could be retrieved by two distinct SQL expressions each involving a single SELECT-FROM-WHERE block. We leave this to the reader as an exercise.

Retrieval-15 In what departments are there at least two distinct salaries?

```
SELECT DISTINCT DEPT#
FROM EMPLOYEE X-EMPLOYEE
WHERE DEPT# IN (SELECT DEPT#
                 FROM EMPLOYEE
                 WHERE SALARY NOT = X-EMPLOYEE.SALARY)
```

The result is D4 and D6. This expression involves a relation label, namely, X-EMPLOYEE.

To see how the expression works, imagine that the system scans through EMPLOYEE records one by one, checking each for acceptability. Suppose that we are checking out the first record, namely, that for employee E2 in department D4. We consider this current record to be the X-EMPLOYEE record. In the inner block we then acquire the department numbers from the EMPLOYEE records where the SALARY field is not the same as that in the E2 record, that is,in the X-EMPLOYEE record. These are the set {D6, D4, D5}. The current record has department value D4; since it is among this set, it must satify. The whole thing is repeated again for employee record E3, and so on, for the entire EMPLOYEE relation.

Retrievals Involving Computations

In the previous section we gave examples of retrievals where data that was in the file was retrieved. In this section we look at retrievals with the following conditions:

1. The data retrieved may need processing to get the result
2. Processing may be needed before records can be selected for retrieval
3. We have a combination of 1 and 2

We use SQL functions MAX, MIN, AVE, SUM, and COUNT. The following retrievals show how we use these.

Retrieval-16 How many employees were hired in 1987?

```
SELECT COUNT(*)
FROM EMPLOYEE
WHERE YEAR = 1887;
```

The result is 3. The COUNT function simply counts records. Ignoring the COUNT, the records that satisfy the WHERE condition are first retrieved. Then they are counted to give the final result.

Retrieval-17 What is the total payroll paid to employees hired in 1987?

```
SELECT SUM (SALARY)
FROM EMPLOYEE
WHERE YEAR = 1987;
```

The SALARY values $18,000, $25,000, $25,000 are first retrieved and then summed to get the final answer of $68,000. Notice that if you use DISTINCT to get only unique values, as below, you get the sum of $18,000 and $25,000, which is wrong:

```
SELECT SUM (DISTINCT SALARY)
FROM EMPLOYEE
WHERE YEAR = 1987;
```

Retrieval-18 What is the average salary at department D6?

```
SELECT AVE (SALARY)
FROM EMPLOYEE
WHERE DEPT# = 'D6';
```

The SALARY values are first retrieved ($18,000 and $21,000) and then averaged to give $19,500. Had we replaced AVE by MAX (or MIN) we would have gotten the maximum (or minimum) salary at department D6.

Retrieval-19 What employees at department D4 make more than the maximum salary at department D6?

```
SELECT EMP#
FROM EMPLOYEE
```

```
WHERE DEPT# = 'D4' AND
             SALARY   (SELECT MAX (SALARY)
                        FROM EMPLOYEE
                        WHERE DEPT# = 'D6');
```

In the inner block we get the maximum salary at D6, namely $21,000. In the outer block we get the employees at D4 who make more than this $21,000. The result is E2, E5, and E9.

Retrieval-20 Find the total number of employees at department D4 who make less than the average salary at department D6.

```
SELECT COUNT(*)
FROM EMPLOYEE
WHERE DEPT# = 'D4' AND
        SALARY < (SELECT AVE (SALARY)
                  FROM EMPLOYEE
                  WHERE DEPT# = 'D6');
```

The result is 3. In this retrieval we need a computation to select the required records, and then a further computation to count them, once selected.

Retrieval-21 For each department find the maximum salary.

```
SELECT DEPT#, MAX (SALARY)
FROM EMPLOYEE
GROUP BY DEPT#;
```

The result is as follows:

DEPT#	SALARY
D4	30000
D6	21000
D5	25000

The GROUP BY clause is used to partition the relation by DEPT# and then to apply the retrieval to each partition.

Retrieval-22 For each department other than D5, find the minimum salary.

```
SELECT DEPT#, MIN (SALARY)
FROM EMPLOYEE
WHERE DEPT NOT = 'D5'
GROUP BY DEPT#;
```

The result is as follows:

DEPT#	SALARY
D4	22000
D6	18000

Retrieval-23 For each department give the minimum salary, provided that minimum exceeds $19,000.

```
SELECT DEPT#, MIN (SALARY)
FROM EMPLOYEE
GROUP BY DEPT
HAVING MIN (SALARY) > 19000;
```

The result is as follows:

```
DEPT#  SALARY
D4     22000
D5     25000
```

The HAVING clause is used to decide which groups of records (with the same DEPT#) are to be selected.

UPDATING A RELATION

A relation can be updated at a terminal using the SQL INSERT, UPDATE, and DELETE commands. INSERT is used for inserting a new record into a relation. UPDATE is used for changing a field value in one or more records. DELETE is used for deleting one or more records. With both UPDATE and DELETE we can use an SQL condition to determine what records are to be affected; the result is that a single UPDATE or DELETE command could affect every record in the file. We also look at the ALTER command, which is used to add additional fields to the records of a base table.

INSERT Command

We dealt with this command earlier in the chapter. It is simple and merely inserts a single record into a relation. A point not covered is what happens if we do not enter data into all the fields of a newly inserted record. For example, if we submit the following INSERT expression, a new record is inserted, but the field SKILL merely gets a NULL value:

```
INSERT
INTO EMPLOYEE (EMP#, DEPT#, SALARY, YEAR)
VALUES ('E8', 'D7', 24000, 1988);
```

The UPDATE Command

The UPDATE command can be used either for updating a single record or for updating a collection of records. We first consider the case of updating a single record.

Suppose that we wish to change employee E6's department to D10. We enter the following:

```
UPDATE EMPLOYEE
SET    DEPT# = 'D10'
WHERE EMP# = 'E6';
```

Following SET we list the fields to be changed; following WHERE we give the condition that selects the record or records to be affected by the update. In the above case, only one record is affected since EMP# is the primary key.

To increase employee E3's salary by $1,000 and also change the employee's skill to secretary, we enter the following:

```
UPDATE EMPLOYEE
SET      SALARY = SALARY + 10C0
          SKILL = 'SECRETARY'
WHERE EMP# = 'E3';
```

In dealing with a numeric field, an algebraic expression can be used for updating. For example, with numeric field X, we might code SET X = X*X*25 - 16.

The above SQL expression also selects only one record for updating, since EMP# is a primary key. But now suppose that we want to give everyone in department D4 a 10 percent raise in salary. Clearly many records could be affected. We can code the following:

```
UPDATE EMPLOYEE
SET     SALARY = SALARY * 1.10
WHERE DEPT# = 'D4';
```

Updates of this type are dangerous at a terminal with an important file, especially with a complex condition following WHERE. It is easy to get the SQL condition wrong, thus selecting the wrong records for update.

Update expressions for multiple record updates are best embedded in COBOL programs, where the expression has been thoroughly tested for correctness beforehand. At a terminal it is usually a better idea to first retrieve and check or confirm the records to be updated, and only then update them—maybe one by one, to be on the safe side. For example, instead of the above expression we might code the following:

```
SELECT *
FROM EMPLOYEE
WHERE DEPT# = 'D4';
```

This gives us the records for E2, E5, and E9. Having checked the records, and particularly the SALARY field, we might then enter the following:

```
UPDATE EMPLOYEE
SET     SALARY = SALARY * 1.10
WHERE EMP# IN ('E2', 'E5', 'E9');
```

As a final check, following the update we might retrieve the records affected just to make sure that the update had been carried out as intended.

The DELETE Command

The DELETE command can be used either for deleting a single record or for deleting multiple records. As an example of the single- record case, suppose that we want to delete the record for employee E3. We enter the following:

```
DELETE
FROM EMPLOYEE
WHERE EMP# = 'E3'
```

The condition following WHERE selects the record or records to be deleted. Because EMP# is a primary key field, only one record is selected in this case.

If we want to delete all the records for employees in Department D4, we an enter the following:

```
DELETE
FROM EMPLOYEE
WHERE DEPT# = 'D4';
```

This deletes records for employees E2, E5, and E9. As with update, SQL DELETE expressions that cause multiple record deletions are dangerous at a terminal. It is too easy to get the WHERE condition wrong and delete the wrong records. Such expressions are better embedded in COBOL programs for routine use, where it is expected that the SQL expressions have been thoroughly tested beforehand. Where the multiple record deletion must be carried out at the terminal, as with UPDATE, it is a good idea to retrieve the records first and delete them only after a thorough check that they are the correct records.

Note that the expression

```
DELETE
FROM EMPLOYEE;
```

will delete all the records in EMPLOYEE. The relational file still exists, however. To remove the file from the system we must enter the following:

```
DROP TABLE EMPLOYEE;
```

Use of the ALTER Command

Suppose that after the file EMPLOYEE has been in use for some time, a need arises for an additional field (TEL), which gives the employee's 4-digit internal telephone number. It is not necessary to create an entirely new file and reload the records, as would be the case with conventional file processing. If we issue the ALTER command as follows

```
ALTER TABLE EMPLOYEE
     ADD TEL CHAR(4);
```

each record of employee will be extended with the addition of a new field, TEL. In each record, TEL will have a null value. Later TEL can be updated by means of the UPDATE command. For example, the following records E3's telephone number:

```
UPDATE EMPLOYEE
SET TEL = '1234'
WHERE EMP# = 'E3';
```

As we can probably see from the structure of SQL retrieval and update expressions, SQL expressions embedded in a COBOL program prior to using ALTER to extend the records will still function correctly after the records have been extended. With conventional file processing the COBOL program must be rewritten with an extension of the buffer and working-storage variables required to hold individual records. This makes an existing program independent of the structure of a file that it manipulates; the program thus is said to have *data independence*, a subject we return to in chapter 13.

VIEWS

A **view** can be looked upon as an **external file** and can be constructed from a conceptual file simply by selecting certain fields. For example, suppose that for security purposes certain users are not allowed to see the SALARY field in EMPLOYEE. For these users a view EMPLOYEE-R can be constructed. We need simply enter a CREATE VIEW command at a terminal as follows:

```
CREATE VIEW    EMPLOYEE-R(EMP#, DEPT#, SKILL, YEAR)
AS             SELECT(EMP#, DEPT#, SKILL, YEAR)
                FROM EMPLOYEE;
```

The result is a relation (relational file), EMPLOYEE-R, that is the same as EMPLOYEE except that it does not have a salary field.

The relation EMPLOYEE-R is not a base table, for it is not implemented as a storage file on disk, as is the case with EMPLOYEE. Instead the system simulates the existence for a user on the basis of the data in EMPLOYEE. This is the essence of a view or external file. It is a relation, or relational file, abstracted from the underlying conceptual file or base table. (The concept of an external file or view is illustrated in Figure 12.1.)

A view can be used for information retrieval. Thus the following expression will retrieve the employees and skills in department D4:

```
SELECT EMP#, SKILL
FROM EMPLOYEE-R
WHERE DEPT# = 'D4';
```

Views abstracted from a single file can usually be updated as well — provided they contain the primary key of the underlying base table. The effect is to update the underlying base table.

SUMMARY

A relational data base system is convenient to use for file manipulation. The manipulation language is SQL. SQL expressions can be used directly at a terminal, or embedded in COBOL programs. SQL is a nonprocedural language. That means that an SQL expression merely defines what is wanted and does not contain the procedure for obtaining the required result. The data base system can convert an SQL expression into a procedure that will process a file. As a result the use of SQL reduces the need for programming effort.

A relational data base system manipulates relations. A relation is a file of a specialized but simple type. A group of cross-referenced relations forms a typical data base, which can be manipulated by the data base system. When we are manipulating only a single isolated relation, we are essentially using the data base system for file processing.

A conceptual file contains only data of interest to the business user (no pointer fields, and so on). A relation is a conceptual file where that file, in addition, has only fixed-format, fixed length, unique records. For every relation there is an underlying storage file on disk. A relation is thus an imaginary file—only the underlying storage file physically exists. With some relational systems a conceptual file that is a relation is called a base table.

A view is a base table from which some of the fields have been removed. A user of a view thus has restricted access to the base table.

The SQL language can be used for information retrieval and for change, insertion, and deletion updating. A single SQL expression can retrieve multiple records or update multiple records.

EXERCISES

Give SQL expressions for the following:

1. Retrieve the salaries of employees who work in department D4 and D5.
2. Retrieve all data about employees making $25,000.
3. Retrieve the employee number and the year hired for employees in department D4 making less than $28,000.
4. Find the salary and employee number for employees other than engineers and managers.
5. Find out everything about employees in departments D6 and D4.
6. Find out everything about employees in departments D4, D5, and D6 (using the SQL IN construct).
7. Find the employee numbers, year hired, and department, for employees making more than $21,000; display the data in ascending year hired and secondarily in descending department.
8. Find out the average salary at department D4.
9. Find the number of people hired in 1987.
10. Find the total payroll for engineers and managers.

11. Find the average salary for the firm.
12. Find the maximum salary for employees in department D4.
13. Find the departments with employees who make more than the average for the firm.
14. What employees in department D6 make less than the minimum salary in department D4?
15. What employees hired in 1987 make less than employee E6?
16. Increase the salary of D4 employees by 15 percent.
17. Employees who make more than $24,000 are to be transferred out of the company. Delete their records.
18. A new employee (E9 D6 27,000 ENGINEER 1988) is hired. Add the engineer's record to the files.
19. In what departments are there at least two distinct skills?

13 FILE PROCESSING WITH SQL EMBEDDED IN COBOL

Because structured query language (SQL) is a nonprocedural language, a few lines of SQL are often sufficient for carrying out a great deal of processing that would take many lines of COBOL code. Not all code in a COBOL file processing program has to do directly with file processing, however; therefore SQL cannot entirely replace COBOL programming. Nevertheless those parts of a COBOL program that are directly involved in file processing can often be replaced by embedded SQL expressions, thus saving a great deal of programming effort.

An additional advantage of using SQL for the file processing parts of a COBOL program is that the SQL expressions can often be independent of the number of fields in the relational file being processed. For example, if the number of fields in an existing relational file (base table) is extended by use of the ALTER command, existing COBOL programs that process this file using embedded SQL are not affected. Such SQL COBOL application programs are said to be **data independent**, or to possess **data independence**. Data independence is one of the significant benefits of using a data base system for file processing.

As we saw in chapter 12, SQL can be used for dealing with either a single record at a time or with multiple records. COBOL, on the other hand, can handle only one record at a time. There are thus some technicalities in the interface between COBOL and SQL.

The best way to learn about the SQL/COBOL interface is to consider first how to embed SQL expressions that deal with only a single record. Later we can consider embedded SQL expressions that deal with multiple records.

In this chapter we assume that the relational data base system being used is IBM's DATABASE2. The details of the SQL/COBOL interface have not yet been standardized, so that they differ from one system to another. However, in most cases the details are not all that different from those encountered with DATABASE2.

EMBEDDING SINGLE-RECORD SQL EXPRESSIONS

In this section we examine how to embed SQL retrieval and update expressions that deal with only a single record. We begin with information retrieval. We use the same EMPLOYEE relation as in the previous chapter, shown again in Figure 13.1

EMP#	DEPT#	SALARY	SKILL	YEAR
E2	D4	30000	ENGINEER	1988
E3	D6	18000	TYPIST	1987
E5	D4	25000	PROGRAMMER	1987
E6	D6	21000	SECRETARY	1986
E7	D5	25000	MANAGER	1987
E9	D4	22000	TECHNICIAN	1988

EMPLOYEE

Figure 13.1 Contents of the base table EMPLOYEE.

Embedding SQL SELECT Expressions

Suppose that we want to use a COBOL program to retrieve the EMPLOYEE record for employee E3 and print out the employee number and salary. The program reads E3 as input data. We can use the following SQL expression for retrieving the SALARY data from EMPLOYEE:

```
SELECT EMP#, SALARY
FROM EMPLOYEE
WHERE EMP# = 'E3';
```

Unfortunately we cannot embed this expression in a COBOL program as it stands. Some modification is necessary.

First of all every SQL expression, including those allowed only in COBOL programs, must be sandwiched between EXEC SQL and END-EXEC, as follows:

```
EXEC SQL
```

```
    SQL-expression
END-EXEC.
```

When used in the procedure division, such a sandwich can then be treated like a normal COBOL sentence.

In the COBOL program, we will have a normal identification and environment division. However, in the working-storage section of the data division, we need to specify a **host data structure** and insert two EXEC SQL specifications.

The host data structure is used to receive the data retrieved by the SQL expression. We are going to retrieve EMP# and SALARY fields, so that we can use host variables, HEMP# and HSALARY, specified as follows:

```
WORKING-STORAGE SECTION.
    77  HEMP#     PIC X(5).
    77  HSALARY   PIC S9(9) COMP.
```

These are ordinary COBOL variables and can be used in any normal manner within the COBOL program.

Continuing with the working-storage specifications, we must now specify the field names for the base table EMPLOYEE as follows:

```
EXEC SQL
    DECLARE EMPLOYEE TABLE
        (EMP#         CHAR(5)  NOT NULL,
        DEPT#         CHAR(4),
        SALARY        INTEGER,
        SKILL         CHAR(15),
        YEAR          SMALLINTEGER)
END-EXEC.
```

Note that the field names EMP#, DEPT#, SALARY, SKILL, and YEAR are not COBOL identifiers or variables and cannot be used in conventional COBOL sentences. They can be used only within SQL expressions.

Still in the working-storage section, we end with the following:

```
EXEC SQL
    INCLUDE SQLCA
END-EXEC.
```

SQLCA is an agreggate COBOL variable that contains the variable SQLCODE. SQLCODE is available to the COBOL program and is used for error checking. Following execution of an SQL expression within the program, the system places a completion code in SQLCODE. A 0 means that all went well; the value 100 is returned if no data is retrieved. Within the COBOL program there must be sentences for checking the value of SQLCODE and taking corrective action if things did not go well with the execution of the previous SQL expression.

The procedure division for the processing can be the following:

```
PROCEDURE DIVISION.
    ACCEPT X.
** X contains value E3.
    EXEC SQL
        SELECT EMP#, SALARY
            INTO :HEMP#, :HSALARY
        FROM EMPLOYEE
        WHERE EMP# = :X
    END-EXEC.
** Values E3 and 18000 now in working-storage variables
** HEMP# and HSALARY, if all went well.
    IF SQLCODE = 0 THEN
        DISPLAY "EMPLOYEE:", HEMP#, "SALARY:", SALARY
    ELSE
        PERFORM ERROR-ACTION.
    STOP RUN.
ERROR-ACTION.
    . . .
```

There are two things to notice about the SQL SELECT expression in the program. First there must be an INTO clause, which specifies where in working storage the retrieved data must go. Second every working-storage variable used in the expression—that is, each variable not declared in the actual base table specification—must be prefixed by a colon.

Embedding SQL UPDATE Expressions

Suppose that we want a COBOL program that updates EMPLOYEE by increasing E3's salary by $1,000, where the E3 and 1,000 values are read into COBOL working-storage variables X and RAISE. We do not need the host structure variables HEMP# and HSALARY this time; these can be omitted from the working-storage specifications. However, we still need the DECLARE and INCLUDE specifications described in the previous section. The procedure division can be the following:

```
PROCEDURE DIVISION.
    ACCEPT X.
    ACCEPT RAISE.
    MOVE RAISE TO CRAISE.
** Assume RAISE in DISPLAY format, CRAISE in PIC S9(9) COMP.
** Value E3 in X and 1000 in CRAISE.
    EXEC SQL
```

```
        UPDATE EMPLOYEE
        SET SALARY = SALARY + :CRAISE
        WHERE EMP# = :X
    END-EXEC.
    IF SQLCODE > 0 THEN PERFORM ERROR-ACTION.
    STOP RUN
ERROR-ACTION.
```

Notice again that the working-storage variables CRAISE and X must have a colon prefixed when used in the SQL UPDATE expression.

Embedding SQL INSERT Expressions

If we want to insert a new record into the EMPLOYEE relation, or load the relation with records initially, we need to use the embedded INSERT command. For example, if we are loading records in EMPLOYEE, we might use a COBOL READ to read a record from a tape file TAPE-EMP into a working-storage structure EMPLOYEEREC. The SQL INSERT command is then used to load a record from EMPLOYEEREC into the base table EMPLOYEE.

Suppose that the working-storage structure EMPLOYEEREC is specified in working storage as follows:

```
01  EMPLOYEEREC.
    02 HEMP#    PIC X(5).
    02 HDEPT#   PIC X(4).
    02 HSALARY  PIC S9(9) COMP.
    02 HSKILL   PIC X(15).
    02 HYEAR    PIC S9(4) COMP.
```

Then to read the next record from TAPE-EMP and place it in EMPLOYEE, we can code the following:

```
READ TAPE-EMP RECORD INTO EMPLOYEEREC,
             AT END ...
EXEC SQL
    INSERT
    INTO EMPLOYEE (EMP#, DEPT#, SALARY, SKILL, YEAR)
    VALUES (:HEMP#, :HDEPT#, :HSALARY, :HSKILL, :HYEAR)
END-EXEC.
```

Again we see that working-storage variables used with an SQL expression need a colon prefix. Note that the values clause in the above expression can be replaced by VALUES (:EMPLOYEEREC).

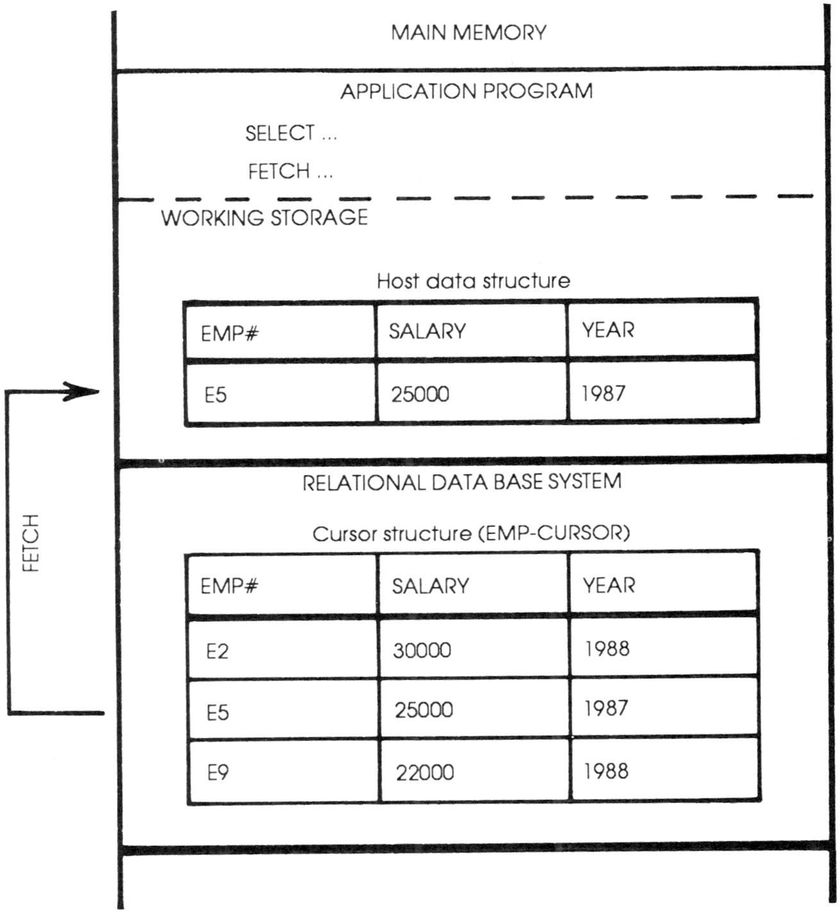

FIGURE 13.2. **Showing how multiple records retrieved by the data base system as a result of executing an embedded SQL SELECT command are placed in a cursor structure within the data base system. Execution of a FETCH command by the program moves the next record in the cursor structure to the host data structure in the program's working storage.**

In the working-storage section we need the same SQL DECLARE and INCLUDE expressions as when an SQL SELECT is being embedded in the procedure.

Embedding SQL DELETE Expressions

Suppose that we want to delete the record for employee E3, where E3 is read into a working-storage variable X. In the procedure division we can code as follows:

```
ACCEPT X.
EXEC SQL
    DELETE
    FROM EMPLOYEE
    WHERE EMP# = :X
END EXEC.
IF SQLCODE > 0 THEN PERFORM ERROR-ACTION.
```

Again the working-storage variable within the DELETE expression needs a prefixed colon.

EMBEDDING MULTIPLE-RECORD SQL EXPESSIONS

When dealing with multiple-record SQL expressions, major interface difficulties show up with the SELECT expression. A SELECT expression that retrieves multiple records will retrieve a number of records that varies with the state of the base table. There is thus no COBOL structure that such a varying quantity of retrieved records can be placed in.

The relational data base system itself provides a structure to hold records retrieved by a multiple-record SELECT expression. This structure is called a *cursor structure* (see Figure 13.2). The cursor structure is under the control of the data base system and may not be accessed using ordinary COBOL.

The Cursor Structure Concept

To understand the idea behind the use of the **cursor structure**, suppose that within a COBOL program we execute the equivalent of the ordinary SELECT expression as follows:

```
SELECT EMP#, SALARY, YEAR
FROM EMPLOYEE
WHERE DEPT# = 'D4';
```

Referring to Figure 13.1 we see that three records are retrieved (for employees E2, E5, and E9). These three records are placed in the cursor structure by the data base system. Although we cannot access the records in the cursor structure using ordinary COBOL (as we shall soon see), nevertheless beforehand we still must place the definition of the cursor structure in the working-storage section of the COBOL program. (This cursor structure definition counts as an SQL expression and is sandwiched between the usual EXEC SQL and END-EXEC.)

We want to get the records out of the cursor structure one by one. As each record is extracted from the cursor struture, it can be placed in an ordinary working-storage structure (which is usually called the host data structure), as in the case of single record retrieval in the previous section. We are provided with an SQL FETCH command, for use only within application programs, that will extract a record from the cursor structure and place it in the host data structure (Figure 13.2).

Normally the FETCH command is placed in a loop. The first execution extracts the first record in the structure, the next execution extracts the next record, and so on. Once a record is in the working-storage (or host data) structure, it can manipulated by ordinary COBOL. The next section gives the details of this.

Embedding the Multiple-Record SELECT Command

Assume that we want to have a program that prints out the employee number, salary, and year hired data for the employees of a department, where the department number is read into a working-storage variable (D) by the program. We thus want to embed the SQL SELECT expression as follows. As we have seen, this expression can retrieve more than one record.

```
SELECT EMP#, SALARY, YEAR
FROM EMPLOYEE
WHERE DEPT# = 'D4';
```

In working storage we must define a host data structure that can hold a retrieved record; in working storage we also need an SQL DECLARE and and SQL INCLUDE, as with the case of single record retrieval. Finally in the working-storage structure section we must define the cursor structure. The working-storage structure specification can thus be the following:

```
WORKING-STORAGE SECTION.
```

```
    77 D        PIC X(4).
    77 HEMP#    PIC X(5).
    77 HSALARY PIC S9(9) COMP.
    77 HYEAR    PIC S9(4) COMP.
    EXEC SQL
      DECLARE EMPLOYEE TABLE
      (EMP#    CHAR(5),
      DEPT#   CHAR(4),
      SALARY INTEGER,
      SKILL   CHAR(15),
      YEAR    SMALLINTEGER)
    END-EXEC.
    EXEC SQL
      INCLUDE SQLCA
    END-EXEC.
**Cursor structure definition follows.
    EXEC SQL
      DECLARE EMP-CURSOR CURSOR FOR
            SELECT EMP#, SALARY, YEAR
            FROM EMPLOYEE
            DEPT# = :D
    END-EXEC.
```

In the cursor structure definition, which must be defined in the working-storage section, we specify a name (EMP-CURSOR) for the structure. We also specify the SELECT expression that will retrieve records and place them in the structure. However, this specification does not cause the SELECT expression to be executed. That is triggered in the procedure division only when we execute an SQL OPEN command to *open* the cursor structure.

In the procedure division we first read in a value for D (which will contain D4). Then we open the cursor structure. This causes the SELECT expression (specified in working storage!) to be executed and the records retrieved to flow into the cursor structure. We then use the SQL FETCH command to extract the first record, move it to the working-storage host structure, and then print it. We repeat for the next record in the cursor structure, and so on, as shown below:

```
PROCEDURE DIVISION.
ACCEPT D.
EXEC SQL
OPEN EMP-CURSOR
END-EXEC.
** SELECT expression executed, records in EMP-CURSOR.
      EXEC SQL
        FETCH EMP-CURSOR
        INTO :HEMP#, :HSALARY, :HYEAR
      END-EXEC
```

```
** First record from EMP-CURSOR to working storage.
    PERFORM EXTRACT-AND-DISPLAY
        UNTIL SQLCODE = 100.
** When FETCH tries to extract past the last record
** in EMP-CURSOR the SQLCODE value returned is 100.
    EXEC SQL
        CLOSE EMP-CURSOR
    END-EXEC.
** CLOSE empties EMP-CURSOR.
    STOP RUN.
**
    EXTRACT-AND-DISPLAY.
        IF SQLCODE > 0 THEN
            PERFORM ERROR-ACTION
        ELSE
            DISPLAY HEMP#, HSALARY, HYEAR.
** Now extract next record from EMP-CURSOR.
    EXEC SQL
            FETCH EMP-CURSOR
    INTO :HEMP#, :HSALARY, :HYEAR
    END-EXEC.
**
ERROR-ACTION.
    ...
```

Notice that any working-storage variables used with a FETCH command must have a colon prefixed. Notice also that a SQLCODE value is returned after each execution of FETCH.

In passing it is worth pointing out that once the CLOSE is executed, the cursor structure is emptied but can be filled again by executing an additional OPEN. If this time the value in D is different, we get a different set of records filling the cursor structure.

Updating and Deleting Records Retrieved in a Cursor Structure

It often happens that some of the records retrieved in a cursor structure should be updated in the base table. Suppose that for employees in department D4, we want to increase by $1,000 the salary of those employees hired in 1988 and delete those hired in 1987.

Assume that the values D4, 1,000, 1988, and 1987 are read into working-storage variables D, RAISE, YR8, and YR7 respectively. Also assume working-structure variables HEMP#, HDEPT#, HSALARY, HSKILL, and HYEAR that can hold a complete EMPLOYEE record. We can use the working-structure EXEC SQL definitions for defining the EMPLOYEE relation and for SQLCA used in the previous section. The definition of the cursor structure (also in working storage) can be the following:

```
EXEC SQL
     DECLARE EMPLOY-CURSOR CURSOR FOR
     SELECT EMP#, DEPT#, SALARY, SKILL, YEAR
     FROM EMPLOYEE
     WHERE DEPT# = :D
END-EXEC.
```

In the procedure division we first read in the values D4, RAISE, 1988, and 1987. Then we open the cursor structure, causing the SELECT expression in the cursor structure definition (in working storage) to be executed. Then we use a FETCH to extract the first record and place it in working storage. If the YEAR value in this record is 1988, we use an UPDATE to update that record in the base table EMPLOYEE. If the YEAR value is 1987, we use a DELETE command to remove the record from the base table EMPLOYEE.

This FETCH and UPDATE/DELETE/**do nothing** sequence is repeated for each record in the cursor structure. The following procedure division code thus illustrates the use of both embedded UPDATE and DELETE commands with a cursor structure:

```
  PROCEDURE DIVISION.
       ACCEPT D.
       ACCEPT RAISE.
       MOVE RAISE TO CRAISE.
** Assume RAISE in DISPLAY format, CRAISE in PIC S9(9) COMP
       ACCEPT YR8.
       ACCEPT YR7.
       EXEC SQL
          OPEN EMPLOY-CURSOR
       END-EXEC.
       EXEC SQL
          FETCH EMPLOY-CURSOR
          INTO :HEMP#, :HDEPT#, :HSALARY, :HSKILL, :YEAR
       END-EXEC.
       PERFORM RECORD-DECISION
               UNTIL SQLCODE = 100.
       EXEC SQL
          CLOSE EMPLOY-CURSOR
       END-EXEC.
       STOP RUN.
**
  RECORD-DECISION.
       IF SQLCODE > 0 THEN PERFORM ERROR-ACTION
       ELSE
         IF HYEAR = 1988
         THEN EXEC SQL
                UPDATE EMPLOYEE
```

```
                SET YEAR = YEAR + :CRAISE
          WHERE CURRENT OF EMPLOY-CURSOR
          END-EXEC
     ELSE IF HYEAR = 1987
           THEN EXEC SQL
                    DELETE EMPLOYEE
                    FROM EMPLOYEE
                    WHERE CURRENT OF EMPLOY-CURSOR
                END-EXEC
             ELSE NEXT SENTENCE.
EXEC SQL
     FETCH EMPLOY-CURSOR
     INTO :HEMP#, :HDEPT#, :HSALARY, :HSKILL, :HYEAR
END-EXEC.
```

In both the UPDATE and DELETE expressions, the clause CURRENT of EMPLOY-CURSOR means the most recent record that was extracted from EMPLOY-CURSOR by a FETCH expression.

Updating and Deleting Multiple Records without Using Cursor Structure

It is not always necessary to use a cursor structure for multiple record update and deletion. For example, suppose that we want to update the SALARY field of all records for department D4, with all records getting the same update. The update is a salary increase of $1,000, with the value 1,000 held in the variable CRAISE; the value D4 is held in the variable X. In this case no cursor structure need be declared in working storage. We simply use EXEC SQL statements in working storage for the EMPLOYEE relation definition and SQLCA definition, as usual, and then place the following in the procedure division:

```
EXEC SQL
    UPDATE EMPLOYEE
         SET SALARY = SALARY + :CRAISE
    WHERE DEPT# = :X
END-EXEC.
IF SQLCODE > 0 THEN ...
```

Likewise, if we want to delete all the records for department D4, we simply place the following in the procedure division, without need for a cursor-structure definition in working storage:

```
EXEC SQL
    DELETE
    FROM EMPLOYEE
    WHERE DEPT# = :X
END-EXEC.
```

```
IF SQLCODE > 0 THEN ...
```

As we mentioned in the previous chapter, update and deletion of multiple records with a single SQL expression can be dangerous, since it is easy to get wrong the condition that selects the records affected. Nevertheless such multiple record updates and deletions are much less dangerous when caused by a COBOL embedded SQL expression. We can assume that thorough testing will be carried out to ensure that the SQL works as intended, before the program is released for production. It goes without saying that such testing *must* be carried out.

RUNNING A COBOL SQL PROGRAM

The major difference between running a conventional COBOL program and a COBOL SQL program is that with the COBOL SQL program you cannot submit the program directly to the COBOL compiler for translation. You first must use the system precompiler.

Let us take the steps in turn for entering and executing a COBOL SQL program. With DATABASE2 and IBM systems you enter a COBOL SQL at a terminal using an editor (which is a subcomponent of TSO, if you are using IBM's OS/MVS operating system). Then you have the source program precompiled by the DATABASE2 precompiler. Essentially this removes the statements EXEC SQL through END-EXEC from the program and replaces them with COBOL code. In the case of an SQL SELECT, UPDATE, DELETE, or INSERT expression, the replacement is simply a COBOL CALL to a submodule. (To cut a long story short, such a submodule is the procedure resulting from a translation of one of those SQL expressions. The translation of an SQL expression such as SELECT takes place as a separate step, and is carried out by a sophisticated system called BIND.)

Once the precompiler has replaced the EXEC SQL statements in the program with COBOL, the source program can be submitted to the COBOL compiler. When the program executes, it calls up the submodules resulting from the earlier translations of SQL expressions. The submodules are kept on disk and are loaded into main memory as required by the program.

The details about how DATABASE2 works are beyond the scope of this book and belong to the subject of data base systems. However, getting a COBOL SQL program submitted and executed is not that difficult. To get things done users simply select options on menus. The details are best learned by working with the menus at a terminal. A more detailed coverage of this area can be found in Ref. 1. Business cases involving SQL appear in Ref. 2.

SUMMARY

Every SQL expression embedded in a COBOL program is sandwiched between EXEC SQL and END-EXEC and can be used as a COBOL sentence. Distinction must be made between SQL variables and working-storage variables that can be used in an SQL expression. Such working- storage variables must be prefixed by a colon if used within an SQL expression.

There is little difficulty in using embedded SQL where only one record is being retrieved by the expression. Where multiple records are being retrieved, a cursor structure must be defined to accept the multiple records. A special SQL FETCH command is used to bring records one by one from the cursor structure to working storage.

COBOL programs containing embedded SQL must first be precompiled by the data base system precompiler before being submitted to the COBOL compiler. The precompiler replaces each SQL retrieval or update expression with a call to a submodule corresponding to the SQL expression. This submodule is generated independently by a translation component of the data base system.

EXERCISES

A COBOL SQL program should be written for each of the following, using the EMPLOYEE relation:

1. What is the skill and salary for an employee number entered at a terminal?
2. What is the year hired and skill for an employee number entered at a terminal?
3. Delete data for an employee number entered at a terminal.
4. Insert new records from a tape file NEW-EMP.
5. What are the employee numbers and salaries for employees hired in a year entered at a terminal?
6. What are the employee numbers and skills of employees making less than $X and working in department Y where X and Y are entered at a terminal?

7. For employees in department X, increase salaries by 10 percent if they are less than $Y and by 5 percent otherwise. Use a cursor structure in the program. Both X and Y are read in.
8. For employees hired in year Y, delete their records if the salary is less than $X, otherwise increase the salary by 10 percent. Both X and Y are read in by the program.
9. For employees hired in year Y, increase the salaries by $X, where both X and Y are read in.
10. For employees that have either skill A or B, delete their records. Both A and B are read in.

REFERENCES

1. Bradley, J. *Introduction to Data Base Management in Business, 2nd Edition.* New York: Holt, Rinehart & Winston, 1987.

2. Bradley, J. *Case Studies in Business Data Bases.* New York: Holt, Rinehart & Winston, 1988.

APPENDIX: IBM DISK DATA

In this appendix we give relevant specifications and calculation methods for the IBM 3380 disk. We also give specifications for the IBM 3350 disk. Commonly required specifications for both disks are given in Table A.1.

	IBM3350	IBM3380
Tracks per cylinder	30	15
Cylinders per drive	1,770	555
Nominal track capacity (S) in bytes	19,254	47,968
User track capacity (bytes)	47,476	19,069
User cylinder capacity	712,140	572,070
Count-data constant (c)	185	480
Count-key data constant (r)	267	704
Nominal data transmission rate (s) (in bytes/sec)	1.198.000	3,000,000
Rotation time (R) in milliseconds	16.7	16.7
Average seek time in milliseconds	16	25

TABLE A.1 Parameters for the IBM 3350 and 3380 disks.

TRACK CAPACITY CALCULATIONS: IBM 3380 DISK

We go about track capacity calculations with the IBM 3380 disk in almost the same way as for the IBM 3350 disk (chapter 2). However, there are a few modifications, which are caused by the following:

1. There are an additional 12 bytes in both the key and data subblocks, for system purposes
2. In addition to the 12 bytes of system data per subblock, subblocks are padded with further bytes to make them a multiple of 32 bytes in length

Count-Data Format Calculations

If B is the length of the data subblock in bytes before addition of the 12 bytes of system data, or rounding up to a multiple of 32, the number of blocks (n) that can fit on a track will be as follows:

n = nearest integer below S/(c + B')
where B' is 32 times the nearest integer above (B + 12)/32

Count-Key Data Format Calculations

If B is the length of the data subblock in bytes, and k is the length of the key field in bytes, both before addition of the 12 bytes of system data and rounding up to a multiple of 32 bytes, the number of blocks (n) that can fit on a track will be as follows:

n = nearest integer below S/(r + (k' + B'))

where B' is 32 times the nearest integer above (B + 12)/32,
and k' is 32 times the nearest integer above (k + 12)/32

Track Capacity Table

If we consider the number of blocks per track to be given, there will be a maximum and minimum block size (B) that will give the number of blocks per track. In Table A.2 we give these maximum and minimum block lengths versus number of blocks for the case of both count-data and count-key data format. (Note that we consider B to be the subblock length before addition of the 12 bytes of system data and rounding up to a multiple of 32 bytes.)

Timing Calculations

Timing calculations with the IBM 3380 disk are carried out as with the IBM 3350 disk (chapter 2). However, the parameter values are different (Table A. 1).Note on the Subblock Length with Count-Key Data Format.

With count-key data format, to get the data subbblock length B, it is only a good approximation to multiply the record length L by the blocking factor b. In reality B = L*b + k where k is the length of the key field. The system attaches this key field to the subblock. The value B = L*b

+ k should be used in all count-key format track capacity calculations for both IBM 3350 and 3380 disks.

TRACK CAPACITY: IBM 3380 DISK

COUNT DATA BLOCK LENGTH (B)		BLOCKS PER TRACK (n) (key length between 1 and 20 bytes)		COUNT-KEY DATA BLOCK LENGTH (B)
MIN	MAX	MIN	MAX	n
23,477	47,476	23,221	47,220	1
15,477	23,476	15,221	23,220	2
11,477	15,476	11,221	15,220	3
9077	11,476	8821	11,220	4
7477	9076	7221	8820	5
6357	7476	6101	7220	6
5493	6356	5237	6100	7
4821	5492	4565	5236	8
4277	4820	4021	4564	9
3861	4276	3605	4020	10
3477	3860	3221	3604	11
3189	3476	2933	3220	12
2933	3188	2677	2932	13
2677	2932	2421	2676	14
2485	2676	2229	2420	15
2325	2484	2069	2228	16
2165	2324	1909	2068	17
2005	2164	1749	1908	18
1877	2004	1621	1748	19
1781	1876	1525	1620	20
.	.	.	.	.
.	.	.	.	.
.	.	.	.	.

Table A.2 Maximum and minimum block sizes versus number of blocks per track. (Note that with count-key data format, if the key length (k) is between 21 and 54, reduce each entry by exactly 54.)

INDEX